D1134701

CAPTIVE SPIRITS

Prisoners of the Cultural Revolution

CAPTIVE SPIRITS

Prisoners of the Cultural Revolution

YANG XIGUANG

AND

SUSAN MCFADDEN

HONG KONG
OXFORD UNIVERSITY PRESS
OXFORD NEW YORK
1997

Oxford University Press

Oxford New York
Athens Auckland Bangkok Bogota Bombay
Buenos Aires Calcutta Cape Town Dar es Salaam
Delhi Florence Hong Kong Istanbul Karachi
Kuala Lumpur Madras Madrid Melbourne
Mexico City Nairobi Paris Singapore
Taipei Tokyo Toronto

and associated companies in
Berlin Ibadan

Oxford is a trade mark of Oxford University Press

First published 1997
This impression (lowest digit)
1 3 5 7 9 10 8 6 4 2

Published in the United States
by Oxford University Press, New York

British Library Cataloguing in Publication Data
available

Library of Congress Cataloging-in-Publication Data

Yang, Xiguang, date–
[Niu kuei she shen lu. English]
Captive spirits : prisoners of the Cultural Revolution / by Yang
Xiguang and Susan McFadden.
p. cm.
ISBN 0-19-586845-5
1. Yang, Xiguang, 1984– . 2. China—History—
Cultural Revolution, 1966–1969—Personal narrative.
3. Political prisoners—China—Anecdotes.
I. McFadden, Susan, date– . II. Title.
DS778.7.Y4313   1997
951.05'6—dc21   97–10203
CIP

Printed in Hong Kong
Published by Oxford University Press (China) Ltd
18/F Warwick House, Taikoo Place, 979 King's Road,
Quarry Bay, Hong Kong

To Liu Fengxiang, Zhang Jiulong,
and my parents

YANG XIGUANG

Foreword

▼

Captive Spirits offers a fascinating window into hidden aspects of Chinese society and politics—aspects that even China specialists have known very little about. Yang Xiguang inhabited a succession of gulags for a decade from 1968 to 1978, and his intimate portraits of fellow prisoners introduce us to worlds within China not previously touched upon by writers. Yang's portrayals reach into the hidden heart of the Maoist regime's most vicious side, and the spirits of its victims.

Parts of these prison memoirs focus on the imprisoned instigators of the violence that had racked the Cultural Revolution of 1966–8, and the book provides new insights into the social roots and psychology of the Cultural Revolution turmoil. Yang's vignettes of cellmates bring to life the stories of militants from both the radical Rebel camp and their antagonists, the violently extremist defenders of the pre-Cultural Revolution *status quo*. In other chapters Yang discusses secretive underground political parties that the Communist government was determined to wipe out. He provides vivid accounts of the past lives and the ideas of imprisoned leaders from the pro-Soviet Labor Party, the pro-Western Democratic Party, and the pro-Taiwan 'Anti-Communist Salvation Army.' He relates the poignant stories of men who landed in jail for their religious beliefs or for the crime of being entrepreneurial. He illuminates the world of the marginal men of Chinese socialist society: pickpockets who spoke an argot of their own and lived by a separate group ethic; and madmen whose psychoses reflected and mimicked and mocked the political world outside the prison gates.

Young, anxious to communicate, and eager to broaden his knowledge, Yang befriended his fellow inmates from all these backgrounds and states of mind. Through them his own views of China and of its political and economic system changed year by year, as he moved through a succession of prisons: the Zuojiatang detention center, the labor camp at Dongting Lake, and Model Prison in Changsha.

Yang Xiguang himself was no ordinary prisoner. He was one of the most influential and one of the most famously condemned of China's Rebel Red Guards. Few other prisoners had been openly denounced by name by Chairman Mao as 'counterrevolutionary'; few others had been publicly condemned by Premier Zhou Enlai, by Mao's wife Jiang Qing, and by the chief-of-staff of the army. Because of this notoriety, Yang faced the terrifying possibility of execution in prison each time a major political 'struggle campaign' erupted in the early 1970s.

What had landed Yang in these extraordinary circumstances were his ideas. As a nineteen-year-old Rebel Red Guard, he had circulated in early 1968 an essay entitled 'Whither China?' In it, he had proclaimed that the major conflict engulfing China was not between Mao's supporters and enemies, nor between China's proletariat and the formerly wealthy classes. Rather, akin in many ways to the Yugoslav dissident Djilas' notion of a 'new class,' Yang had written in 1968 that the major conflict lay between a 'red capitalist class' and the masses of the Chinese people:

> At present over 90 percent of our high-ranking officials have formed into a unique class—the red capitalist class. . . . It is a decadent class impeding historical progress. Its relationship with the people has changed from that of leaders and followers to rulers and ruled, to exploiters and exploited, from equal, revolutionary camaraderie to oppressors and oppressed. The class interests, prerogatives, and high income of the red capitalist class is built upon repression and exploitation of the masses of the population. *

A not entirely dissimilar view of the polity, though broached in non-radical terms, brought a million people into Tiananmen Square in 1989. But two decades earlier, much as in the tale of the small child and the emperor's clothes, Yang Xiguang's observations had stepped outside the ideological paradigm that people permitted themselves to entertain. He was not just

---

* A slightly abridged English translation of 'Whither China?' (using different wording than I use here) is contained in Klaus Mehnert, *Peking and the New Left At Home and Abroad* (Berkeley: Center for Chinese Studies, China Research Monograph No. 4, 1969), pp. 82–100. Mehnert's book focuses largely on Yang Xiguang's essay and the response that it and a couple of other related essays elicited from the Chinese communist Party leadership.

expounding heresy—it was heresy of a sort the students of Yang's generation had never imagined could exist.

The Cultural Revolution turmoil, though, was beginning to stir questions in the minds of many young people by the time 'Whither China?' was penned in late 1967. Passed hand to hand by Rebel Red Guards during 1968, and further spread by the national leadership as 'material to be criticized,' Yang's essay ultimately reached a readership of many hundreds of thousands. It was with a rush of sudden recognition that young people across the breadth of China read it. It was a moment of enlightenment that was remembered in the late 1970s and early 1980s by the leaders of China's dissident Democracy Wall Movement, who looked back to Yang's essay as one of the key formative elements in the development of their own views. The well-known dissident writer Wang Xizhe observed in a 1980 essay that 'the Yang Xiguang group was the forerunner of the Thinking Generation.'

YANG XIGUANG'S BACKGROUND

Yang Xiguang was born into the class that he later was to condemn. His parents had been among the leading members of Hunan Province's political elite, the rulers of several tens of millions of people. During the 1950's, Father sat on the province's governing Party committee and headed the Party committee's Secretariat. Mother served as deputy head of the provincial trade union organization.

Father was at once a Communist official and descendant of China's literati, and he endeavored to pass on to his children the aspirations and the ideals of both. Grandfather had been an imperial degree holder, and Father had, in turn, been schooled in the Confucian morality. Like other wealthy young men of the period, Father had been sent on to a Western-style secondary school, and then to a university in Shanghai where he became involved in the Communist underground. From there he was promoted to the Revolution's headquarters at Yan'an and high-level positions in the new Communist government. But true to his own upbringing, he obliged young Xiguang to learn the Confucian analects before the boy entered primary school.

Mother, like Father, had worked in the underground Party in Hunan before fleeing to the Communist headquarters in Yan'an. She was intellectually more modern than Father. As the mark of a liberated woman, she had even published an article in 1942 on Ibsen's *A Doll's House*. She made it a point to hold political and intellectual discussions with her children, and to impart to them her liberal notions on the value of the individual and empathy for those less fortunate than themselves.

Father, more than Mother, had been aware of the tragedy that was developing in the Hunan countryside under the radical policies of the Great Leap Forward, and spoke out in warning in 1959. Within months, he was declared a right-wing opportunist, and sent off in disgrace to the countryside. But his opposition to the Great Leap Forward's excesses was vindicated by the collapse of the Leap into economic depression and starvation. He was politically 'rehabilitated' in 1962, and was reinstalled on the Provincial Party Committee. But he would end up paying dearly for his views in the Cultural Revolution.

Throughout Yang Xiguang's years at Hunan Province's elite secondary school, Changsha First High, which he entered in 1962, classmates looked up to him as the son of a top leader. Most of his schoolmates were from the families of doctors, teachers, and engineers, holding a class designation that most Chinese referred to as 'middling class.' Others were the offspring of Party officials, admitted by the school mainly for their ultra-red family pedigree. Such children usually found themselves in classrooms with students academically superior to themselves. Refusing to resign themselves to a rank in the bottom half of their class, they tended to disparage their middling-class schoolmates' academic success; when the Cultural Revolution erupted, they formed Red Guard groups based entirely upon red-class parentage.

Yang, however, was an exception. He had no need to feel defensive about his academic work. Even in a classroom containing the brightest of the bright, he stood at the top of his class. The animosity that others of his station felt toward their non-red-class schoolmates never applied to him.

The animosities among China's high-school students of different class backgrounds would, at the start of the Cultural Revolution in the spring of 1966, contribute greatly to the outbreak of violence among them. As we shall see, Yang would later meet several of his schoolmates in prison, incarcerated for having participated too militantly on one or the other side of the barricades in this internecine student warfare: the red-class students as Conservative-faction Red Guards and the non-red-class students as Rebels.

ENTERING THE CULTURAL REVOLUTION

The momentum of the earliest months of the Cultural Revolution encouraged the exclusivist red-class feelings of pride that the officials' children had long nurtured: for Mao and the

Party were placing the so-called 'revisionist' line of 'white experts' and 'bourgeois educational authorities' under attack. At Changsha First High School, a self-selected group of a dozen students of sterling red parentage excitedly formed a group in early June 1966 in response to the national lead. Yang was allowed to participate. But suddenly in early August the boom was lowered on his parents. The provincial Party leaders had decided to use Chairman Mao's new campaign to attack their rivals within the Party, and Father provided an easy target. When his parents first came under official attack, Yang rushed to their bureaus to read the posters that had gone up criticizing them as 'counterrevolutionary revisionists.' It was a devastating blow to his self-esteem and future prospects; his world had been turned upside-down. He has told me:

> I felt terrible, that there was no longer any position for me in society, that there might be no way for me to survive. When I read the posters, for example ones denouncing my mother for opposing the class line and the Great Leap Forward, I knew these denunciations were consistent with my parents' opinions, and I felt that my parents must be wrong. In China then, the influence of the school's teachings was greater than those of one's parents. I felt confused. I couldn't argue against my own sudden bad status, yet I felt aggrieved. I desperately started reading Mao's writings and pronouncements to find something that would sustain me in my terrible situation.

At school, events were continuing to go badly for him. That August the red-class students, under the leadership of the daughter of the provincial Party's Second Secretary, were emulating their peers in Beijing by forming a Red Guard group to demonstrate their loyalty to Party authorities and their own red-class superiority. Yang witnessed their inaugural meeting, and was perturbed. They were promoting what was called the 'blood-line couplet':

> If your father's a hero you're a good man;
> If your father's reactionary, you're a bastard.

The couplet seemed to Yang like a dagger directed at himself, since his father was now enmeshed in deep political trouble.

THE RISE OF THE REBELS

When directives from Beijing in October permitted rebellion against Party 'powerholders' by those professing to uphold

Chairman Mao's Thought, a great many people who had felt persecuted either before the Cultural Revolution or during its first months seized at the opportunity. They formed small groups in Changsha which quickly allied in a citywide omnibus 'Rebel' organization titled the 'Xiang River Storm.' Its ranks expanded with incredible speed. By the end of December 1966, it could count hundreds of thousands of members: disgruntled students, teachers, workers, and white-collar personnel alike. In particular, Xiang River Storm found partisans in the factories, where many workers were unhappy about the tight controls exercised upon them over the years by Party cadres from the factories' Political Departments.

Initially, Yang Xiguang did not dare to affiliate himself with any group, since his family was in deep trouble, but on his own he busily wrote and pasted up posters. By January 1967, when Party authority had collapsed and Rebel organizations were 'seizing power' throughout China, he felt daring enough to ignore his parents' pleadings and organized a group of seven students to support the Xiang River Storm.

The Rebel euphoria was short-lived. Yang surmises that by the end of January, Zhou Enlai had been able to convince Mao that the massive organizations cropping up nationwide too closely resembled political parties and might ultimately challenge the principle of Communist Party hegemony. In what Rebels later titled the 'February Countercurrent,' Mao gave the go-ahead for military crackdowns against 'counterrevolutionary organizations.' In Changsha, as elsewhere in China, vast numbers of the activists in Xiang River Storm and allied Rebel groups were imprisoned, over-crowding places of detention, amidst popular resistance to the troops in the city's streets. Yang wrote angry posters denouncing the turn of events, and found himself among those arrested and beaten.

Mao soon reversed tactics. He wanted to continue to make use of Rebel groups to carry out his campaign against the Party apparatus, and in March 1967, after forty days in prison, Yang and other students were released. Once again, the Rebels' numbers swelled—with members of Red Guard organizations representing middling-class students; Red Guard groups of working-class youngsters; and the majority of workers in the city's large factories. But the most militant of the work-sector Rebel organizations represented workers at small enterprises and at the other workplaces that had received unfavourable treatment before the Cultural Revolution: underpaid handcart haulers, construction workers, and handicraft artisans.

In many other cities in China, Conservative-faction worker groups dominated the large factories; but in Changsha, the Rebels were the clear majority. In June of 1967 they launched an attack on the headquarters of the Conservatives' university-level organizations, after which the Conservative faction began fighting back with military weapons. The Conservatives had access to such weapons because their membership included the trusted 'backbones' of the pre-Cultural Revolution work-unit militias.

Momentarily the Conservative faction gained the upper hand, but from early July onward, the Rebels seized weapons from the Military District garrisons. The first Rebel groups to make the attempt were the Youth Guardian Army, an organization of poorly paid apprentices, and the Changsha Youth, a Rebel organization of young pickpockets who had been in labor camps. Young Bandit Xiang (featured in Chapter Five) was part of this violent group. When army officers obeyed commands from Beijing not to intervene in these raids on military warehouses, other Rebel groups joined in. Both the Rebel and the Conservative camps were desperate to triumph in Changsha, partly from a pragmatic realization that the losing faction in the Cultural Revolution was likely to be labeled 'counterrevolutionary.'

As casualties mounted in this civil war, the outnumbered Conservatives fled Changsha for the industrial city of Xiangtan. Located in the part of Hunan that Mao came from, Xiangtan had become an armaments manufacturing center after 1949. As such, its workforce had been granted a higher status than other workers, and they felt loyal to the Conservative *status quo*. In the pitched battles between the Rebel worker/student armies of Changsha and their Xiangtan-based Conservative rivals, some of the most hot-headed of the militants from both sides, such as Fire-soldier Mao (Chapter Six), ultimately ended up alongside Yang behind bars.

The triumph of the Changsha Rebels was short-lived, destroyed this time by infighting. In August 1967, some of the Cultural Revolution's leaders in Beijing invited the heads of Hunan's red-class Rebel groups, including those from the large factories, to join a new official committee to govern Hunan. The excluded non-red-class Rebel organizations, finding themselves once again deemed illegitimate, and dangerously beyond the pale of recognized political activity, refused to accept the new arrangement. By September 1967 the Rebel faction was pitched into conflict between two antagonistic camps. The

Conservative-faction organizations in Changsha were dissolved by Beijing; most of their members quickly joined forces with the newly legitimate red-class Rebel organizations.

The lines were now drawn more clearly than ever between the social groups who had been disadvantaged before the Cultural Revolution and those who had not. Yang Xiguang was now aligned firmly in the camp of the former—and was acutely aware that their cause needed to be explained and justified ideologically.

The organizations of the political have-nots quickly banded together in a new umbrella group, titled 'Shengwulian,' shorthand for the 'Hunan Provincial Proletarian Revolutionary Alliance Committee.' By 1968, Shengwulian would be known throughout China, partly through the writings of Yang Xiguang, as the most famous of China's 'ultraleftist' groupings.

Shengwulian consisted of more than twenty loosely affiliated organizations, each with its own particular grievances. Besides the rump Xiang River Storm of the ill-favored poorly paid trades, member groups included: non-red-class student Red Guards; teachers who had been persecuted as Rightists and now desperately demanded political rehabilitation; the Red Banner Army composed of disgruntled ill-employed army veterans; and Tertiary Education Storm, headed by Zhou Guohui, whom we shall meet several times in the following chapters. His group was comprised of students who were in trouble before the Cultural Revolution due to unfavorable family backgrounds or to personal political black marks.

TOWARD 'WHITHER CHINA?'

These groups' alliance began to clarify for Yang the underlying causes of the mass upheaval in which he was engaged. Trying to frame his thinking in terms drawn from Marx, he felt that the common thread in the Shengwulian members' struggle must be their prior and ongoing manipulated persecution by a ruling class eager to maintain its power.

Yang began to seek out complaints at the bottom of society, searching idealistically for alternative ways of organizing society that would avoid inequalities and repressive hierarchy. He traveled into the countryside to interview peasants, and also met with groups of angry youths who, during the several years before the Cultural Revolution, had been sent from Changsha to the countryside to settle. He studied Lenin's 'State and Revolution' and the 1966 Cultural Revolution articles that had commemorated the 95th anniversary of the Paris Commune.

The ideas in these writings seemed to Yang consistent with the crying need to transform the Chinese polity, not just to oust particular officials.

Armed with such ideas, Yang commenced work on 'Whither China?', which he completed the first week of January 1968. He framed the essay as a potted history of the Cultural Revolution's development through the prism of a class struggle between the new bureaucratic class maneuvering to stay in power and the powerless masses. The latter, Yang, claimed, were learning to comprehend the nature of their oppression and the possibilities of mass power. As Yang noted in 'Whither China?':

> The storm of the January Revolution of 1967 within a very short time . . . wrested the destiny of our socialist nation and the administration of the cities, industry, transport, and finance . . . away from the hands of the bureaucrats and into the hands of the enthusiastic working class. The members of society suddenly found, in the absence of bureaucrats, that they could not only go on living, but could live better and develop more quickly and with greater freedom.

In order to attain this freedom permanently, the masses must seek to overthrow not only the bureaucratic 'class of red capitalists' (whose 'representative' was Zhou Enlai), but also the military officialdom, the armed appendage of this elite class. In place of the structures of state machinery, a 'new society' would arise, whose officials would 'be produced in the struggle to overthrow the decaying [ruling] class':

> These officials . . . will have no special privileges. Economically, they will receive the same treatment as the masses in general. They may be dismissed or replaced at any time at the request of the masses.

Such ideas were being bandied about in other provinces, too, in groups similar to Yang's. 'Whither China?' circulated far more widely, though, and gained a far broader influence than these other groups' writings, in part because it was better written and its argumentation more easily remembered. But its fame also owed to the fact that condemnations of Yang Xiguang and Shengwulian became the focus of a conference in Beijing that January attended by the Cultural Revolution's leadership. In the wake of that conference. 'Whither China?' and two other Shengwulian essays were distributed nationally by the Party as 'materials to be criticized.'

As soon as word reached Changsha of the Beijing conference, Yang went into hiding. He stayed underground for a month in Changsha, hidden by one family after another, and then fled to the city of Wuhan in neighboring Hubei Province. There, 'all that anyone knew was that I belonged to a counterrevolutionary organization that had been denounced by high-level Cultural Revolution leaders. They turned me in.' He ultimately endured ten years of prison as punishment for having written 'Whither China?'

STRUGGLE CAMPAIGNS

Yang's prison experience, which is vividly conveyed in this book, will both shock and inspire readers. While reading about the personal travails of the prisoners, it should be borne in mind that his decade-long period of imprisonment was punctuated by a frightening series of nationwide 'struggle campaigns.' These embroiled all of China, from urban factories to small towns to remote villages. In these campaigns, political dissidents, social non-conformists, the losers of local power struggles and bad-class scapegoats were forced on to platforms and abused. They were often summarily consigned to labor camps. Each of these campaigns introduced vast numbers of prisoners into the gulag—and put the lives of many political prisoners already there at risk.

There was the Purify the Class Ranks Campaign of the latter half of 1968, in which the State turned to mass terror to bring the turmoil of the Cultural Revolution to an end; millions of victims were 'struggled' against in the brutal rituals of mass meetings and then jailed in make-shift prisons called 'cowsheds.' There were the so-called 'Anti-May Sixteenth Conspiracy' purges of the early 1970s during which, as Yang recalls, vast numbers of former Rebels were imprisoned and tortured. There was the equally terrifying Strike One–Oppose Three Campaign of 1970, in which huge numbers of activists from the losing factions of the Cultural Revolution, along with persecuted people from the so-called 'bad' classes, were beaten and, in all too many cases, executed.

Yang Xiguang himself came close to being a terminal victim of this latter campaign. In transit from his labor camp to an urban interrogation center, he spotted an official-looking poster demanding his execution; and in the days and weeks that followed, as he tells here, he spent a very frightening period on death row, awaiting a massive public gathering at which he and others would be shot for the political edification of spectators.

In the event, of course, he did narrowly survive the Strike One–Oppose Three Campaign; but a few of his closest friends were sacrificed on its altar. Who those friends were, and how they died, is grippingly related in the memoirs that follow.

THE LEGACY OF 'WHITHER CHINA?'

Despite the crushing of Shengwulian and the jailing of all of its leaders, and despite the terrible repressions of the late 1960s and 1970s, dissident ideas that were kindled during the Cultural Revolution could not so easily be eradicated. As Yang Xiguang sat in prison, 'Whither China?' circulated from hand to hand and had a considerable effect on the world outside. In 1980, the Canton-based Democracy Wall Movement writer Liu Guokai published an underground, book-length essay entitled 'A Brief Analysis of the Cultural Revolution,' in which he observed:

> 'Whither China?' struck a responsive note in the hearts of many people. . . . People hid copies of writings reflecting such ideas and passed them around among those they trusted, holding lively discussions. The great suppression of 1968 [when the Cultural Revolution was crushed] infuriated many people and caused them to change their outlook. Ultraleftist thought won more followers and supporters. Many who had missed the opportunity to read the article 'Whither China?' searched for it. Those who read it told others about it in secret. Quite a few students and educated young workers accepted ideas in the article and developed them further. They lost interest in factional struggles and turned their attention to the larger issues of the existing system. They analyzed essentials behind appearances in an effort to find the root cause of social problems. [Translated in *Chinese Sociology and Anthropology*, 19, 2 (Winter 1986–7).]

The influence of Yang's essay, ironically, outlasted Mao's regime. A great many in China came to see the essential conflict in China as one between a manipulative class of Party officials intent upon preserving their power versus a powerless mass of ordinary people, who had been repeatedly conned into seeing the Party apparatus as their champions against imaginary foes. If the problem lay with the monopoly on power of a Leninist *nomenklatura*, then only institutionalized means could thwart these political *apparatchiks*. A more pluralistic and democratic polity was necessary.

The ultimate impact of 'Whither China?' was not to promote armed, ultraleftist revolution by the masses, as its young author had urged. Rather, its argumentation inadvertently helped to lay the intellectual foundations for the 'bourgeois liberalism' of the 1980s. The irony of this did not, however, prove disappointing to Yang, for he had traversed an intellectual odyssey similar to his peers. Indeed, in the latter part of the 1980s, writing under the name Yang Xiaokai in journals such as Shanghai's *World Economic Herald*, he developed a reputation in China as a champion of 'bourgeois democracy' and of a decentralized, indeed privatized, economy. It was a long, curved road, but one whose outlines are clear.

As reflected in these memoirs, the Cultural Revolution dragnet had forced a great many bright intellectuals into the gulag, and Yang Xiguang benefited greatly there from their coaching in mathematics, engineering, and English. Not many years after his release from prison, he won a fellowship from Princeton University to undertake Doctoral studies in Economics. Today he teaches at a university in Melbourne, attracted more to Milton Friedman than to revolution from below.

JONATHAN UNGER
January 1997
Canberra, Australia

Author's Preface
▼

'WHITHER CHINA?'

Absorbed with the daily challenges of being a new graduate student on foreign soil, I had virtually forgotten about my previous identities, both revolutionary and counterrevolutionary, until one day when I was in Princeton University's Gest Library looking for sources on the origins of the Cultural Revolution. There it was, tucked away in the stacks of Chinese and English text: 'Whither China?' To my surprise, I discovered three or four different English versions extant. Sometimes the author was listed as 'A soldier of the Steel 319 Corps, "Seize Military Power"'; in others, 'August 12th Squad of Seize Military Power'; in still others, simply 'Shengwulian.' Yet each of the various Sinologists I would encounter somehow knew that the author of the essay was a Changsha First High School student named Yang Xiguang.

Nowadays, 'Whither China?' is generally accepted to be the first essay published in China to criticize the Communist elite class and advocate a total change in the political system, a fact which has prompted many scholars to focus their research on Yang Xiguang. English translations began circulating in the West in 1968, along with several other Shengwulian documents. 'Whither China?' seemed to strike a particularly resonant chord among America's New Left. There were those who believed that the author was attacking the Communist system from an 'anarchist' perspective; others claimed that he was interested in 'egalitarianism.' When the China-watchers and the other scholars who had come of age during the radical sixties visited with me at Princeton's Department of Economics, they were patently skeptical, not only of my identity, but of my integrity. Was it conceivable for an ultraleftist who once advocated using revolutionary violence to overthrow the oppressive 'red capitalist class' to turn around and suddenly embrace Milton Friedman? *Captive Spirits* records the lives of many of the 'counterrevolutionaries' with whom I shared cells during my decade behind bars, as I negotiated each of the three large systems within the Chinese gulag: the detention center, the labor reform camp, and the prison. Ironically, by the time I was sentenced in 1969 I had already abandoned my faith in revolution and had begun pondering the paradoxical coexistence of conservatism and rebellion. The Sinologists interested in Yang Xiguang may also be interested in the tales about underground political leaders, entrepreneurs who were involved in illegal, free-market activities, pickpockets, thieves, persecuted writers and religious devotees, and members of the Nationalist upper crust, for their stories *are* my story. At the end of this journey, they will perhaps not only better understand my transformation, they will also undergo a transformation of their own.

YANG XIGUANG
January 1997
Melbourne, Australia

Preface

▼

The magical spirits of traditional Chinese mythology take myriad shapes and forms. They can appear as animals or humans, as demons and tricksters of the underworld, and as benevolent powers bringing bountiful harvests and resolving unhappy love affairs. In modern times, the language of the supernatural has often been borrowed to describe human behavior. In China as elsewhere, it is not unusual for a people to cloak the unfathomable in more familiar terms. Thus, during the Great Cultural Revolution of 1966–8 the creative forces representing divergent ideas were identified as the malevolent 'cow-ghosts and serpent-spirits': counterrevolutionary creatures who were deprived of their rights and sometimes their lives when they offended the prevailing political forces. Up until the late 1970's, individuals who found themselves 'capped' and 'labeled'—permanently separated from the comfortable orthodoxy of the 'people'—suffered the cruelest form of discrimination, at once social and political. It is the stories of these men and women that are told within the pages of this book.

The reader will not find all incarnations equally congenial. Some are frightening; some comical; others hopelessly pedantic. In the act of translation, I embraced them all. Each defied me to capture it alive and bring it into the Western world. Occasionally, I would grapple with a snake-spirit, pin it down on the page, only to watch the creature slip through my fingers moments later, as it became a stereotype, or worse, an empty name, lifeless and flat. Fortunately, in those cases, Yang Xiguang was standing by to serve as patient medium. As he tells us at the end of the chapter 'The Exit Brigade,' he feels very much at home among all of these spirits.

I must confess that, even now, I do not. About halfway during the long process of our collaboration, spirits began to visit my desk at unexpected moments, eventually crossing time and space so often that by now they have become part of me. Still, they trouble me and touch me. The unseen faces, the unspoken voices of real people—each insisted to me that it was unique. The reader may find, as I did, that the particular experiences and fates of many of these individuals can provide new insights into the larger experience of China during the ten years of chaos.

It is my hope that within this volume, not only the spirit, but the flesh of those held captive will come alive, if only for a fleeting moment, so that the reader can come away with a sense of the dignity and diversity that characterized the vast underworld of the Cultural Revolution. Should readers find that they too have been touched or troubled perhaps I will have succeeded to some measure.

This translation has benefited greatly from the assistance and support of many individuals. Among these, I am indebted to Eric Perkins for his insights into Marxist historical interpretations of the ultraleftist movement; to James Farr for his helpful analysis of the Paris Commune; and to Seth Sicroff, who provided a careful reading of an early draft. Special thanks to Elene Kolb, a source of visionary pragmatism on more than one occasion. At Oxford University Press, I wish to express my gratitude to Mary Child, whose incisive editorial reviews and tireless critiques have significantly improved this manuscript. Finally, thanks are due to my family, who during the long writing of this book, put up with microwaved takeout on many an evening.

SUSAN MCFADDEN
January 1997
New York

Contents

▼

Names in the Book

▼

Bi Jian—Head of the Red Banner Army and inmate at Zuojiatang.

Bin, Master—Bin Lanting, petty proprietor 'Rightist' inmate at Model Prison.

Chen Boda—Head of the Central Cultural Revolution Group.

Chen, 'Professor'—Chen Guangdi, mathematics professor at Hunan University.

Chen Lingmei—Head of the Shengwulian Special Investigation Team.

Chen Sancai—'Rightist' indicted in the Shengwulian case.

Cheng Deming—Conservative convert and Yang's classmate from Changsha First High School.

Chiang Kai-shek—Nationalist leader from 1927; led the Nationalist forces to Taiwan after the Communist victory.

Ci Xi—Empress Dowager of the Qing Dynasty, 1835–1908, whose reign in 1905 led to the Boxer Rebellion.

Deng Xiaoping—During the Cultural Revolution, Secretary-General of the Secretariat of the Communist Party; criticized for his economic ideology. Subsequent Premier and father of China's 'Open and Reform' policy.

Fu Zigeng—Peasant labeled as a 'counterrevolutionary fugitive' and executed at Reconstruction Farm during Strike One-Oppose Three.

Gao Jianjun—'Build-an-Army' Gao, girlfriend of Fire-soldier Mao, and fellow member of Red Angry Fire.

Guan, Political Director—A rehabilitated capitalist roader who served as political director at the Third Brigade of Reconstruction Farm and improved conditions.

Guo Zhongzhu—Yang's assistant mason in the Construction Group.

He, Counselor—Political counselor of the First Detachment of the Third Brigade, Reconstruction Farm.

Han Xin—One of the founders of the Han dynasty, whose ambition led to his demise.

He, Dumbbell—Peasant prisoner at Reconstruction Farm who witnessed the Dao County Massacre.

He, Teacher—He Minhe, former engineer and 'Rightist' who tutored Yang at Reconstruction Farm.

Hongyan—Conservative Red Guard girlfriend of Cheng Deming.

Hou Xiangfeng—'Rightist organization criminal' implicated with Liu Fengxiang in the Shengwulian case.

Huang, Spectacles—Rebel author who is imprisoned for criticizing Mao and who circulates his novels at Reconstruction Farm.

Huang Wenzhe—'Practicing counterrevolutionary' at Reconstruction Farm.

Huang Xingying—Female classmate of Yang and inmate at Zuojiatang.

Ji, Detachment Leader—Director of the Third Detachment, Third Brigade, Reconstruction Farm.

Jiang Qing—Ultraleftist wife of Mao Zedong arrested in 1976 as a member of the 'Gang of Four'.

Kang Sheng—Politburo member and Deputy Head of the Central Cultural Revolution Group beginning May 1969.

Lei Techao—'Rightist' suspected of being part of a counterrevolutionary organization along with Liu Fengxiang.

Lei, Thundergun—Nationalist progeny ëweedí and prisoner at Reconstruction Farm.

Li, Counselor—Political counselor of the First Detachment, Third Brigade, Reconstruction Farm.

Li, Farm Director—Director of Reconstruction Farm.

Li Liang—Rebel commanding officer of the Changsha Youth at the battle of Yijiawan.

Li, Preacher—Li Anxiang, lay Catholic minister who worshipped underground in Changsha.

Liang Qi—Wife of Director Song Shaowen.

Lin Biao—Red Army general designated as Mao's successor but who later died mysteriously in a plane crash.

Little Boss—'Rice broker' at Zuojiatang.

Little Du—Labor prisoner at Reconstruction Farm who related the story of Su Yibang the elder's death.

Little Li—Girlfriend of Doctor Wang.

Little Li—Young prisoner from Changsha who is in the Exit Brigade with Yang.

Little Liu—Liu Chengning, boyfriend of Missy Jian at Reconstruction Farm.

Little Ma—Prisoner at Reconstruction Farm accused of membership in a Labor Party.

Liu, Brigade Leader—Leader of the Third Brigade, Reconstruction Farm.

Liu Fengxiang—'Old Liu', 'Helmsman', Yang's 'Rightist' friend and mentor.

Liu Guinong—'Counterrevolutionary' peasant prisoner struggled against at Reconstruction Farm.

Liu, Grandpa—Old Nationalist, former secretary of Chiang Kaishek, prisoner at Reconstruction Farm.

Liu Jiajin—Machine repairman in story told by Old Yu.

Liu Manman—Prostitute detained at Zuojiatang.

Liu, Political Director—Political director at the Third Brigade, succeeded by Political Director Guan.

Liu Shaoqi—President who tried to change Mao Zedong's Great Leap Forward policy; the major target of the Cultural Revolution.

Liu, Warden—Warden at Zuojiatang when Yang is detained in 1968; eventually sent to a May Seventh cadre school.

Liu Zhenyu—'Rightist' forced to confess at Reconstruction Farm.

Long, Lawyer—Long Caizao, a former lawyer imprisoned at Reconstruction Farm.

Lu, Blindman—Changsha capitalist and inmate in Zuojiatang.

Lu Guoan—Yang's 'Apprentice brother' and fellow mason in the Construction Group at Reconstruction Farm.

Luo Gang—'Spartacus', pickpocket inmate at Zuojiatang.

Mao, Fire-soldier—Yang's fellow inmate at Zuojiatang; member of radical Conservative Red Angry Fire.

Mao Zedong—1893–1976, creator of the People's Republic of China in 1949.

Missy Jian—Zhao Jian, Little Liu's girlfriend.

Peng Dehuai—Defense Minister who criticized the Great Leap Forward policies and angered Mao, who retaliated during the Cultural Revolution.

Peng Zhen—Beijing Mayor criticized as a revisionist during the Cultural Revolution for his evaluation of the Great Leap Forward.

Qin Shihuang—259–210 BC, the first emperor of the Qin Dynasty.

Qiu, Baby—Prisoner at Reconstruction Farm; 'executioner' at the Dao County Massacre.

Shen Ziying—Outspoken 'counterrevolutionary' prisoner at Reconstruction Farm.

Song, Director—Song Shaowen, former actor/playwright and Rebel member of Shengwulian.

Su Yibang, the younger—Classmate of Yang's at Changsha First High School.

Su Yibang, the elder—Sentenced at Zuojiatang for membership in a counterrevolutionary organization known as the Democratic Party.

Sun, Big-head—Former Chinese opera star who was imprisoned for criticizing Mao after Peking Opera was declared reactionary.

Tang, Counselor—Political counselor of the Third Detachment, Third Brigade, Reconstruction Farm.

Three-haired Kid—Blinded a Conservative cadre during a factional clash during the Cultural Revolution.

Wang Baiqiu—Prisoner at Reconstruction Farm who is caught stealing vegetables.

Wang, Doctor—'Little Wang', prisoner doctor at Reconstruction Farm.

Wang, Master—Wang Jinguo, Rebel and Yang's 'master' mason in the Construction Group.

Wu, Study Leader—Third Detachment, Third Brigade, Reconstruction Farm.

Xiang, Bandit—Xiang Yuanyi, Rebel imprisoned for blowing up a large building.

Xiao Fuxiang—Machine technician and prisoner at Zuojiatang.

Xu, Whiskers—Warden at Zuojiatang and successor to Warden Liu; former Army officer.

Yang Dayi—Conservative Hunan Provincial Party Secretary and Commander of the Hunan Military Region.

Yang Guochang—'Die-hard' counterrevolutionary prisoner; struggled against at Reconstruction Farm.

Yang Hui—Yang Xiguang's sister.

Yang, Instructor—Political instructor, Third Detachment, Third Brigade, Reconstruction Farm.

Yang, Master—Yang Zili, Rebel and 'master' mason who oversaw Lu Guoan in the Construction Group.

Yang Shuguang—Yang Xiguang's older brother; persecuted as a 'Rightist'.

Yang, Supervisor—Ideological supervisor at the Third Brigade, Reconstruction Farm.

Yang Taonian—'Soothsayer' at Reconstruction Farm who advocates a 'legal system' composed of Buddhist and Taoist ethics.

Yang Xiaowen—Landlord's son and who chooses to remain at Reconstruction Farm after his release.

Yang Xuemeng—cousin of Yang Xiguang; sentenced at Zuojiatang for his involvement with the Great Harmony Party.

Yao, Baby—Son of a top Nationalist leader; sentenced to Reconstruction Farm for 'counterrevolutionary slander'.

Ye Xiangzhen—Daughter of Ye Jianying.

Yu, Old—Yu Yuyi, 'Chief Engineer' Yu; Model Prison 'Rightist' and tutor to Yang Xiguang.

Zhang Bolun—'Rightist' inmate in Zuojiatang.

Zhang, Commander—Zhang Jiazheng, leader of the Rebel Xiang River Storm.

Zhang Chunqiao—Ultraleftist official and member of 'Gang of Four'.

Zhang, Iron-soldier—Zhang Tiejun, Rebel wife of 'Old Liu', Liu Fengxiang.

Zhang, Nine Dragons—Zhang Jiulong, Yang's fellow inmate and go partner at Zuojiatang.

Zhang Yugang—Author of Shengwulian's 'Manifesto'.

Zhao Jinxiang—Female teacher at the Reconstruction Farm school for cadre children.

Zhao, Secretary—Inmate at Zuojiatang; former Party cadre.

Zhao Ziyang—Advocated economic reform in his capacity as Party Secretary.

Zhong, Master—A leading master of the Construction Group at Reconstruction Farm.

Zhou, Counselor—Political monitor at Reconstruction Farm with urban experience; successor to Director Guan.

Zhou Enlai—Premier of the People's Republic of China from 1949 to 1976.

Zhou, Fatty—Venal cadre in the Exit Brigade responsible for making decisions about where released prisoners will go.

Zhou Guohui—Student leader of Shengwulian's Tertiary Education Storm.

Zhou, Rambling—Reconstruction Farm prisoner and sympathizer with Conservative cause.

Zhu, Teacher—Yang's electrical engineering instructor; 'Rightist' inmate at Zuojiatang.

Part I

Zuojiatang Detention Center

FEBRUARY 1968–DECEMBER 1969

▼

1

The Lower Depths

▼

Satisfied that the paperwork is in order, Warden Liu places his pen on the table and looks up, first at me, then at the olive-grey light at the window. Rising, he switches off the lamp and rubs his knuckles. 'Yang Xiguang, let me tell you something. This place is nothing but a giant dye vat. It doesn't matter if you're pure white when you come in; by the time you leave here, you'll be covered with stains.'

I do not respond. The interrogation is over.

We are halfway down the southern corridor when he pulls me aside nervously, a curious gleam in his eyes. 'See here, this place is packed full of cow-ghosts and serpent-spirits—not what *you're* used to. Mind they don't lead you astray.' Then his face hardens, and without another word, he marches me over to Number Nine and unlocks the door.

Where is this Number Nine?

Hours pass, maybe even a day, before the full weight of realization comes home to me—it is February, 1968 and I am at Zuojiatang.

◆

Mechanically, and yet as in a dream I recall the events of the past forty-eight hours. I am sitting on a train from Wuhan to Changsha and can see nothing—my eyes are covered with a towel, my hands handcuffed behind my back. Every couple of minutes the smell of urine floats by, as do the soft voices of a young woman and my two guards. I know they are mocking me, Yang Xiguang, the student who wanted to smash the government machine.

I can hear their words but shut them out, thinking of how last month, before I ventured out into the rural areas of Hunan, I had delivered a week's worth of newspapers and clean clothes to the place where my mother had been placed under house arrest. It was the last time I would see her. She had been acting strangely—nervous and distracted—asking again and again about me and my younger sister Yang Hui. I did not know then that these were the actions of a woman who knew she would never see her children again, who had already resolved to hang herself, and yet could not quite let go.

Just weeks ago Kang Sheng, Jiang Qing, and Zhou Enlai have met in Beijing to convene a special session of the Hunan Provincial Preparatory Revolutionary Committee. At the meeting they announced that my essay 'Whither China?' was an ultrarightist, reactionary document.[1] It could not have been written by a high school student—not even by a college student—they declared: it must have been composed by a 'black hand' operating behind the scenes. Someone in a high position within the Party, someone like my parents. At the same meeting Shengwulian, the Rebel umbrella organization to which I belonged, was declared to be a counterrevolutionary organization. Throughout Hunan, and throughout all of China, a massive witch-hunting began in earnest.

The residents of Changsha are sympathetic to Shengwulian; friends had arranged for me to stay low at the homes of the Rebel group Red High School Committee. Days, I remained indoors reading; nights I disguised myself in a leather overcoat, a large fur cap, a surgical mask, and a pair of plain glasses then combed the streets, flashlight in hand, reading the big-character posters. One night I stayed at the home of one of Yang Hui's classmates, where I learned the details of how my sister had gone to collect our mother's body. My mother, it would seem, had been accused of being the 'black hand' responsible for writing 'Whither China?' Before a public gathering, her hands had been dipped in black ink, and she had been 'struggled against' as she knelt on the ground. I dared not imagine my mother's appearance in death. I took from my bag the last picture she had given me, her loving smile untouched by house arrest and struggle sessions. Tears filled my eyes.

The voices of the guards interrupt these memories, and I catch the words 'famous reactionary.' These words sting me. I will not accept such a destiny.

---

[1] Kang Sheng was a Politburo member and Deputy Head of the Central Cultural Revolution Group from May 16, 1969 through the Ninth Congress of the Chinese Communist Party, held in 1969. Mao's wife Jiang Qing was acting in her capacity as Deputy Head of the Central Cultural Revolution Group during this time.

◆

I was born in heady times, in the autumn of 1948, as the Civil War was nearing an end, and the tide was turning in favor of the Communist camp. My parents had just been transferred from the caves of Yan'an to northeast China. The Communists had just won a minor battle in that area, so I was familiarly called 'Xiaokai,' or 'little victory.' It was only when I began school that my parents addressed me by my formal name, 'Xiguang,' meaning 'light at dawn.'

My father was a member of the Hunan Provincial Party Committee; my mother, Deputy Head of the Provincial Trade Union organization. I had grown up among the Communist aristocracy and drunk at the well of communism. Up until high school, I was in awe of the revolutionary heroism of the Communist Party which had conquered the Nationalists. The novels and the revolutionary memoirs that all children read were steeped with the dogma of revolutionary violence as a means to overturn unjust regimes.

Though not immediately apparent, political upheavals continued within the Communist Party after 1949. My family's first setback occurred in 1957, for that was the year my brother and uncle, like so many others, were labeled 'Rightists.' Then, in 1959 we said goodbye to my father as he retreated to the countryside; he had spoken out against the Great Leap Forward. Three years later the Party reversed its policy. My father's name was completely cleared by Party Central, and our family was reunited. With the new emphasis on knowledge and grades, I was accepted to the competitive Changsha First High School. Like the rest of my family, I was a beneficiary of those relatively 'rightist' policies.

But in 1964 politics took command and once again I felt myself being pulled to the left. My parents, especially my mother, tried unsuccessfully to temper my leftist bent. When the Cultural Revolution began several years later, I threw myself into anti-work group activities. The 'work groups' were teams sent by Communist authorities, at the direction of President Liu Shaoqi, to regain control of university campuses which had been paralyzed by rebelling students. During that same period both my parents were criticized by the Hunan Provincial Committee. My father was pronounced a 'counterrevolutionary revisionist.' I was persecuted by the work groups and the original 'pure-red' Red Guards looked down on me because of my parents' bad name. It was only natural for me to oppose the 'blood line,' the

caste system based on 'pure' class origins. I joined the Rebel
faction of Red Guards composed of students coming from 'bad'
class origins.

Then, in the autumn of 1966, I became active in the city-wide
efforts to rehabilitate the 'counterrevolutionary' Rebel workers
and began to support Xiang River Storm—the first Rebel, quasi-
political party in Hunan to contain, not just students, but also
individuals from different professions.

The Conservatives and the military had combined forces
during the February Countercurrent to crush most of the Rebel
organizations, including Xiang River Storm. During that period
I continued to protest against the persecution of the Rebels and
was briefly imprisoned by the military. As soon as I was released,
I rushed off to the nation's capital to gather information and
speak with the Red Guard groups there; it was in Beijing that
I first encountered the big-character posters critical of the
privileged class of Communist society. I decided to investigate
the social origins of the Cultural Revolution, confident that my
findings would fit nicely into Marxist-Leninist theory.

My data collection began with an interview of our family
nanny, who had surprised us at the beginning of the Cultural
Revolution by suddenly joining the Rebel organization for
nannies. We had been exploiting her, she announced. She made
it clear that the deference she showed my parents had been
completely feigned; deep down, she and most of the other
Changsha residents hated the Communist cadres and their
arrogant ways. Troubled, I recorded my findings, for her hatred
for those at the top could not be explained in terms of Mao's
'protracted revolution under the dictatorship of the proletariat'
or 'the struggle between the two lines.' I continued to pore over
the works of Marx.

Then I went into the countryside to carry out a series of
interviews. I spoke to the educated youth demanding to return
to the cities and to workers who were forming union-
like organizations. I spoke with peasants as well, who
were surprisingly vocal about their unhappiness with the
Communists' land tax policies. In 'Whither China?' I recorded
my conclusions—that a new privileged class had formed, which
was, as Marx put it, 'suppressing and exploiting the people.'
Nothing short of a violent, Paris Commune-style revolution
would remove this class, paving the way for open elections and
a democratic state.

China's top leaders in Beijing had assumed that by throwing
token support to the Rebels at strategic moments, they could

neutralize their political adversaries. They had never dreamed that a Changsha High School student would take the call for revolution seriously enough to attempt to define a defiant, new Rebel vision. To them, my essay appeared as if from nowhere.

◆

A screech of the brakes and the train comes to a halt. I am led off the platform into a vehicle, but in what direction, I cannot be sure. Surely this must be Changsha. I begin to imagine what detention will bring. Images of the lower classes described in Gorky's *Lower Depths* and *My Universities* fill my head. Before the Cultural Revolution my life had lacked for nothing materially, yet to my sixteen-year-old mind, my days had been empty. Now, two years later, a part of me aches to plunge into the 'lower depths' and investigate these colorful people. Until the nation's political chessboard changes, that will be my game plan.

My blindfold is removed, and I find myself in a small, dark room, squinting at a flickering light.

2

Spartacus

▼

At my first meal the inmates cling to me. One in particular seems very unwilling to leave.

'It's tough for you newcomers when you first come in. After a while, though, you'll get used to it—everyone does. Come on, try to eat.' Tall, muscular, and attentive, this man who hangs by my elbow gives me the creeps.

'I really don't feel like anything.'

'It won't get any better,' Luo Gang continues gently, sweeping his arm broadly to one side. He flicks his wrist and points to my bowl. 'You may be in here awhile. I mean it: if you don't eat something soon, you'll collapse.'

His words drift past. My thoughts are occupied with the political situation in Beijing. How long will it take this time before Shengwulian is rehabilitated? It is February, the beginning of the lunar year. Though I am inwardly moved by his concern, I do not reply.

'Well, then let me help you clean up,' he says, removing the enamel bowl from my hands as he speaks. As I turn away, he lifts his chopsticks and hastily shoves the bowl's contents into his mouth.

Three days later, I begin to appreciate exactly what I have forfeited. Too late.

One month passes. The pit in my stomach is now a source of constant pain, and my heart races wildly. In June I learn that this man who appropriated my food with such finesse is a professional pickpocket.

Like every child who learned to read during New China's first decade, my mental image of prison was imprinted by the dark dungeons of *Red Cliffs* and its riveting tales about the Nationalists' wartime political prisons. They were vile places, we knew, where hunger and terror reigned.

Though Zuojiatang Detention Center is a product of socialist

construction, it has a certain reputation of its own. Conservative
Red Guards bandy the name to intimidate Rebels, 'black
capitalists,' and 'reactionaries'; parents, to chasten disobedient
sons and daughters. For many years, Zuojiatang [Zuo Family
Pond] was nothing but a little plot of land surrounding a pond
in the southeastern outskirts of Changsha belonging, one
assumes, to a family named Zuo. It grew in time into a
dingy residential area. By the late 1950s, however, the name
'Zuojiatang' meant only one thing: the massive and forbidding
detention center where I have landed. By now the red-brick
buildings have turned purple with age, though the roof tiles
remain their original dark red. It is said that the layout of the
facility is modeled after Soviet prisons.

◆

Luo Gang is an enigma. It's almost uncanny, the resemblance
he bears to the Western actors in *King Arthur and the Knights
of the Roundtable*. His skin is fair, almost translucent; he has
large eyes and long, thick eyebrows. And like the Occidentals I
have seen in movies, he uses exaggerated gestures, opening his
mouth very wide and jutting out his chin when he wishes to
show surprise or disdain, or to indicate that something is out of
the ordinary. If he is feeling down, he shrugs his shoulders
dramatically in resignation, or rolls his eyes up to the ceiling.
Such hyperbole is simply not Chinese; it makes one jumpy, and
gives the impression that the person is frivolous and doesn't
know his place. And yet somehow I find myself befriending this
man.

Though at first he won't admit what it is he does for a living,
he speaks freely of all sorts of things only a pickpocket could
know. Practically every word out of his mouth is 'black
language,' the filthy argot of the bandit. Half of it I can't even
understand: no one at school or in the Provincial Committee
compound ever talked like this. Instead of 'soldiers,' he says
'grain-eaters'; to him, they are nothing but big 'rice barrels' who
sit around, waiting for meals. Paper currency is 'big leaves'; grain
coupons are 'little leaves.' There are even special words for the
numbers one to ten.

One problem plagues him; he is *milao*—starved—in every
sense of the word. There is no smoking in the *haozi*. Luo Gang
spends his waking hours fantasizing about 'chasing dogs,'
picking up old cigarette butts. He can be sure of netting a
cigarette for every question answered at pre-trial interrogation,

but these never last very long; one needs a steadier supply. But he's in luck, for a fresh opportunity arises every time he is paraded around the streets for criticism, a common enough occurrence these days. That's when Luo Gang chases down a lot of dogs.

But since matches, too, are prohibited, creating a fire is even more problematic than obtaining tobacco. First you pull tiny bits of straw from the mats used as summer bedding, twist them into a thin 'braid,' pull a tuft of wadding from a quilt, and carefully wrap it around the straw. Then one has to remove a plank from one of the beds, ever so quietly, and rub it back and forth like crazy until the cotton fibers begin to smoke. By blowing gently, it is possible to bring the little ball to flame; if you blow too hard, though, you have to start all over again. The process can take hours. Luo Gang has never been much at playing chess, guessing riddles, or solving brainteasers, but when Number Nine is out of matches, he is the first one we turn to. You have to respect a guy who can make fire.

My sleep is fitful, riddled with dreams. I am betrayed by someone I trust. I am arrested. A driver and two rifle-bearing privates escort me to the Wuhan train station. I sit in the train for hours. When my blindfold is untied, I see a man in a faded green shirt and blue pants. Warden Liu. 'This detention center is run by the Military Control Commission of the Bureau of Public Security,' he announces stiffly. Then I wake up.

When it comes to food, we are all *milao*. The three daily meals we are given are calculated to keep us just barely alive, so that about an hour before mealtime, everybody gets up and stands in the middle of the *haozi*, excitedly, as if a great event is about to take place. What we are waiting for is five ounces of rice—a child's portion—and a ladleful of vegetables cooked in water laced with a few drops of oil. The rice has been carefully premeasured, steamed in individual bowls, and stacked up on a wheeled cart; the vegetables are dumped in one large wooden bucket carried about on a shoulder pole.

The turn of the lock and a rush for the door. It is the biggest and the bravest, men like Luo Gang, who end up with the bowls that seem to be just a little bit fuller than the rest. He stares at each ladle of vegetables, wide-eyed, like a water buffalo. Sometimes the portions aren't even close to being equal and there are fights.

Xiao Fuxiang, a machine technician arrested in 1965 as a 'class enemy,' holds the *haozi* long-timers' endurance record. After four years in Number Nine, he scarcely looks human. I marvel at the transforming power of hunger. Within six months fat people become unrecognizable. Thin people soon take on the appearance of mummies.

My sexual urges have all but disappeared. As flesh melts away, my wet dreams decrease from once a week to once or twice a month. There are no secrets in Number Nine. Under the tutelage of Xiao Fuxiang, one of the mummies, inmates routinely jump out of bed after their nocturnal adventures, wash themselves, and put on clean clothes. I am much too embarrassed to follow suit. Only gradually am I emboldened by the example of Xiao Fuxiang, who on such occasions never fails to trumpet the glad tidings, disclosing as a matter of course the woman of his dreams on that particular evening.

For large men like Luo Gang, the accumulated effect of hunger is not merely a matter of comfort, but of life and death. He knows it. There is little he can do. Whenever he is allowed to go in the courtyard, 'out into the open air,' a privilege once granted prisoners every month but all but forgotten after the chaos of the Cultural Revolution—he yanks up tiny bunches of weeds to chew on. One day he finds a toad hopping about the courtyard. He skins it the moment he returns, grinning all the while, and before it stops twitching, pops it into his mouth. To get it down, he pats his chest and stomach.

Real meat exists only at our imaginary dinner parties, the spontaneous festive gatherings we hold whenever we get punchy and dizzy. One inmate who is familiar with Changsha's better restaurants begins by reminiscing enthusiastically about the three-delicacy and spicy beef noodles at the Yang Yu Xing. Others think back fondly on feasts of Hunan-style roast duck at Qi Zhen Pavilion, the steaming, meat-filled buns at the Garden of Virtue, or the twenty-odd varieties of rice noodle soup at the Peaceful Haven. As privileged residents of the Provincial Committee compound my family had eaten well, but I had never known the extent of Changsha's wonderful cuisine.

Luo Gang tells me how, on a good day, he and his friends would spend a small fortune on gourmet banquets; it is not surprising that the pickpockets are active participants at all our imaginary parties. They can relate the definitive method of preparing mouthwatering fare such as tiger-skinned pork shoulder, detailing how to select the best cut of meat and how to sear the skin to an appetizing golden brown; for steamed pork with seasoned rice powder, they share their secret method of slicing the pork belly into wide but thin slices; they explain to us how to prepare pork skin for mock shark fins. The longer we listen, the hungrier we become. These evenings conclude with a solemn pledge: as soon as we get out, the first thing we are going to do is to make a grand tour of the city's restaurants, making sure we sample each and every one of these notable dishes.

Ever since the onset of the Cultural Revolution, it has been forbidden to send care packages. This does not keep inmates from quietly passing the word to their families: 'Put lard in toothpaste tubes, dried shredded pork in the linings of jackets and quilts, glucose in medicine bottles.'

If you are connected, you can buy rice. Those prisoners whose relatives are too poor to send clothing, and whose appetites permit, find out quickly that a bowl of rice is the most precious commodity in the *haozi*. The secret rice trade flourishes.

Luo Gang is supplied by Little Boss, a short man in his early thirties whose family had been important Changsha capitalists with Nationalist ties. In 1949 the Little Boss lost his source of income and some ten years later got involved in the grain coupon 'business,' brokering grain coupon transactions. These, of course, were quite illegal, and he soon found himself a 'guest' at Zuojiatang. His business instinct serves him surprisingly well here, where a bowl of rice can be exchanged for a piece of clothing, or for a two-kuai prison coupon, the mimeographed prison currency which can in turn be used to acquire toothpaste, paper, and soap. That means a bowl of prison rice is worth the daily wage of a typical worker—ten times more than the price of rice on the outside.

Although demand is high, Little Boss is forced by hunger to limit his sales to one bowl a week. On the appointed day, he stays in bed late, forgoing breakfast, until almost lunchtime. By noon he is so weak he can barely stand. It goes without saying that transactions of this sort violate prison rules, so Luo Gang discusses terms with Little Boss in a corner where nobody can hear them. In less than a month's time Luo Gang has traded in all the clothes but the ones he has on.

He has become almost crazed with hunger, at times laughing bitterly, then suddenly silent. Or he sinks into depression, wailing out endless verses of 'Night Song,' a bandit's dirge that I have never heard before:

> Life on this earth is not so great,
> We're worse off than roadside grass,
> The grass, it dies, but comes back in spring,
> People die, and are never seen again.

The door suddenly swings open. 'Xiao Fuxiang, you're wanted for questioning.' At the sight of Warden Liu, Xiao quickly jumps from his bunk to the floor and scrambles to pull on his shoes. 'Just what do you think you're singing?' bellows the warden.

'Cadre, sir,' Luo Gang replies, rushing to the door, 'I'm so hungry I'm ready to hang myself. Whatever I've done, if you're going to sentence me, do it now. Take me out, tie me up, hang me from my wrists, and paddle me fifty times—it's all right with me. Anything would be better than slowly starving to death in here.'

The warden knows very well that Luo is one of Zuojiatang's 'frozen bean curds'—even when you fry them, the oil and salt never get to them. Smiling weakly, he replies, 'So, you still think you can lead a decadent, revisionist life? Now then, that's exactly why we want to remold your thoughts. We communists don't ever beat anyone, nor do we ever sentence wantonly or kill . . .'

'You just keep us hungry and helpless,' mutters Luo Gang.

'Straighten up!' The warden's face flushes with anger. 'You're out of line.'

As it turns out, Warden Liu is not one to talk. Soon after this incident he himself is packed off to a May Seventh cadre school for remolding by individuals who are more radical and more revolutionary than he. His replacement is a military man, a bearded lieutenant in the 47th Army whom we privately refer to as 'Whiskers.' By midyear, all the regular Public Security prison staff, the Conservatives who are affiliated with the Public Security Bureau, the Procurate, and the courts, are gone. The first notable change brought about by the Hunan Military Control Commission is the frequency of beatings.

Since the door to the detention center office is usually left open, we always know when Whiskers is laying into someone. Several weeks after his arrival, I climb up onto the front window bunk, where I can just make out the silhouettes of our bearded new warden, wielding a club, and another man, trying to protect his head and glasses with his hands. The glasses look vaguely familiar—they remind me of the ones worn by a Hunan University student leader of Shengwulian's Tertiary Education Storm.

'Zhou Guohui!' My voice rings throughout the quadrangle. When Zhou looks in my direction, Whiskers beats him harder than ever. Angrily, I cry out again, 'Don't hit him!' Several other inmates watching from their windows began to chant, quoting from Mao, 'Fight with words, not weapons!'

Whiskers begins to walk in the direction of Number Nine and I know I am in for a bad time. Watching quietly as I put on an extra shirt, Luo Gang tries to stuff his cap on my head, but I won't let him.

'All right,' he whispers, 'but when he hits you, remember to cover your belly and your head with your hands—the other places all have bones to protect them. Whatever you do, don't let them bust up your head and belly.'

In a matter of moments we are in the detention center office, where Whiskers loses no time in pummeling my head. I concentrate on cushioning his blows, aware nevertheless that out in the courtyard dozens of inmates are squatting or kneeling on the upper bunks, their angry faces pressed to the bars.

'Don't beat prisoners!'

'Fight with words, not weapons!'

The guards who have been standing by in the courtyard start to hurl stones at any prisoner they catch shouting. As the blows continue to shower down, I can see guards jumping all around. No sooner do they aim at the north wing than the southern *haozi* start up. Stones and voices fly back and forth, with Luo Gang's voice the loudest of them all, until the guards finally call for reinforcements, and the heavy, iron gate swings open. Mounted machine guns roll in. Soldiers carrying loaded rifles rush through the massive iron gate and spread quickly throughout the courtyard, positioning themselves at the doorway of each of the twenty-four *haozi*. Only then does Whiskers finally put down his club. The entire incident has lasted about fifteen minutes.

Zhou Guohui and I are subsequently led by two important-looking officers through the corridor, out of the quadrangle, and into a nearby pre-trial interrogation room. They are surprisingly polite. 'If you have an opinion, you can communicate it to me,' says one of them, looking at me. 'But don't be starting trouble.'

'The last couple of weeks the guards have been beating people almost every day. Chairman Mao says to fight with words and not with weapons. Don't these people carry out their work according to the directives of the Chairman?'

'Beating people is not acceptable, it's true,' the officer replies. 'But creating a disturbance is worse.'

It is the summer of 1968. The political situation that seems to be shaping up throughout China is extremely delicate, for the balance of power between the Rebel and Conservative factions has just begun to shift in favor of the Rebels. It's a good time for the members of Shengwulian to push for rehabilitation. The 47th Army can't be sure which way the political tide will drift next:

everybody remembers how, just last summer, the radical Rebel group Xiang River Storm was officially cleared in a similar face-off, so the military has adopted a very cautious wait-and-see attitude toward Shengwulian celebrities such as Zhou and myself.

Perhaps that is the reason we are not punished further for our defiant behavior. The beatings subside for a while. And Luo Gang takes a fresh look at 'weak scholarly types' like me. He begins to open up.

The chaos of the last couple of years was a pickpocket's dream. 'Didn't Lenin say, "Revolution is the people's carnival?"' he winks. Luo Gang joined Xiang River Storm and had been on the scene when the Rebels seized the guns. In ordinary times everyday citizens were not permitted to get their hands on weapons, and the pickpockets had a field day. When he was wounded in the 24th High School Incident, the final battle in a series of military confrontations between Changsha Rebels and Conservatives in 1967, he was treated like a war hero. Along with his comrades-in-arms, Luo Gang had a chance to try out some of the .59 millimeter pistols and semi-automatic rifles, and to steal several trucks from the arsenal. He taught himself how to drive. Too bad, he recollects wistfully, he never did figure out how to use high gear.

I seldom hear the word 'pickpocket' used within the confines of Number Nine; the preferred term is 'Master Pincers.' But in the parlance of Luo Gang, what he does is 'catching fish.' When he returns from being marched around town, he will say things like, 'A lot of fish out there today—too bad my pincers were all cuffed up. Damned if I wasn't just like a fly sitting on a bull's balls—I had to move where they did.'

In my heart I know he is treating me particularly well, both because I am a celebrated political underdog and because I am relatively young. Even so, he gets on my nerves. I simply cannot stand the boundless enthusiasm with which he talks about women. 'Take off your dust mask, let me take a look,' he chants again and again. 'If you haven't married anyone yet, you'll have to marry me!' The song drives me absolutely crazy.

Even less amusing is his tale about how he and a friend became obsessed with the gradually swelling breasts of their female classmates in elementary school. Luo's friend had made him a bet: If Luo could touch one of those 'things' without making the girl angry, he would win one *kuai*.

'It's a deal,' Luo said without hesitating.

The next day after school, while they were walking around,

they spotted a couple of girls heading in their direction. Luo Gang quickly looked away, he tells me with a smirk, and cocked his head toward his friend as if he were in the midst of a serious conversation. Then, just as the girl closest to him brushed past his shoulder, he turned around, and spat right in the middle of her chest. Losing no time, he pulled out a handkerchief and dabbed furiously at her blouse, apologizing all the time. Spitting in public was not unusual in those days, and the practice was by no means limited to men, so it didn't occur to the girl to be angry. She was even a little embarrassed at all the fuss he was making and kept protesting, 'It's all right; it's really all right.'

Luo Gang grins at the memory of his victory: He had, at the age of thirteen, maintained his honor, won a sizeable amount of money, and satisfied his curiosity all at the same time.

So vulgar does he seem to me that I actually feel ashamed for him. 'No game on earth is more fun than "playing women,"' he says. Graphic descriptions of his various exploits dominate his conversations to such an extent that I begin to suspect the *haozi* gossip is true, that picking pockets is not the only reason he is in prison. Though I never inquire as to his specific charge, whatever it is, it is bad enough for him to avoid mentioning it. If one is to believe the rumors, he did something in a hospital involving a nurse.

'It was some sort of sex crime,' whispers Xiao Fuxiang to me one day.

'How do you know?'

'Last week he came back from pre-trial interrogation pretty shaken. The prosecutor was a woman—Can you imagine?—and I guess she was pretty tough. She even asked if he "got in" and if "liquid" came out! A woman! So he must be in for rape, or something close to it, don't you think?'

Luo Gang's class origin was bad; not 'red' enough to go on to high school. With no money and a lot of time on his hands, he had loafed around for a spell, then started to steal. When he first began his apprenticeship with an old pickpocket, Luo approached his targeted victim six times, only to walk away five. The sixth time, he returned with what he was after. Half of the money went to the old man and Luo Gang had spent the rest the same day. After that, he tells me, 'catching fish' became his life.

'It must be hard to take a wallet from people who are wide awake without them feeling anything,' I ask somewhat self-consciously, knowing that I must sound naïve. 'Do you have special tools?'

'Course we do—razor blades. You hold them between your

index and middle fingers, so with a flick of the wrist you can open up a slit for the fish to come out. But most of the time we don't need any tools.'

With great excitement, Luo proceeds to describe his life during the early sixties. There had been a girl pickpocket on a train; her fish-catching skill was unerring, and Luo Gang fell for her, head over heels. They wandered around for a couple of months, stealing together by day, sleeping together at night. Then one day when he opened his eyes, she wasn't there. 'The damn whore,' he mutters bitterly, 'once you came, she didn't even know you were alive.'

On the road he often awoke feeling panicked, haunted by the feeling that he was being pursued. One afternoon another pickpocket ran up to him, pushed a watch into his hands, and ran off again. Before Luo Gang had realized what was happening, he was surrounded by an angry mob and beaten until he was almost unconscious. 'When brown mud drops into your pants, it always looks like shit,' he grumbles.

Recalling the violence of that day and others, Luo surprises me by speaking almost affectionately of the Public Security Bureau. 'You know, whenever I'm caught in the act, I always try to get to the nearest branch as soon as I can,' he says earnestly. 'Otherwise my hands, my legs—my whole body gets smashed up.'

It was the Public Security Bureau who subsequently sent Luo Gang to a home for juvenile delinquents too young to be sentenced, where he stayed until he was assigned to a factory as an apprentice worker. Since the hours were long, 'fishing' had to be fit into his spare time. But he was strong and full of life, and quickly became popular with the factory girls, who called him 'Spartacus' because he reminded them of Kirk Douglas. Factory life brought men and women into constant contact, and incidents involving 'moving hands and feet' were common. During the numerous weekend trips into the suburbs of Changsha, it was inevitable that he would have 'romantic' interludes. Yet when he recalls his trips to places like Yelu Mountain or Liuyang River, he makes a point of telling me that what he had enjoyed most was 'discussing his beliefs.'

'What?' I interrupt. 'Did you say *beliefs*?' I can't possibly imagine what beliefs Luo Gang might have, unless it was that 'there's nothing more fun than playing women.'

'All my girls know I believe in "The Vagabond."'

'That Indian movie?' It slowly occurs to me what he means. It's not a bad movie; I saw it in the late fifties when it ran not only in China, but in the Middle East and the Soviet Union. The story of a judge who believed in the 'blood line,' or the 'theory of lineage,' Raj Kapoor's 'Vagabond' had everything necessary for mass appeal—a poignant love story, an intricate plot, biting social commentary, spectacular song-and-dance numbers, and, not incidentally, a likable anti-hero named Raj—a pickpocket who lived on the streets of New Delhi.

Convinced that 'thieves beget thieves,' the movie begins with an Indian judge unjustly convicting Jagga, a man whose father and grandfather were notorious bandits, but who himself is innocent of any crime. Now embittered, Jagga plots to teach the judge a lesson by abducting his pregnant wife and raising the child—the young Raj—to be a robber. The judge is unaware that he has a son, and adopts a girl named Rita, who being as intelligent as she is beautiful, becomes a dedicated attorney. In a strange twist of fate, Raj and Rita meet each other outside the courthouse, then again in her opulent home. They fall in love and Raj proposes, only to be driven away by her father. When Raj is arrested a second time, Rita learns of his real identity, and in an eloquent closing statement reveals to the courtroom Raj's hidden past, whereupon Raj receives a relatively mild sentence of three years.

'I like the ending the best,' Luo Gang tells me. 'You know, when Rita sees Raj off to labor reform camp. Remember?' I nod with a faint smile. 'She says, "I'll be waiting for you, Raj."' Luo's expression is radiant, as if there were really a beautiful woman standing right next to the bunk. He has forgotten, of course, that there aren't any 'labor camps' in India, nor do I remind him.

It is only natural that he identifies with Raj, I reflect. Luo Gang, too, was deprived of an education because he lived in a society that embraced the 'class line.' But though he recognizes the inequity of all this, he doesn't dwell on his lot. For better or for worse, he is already a pickpocket, and seems to thrive on the defiant lifestyle that he leads.

'The Vagabond' and its music has reached out to more than just prison inmates—even small children know the melodies and can sing the Chinese lyrics. 'Rita's Song,' a soft, romantic tune, seems to be especially popular among the pickpockets and is often heard in Number Nine. Ever the free spirit, Luo Gang has his own favorite, the title song, 'Raj's Song,' or 'Vagabond,' with its snappy rhythm reminiscent of the pulse of a large, prosperous city and the pickpocket's turbulent life. Rocking his shoulders to the beat, he hisses, 'Damned if I'm not just like a beggar screwing an asshole—it's a poor sort of happiness we're stuck with on this earth.' The muscles on his face twitch.

Labor camps are not new to Luo Gang, and this is his fourth stay in the detention center. He pulls me aside one day and says quietly, 'That guy Liu is "KGB"; he's always sending snitch reports to the cadres. I think he needs to understand some flavor.' 'Flavor,' of course, refers to the 'flavor of human kindness.'

'Him?' I ask, looking over this man in his late fifties who is said to have served as a Nationalist official and is in Zuojiatang on a charge of graft. Although Old Man Liu has always been extremely polite to me, come to think of it, he does seem to act excessively meek when the authorities are around, and he is downright rude to the pickpockets.

'Sure. He's an historical counterrevolutionary. The Communists always use old guys like that to keep an eye on the practicing counterrevolutionaries. Sure. The same way they use common criminals to keep the counterrevolutionary criminals in line. Haven't you noticed every morning how Old Man Liu is always one of the first ones up? How he always wants to be the one to dump the pot or to bring in the hot water? What, you thought he was a hard worker?' 'Historical counterrevolutionaries' were individuals who had been pronounced guilty of political crimes before 1949—usually individuals associated with the Nationalist regime; 'practicing counterrevolutionaries' referred to individuals who committed 'counterrevolutionary crimes' after that time.

One or two days later, Luo Gang magically acquires one of Liu's 'reports' and shows it to me. On special paper available only to the pre-trial interrogation officers I read the carefully written words:

Cadre, sir: In Number Nine, Wen Liusheng recited aloud and wrote from memory the feudalist weeds *Three Hundred Tang Poems* and Zhu Geliang's 'Great Generals.' On June 7th, Luo Gang introduced his pickpocket experiences to another prisoner. On June 11th, in an attack against our new society and socialism, Zhao Dewen said that his present salary could have bought twice as many things before Liberation. Signed, Liu.

One after another, Old Man Liu's fountain pen, ink, and paper all take off without wings. I never see Luo Gang make a move, just Old Man Liu rushing about, muttering and cursing, 'Who took my pen?' Then it finally hits him, and as the pickpockets later joke, he is 'like the blind man who has finished a bowl of

sweet dumplings—he knows exactly how many he has eaten.'
Somebody is trying to get even, of that he is sure—but 'like a
mute who has swallowed an herbal tonic, he is unable to tell of
the bitterness.'

Old Man Liu has had ample occasion during his lengthy
tenure as an 'historical counterrevolutionary' to witness
pickpockets gang up and beat 'KGBs,' or snitches, to death, so
he isn't going to pursue the matter. In light of the possibilities,
he figures, losing a pen isn't so bad.

In the next nationwide anti-crime campaign that comes along,
Old Man Liu is sentenced. Life: a term so heavy that it is clear
that the authorities have judged him not only on the matter of
misappropriating public funds, but on his 'historical' background
as well.

'It's just not fair!' he cries out over and over. 'This society eats
people alive!' Only then does Luo Gang's resentment toward him
dissipate. Old Man Liu moves over to the transit cell.

Not long afterwards Luo Gang, himself, is handed ten years
for whatever it is that he has done. At the age when he still needs
'growing rice'—men being considered fully 'grown' at twenty-
five, women at twenty—he is now so thin that he bears no
resemblance to the man I first met. His sentence is read aloud
to him in one of the pre-trial interrogation rooms, as is the
standard practice, and when he shares the news back at the
haozi, everybody starts shouting, insisting that it's too severe.
But Luo Gang is beaming with pleasure and relief. He calls a
friend in Number Ten, shouting at the top of his lungs, 'Well, it
looks like the Public Security organs just got themselves another
free piece of good muscle. Hey, hey! I'm off to the labor camp
brigade to eat "growing rice"!'

During an inmate's final weeks, family members are
permitted a single visit to Zuojiatang. It is the only time that
such a meeting can take place, regardless of how long one is
detained. Since the authorities are the only ones who know the
actual departure date, most relatives report to the prison soon
after sentencing.

Luo Gang waits in vain for the guards to announce that he has
a visitor and then leaves quite suddenly, on a blustery, rainy
morning in December 1968. From atop my bunk, I try to picture
him filing out the main gate with the other prospective laborers,
slowly making the thirty-minute walk to the train station,
accompanied only by a few guards, who must be cursing the
inclement weather. It dawns on me that none of his 'Ritas' ever
showed up. There will be no one waiting for Spartacus Luo.

3

Blindman Lu

▼

No one can remember his real name, not even our guards; everybody calls him Blindman Lu. He wears funny, round, mock tortoise-shell spectacles, the kind people wore before Liberation, with lenses as thick as the bottoms of bean-paste jars. From a normal distance all you see are short, narrow slits behind the blurred glass. But if you stand right next to him, the lenses work the other way, revealing two dark eyes peering out intensely at the world.

Blindman Lu is not very tall, and he is thin even by prison standards. Regardless of the temperature in Number Nine, he keeps himself bundled up like a cocoon. Mornings without fail he dons an expensive brown woolen suitcoat with a high Mandarin collar, then carefully pulls on yet another Chinese-style jacket made of coarse blue cloth, the kind once worn exclusively by workers. To look at this ragged outer garment and his dirty wisp of a beard, you would think he was nothing but a vagabond, down on his luck. Who could guess that Blindman Lu owns a fancy piece of real estate in the Octagonal Pavilion downtown? He admits to owning a three-story building and sophisticated machinery for manufacturing leather shoes, and the resident pickpockets swear that he's got vast quantities of gold bullion tucked away. There is no denying it, Blindman Lu is a capitalist.

Like the pickpockets who use Zuojiatang as a hotel, he is a frequent patron of the establishment and knows most of the other guests by sight. He seems affable enough, speaking at length with just about anyone, boundlessly interested in everything. He will exhaust a topic, from the cut of a suit to the best brand of toothbrush, from the composition of a stool sample to the political movement of the day. I soon discover, though, that this amiability is not totally ingenuous, but rather a habit that has gradually evolved from his philosophy of business. As

he later explains to me, he believes that all events are in some
way related to one another. The more a person can take
advantage of little scraps of information, indications of how
separate events interconnect, the more opportunities will arise
for him to make money.

But if Blindman Lu is the wealthiest man in Number Nine,
he is also the tightest. He has never used either toothbrush or
toothpaste. Instead he carries around a sliver of bamboo that he
unwraps once a day to scrape his tongue, and he cleanses his
teeth with water. Some of the pickpockets openly jeer at him,
saying that he is willing to totally disregard modern hygiene in
order to save a few cents. Others say this practice is simply a
habit which he acquired as a child and can't shake, that a rich
man like Lu certainly wouldn't care about such a pittance.

Lu is my first capitalist to meet face-to-face, although I have
read about them in books, of course. Ever since Lu joined our
ranks I have been dying to hear the story of his life and how he
made his fortune. But Blindman Lu seems unwilling to share his
experiences with mere students; we lack knowledge of the real
world. Whenever I bring up the subject of capitalism, he tries to
cut the conversation short, nodding vaguely, in a polite but
visibly impatient manner.

One day, however, he overhears Spartacus Luo mention that
I am the author of 'Whither China?' and that changes everything.

'I've often thought about where China is headed myself,' he
volunteers.

'Have you read the essay?' I ask skeptically.

'No, no.'

I laugh to myself. This man can hardly be interested in a Paris
Commune-style democracy; it's more likely that he is thinking
about the system of private ownership, assuming that I have
compared the relative advantages of capitalism and socialism.
But I am in no hurry to set him straight; I do not wish to alienate
this interesting man.

Blindman Lu eventually begins to talk about his enterprises,
but I suspect this is less in response to my own questions than
to the unceasing assaults of the pickpockets. The 'pincers' take
as their sacred creed, 'Blessings should be enjoyed together;
misfortunes should be suffered together.' They can neither
understand nor forgive Blindman Lu's solitary existence and
'stinginess,' nor do his unusual habits help very much.

He is known throughout the *haozi* for never washing his feet
and for refusing outright to change his socks. Worse still, every
couple of days he takes off his smelly socks, picks the lint from

between his toes, and holds it up to his nose to savor at length. Somehow he finds the odor appealing; it seems to stimulate his senses.

One afternoon several of the pickpockets catch him in the middle of this strange ritual and rush over to seize his glasses. He'll never get his socks back, they threaten, unless he promises not to take them off when they are around. Blindman Lu howls in protest, but, at length, seeing that the pickpockets are not inclined to negotiate, he gives in, pledging solemnly never to let another man in Number Nine witness him remove his dirty socks.

Equally irritating, Lu snores. In our cramped quarters Blindman Lu's snorts seem to shake heaven and earth; his upper torso lifts and falls so violently that it is hard to believe he is really sleeping. All of this is just too much for the pickpockets. Whenever he begins to snore, they roll up tiny paper cylinders, squat by his side, and poke at the hairs protruding from his nostrils till he is wide awake and hopping mad.

Compared with these antics, my own sort of probing must seem far less objectionable. Blindman Lu finally tells me about his life. In 1950 at the age of eighteen, just after graduating from high school, Lu went into business. He tried selling all sorts of things, beginning with 'Sesame Pull,' a caramel-like candy mixed with white sesame seeds. Children would crowd around his pushcart, waiting for a chance to grab onto the end of the long, sticky mass. When Blindman Lu cried out, 'All right, pull!', a child would yank at the candy until a chunk broke off. You could keep whatever you pulled off, and the price was always the same. It was a popular game with the throngs of kids lining the streets and alleyways of Changsha, and profitable.

Then he introduced a 'variety pack' of sweet and savory snack foods, again catering almost exclusively to school children. Slung on his neck was a wooden box divided into a dozen or so square compartments, each housing a different treat, such as salted ginger, candied perilla leaves, hawthorn wafers, and various preserved fruits. Five pennies would buy a small paper packet containing a sampling of all twelve, eliminating for the greedy child a difficult choice.

For the adults, Lu developed a primitive sort of peepshow called the 'Western glass.' During one of his frequent visits to Shanghai he got his hands on color slides of world-famous historical landmarks—pictures of the Eiffel Tower, the pyramids, the canals of Venice. For good measure he also included in his collection several poses of Western women, noteworthy for the fact that they were naked from the waist up. The portable peepshow consisted of a square box mounted on a revolving wheel that could be turned by hand. At the top of the box there was just enough room for one person to view the series of slides through a small lens. A black cloth was draped over the box and Lu had confected an imposing sign:

SEE THE FAMOUS SIGHTS OF THE WORLD!
WESTERN BEAUTIES!
TOUR THE WORLD'S FAMOUS CITIES!
ENJOY SEEING MODERN YOUNG WOMEN!

During these early years Blindman Lu tried his hand at countless other small businesses. He was constantly going back and forth to cosmopolitan Shanghai, scouring the city for new ideas and equipment. On one such trip he learned of an opportunity involving a monosodium glutamate factory only recently established in Shanghai. The plant was preparing to market its product nationwide and Lu was able to secure exclusive rights for distribution in Hunan. He set up his operation step by step. He bought a typewriter, hired his cousin as secretary, and started mimeographing flyers.

A key element of the promotion was a personal letter from Lu asking all interested stores to respond as soon as possible. The office address on his letterhead was in fact Blindman Lu's home address; the phone number was that of the nearest phone booth. The shopowners had complete confidence that the MSG was coming out of a respectable establishment of long standing.

Lu tells me that, for the Chinese entrepreneur, the period immediately following the Civil War was an especially prosperous one. Imports from potential foreign competitors had disappeared with the onset of the American blockade; the Party was actively fostering private capital investments. The Shanghai factory's MSG quickly penetrated the national market and the twenty-four year old Lu found himself a member of Changsha's nouveau riche.

His daily routine was surprisingly simple. He had only to send the incoming orders on to the Shanghai plant and wait for the goods to be shipped to Changsha. As soon as the cartons arrived, he would rickshaw them over to the main post office and distribute the MSG throughout the province. He didn't even need a warehouse.

Then came his biggest break of all, when the factory decided to expand its operations and drastically cut its prices. For one reason or another, the managers allowed Lu to buy a large quantity of MSG at the reduced price early on, so that he was able to sell it all at the original retail price before the factory reduction was announced to the general public. This factory discount was a windfall for Blindman Lu, providing the capital for his subsequent endeavors. He was able to purchase prime storefront property in the Octagonal Pavilion, remodel the three-story building that stood on it, and go into business in earnest. Soon he was not only selling MSG, but all types of machinery.

True to the old Chinese saying that good times never last for long, the year of 1956 brought with it the State–Private Joint Enterprise Movement and trouble for Lu. Businessmen had already suffered five years earlier during the Three Antis (1951–52) and Five Antis (1952): the respective campaigns against corruption, waste, and bureaucracy within the Party, government, army, and mass organizations; and against bribery, tax evasion, theft of state property, cheating on government contracts, and stealing of economic information. Most enterprises had never fully recovered. As the Communist Party increased its pressure once again ever so slightly, private investors handed their businesses over to the State without so much as a peep of protest.

Blindman Lu was not about to give up his newly acquired building. In fact he didn't even consider the idea, proclaiming, 'The Communist policy of State–Private Joint Enterprise is based on voluntary participation for mutual benefit, and I choose not to participate!'

The MSG factory in Shanghai had long been converted into a 'semi-private' enterprise. They offered Blindman Lu a steady position at 40 yuan a month. Of course, they said, he must work in Shanghai. Again, he flatly refused. Instead he purchased a large machine for manufacturing shoes and immediately began production in his own shop. By this time his entire building was devoted to manufacturing or sales of one kind or another.

The Party was annoyed. Not only was Blindman Lu not participating in their program, he actually seemed to be thriving on his own. Clearly a time for action, the Communist officials began to squeeze Lu's employees. Among them were a few who were relatively sympathetic to the Party. Soon these could be heard complaining about their boss, saying that he exploited them. The hours were too long, the benefits too few.

Blindman Lu parlayed by firing all the workers. The Party responded: such an action was expressly prohibited. Lu decided to take the matter to court. Gathering up all the official documents he could lay his hands on, he eloquently defended his right to dismiss the workers. The court waited for him to finish, decided in favor of the workers, and imposed a stiff fine on Blindman Lu, labeling him a 'reactionary capitalist who refused to be molded by socialism.'

Still Lu did not give up. He halted indefinitely all operations requiring outside workers, refusing to pay any more salaries. Keeping one machine on which his wife could make cotton soles, he went to the Hunan Provincial High Court to appeal his case. This court ignored him completely, so he tried another organization—the Standing Committee of the Provincial People's Congress. There he was turned away by the petty official in the reception room, who also took the occasion to rebuke him for not accepting the molding influence of socialism.

To Lu this was sheer propaganda, certainly not something to take very seriously. 'In cases like these you must use only legal criteria,' he continued to counsel the bureaucrat patiently, 'and only facts as evidence. Isn't that what the Premier of your Communist Party said in his political work report?' The official blinked and ignored him. But before too long Lu became a familiar face and was not even permitted to enter the reception room. This made it more difficult than ever for him to gain access to public officials.

Just about the time when Lu had his fill of being rebuffed, he began to notice that whenever ordinary civilians like himself wore clothes made of wool, they were treated with hostility by government organizations. In the 1950s, he tells me, wearing well-tailored clothes was a privilege reserved for high-ranking cadres. If ordinary citizens dressed 'lavishly' they were condemned as bourgeoisie who exploited the people. On the other hand, expensive suits on the persons of high-level officials evoked from the masses respect and even envy.

Once Blindman Lu had cracked the subtle dress code, he began wearing a tattered old shirt on top of his woolen suits, a practice which, sure enough, magically enabled him to approach the highest of Hunan officials. On hearing that an important figure such as the mayor of Changsha or the municipal party committee secretary would be attending a function at a particular public place, Lu would rush to the scene and pass the individual his formal written appeal. When the officials present saw that Lu was a man of humble status, they invariably treated him quite well. In this way Lu's petition was finally accepted and submitted to the appropriate authorities for review. He was told to wait, that his case would be 'investigated.'

The results of the investigation came only too soon. In 1958, during the final stages of the Anti-Rightist Campaign, Blindman Lu was officially labeled a 'bad element who refused to be molded by socialism.' While his reform was overseen by the neighborhood police substation, several political officials would occupy Lu's building. They publicly announced that the first and second floors would be reserved indefinitely for Communist Party use.

Then in 1964 a new policy calling for the 'transformation of private homes' was adopted and Blindman Lu's building was confiscated altogether. Undaunted, Lu traveled to Beijing to lodge a complaint. He was taken into custody by the Ministry of Public Security and held for one year, on the grounds that he was a 'bad element who refused to submit to authority.' Since he had not committed a criminal offense, he was released in 1965. During the Cultural Revolution, his building was ransacked by the Red Guards, who seized his gold and drove him out onto the streets to live. Once again he made the pilgrimage to Beijing to petition the authorities; this time he was made to serve a double prison term.

In Zuojiatang, secure in the knowledge that he has not broken any laws, criminal or otherwise, Blindman Lu calmly awaits the day of his release. He delights in reciting, in their entirety, the articles of the 1954 Constitution providing for the protection of citizens' property.

'If the Communists are the ones exploiting workers,' he grumbles, 'it is said to be the "work of the proletarian revolution" and the workers are said to be "making a contribution to society." But let ordinary people employ workers—no matter that the salaries are much higher—and those people are considered bourgeois and reactionary. When you're the one doing business, you're called a dirty profiteer; when it's them, it's all right. If you aimed a three-barrel gun at me, I still wouldn't accept this Communist logic as truth.'

He cites examples of the Communists' monopoly on foreign trade and the various movements to 'increase productivity' and 'economize on resources.' 'Look how the State conducts foreign trade,' he begins, 'It buys low and sells high, in extremely speculative business deals that easily yield a hundred, often three hundred percent profit—perfectly legal. But just try and let a private citizen do the same thing, for a lot smaller profit; he's a dirty profiteer.' Or he says, 'In Communist factories, there are productivity movements all year round. The first season has "The Open Door is Red—Get Off to a Good Start Movement," midyear it's the "Every Month is Red Movement," and at year's end it's the "War for Red Throughout the Year Movement." The purpose of every single one of these is to get workers to work more for less.'

Blindman Lu's mind never stops moving. Never in my circles have I met anyone as receptive to new information. One minute he is talking shop with a sales engineer about the principles, parts, and mechanics of a flocking machine. Then he turns around and shows the same enthusiasm for subtle legal matters. He is even interested in *Das Kapital*. I share with him my secret copy, and the two of us finish the three-volume set within hours of each other, when I can hardly wait to tell him my epiphany: The labor theory of value is invalid because it ignores another factor determining price—Marx's 'use value,' the concept now known as 'utility.' And after reading Marx's discussion of Adam Smith, I say to myself, 'Smith's theory of the division of labor is inconsistent with the labor theory of value.' I decide to become an economist.[1]

When Blindman Lu returns the book to me, he is also smiling, but for different reasons: within its pages he has found several descriptions of two-party legal suits involving wage disputes.

◆

Throughout the years of his detainment, Blindman Lu remains optimistic, never doubting for a minute that he will some day be freed. Nor is he terribly unhappy in prison; in fact he considers himself almost lucky. Many a 'free' industrialist is reported to have disappeared under mysterious circumstances; many have died by their own hands. And as I prepare to walk out of Number Nine for the last time to hear my own sentence, I catch myself thinking about this odd little man with a measure of irritation. No doubt I envy him his comfortable and eminently tenable position.

It was Blindman Lu's fate that showed me how the Communists once treated private business owners, the cruel and arbitrary way in which his property was taken away. To him, the

[1] While in Number Nine I decided to accomplish three things during my career as an economist: first, to develop a theory of value that would take into consideration 'use' value and the cost of goods; second to develop a theory that could explain the relationship between the division of labor and the determinants of value; and finally, I hoped to formalize the theory of value using calculus, an idea which I got from a large-character poster at Beijing University in 1966. During my time in prison I wrote several essays on these subjects and eventually was able to achieve all three of my objectives.

right to own property was a natural, legal, and logical matter;
but as natural as it was, it was incompatible with the ideals and
the ideology of the Communist Party at the time. The tenets
of communism that I had always held sacred manifested
themselves through his stories as things that could not coexist
with humanity and justice. The older I get, the more I appreciate
his tenacious conviction that justice and fairness will ultimately
prevail.

4

Nine Dragons

▼

The repeaters, those who are 'twice-in-the-palace,' know instinctively that Zhang Jiulong was involved in some sort of underground activity. He is treated badly, which means that he is important. And he is the only man in Number Nine who doesn't ignore the numerous and, for the most part, inconsequential house regulations.

Whereas the rest of us entertain ourselves daily in creative, if somewhat disreputable ways—memorizing classical poetry, telling lewd stories, and playing poker, or 'paper strips'—Nine Dragons Zhang leads a Spartan life, allowing himself but a single indulgence. This is *weiqi*, 'surrounding chess,' the Chinese game that has come to be called 'go' by the Japanese. For Zhang it is a preoccupation which entails no small risk.

No matter that our activities routinely escape the attention of the guards, the games remain 'strictly prohibited,' and an exceptionally stealthy patrol that succeeds in catching the players red-handed can be expected to confiscate all the pieces. Then, even before the lock clangs shut, a series of miniature production lines spring into action. Political fliers will be deftly transformed into chessmen, black and white go 'stones,' and poker cards, all with the aid of just a pencil and a few grains of sticky rice. On occasion, the younger pickpockets refuse to give up their contraband, claiming they haven't been playing games, merely sitting on their beds looking for bedbugs and fleas. 'If you want, we can turn over our fleas to you,' they volunteer cheerfully, knowing that the guards will probably leave it at that. Such unorthodox behavior, I am to learn, is the privilege of common criminals: Nine Dragons Zhang makes very sure he never gets caught.

It is at the go board that I first meet him. We are well matched, I note silently; surprisingly so. Like the others, I tend to look down on this shadow of a man for his patently counterrevolutionary bent, but he is able to beat me at go, and does so frequently. Because it has many more possible configurations and manipulations than its Western cousin, chess, go requires a better memory and more intelligence. Good partners are not easily come by. Soon Zhang and I can be found once or twice a day up on somebody's bunk, legs crossed, fiercely contemplating the relative positions of black and white. And whereas a game between inmates ordinarily lasts about an hour, for Zhang and me three hours often pass before all of our regional confrontations are resolved and the points can be counted.

I plan my attacks with care, glancing up from time to time, trying to read his deep, brooding eyes that at times flash with unconcealed cruelty. It is impossible to know what he is thinking. He seldom waits very long between moves; his reflexes are quick, his calculations accurate. And he can see more than ten moves ahead. Though we go at it again and again, our matches are never dull, for his style of play is characterized by what in Chinese we call 'leaving very little air.' Playing each configuration close to the wire, he leaves only one or two points at liberty. Then, just when his divisions appear to be hopelessly besieged, one of these seemingly 'dead' clusters opens up suddenly and swallows a giant piece of what should rightfully have become my territory, killing off any of my men that happen to be trapped inside.

Pre-trial interrogation is intermittent and always unannounced. A guard appears one morning, calls out a name or two, and the people are taken away. If the name is Zhang's or mine, our game has to wait until the next day, when play resumes as if nothing had happened. There is no mention of the men at Public Security, or of the sentencing that will inevitably follow.

Sometimes I win. Perhaps because we respect each other's abilities and silences, a measured but very real sense of trust evolves: we are adversaries, but we are friends. He, too, knows of 'Whither China?' and asks about it. Ever so cautiously, he begins to reveal bits of information about his own past.

Zhang's father was trained as a machinist and became skilled in the use of lathes, pliers, planes, and milling machines. An uncle, his father's older brother, who was also mechanically inclined, opened an automobile repair shop shortly after Liberation, the first of its kind in the province. Business was so good that Zhang's father soon set up his own machine shop. Though his facilities were limited, he accepted just about any kind of metalworking job he was offered. Except for a belt-driven lathe and a small milling machine made of lead, he did all his polishing and filing using his bare hands and a little vise. When he ran up against a task that he couldn't manage alone, he relied on a large factory and rented the equipment he needed. His ingenuity soon paid off. Business picked up and his mother and older brother began to help out full-time. By the time Zhang was in college, his father had acquired three sets of custom metalworking tools and he employed two assistants.

According to Zhang's accounts, they could do more work than a state-run factory with one hundred workers and state-of-the-art machinery imported from the Soviet Union. It was no secret that the workers in big factories of this sort just sat around much of the day waiting for the people at the top to send down 'planned tasks.' The booming machine industry had become too sophisticated for the central planners to comprehend, and the independent outfits that were sprouting up everywhere could not always find suitable factories to help them with special orders. Since state-run factories had little incentive to seek out the independent workshops, much of their expensive equipment lay idle day after day.

But then the State–Private Joint Ownership Movement came along, and the Zhang family stopped worrying about things like efficiency since their shops were now the property of the State. They had new problems. Nine Dragons' uncle was branded a capitalist, and his father fared only somewhat better, being labeled a 'petty proprietor,' sandwiched between the petty bourgeoisie and capitalists.

His family thus blackened, the young Zhang Jiulong spent a lot of time thinking about the different types of economic systems. Predictably, he came to the conclusion that private enterprise was the most efficient form of economic organization. Zhang was an ultrarightist. In those days it was bad enough to be called a 'Rightist,' the title applied to the various right-wing intellectuals who had strayed down the path of revisionism, but who nevertheless subscribed to Marxism-Leninism and accepted axiomatically that the socialist economic system was superior to the capitalist one. Mildly tolerant of these generic rightists, the authorities have been ruthless in their persecution of ultrarightists, a fact of which Zhang Jiulong is very much aware. I almost never hear him register his opinions in the confines of Number Nine.

He was a gifted child who loved to read, placing into Xi'an's Aeronautical Institute before he turned fifteen. By his junior year, however, he found the political atmosphere so oppressive that he had to transfer to a non-military school. It was not acceptable for a son of the bourgeoisie to stay on at an institute so closely linked to national security.

Then, dropping out of school altogether, he had returned to Changsha. The bottom had already fallen out of the Great Leap Forward economy and the provincial capital was in chaos. Angry and lonely, he began to mingle with rightist students and with the machinist drifters who, without steady employment, floated aimlessly about the province. Many of them had been trained as engineers and picked up odd jobs where they could.

Zhang learned that some of the drifters were starting up underground factories. By frequenting teahouses and restaurants, the aspiring underground entrepreneur could make contacts with commune 'businessmen' and purchasing agents for state industries and find metal-processing jobs. If the job could be managed with just a crude file and long-nosed pliers, the drifters stayed at home. When expensive tools and machines were needed, they went to their friends at state-run plants, made a sufficiently gracious financial gesture, and worked in the state plants at night. All the lathes, planing machines, grinders, and electric welders were at their disposal for free, or for a small fee. Machinist drifters were able to make a good living, as much as two or three times more money than high-ranking cadres.

The underground factories were managed in much the same manner as their state counterparts, except when it came time to issue salaries, which entailed a more complicated procedure. After deciding on a local collective industry or a commune in the outlying suburbs, an underground manager would buy off the appropriate officer in order to use the unit's bank account. Once the underground enterprise had received payment from the buyer (in most cases a state-run factory), it deposited the money into the cooperative's account. The cooperative subsequently deducted from thirty to fifty percent of the gross, and the remainder was paid out in the form of salaries to the underground factory workers. The entire process basically amounted to 'renting' a bank account at a very high premium.

More obscure to me are the activities of his Rightist friends. Time after time, Nine Dragons evades my questions about what is rumored to have been a very active group. Yes, he acknowledges, it is true that there were some college students of his generation who had been persuaded by the Anti-Rightist Campaign that Western-style parliamentary democracy would never evolve peacefully in China. Yes, he admits, the group believed that the only way to achieve democracy was to set up a clandestine organization. No, he insists, he is sorry, but the exact details are not clear to him.

Their activities are evidently so secret that the Public Security has never been able to prove the existence of an organization per se. They noticed initially that a group of right-wing intellectuals frequently got together to discuss politics; they observed that the same bunch later joined the Rebel forces during the Cultural Revolution, taking possession of large numbers of weapons. The cadres have been keeping detailed dossiers on questionable individuals since 1959, staging crackdowns and tracing the subtle signs of any underground movement. Zhang and the others were part of some sort of formal organization—of that the public security cadres felt sure.

Whatever it was, Zhang Jiulong must have gotten involved knowing full well that for the rest of his life he would live in danger, 'carrying his head around in his hands.' His family was not aware of his work. And if his group has a name, no one seems to know what it is. There is no charter, nor are there officers.

I look at this man across from me at the go board. I want to know more. During the Cultural Revolution, I had observed many political organizations on the scene, but not a single one of those claimed to be a 'party' nor was recognized officially. When Zhang Jiulong and his family were persecuted in 1956, however, Zhang's gut response was to organize an opposition group—perhaps a party. It was his only recourse. The authorities' utter incompetence in managing the economy both enraged and encouraged him. And he would not have been alone.

Zhang monitors himself relentlessly day after day. Naturally sociable, he must love a good debate. Inevitably, although his lips are sealed on the subject of the 'organization,' some things do emerge from our roundabout conversations about his father's shop.

One afternoon, while I am pressing Zhang for details about his father, one of my classmates from Changsha First High School overhears Zhang's quiet responses. His name is Cheng Deming, and he is said to be a member of United Action, an elitist organization composed of the original Beijing Red Guards, the sons and daughters of the highest ranking cadres. Cheng is a devotee of Liu Shaoqi and the 'Soviet revisionist line,' so of course he believes socialism is superior to capitalism.

'Mao's agrarian socialism isn't really socialism at all,' argues Cheng. 'It's left-wing opportunism, the root of all our problems in China today.'

It is probably because Cheng is so very outspoken that Zhang feels secure enough to let down his guard today.

Their conversation starts innocuously. Everything is fine until Nine Dragons leaves the realm of the abstract to speak of his father's workshop and of how amazingly efficient it had been. As always, he keeps his voice very low, so low that Cheng and I can barely hear what he is saying, but there is a new intensity. After a few minutes, Cheng Deming has had enough.

'There's no way in the world that private businesses like your father's can help a country like China become modernized!' he says rather loudly, causing some of the inmates at the other end of the *haozi* to look nervously in our direction. Unlike Zhang, Cheng needn't be too concerned about being overheard, for he knows that many prisoners, and even some of the guards, share his beliefs.

'I'll give you a good example,' Cheng continues enthusiastically. 'The machine industry depends on the development of the emery wheel, because the emery wheel is the basis for precision machining. And the emery wheel depends on the advanced technology required to manufacture synthetic diamonds. Just look at the economy of scale you need! But with the help of the Soviets and the first Five-year Plan, we constructed more than 156 large-scale projects, plus a good-sized emery wheel factory at Zhengzhou that we built with the Germans. That plant provided lots of emery wheels—cheap ones—very early on. If we had to rely solely on a free-market system, how long do you think we would have had to wait for specialized emery wheel factories to appear?'

Nine Dragons is not to be swayed. 'Wake up,' he says sarcastically. 'All that fancy equipment spends most of the time sleeping in the shop. State-run industries aren't going to kill themselves looking for new work. Sure, they build a bunch of factories, produce a whole new line of machine tools—but they don't produce the things that people really need.'

Private business is the answer to China's economic problems, Zhang is sure, for although shops like his father's were small, they could bring in money quickly enough to compensate for their size.

'You don't understand,' responds Cheng, frustrated, but unwilling to give up. 'Everyone knows that in capitalist economies, there's a huge financial crisis every ten years that destroys all the wealth society has accumulated.' He pauses. 'You're not thinking of courting disaster by restoring capitalism in *China*?'

Nine Dragons pales, realizing that the discussion has gone too far. None of us speaks, but I can see Zhang's bloodshot eyes moving about the periphery of the *haozi*. He wills himself to suppress his emotions and doesn't refute Cheng Deming, but I sense that he is armed with other, more telling theories which he could easily use to counter Cheng. Cheng's last remark has made explicit reference to the ideological 'cap' on Zhang's head, a cap to which Zhang is particularly sensitive. In the official Communist dictionary he is considered an 'ultrarightist with capitalist leanings,' a more dangerous cap than the 'rightist revisionist' one worn by Cheng Deming.

Nine Dragons' face is somber. His pride has been damaged and I am embarrassed for him. But I know too that Cheng is sincere in his beliefs and isn't throwing his political weight around— that he doesn't despise Zhang the way the Communists do. I want them to continue their debate; I resent the fact that Zhang has been silenced.

Conversations like this are exciting, fresh, and seductively dangerous. Nowhere have I heard viewpoints as radical—not in private discussions of my 'ultraradical' student groups, not in the intimate surroundings of high-ranking Provincial Party cadres' homes. It's enough to make one thankful to be in prison.

Still, I reflect, how can a *rightist*—Cheng—believe that socialism is superior to capitalism? And how can anyone in China really believe in private enterprise? As a new leftist, although I share Marx's negative appraisal of capitalism, I am critical of the authorities, as is nearly everyone who lives in the Rebel-dominated Number Nine. It is my feeling that the privileged class within the Communist Party are none other than 'red capitalists,' who oppress and exploit the people, and are every bit as evil as the 'white' variety. The tenor of the conversation reminds me that there are substantive differences between communism and capitalism, and I am struck by my inability to clarify in my own mind just exactly how they differ. Any heretical 'ism' that challenges the prevailing political discourse is certainly worth thinking about. Still, though Zhang's courage has earned my respect, I feel sorry for him. Surely his radical claims will never attract any attention. Few people will even know what he is talking about.

Precisely for these reasons, it seems very odd that the authorities are taking him so seriously. Though Zhang is unusually intelligent and ambitious, I doubt that he could ever constitute any real threat to the State. Unless there is more to him than meets the eye. Unless the pickpockets have something.

I watch for opportunities to fill in the gaps. Sensitive to the fact that the details threaten his survival, I never ask him directly about the underground. Instead I get him to tell me stories, hoping that from these I can piece something together. Nine Dragons falls right into my trap.

In a long story about a man named 'Bluebird,' he tells me about a 'professional politician' in the Russian Social Democrat Party who had organized an extensive political network. It had been Leninist in nature, composed of secret revolutionary cells. Zhang speaks knowledgeably and passionately, and as I listen, I recognize the same hushed tone of voice he uses when he describes his father's little machinery workshop. When his story is over, we are both very quiet. I know that his commitment to the organization has been total and irrevocable.

It is probably the first time in my life that I have heard the words 'underground professional politician,' a title, which when he utters it, seems worthy of emulation and respect. To a man of Zhang's ambitions, upstart political theorists like Cheng Deming and myself must seem incredibly impotent.

Suddenly it hits me—why he is always so cautious. But his determination frightens me as well, for Communists despise and fear more than anything else the uncompromising dedication of people who devote themselves to underground organizations.

◆

I have never been one to worry about regulations; I am always breaking one rule or another. I love, for instance, to 'make calls' to other cells by crawling up onto the window ledge and speaking softly to the inmates at the window next door. Or I stand up on an upper bunk and use my arm to draw large characters in the air, effectively communicating with the *haozi* on the opposite side of the courtyard, some fifty yards away.

My calls continue quite regularly until one morning, when a guard on patrol spots me. I listen to his footsteps with a certain amount of detachment as he runs to the office to fetch Whiskers Xu. Soon the door opens and the two of them stride in. Whiskers looks around and shouts out, 'Who was standing at the window just now?'

A couple of inmates shift nervously around.

'Everybody on your knees!' Whiskers commands, his bushy eyebrows twitching. Nobody even considers disobeying an order given by an officer of the 47th, who would require little provocation to lash out at us with stinging strips of bamboo or a leather belt. For some reason, Nine Dragons is one of the last people to climb down from the bunk and happens to catch Whiskers' eye. 'Zhang Jiulong, get down here and tell me who it was making a call!'

'I don't know,' he replies evenly.

'Who was it?' Whiskers repeats.

'I wasn't paying any attention.'

Whiskers flicks the belt high in the air and pelts him three times.

'I was the one,' I intercede finally. Without a word, Whiskers spins around, and as the guard looks on, decorates me with what is known as a 'precious sword on the back.' Twisting my arms behind me so that one hand is forced excruciatingly on top of the other, he attaches a pair of handcuffs, then drops me on the floor. The arm wrapped around my neck is pulled so tightly that I can't get up off the ground or raise my head. If I try to alter my position, the pain races down my spine, radiating into every part of my body. Having watched other prisoners, I know that before long I will lose consciousness.

'There, see if you can behave yourself now,' Whiskers chuckles. He disappears out the door, followed by the guard.

Forty minutes later, perspiration soaks my shirt. I can't take it anymore. Zhang Jiulong and another, older inmate prop a couple of pillows under my legs, allowing me to lay my head on the floor for awhile. He looks down at me for several moments before stepping over to the window. 'Cadre, sir, somebody's fainted in here,' he calls out nonchalantly. Then he goes back and sits on his bed.

How to put into words the way I feel as I lie half-conscious on the floor, recognizing a voice I know to be Nine Dragons', speak up on my behalf—relief and fear and gratitude. It is the only time I witness him drop his guard.

Not long afterwards Whiskers returns to unfasten the handcuffs. 'The next time you're tempted to make a call, remember what this feels like,' he says without emotion.

I really don't mind Whisker's scoldings. Warden Liu, like most of the guards, dedicated his life to reforming prisoners' thoughts and preached at us endlessly. Perhaps because Whiskers is a military man, he satisfies himself with punishing our bodies and leaves our minds alone.

Judging from the fact that Zhang is so well-informed about life in the United States, and from his attitude toward the Soviet–American split, it is clear that he is pro-American. If Nixon is elected, he confides, it will not bode well for the United

States, for Nixon is a man with 'great ambition and little talent.'
On the other hand, he is crazy about Kennedy. When a group of
inmates gets onto the subject of the Cuban Missile Crisis and
how easily the Americans were able to drive away the Soviets,
I watch Zhang, waiting for him to comment. In fact he says
nothing, but he is grinning.

Then there is the Rosenberg affair, which by this time has
been forgotten by virtually everybody in China. The somewhat
older intellectuals, one generation before mine, tend to believe
the official story in the papers, that the United States
government murdered an innocent American scientist. My peers
have no idea what the case was all about. Nine Dragons,
however, seems to remember every little detail. He tells me that
Rosenberg had given the Soviets vital information about how to
build an atomic bomb. He goes on and on, finally informing me
that Rosenberg and his wife were executed in the electric chair.

Taiwan is another of his favorite topics that no one else ever
seems to mention these days. In fact, when he and I discuss
China's future, he insists that Taiwan will play a major role, for
the continued existence of a government on the island will have
the same effect as if there were two parties on the Mainland.
This is crucial, he explains to me, because it means that the
Chinese political situation will develop very differently from
that of the Soviet Union.

Listening to him hour upon hour, I realize that I know almost
nothing about the island across the strait from Fujian. Except for
what I have gleaned from Chiang Kai-shek's 'A Message to My
Countrymen on the Mainland' in *Reference News* in 1967, I
know only what I have read in the scathing reports in the *Hunan
Daily*. I try to evaluate Taiwan's economic progress indirectly,
from articles such as the one about a group of unhappy pedicab
drivers who were protesting, it seemed, because the government
had adopted a new policy of using automobiles instead of
pedicabs. This new item had absolutely floored me. On the
Mainland, pedicabs were still a relatively uncommon and highly
desirable form of modern transportation. In Hunan, at least,
transportation continued to rely on wooden pushcarts; it was
hard to believe that in Taiwan pedicabs were already on the way
out.

But when I tell Nine Dragons this story, he does not seem
surprised. 'Do you know the only two governments in the world
that did not lower their flags when Kennedy was assassinated?'
he quizzes me.

I shake my head.

'Communist China—and—Nationalist China. Old Chiang was still bitter over an incident in 1962 when Kennedy refused to support him in his plan to counterattack the Mainland.' Where is Zhang getting all his information? At home, my own best sources were the *Reference News* and *Confidential Reference News*, which my parents as Party members received regularly, but even these papers for the Communist elite had never carried such stories. Perhaps by paying close attention to the briefest of news briefs about US–Taiwan relations, Zhang has been able to draw subtle inferences about the political picture in China. More than ever, I long to hear about the inner workings of the organization in which I was certain he has played a leading role.

◆

Just as summer is turning to autumn, Whiskers orders all the men in Number Nine out into the corridors one day to hear Central Committee directives 7.3 and 7.24. The news is very good or very bad, depending on the person you talk to, but no one will dispute that a big change is in the offing. Large-scale armed confrontations have been breaking out among the different political factions, and more weapons have been seized. The situation is so serious that the army has been called in. Nine Dragons must be silently rejoicing at the authorities' inability to keep order. I am worried, nevertheless, and I know he must be too. The escalation means that Zhang's future is darker than ever.

'So what do you think will happen?' I ask him after we get back to the *haozi*.

'It's not unlike the Cultural Revolution,' he says calmly, referring to the summer of 1966. 'Chaos always helps the Communists consolidate their power.' When I ask him why, he flashes a rare smile. 'As a matter of fact, I wrote a piece on this very same topic about a year ago.'

He says nothing further that day. Later I learn that the article was a political analysis that had been widely circulated among the members of his party, only to fall into the hands of Public Security. It was the first and only piece of physical evidence they would find.

It occurs to me that Zhang would likely not talk about his activities very much, even if he were not in danger. Like a bankrupted entrepreneur, he is loath to go into detail about the reasons for his failure. But Zhang plainly enjoys discussing the

contents of his article, and goes back to it time and time again.
He believes that the common people's dissatisfaction with the
authorities is a phenomenon not unlike pent-up sexual desire
and that democratic countries allow emotions of this sort to
be vented on a regular basis, so that no revolutionary thoughts
ever form. On the other hand, because totalitarian countries
have no escape valves, strong revolutionary feelings are able
to accumulate—the ideal conditions for revolution, Zhang
explains. When Mao launched the Cultural Revolution, it
suddenly became possible to vent the revolutionary urges which
had been building since 1959. Then the extreme chaos of 1968
made the people long once again for social order. Not only did
the Cultural Revolution allow the authorities to stave off
an anti-Communist revolution, it unexpectedly stabilized the
regime.

'I don't think the regime is so stable,' I interrupt. 'Even though
you can't openly revolt against the authorities anymore, a coup
could cause a major change in the political situation at any
moment. Look, Lin Biao and Zhou Enlai are bound to go at it
sooner or later.'

Nine Dragons smiles at me mysteriously, but doesn't pursue
the topic. 'You're a lot more mature than you used to be,' he says
simply.

This patronizing tone annoys me to no end—he is only six or
seven years older than I. When we discuss the Cultural
Revolution, I insist vehemently that the factions had been forged
by social forces. The various Conservative factions are people
who wish to maintain the *status quo* and keep the upper hand;
the Rebel factions, people who are being persecuted, or who have
'background' problems. When I am finished, Nine Dragons looks
at me long and hard, and says with visible disgust, 'When are
you going to realize that they're *all* puppets. Every single group
out there is being manipulated by two factions at the very top!'

I tell myself that he is mistaken. The conflicts of the two
factions are very similar to those of the Tories and the Whigs
in England, or the Montagnards and the Constitutionalists in
France: even though the top was exploiting the bottom, the
people at the bottom could nevertheless derive a certain measure
of political benefit out the situation by exploiting the people at
the top at the same time. Zhang Jiulong himself had taken
advantage of the turbulence of the Cultural Revolution to carry
out his own political agenda. But I don't say any of this to him;
it would cut too deeply.

Each time he comes back from interrogation, his face is grey.

And he doesn't eat. At Zuojiatang, this is almost unheard of; we look to the arrival of our five ounces of rice with the same expectation that we look to the ascent of the moon and the stars. I am about to console him until I see the savagery in his eyes and his trembling jaw.

'Have a run-in?'

'They don't have a shred of evidence and they're still insisting that I was a member of some organization,' he says quietly. Unwilling to touch upon his wound, I let the matter drop.

Ever the strategist, during his interrogation Zhang tries hard to turn the incriminating contents of his article into his defense, saying that the document proves he himself doubts the value of anti-government activities. His argument falls upon deaf ears. At a time when the newspapers are calling out for the total eradication of 'political blight,' the specific wording in an essay is less important than the fact that a man who opposes the Communist Party is still living and breathing.

◆

It has been raining all day, and the sound of water dripping off the roof onto the muddy courtyard has made us contemplative and a bit remorseful. Staring past the window, Nine Dragons begins mumbling about democracy, very softly.

'In 1957 there were a lot of intellectuals who thought they could use peaceful means to obtain a parliamentary democracy. But I guess that's impossible.' Is he talking to me? He pauses, then resumes. The rain is coming down harder and harder, making it difficult for me to catch all of what he says, but I don't dare interrupt for fear he will stop altogether.

'In early 1960 some of the younger intellectuals considered going the way of Che Guevara.' He looks at me suddenly and asks, 'Do you know about him?'

I nod silently. *Reference News* had run a story when his body was found.

'Those students did end up following in Che Guevara's footsteps,' he repeats mechanically, turning once again toward the window. We sit together in silence, watching the rain.

Both Nine Dragons and I know that our go matches will come to an end when one of us is sentenced. I am the first to leave and am in the transit cell for three weeks, with one week remaining before I am to be sent down to labor camp, when I learn that Zhang has also been taken from Number Nine. It is what we both feared, but never uttered—the death penalty, suspended for two years.

The day of his sentencing, as he and the others are about to be marched out to the streets, I see his pale face for the last time. He is a man with very clear thoughts; from the surprised expression on his face I surmise that the authorities probably have no hard evidence. The bulletin that comes down later supports my suspicion, for he is charged as the leader, not of a counterrevolutionary organization, but of a counterrevolutionary 'clique.' They must know only that a group of Rightist intellectuals met regularly to discuss politics.

I am laboring at Reconstruction Farm in the spring of 1970 when I hear the news that Zhang Jiulong has been sent up before a firing squad, a victim of the Strike One–Oppose Three Campaign, the movement to 'strike down' counterrevolutionaries and 'oppose' common criminals, corruption, and waste. My shoulder pole drops; fear knots and turns my stomach. Over and over, I picture what he must have looked like, bloodied, in a heap. I will the image from my mind but his face does not leave me. I try to remember our last go game, what the board looked like, or who won.

◆

I must have spent hundreds of hours with Zhang, but many parts of his story remain a mystery. It is doubtful that anyone knows the complete truth about the organization which he most certainly headed, unless of course there are key members who were able to slip through the Public Security net. A quandary, indeed—it is difficult to gain information from dead people.

Soon after the news of Zhang's death, a fellow inmate at the farm confides to me how, during the most intense fighting of the Cultural Revolution, he, Zhang, and a few comrades had joined a Rebel organization and obtained weapons and ammunition any way they could. Having lost virtually all control of the masses, the authorities were allowing political groups to be organized provided they weren't anti-communist or anti-Maoist in nature. It was then that the group's movements became visible, and as soon as the campaign to 'Purify the Class Ranks' was announced in late 1968, the authorities had closed in on them. The first people to implicate Zhang were those who had themselves been members of the Rebel organizations. When it came to purification and purges, the Rebels and the conservative Red Guards were surprisingly consistent in their willingness to expose the perpetrators of anti-communist activities.

As the days go by in the camp, I hear more and more stories

about people who have been accused of being members of counterrevolutionary organizations. With each new account, I sift through my own experiences, thinking back to the essay I wrote in 1967, when I had hoped to organize a seedling party. I reflect in horror that, under the 'Regulations Regarding the Punishment of Counterrevolutionaries,' organizing a political party is a capital offense. Yet in these heady times of the Cultural Revolution, nobody seems to be aware of the fact. Nothing in the written law or in the endless propaganda warns of the possibility of death. Still it is there, unspoken, the silent threat somehow made even more chilling in its effect.

My interest in the underground does not die with Zhang—on the contrary. Yet I will never again approach an 'organization criminal' with such innocence. Though I hate the authorities more than ever, and know now that there is reason indeed to fear them, I am even more terrified of the shape my own thoughts might take if I am not careful. It is, as the older prisoners have learned long ago, much easier to bury one's head and keep men like 'Nine Dragons' Zhang at a distance.

The old politicals—the historical counterrevolutionaries— had shunned him from the start. But then so had the pickpockets, the rapists, the profiteers, and the thieves. They all had their reasons. Officially, Nine Dragons was 'rankless,' so far at the bottom of our criminal hierarchy that he was considered to be outside of it. They had known all along he was a goner, already up to his chest in the yellow earth.

5

Bandit Xiang

▼

Bandit Xiang is not your everyday, run-of-the-mill pickpocket. Despite the fact that one finger is missing and that his right arm juts out at an unlikely angle (testimony to the times he didn't get away), he is simply too ingenuous and too shy for a man of his trade. The worst thing you can say about him is that he's a bit mischievous, a flaw which makes him all the more likable.

The average Hunanese is short. Bandit Xiang is shorter. His face is round and weather-beaten, and his eyes are those of a rodent: small, close-set, and quizzical. The constant weight of a shoulder pole during his early years in the countryside has left him slightly humpbacked.

He's young—can't be more than twenty or twenty-one. And he isn't really a bandit. It is because he comes from a Tujia minority tribe in Xiangxi, a poor county known throughout history for its marauding gangs, that the other inmates affectionately call him 'Bandit.' His real name is Xiang Yuanyi—'Yuanyi' meaning 'far-reaching justice,' which I think suits him quite well. But like the others, I call him Bandit Xiang.

'I'm just meat on the chopping block: this time I'm going to be in for a long stretch,' Bandit Xiang announces with a sigh the day he enters Number Nine. 'Aii-ya, if only my "sixth intestine" hadn't been acting up and I had just controlled myself—I didn't *have* to watch, you know—I wouldn't be here today.'

Although he commands the Changsha vernacular, his speech is heavily accented with the sounds of his native Tujia dialect, and we all laugh. 'It's true, you know,' he continues earnestly, 'the taboo about watching men and women "at work." It's not just a superstition; I don't care what they say. If I had minded my own business, I'd be out on the town "stirring up onions" right this minute.'

In the black argot of the Changsha pickpockets, 'work' means sex. The pickpockets always seem to be talking about somebody 'working.' It's embarrassing. A few days later I hear that the 'worker' in question, Bandit's ex-roommate and fellow carouser, Li Liang, is being held next door in Number Ten.

I seriously doubt that the round-faced 'bandit,' dressed in tidy work clothes of 'blue khaki,' is in jail because he failed to mind his own business. Most of the pickpockets take great pains to appear fashionable, imitating their criminal cousins in Hong Kong; the rest wear tattered old clothes or dress as students. I spot them as soon as they come in, these wolves in sheep's clothing; eyes bright with desire and deceit gleam in their boyish faces. But in the days I have spent with the Bandit, he has never given me any reason to doubt his sincerity. It certainly would never have occurred to me that he was responsible for blowing up the biggest building in Hunan.

Bandit Xiang was ten years old in 1959, when the country was reaping the harvest of the Great Leap Forward. More than twenty of the biggest and strongest young men in his village had already died in the fields. Because their appetites were the largest and their exertions the greatest, they were the first to go.

While Bandit's father lay on his death bed, he had called his wife to him, saying, 'When I die, cut off my flesh and eat it; whatever you do, don't let the children go, too.' In those days, Bandit told me, it truly seemed as if the end of the world were at hand. There was always someone digging a grave. All the women had stopped having periods. The only thing that people thought of was surviving till the next day; it did not matter how. And so, to keep the whole family from starving to death, Bandit and his mother sliced the flesh from his dead father's legs and boiled it with wild grasses.

After his mother had buried the bones that remained, she sent her two children out on the main road to escape the famine. Then she married the man in charge of the village canteen, one of the few men who wasn't hungry. Bandit Xiang walked all the way to Changsha, where he met up with a number of 'little pickpockets' just like himself. In several months he mastered the pincer's art and became popular with the other young pickpockets. Punning on his real name, they called him the 'Just Thief,' for whenever he lifted somebody's wallet, if there was a government identification card or other important document inside, he never failed to mail it back to the owner the following day.

He was picked up many times, and each time reprimanded and released. Finally, he was punished as part of an 'administrative disciplinary action;' without trial or sentence, he was sent down for three years of re-education through labor. When his term ended, it suddenly occurred to him that he had nowhere to go, so he agreed to stay on at the Long Bridge Labor Re-education Farm, where he was guaranteed 25 yuan a month and was close enough to Changsha, some ten miles away, to make day trips on Sundays and holidays.

But at Long Bridge he found that, although his stomach was never empty, neither was it ever really full, and the life of a 'regular employee' wasn't particularly easy. There were four distinct castes: at the top were the cadres in charge, followed by men who, like the Bandit, had already been released from labor re-education programs and were now regularly employed. Next came the people still serving labor re-education terms. Labor reform criminals were at the bottom.

In fact, Bandit tells me, there really wasn't all that much difference between labor reform and labor re-education. The food and the work for the two classes of laborers were basically the same, the only distinction being that re-education candidates were sometimes allowed to return home for the Lunar New Year and other major holidays.

Though Long Bridge Farm produced mostly cotton, it supplied other crops as well. Two or three times a year, after the harvest, a portion of the crops would be allocated to the people who lived on the farm. The highest quality products were distributed to the cadres, the next best to released laborers, and the worst were reserved for labor re-education and labor reform prisoners. The price was the same in each case. Any surplus was sold to the government purchasing agency.

Bandit loves to tell stories about Long Bridge and about the Cultural Revolution. Some inmates sit huddled on the floor, some of us lie on our stomachs atop the bunks, all listening with pleasure as Bandit darts about the *haozi*, waving his right arm at odd angles, reliving his adventures.

One incident he tells of involves a strapping, young pickpocket known as the Three-haired Kid, who contracted a virus and collapsed in the fields. The next morning he couldn't get out of bed. It was 1965, a year when material incentives were rejected as revisionist. With no economic spurs to induce people to work, the authorities observed that the number of workers feigning illness was steadily growing. Before long they simply assumed that any illness was feigned. One of the cadres came to the dormitory, and tried to force the Kid back to the fields, beating him viciously with a cane. The Kid snatched it away from him and struck back, hard. Hearing the commotion, the

other cadres rushed to the scene, tied the Kid up tightly, and left
him to bake in the hot afternoon sun. The Kid, still feverish,
screamed out oaths until he was hoarse.

'One of these days I'm going to get all of you bastards! You'll
see how tough I can be—I'll pay you back ten times over for this.'
Some time in the late afternoon he lost consciousness. His wrists
and arms were permanently engraved where rope cut into flesh.

The Kid's opportunity for revenge came in the spring of 1967
during the Cultural Revolution, when the released re-education
laborers of Long Bridge Farm decided to rehabilitate themselves
and formed a political organization called the Changsha Youth.
As part of the Rebel actions, one of their sworn goals was to get
even with the Public Security cadres who had consistently
suppressed them over the years. Meanwhile, the labor camp
cadres had joined a Conservative political group consisting of all
the security organs, including the Public Security Bureau, the
Procurate, and the People's Courts, anticipating that the released
Rebel prisoners would be 'plotting counterrevolution against
the dictatorship of the proletariat.' Their concerns were not
unfounded.

Conservative and Rebel forces clashed, the Changsha Youth
being among the first to storm the military district and seize
guns. At that time the military sided with the Conservatives,
and the militia's arsenal was used to outfit the Conservatives.
But as soon as it became known that Mao Zedong and Jiang Qing
approved of the initial Rebel gun raids, other Rebel groups in
Hunan quickly followed suit. By late July the Changsha Rebels
had gained the upper hand, and the Conservatives fled to the city
of Xiangtan, a hotbed of conservatism and a military stronghold.
It was during this altercation that the Changsha Youth captured
several Long Bridge Farm cadres, including the one who had
persecuted the Three-haired Kid.

True to his word, the Kid brought the man to the Changsha
Youth 'office of interrogation,' where the cadre was ordered to
sit in a chair across the table from the Kid. He was by now
painfully aware that his punishment of the boy had been
excessive and that the Kid was not going to let him off easy. In
an act of desperation, he lunged for the pistol that had been left
on the desk and fired at the Kid. The enraged laborers rushed
over and knocked the cadre onto the floor. The next morning,
the Kid proceeded to the holding cell and plucked one of the
cadre's eyes right out of its socket.

As the Bandit finishes his tale, I find myself shocked and
troubled, not so much with the raw violence of it, but because

of the motivations leading to it. Throughout my ideological deliberations, I have rationalized such acts of violence, advocating a Paris Commune-style of revolution, regardless of the price. I have read the Chinese translation of *A Tale of Two Cities*, a volume which confirmed for me that the violence of the masses is always provoked by the systematic but equally violent oppression of the lower classes by the upper classes. It is natural for me to believe that the tensions between Conservatives and Rebels have been caused by ideological differences arising from conflicting social forces. But now, in a small, dirty prison cell, this strange little pickpocket who can't speak a word of Mandarin, and in fact can barely manage the Changsha dialect, is making it very clear to me that the bitter enmity of these two organizations is rooted, not in doctrinal contradictions, but in hatred, pure and simple, and mutual oppression. As my eyes are opened to the dark and irrational side of revolution, my lofty political ideals pale.

I now listen very carefully to everything the Bandit says, and gradually realize that in contrast to the other pickpockets, who speak compulsively of the methods and objects of their thievery, he tends to talk about economics and politics, topics very close to my heart. Because he had hurled himself into the maelstrom of the Cultural Revolution, he knows firsthand the twists and turns of many battles, details that never made the press and are relished by everyone in the *haozi*. It takes very little prompting to get Bandit Xiang to while away an afternoon by telling the tales of revolution.

Everyone in Number Nine knows of the famous battle of Yijiawan, and so one day when the Bandit casually mentions that he was part of that action, we become quite excited.

In the summer of 1967, after the Rebels drove the Conservatives out of the provincial capital, they set their sights on the city of Xiangtan. Each ensuing confrontation found the Changsha Youth at the vanguard, and the attack on Xiangtan was no exception. The commanding Rebel officer had been none other than our *haozi* neighbor to the west and Bandit's ex-roommate, Li Liang. Li came from an aristocratic family, and in the early sixties was a college student. Becoming disillusioned during the Great Leap, he had tried to cross the border into Hong Kong several times and was turned back. He was sent down for re-education after his last attempt. To his surprise, when his three years were up, he was forced to stay on as a regular employee. As the only college graduate to join the Changsha Youth, Li Liang was the best educated. Moreover, he had a reputation for being an exceptional tactician; in him resided the mind and spirit of the organization.

Ever since Liberation, Xiangtan, birthplace of Chairman Mao Zedong, has been a center for the munitions industry, supplying the airplanes, tanks, and other armaments for the nation. The workers in these plants all backed the authorities; reinforcing the Conservative position was in their vested interest. In the other camp, the workers and other city residents of Changsha tended to support the Rebels, who were challenging the local Communist authorities. Yet before the Rebels could attack Xiangtan in 1967, they had to pass through the little village of Yijiawan.

'It was right in the middle of summer—so hot, you wanted to crawl out of your skin,' the Bandit begins in a half-serious, half-jesting tone, pacing back and forth. 'Along with all the other mock warriors of the Changsha Youth, I readied myself for war. We set out in different trucks, wearing our heaviest work clothes and fully armed. For weapons, we had the very latest—Chinese-made .56 semi-automatic rifles. And we had some automatics and machine guns, too. We were pretty excited, because we had just gotten hold of all this stuff at the Hunan Provincial Command Arsenal. The trucks started moving, eight of us in all. The first four were carrying us and the Young Guard; the last four, the Red Banner Army. Those old guys even had trench mortars with them.' Composed of Changsha apprentice workers, the Young Guard had been the desperadoes of the Rebel forces; the Red Banner Army was a Rebel battalion of old army veterans who had fought in the Civil War and the Korean War.[1] The authorities were so intimidated by the latter group's military strength that Zhou Enlai declared them to be a counter-revolutionary organization as early as January 1967.

'The whole time the mood of the men was solemn and a little tense. We were acting like military heroes, waiting for the big moment. Then, just as the first truck was about to reach Yijiawan, we heard a large explosion. I was in the cab of the second truck, and as we came around the bend, I could see through a slit in the canvas to a spot way up the road where there were little black dots, but they were getting bigger and bigger. Somebody shouted out, "My god, we're in for it now—like clay buddhas crossing a river! Tanks—tanks!"

[1] The 'Young Guard' derived its name from Fadeyev's novel of the same name, a famous war story about young people involved in the Russian underground resistance in Krasnodon. The book later had to be rewritten to emphasize the role of the Komsomol and the Communist Party in the underground movement.

'I had never seen a tank before. In the movies, tanks were always big, clumsy things. People were always running and jumping up on top of them. But those big black dots ahead, they were moving fast—faster than cars.

'We heard a loud booming noise and then another one. It took a minute or so for us to wake up to the fact that the booming noise was the sound of a tank firing—firing at us. Things were blurry and confused. I sure didn't feel like a hero. Little Gang, a boy who had talked real tough just five minutes before, stuck his head down into the cabin seat, pointed his rifle at the sky, and started shooting. He was out of control, totally out of control—just like a toad trying to prop up a corner of a bed—the harder he pushed, the more he quivered.'

Whenever he tells his stories Bandit Xiang tries to mix prison slang with Changsha colloquialisms, but since his pronunciation is never quite right, he ends up saying things like 'sliver' instead of 'quiver,' making us laugh all the louder. He does not seem to mind, for he grins in return.

'And that's when we crashed into the truck ahead of us. It had already been hit by one of the tanks, but the men were still sitting inside, dazed. We watched the flames swallow it up and then Li Liang called out for us to get down off of *our* truck. He yelled, "Get out quick!" but most of the guys just kept firing their rifles into the air. Then he said, "You dead fish! If you want to want to die, don't do it here!" That's when they finally jumped down.

'After we got out we tried to find a place to hide. We had completely forgotten why we had come. I didn't know what was happening. I didn't know that war was going to be so confusing. It sure wasn't heroic. We never thought to bring along something practical like a walkie-talkie.

'Little Gang and I were lying on top of a grave mound. He was even too scared to shoot into the air. We could see the second tank following after the first, steering off the road to avoid what was left of the burning truck. It was heading straight towards Changsha.

'Suddenly we heard shots coming from the top of another hill, shots from 82-millimeter trench mortars. One shell landed right next to the third tank. There was a big flash of light and a cloud of dust. Yeah, it was the Red Banner Army. These men, they knew what they were doing; they had fought in real wars and it showed. All the time we were shooting like crazy into the sky, they had been dragging their 38's and their mortars up into the hills.

'And they were great shots. They wouldn't touch the new semi-automatic rifles—said the range was too close, only about 500 yards. So instead they used the Japanese 38-millimeter rifles made in the Second World War. Those old guns could reach targets more than 1000 yards away.

'The entire exchange was over in fifteen minutes. The Red Banner Army almost never missed and the tanks couldn't figure out where the mortars were hiding. By the time we calmed down enough to enjoy the fight, the tanks had already swung around in retreat. That's when I looked over at Little Gang. He was so frightened he had peed in his pants.'

We laugh appreciatively.

In September of 1967 the Rebels had split into two camps. Those which had been offered seats in the Provincial Revolutionary Committee Preparatory Group joined the Trade Union faction. Those which had been denied seats, the 'minority Rebels,' formed the Xiang faction. The Changsha Youth quickly became a force within the Xiang camp.

The Xiang and Trade Union troops clashed more than once, and it was in this second phase of the Cultural Revolution, during an armed confrontation at May First Square that the Bandit, true to his prediction, had run into trouble. On that autumn day he had been among the Changsha Youth to occupy the high-rise building facing the Hunan Embroidery Building, which rose impressively on the square. Boasting six stories, the latter was the pride of the city; a showpiece for travelers, it housed intricate handicrafts from all over the province. The Embroidery Building was being held by the Trade Union faction.

As soon as the Rebel split was announced, the fighters in both buildings started shooting at each other. The Changsha Youth were in possession of an anti-aircraft machine gun, which they mounted on the roof. Bandit Xiang took the weapon, loaded it with an armor-piercing, incendiary bomb, and aimed it at the Embroidery Building. After one round of rapid fire, the structure burst into flames. By the time the blaze was extinguished, nothing but ashes remained. Every major regional newspaper had covered the story.

There is no doubt in Bandit's mind that the Embroidery Building disaster was brought on by the two instances in which he witnessed people having sex. Ever since he ignored this inviolable taboo, he tells us, he knew something bad was going to happen to him.

A few days before the battle, as Li Liang was returning from Changsha to the Long Bridge farm, he had met an unusually attractive woman along the roadside. They had hit it off right away and that evening he had brought her home to the camp with him. Although Bandit Xiang and Li Liang shared a dormitory room, Bandit had also been in Changsha that week. On that particular night he decided to go back to the dormitory to get a few things. Just outside the door he heard a woman's voice and hesitated for a moment. But he was curious, and couldn't resist taking a peek. In the darkness he could see the outline of two people making love, the woman sitting on top of the man, in a position the Chinese call the 'umbrella handle with flowing water.' This was bad luck indeed. Bandit Xiang began to worry.

Not long afterwards, a second event occurred. Many members of the Changsha Youth played around with women, and on this afternoon it was proposed that the group go on a field trip of sorts. The late summer weather was just right for outdoor work, it was observed; why not go over to Martyrs' Park, where there were bound to be couples hidden in the bushes, reveling in the balmy weather. 'Yes, let's go investigate,' echoed the others enthusiastically. 'It should be a good time.'

By now Bandit was more reluctant than ever to take part in this kind of activity, and he refused to go along. He knew what he would find. Even at that time overly crowded living quarters created problems for any individuals who hoped to get a taste of what relations outside of marriage would be like. Anyone who was having an affair had long since discovered that Martyrs' Park in summertime was an idyllic spot for the 'pleasure of clouds and rain.' Situated in the northeastern suburbs of the city, the park occupied almost 150 acres, making it the least densely populated area in Changsha. Plantings of various flowering shrubs and trees had been arranged with a touch of the exotic; red and gold pavilions accented the carpet of soft, green grass that matted the ground. Even people from as far as Shaoyang and Hengyang were said to make excursions here in order to sample nature's bounties and escape the watchful eye of their spouses.

Just before midnight the gang returned to Changsha Youth headquarters. Bandit heard the commotion and walked over to the conference room door, joining the others who were filing inside. There to his horror he saw a man and a woman, stark naked, surrounded by half the membership of the Changsha Youth. The couple appeared extremely distressed.

'Why don't you perform one more time for *us*?'

'Yeah, you were probably going to wash the groove again anyway before the night was over. And if you don't cooperate, we're not going to let you go.'

'And if you *do* it once more, we won't turn you in to your units.'

At this last remark the couple looked at each other with grim determination. The man massaged himself slowly with one hand, placing his other hand stiffly on the woman's shoulder. In a few minutes, though, it became obvious that things were going nowhere. Pointing to the woman, one of the onlookers shouted out, 'Hey, you can help him out.'

'Right, right!' someone else cried. 'Stroke him, stroke him!' The spectators then all became very excited, but it was no use. Bandit Xiang hurried out of the crowded room, thoroughly disgusted and frightened.

'And that's why I'm in jail today,' Bandit Xiang tells us wistfully, finishing his story. 'I gained a petty advantage just to meet up with great misfortune.'

Sentenced as a 'counterrevolutionary arsonist,' the Bandit receives only seven years. He is overjoyed that the term is not any longer. Though he had been the one to fire the machine gun, he was merely acting under orders; Li Liang, ever the guiding spirit of the Changsha Youth, is considered the perpetrator. I reflect quietly that the official who made the decision has likely taken into consideration the Bandit's irrepressible good humor, for it is clear to all that the little pickpocket asks nothing from the world.

Li Liang does not fare so well. Like Zhang Jiulong, he is sentenced to death, with a two-year suspension. When Bandit hears the news, he shakes with anger. 'Those guys down at the Public Security Bureau are real bastards,' he cries out. 'A lot of them wouldn't be around today if Li Liang hadn't stopped some of the other members of Changsha Youth from beating them. And now that the tables are turned, they've forgotten all about it. That's 'cause they know he has a "political brain" and he's a threat. They won't rest easy till they've killed him. Guys like that only respond to the Three-haired Kid's approach.'

The Three-haired Kid, like the other members of Changsha Youth who have taken lives, is sentenced to death, effective immediately. The morning of his execution, as he is dragging his foot shackles past Number Nine, we hear him shout, 'Bandit, I'm going down to see the King of Hell and I'm going to save a place for you. When you join me, I won't fail to entertain you royally.' He is smiling impudently, as if to say, 'Eighteen years from now I'll be a hero again!' The Kid doesn't doubt for a moment that he will be reincarnated at the appropriate time, and knowing this, we feel better, at least for a little while. But the Bandit is haunted long after.

6

Fire-Soldier Mao

▼

The initiate to Number Nine steps inside the door. His pupils narrow in the darkness, and he gasps, struggling to maintain equilibrium. Vapors emanating from the festering chamber pot, the mildewing bedclothes, and the many unwashed and diseased bodies come together in this cramped place to produce an air so vile that it can suck the breath right out of a newcomer's lungs. And does so, the instant the warden shuts the door. A vague queasiness travels from the throat into the stomach; he gags, almost in spite of himself: a dry but violent little retch of acquiescence. It is only then that the inmate notices how very small the room is.

Except for a tiny space in the northwest corner reserved for a large vessel of bathing water and the chamber pot,[1] much of the 30-by-10-foot cell is taken up by double-decker bunks. There are six of them in all. Just one year ago, during the February Countercurrent of 1967, more than thirty men—mostly members of the Xiang River Storm—were deposited in this room, one after another, like dumplings dropped into a pot. But on the clear, cold February day that Warden Liu locks me up, the number is down. I count twenty-two men in this room, and quickly realize there aren't going to be any empty beds. Holding my bundle, I stand in the middle of the *haozi* and wait.

The others are silent, frozen in their positions, their faces, masks with flickering eyes. At length a young man—the 'mummy,' Xiao Fuxiang, with his pointy, arched eyebrows and hair prematurely thinned from lack of protein—struts up to me

---

[1] With the chaos of the late 1960s, the monthly privilege of allowing detainees 'into the open air' and trips to the bathhouse were all but forgotten. Most inmates did not bother to wash at all. Those who did, bathed in the small but relatively unoccupied corner reserved for the chamber pot and the giant, olive-colored ceramic tank filled with icy-cold water every morning at seven o'clock.

and grunts, 'What's your name?' When I tell him, every man who is being detained on account of 'problems' related to the Cultural Revolution—in effect, just about everyone present—relaxes.

'You can share a bunk with me.'

The voice comes from the top bunk of the bed against the back window. It belongs to a muscular youth of about seventeen who is wearing faded work clothes patched neatly with little squares of blue cloth. His skin is free of telltale scabs, and he smells clean. When he speaks to me, his manner is serious and deferential—oddly so, I reflect. He is one of the few who remained impassive upon learning who I was. He says very little. I try to discern his thoughts, but can find traces of neither sympathy nor hostility toward the radical leftist politics commonly associated with my name. I decide to accept his offer.

We don't talk much at first; I am in no mood for chatting, nor does my new bunkmate volunteer any information. Evenings he looks out the back window into the courtyard and sings, not political songs, but romantic ones, theme songs of movies from the fifties such as 'Riding the Wind, Breaking the Waves,' and from the early sixties—'Ice Mountain Visitor,' 'Slow Down Little Horse,' and 'Wedding Song.' No one has heard these songs since 1964, when they were declared revisionist. Every evening, just as dusk sets, the younger prisoners settle down to listen to his sad music, each of us with his private thoughts.

Then, on about the third day of my detainment, he finally introduces himself: 'My name is Fire-soldier Mao—I'm a member of Red Angry Fire.' He pauses and smiles. 'And a murderer.'

The red terrorist organization to which he has dedicated himself—and from which he has drawn his new, revolutionary identity, free from the 'color' of the Four Olds—is well known to the residents of Changsha and to the Rebel Camp. Red Angry Fire is said to be unyielding, even ruthless on the battlefield; its members are radical Conservatives, about 180 degrees to the left of the ultraleftist Xiang faction with which I sympathize, and for which the Bandit had fought.

Not knowing exactly what to say, I do not respond at all. That Fire-soldier and I are bedfellows is but one of the many great ironies of the Cultural Revolution, I muse.

His face is chubby and cheerful; he doesn't look like a terrorist. Only his movements, cautious and studied, suggest that he might be anything other than a young worker. Why would someone named 'Fire-soldier' invite an ideological enemy to share his bunk in these already very crowded quarters? Perhaps he was joking. And then again, maybe not.

Fire-soldier wonders if I know about a cartoon he saw once when he was dragged outside for criticism, one in which the artist had drawn me as a baby monster, implying that I was raised in a privileged environment. 'You were in your parents' arms, sucking on a bottle of black poison,' he says hesitantly. 'Is it true, Yang Xiguang? Did you really get to drink milk every day when you were little?' There is no small amount of envy in his voice.

As a matter of fact, I have heard about this particular cartoon; Spartacus saw it one time while he was out 'chasing dogs.' In it, my parents were villainized as 'black ghosts' (revisionists) with green faces and long teeth; I was a 'revisionist seedling.' Fire-soldier, however, seems less interested in my ideological shortcomings than in little details about my family's lifestyle. He poses endless questions; it's as if I come from Mars. I hem and haw, doing my best to change the subject, distracting him for a while. Soon, though, he begins to stare me in the eyes.

'You're not *really* seventeen.'

I had turned nineteen in October, but the Changsha residents sympathized with me, and the wall posters around town routinely reported me as being two years younger. I know, of course, that I look older, and, smiling, tell him my real age.

Then he starts up again, coming back to the cartoon. He is obsessed with my parents. I can tell from the way he talks that he is completely unaware of the political rifts among high-level cadres, that some individuals on the Provincial Committee are still in power, while others have fallen from grace. This young man in blue work clothes speaks glowingly of them all. The Conservatives always have been easily impressed by Communists above a certain rank, I think wearily. My parents, he assumes, were simply a couple of cadres who happened to run into some bad luck during the Cultural Revolution. Suddenly it makes sense: just as everyone with a 'complicated' class background is suspect, Fire-soldier decided from the moment he set eye on me that I am was 'reddest' inmate in the *haozi* and the answer to his prayers.

Actually, when I think of it, his attitude is pretty funny. He is always warning me about the pickpockets and the other members of the black society, not realizing that, as a victim of political persecution myself, I feel only sympathy for them. I know very well that during the 'Red Terror' campaign to 'Destroy the Four Olds' in 1966, the Conservatives killed or maimed untold numbers of the 'black seven'—landlords, wealthy peasants, counterrevolutionaries, 'bad elements,' rightists, capitalists, and bourgeoisie. Most of the survivors joined up with the Rebels. It is no surprise to me that Conservatives like Fire-soldier want to keep their distance from the 'black seven,' but it should occur to him that I might feel differently.

Still, I like him well enough. He is honest, straightforward, and mature for his age. We soon become good friends.

Fire-soldier used to be an apprentice at a large and prestigious mining machinery plant with good benefits and good pay. He was also a member of the Communist Youth League, and his class lineage is as pure as they come, for his father and elder brother were model workers at the same factory. The employees of such factories have tended to profit doubly from the Communists' policy of industrialization; it not only prioritizes heavy industry in the economy, but advocates placing industrial workers in leadership positions within the Party.

As everywhere else in China during the 1960s, the workers of these large industrial factories split into two factions. The ranks of the Conservatives were filled by League and Party core members, model workers, and other 'activists' like Fire-soldier's father and brother, who responded to the call from the top by giving their own grass-roots speeches at formal gatherings. I can see that Fire-soldier readily accepts the propaganda of the Party bureaucracy, in other words, that the Rebels are nothing but a group of Rightists who wanted to use the Cultural Revolution as a means to overthrow the Communist Party and the Loyalists. His 'sacred mission,' he often tells me, is to 'suppress rebellion and protect the red rivers and red mountains.' Fire-soldier had joined the Red Angry Fire in 1967.

Though we are not all 'Rightists,' it is true that each individual in the Rebel camp does have some bone to pick with a political leader or has been a victim of persecution. And almost everyone in Number Nine is linked to the Rebel cause in one way or another. Fire-soldier confides to me that he believes all Rebels are 'bad people,' but he adds quickly, 'You students are different; you're very innocent—you're just responding to Chairman Mao's call to support the Cultural Revolution.'

'There were three of us from the plant who signed up to join Red Angry Fire,' he recollects nostalgically. 'A truck was waiting outside and a lot of people—family and friends and coworkers—

all came to see us off. Yang Xiguang, you can't imagine how moving the whole thing was; people were in tears. It was just like in the movie "Dong Cunrui." '

An heroic soldier, Dong Cunrui had sacrificed his life by sabotaging a Nationalist-held bridge during the Civil War. In the famous scene to which Fire-soldier Mao is alluding, a group of parents in Jilin Province proudly and tearfully send their sons off to join the People's Liberation Army.

'Never forget that our family could not be what it is today if it weren't for the Communist Party,' Fire-soldier's mother said to him the day he left. 'And now those Rightists want to go up against the Party and overturn the dictatorship of the proletariat. We can't let them succeed in their schemes, even if it means making sacrifices.'

When he repeats his mother's parting words to me, he is very melodramatic, as if he is performing on stage. I wince in embarrassment.

Then, he tells me, a toothless old lady that he didn't know had hobbled up to him, urging him to repay his debt to his country. Soon the workshop's Party secretary himself began shouting out slogans, so that before long everyone in the crowd was chanting, 'I'm ready to die for red power!'

In Zuojiatang, confrontations between Rebels and the Conservative minority are inevitable, especially since politics colors every aspect of our lives. But whereas Fire-soldier Mao is willing to confide his personal opinions to me, with others he avoids any serious discussions and will only play cards or dominoes. This makes it somewhat difficult for the Rebels to pick fights with him.

We are out in the courtyard getting some fresh air, when Fire-soldier and Spartacus scoop up a few handfuls of dirt and some weeds. They bring them back to the *haozi*, where they plant them in broken dishes. Faithfully every morning they water the weeds and check their progress. Fire-soldier's is growing steadily taller and has even begun to flower, infuriating Spartacus.

'Even if they aim a triple-barrel gun at us, we Rebels can't let the Loyalists win!' Spartacus whispers conspiratorially into my ear.

When I awaken the next day, the leaves on the Conservative plant are drooping, and by the end of the week the Rebel weed has surpassed its competitor. 'I pissed on Fire-soldier Mao's flower in the middle of the night,' Spartacus confides to me with a grin.

Like Bandit Xiang, Fire-soldier was at Yijiawan, but he was

fighting on the other side, the Loyalist side. Unlike the Bandit, he had been there afterwards, during the 'August Eighth Sacrifice.' During a quiet moment, when the two of us are just sitting around on the bunk, I ask him how they had ever managed to capture any men from the Red Banner Army.

He doesn't answer me directly, choosing instead to begin the story much earlier.

'We were feeling pretty confident with ourselves, having blown up the first Rebel truck. But when the next trucks started to drive up, their men jumped down as soon as they saw our tanks. An old guy from the August First Corps said to me, "Looks like we've run into the Red Banner Army." I was packing a submachine gun and kept looking for a good target. "Listen to the sound of their fire—they're using big old .38s," the old veteran told me. They don't like the new semi-automatic 'cause the range is too close.

'When we charged up the hill trying to close in on them, a lot of our Red Angry Fire soldiers were picked off by the Red Banner Army. I was completely disoriented, didn't know which troops were which. I couldn't find the rest of the Angry Fire, and worst of all, I didn't know where the enemy was. I figured that the only way to keep from being cut down like grass like my buddies was to follow the August First and do whatever they did. There was nothing left to do but collect the bodies of our dead and head back to Xiangtan. Everybody was depressed. We had lost face in front of the Red Banner Army and that made us want more than ever to defeat those old veterans, to prove that we were real fighters. Somebody suggested waiting till nightfall and sneaking into Yijiawan to show them our stuff. So we jumped into the trucks and headed north.

'It was already very late when we finally reached Yijiawan. Our convoy stopped and parked on the outskirts of the village; then most of us walked into the village to have supper and rest for a while. We took off our armbands so nobody could tell who we were, for we were already in "Xiang River mad-dog territory." The guys from the August First Corps all had on old army uniforms, but we were wearing our regular blue work clothes.

'We walked by a teahouse where we saw several men who looked like military vets, so we decided to go in and see what was going on. After we ordered, we struck up a conversation, telling them we were with a unit in the Xiang River mad dogs. They were Red Banner all right. Those rice-mongrels never doubted for a minute that we weren't who we said we were.'

'Rice mongrels'—literally, 'the faction that makes rice'—was a pun on the word 'rebels,' or 'the faction that makes rebellion.'

'Then we all sat down together at big table and somebody poured out the tea. They really were stupid and kept shooting their mouths off about their decisive victory, especially three old "battered red banner" veterans.'

As he tells his tale, Fire-soldier becomes very animated, almost passionate, and starts using derogatory terms whenever he refers to the Rebel camp, forgetting for a minute to whom he is talking. I am privately offended and a little hurt, but remind myself that there is after all a wide ideological gap between us. He must see it in my face, for he resumes a more neutral tone right away.

'They bragged about the fact they were with the August First Corps, and that they'd been able to push back the Red Angry Fire tanks, killing at least a dozen of the enemy. Before we'd even finished eating though, the leader of the August First Corps shouted out a command, and the Red Banner Army men were disarmed. We tied them up and took them to the truck. Then we captured some more of them in the village, this time from the Xiang River Storm. Now at last we could go back to Xiangtan.'

Upon his return Fire-soldier found out that the Changsha Youth had used captured Red Angry Fire soldiers to 'cushion' the coffins of their own dead. Taking eight of the Red Angry Fire prisoners, they had shot them and made them into funerary sacrifices, burying them beneath the caskets. This news incensed the Red Angry Fire, who began to cry out, 'Blood debts have to be repaid in kind!' and 'An eye for an eye!'

And so, as Fire-soldier recounts, on August 8, 1967 eight Rebels were lined up before a firing squad in a sacrificial ritual held to commemorate the eight dead Conservatives. No sooner were the shots fired than the onlookers began to sob—tears, not for the Rebels lying at their feet, but for their friends who had served as coffin cushions in Changsha. Concerned only with revenge, Fire-soldier carried out his orders to 'provide the extra shots,' and one by one examined the bodies to make sure they all were dead. Two had survived, miraculously, their heads still bobbing up and down, in spite of the fact that blood was gushing from the wounds. 'Those two guys just wouldn't die—kept squirming around, so I had to shoot' em each twice more before they finally went up to Western Paradise.' Fire-soldier speaks without any remorse, as if he were describing a completely legitimate activity. He is unaware of my uneasiness and my rage and continues, 'That's what they're charging me for.'

After the Rebels took control of the rest of Hunan, the Red Angry Fire scattered, fleeing to Jiangxi and other nearby provinces before finally being dragged back to Changsha. The new Hunan authorities were in support of the 'orthodox Rebels.' Now the Trade Union faction, with the backing of the Communist Party Central 'Security Headquarters,' was responsible, together with the military, for keeping order throughout the province. Controlled by workers, the Security Headquarters seized, interrogated, and beat people at will; it was much worse than the Public Security Organs Headquarters. The heads of all extremist groups, whether the conservative Red Angry Fire or the Rebel Shengwulian, were rounded up and persecuted as political enemies. There was no concept of law.

Fire-soldier was not as lucky as I had been; before coming to Zuojiatang he had been hung by one wrist from the rafters and beaten on a regular basis. The handcuffs and foot shackles cut into his flesh, leaving permanent red scars on his wrist and ankles; bluish bruises covered his head and body like scales on a fish. Only after he was transferred to a regular detention center was he able to escape this kind of physical abuse.

'When I finally got into Zuojiatang I could relax,' he says, wincing. 'The Public Security Organs Headquarters is on our side; they'll do what they can to take care of me.' Fire-soldier knows that it is only a matter of time before order will be restored, for the world is still a Communist one and he, a Communist. He knows that once the Rebels are conquered, the valiant defenders of the nation will be immune from any further punishment.

And so Fire-soldier has settled into his life in Number Nine, a little edgy about the pickpockets, the counterrevolutionaries, and the other undesirables, but mainly quite content to be out of the hands of Security Headquarters. But what makes him happiest of all is the fact that 'Build-an-Army' Gao, Gao Jianjun, is in Number Thirteen.

The only women's cell in the complex, Number Thirteen, houses the likes of prostitutes, political extremists, unfaithful wives who conspired to murder their husbands, embezzlers, and spies from Taiwan. Not surprisingly, these inmates are of pivotal interest to the rest of us. Many a guest has, privately or publicly, picked out his own 'sweetheart.' Even the least attractive woman who emerges from Number Thirteen on her way for interrogation is unable to do so without causing the inhabitants of every *haozi* to climb up onto the window bars and stare out hungrily.

Three women elicit particular attention. The first of note is Huang Xingying, another of my high school classmates from Changsha First. Like me, she has landed in prison because her political ideas go beyond the limits tolerated by the authorities.

The second is a prostitute named Liu Manman, the kind of voluptuous young woman with smooth, fair skin rarely found in southern China. She winks at the pickpockets, who are very fond of her and talk about her endlessly. I am impressed at how much they seem to know about her. One young Rebel who left the countryside to work as a mason in Changsha tells me he spent a lot time looking for prostitutes. When he finally found one, he was outraged at the price: 'Those people have a lot of nerve asking five yuan a night.' He claims to have slept with Liu Manman. To prove their intimacy, he tells us that although she has slept with countless men, she really loves only one. She has been using her body as a means of repaying his debts—and only when her lover commanded her to do so. Spartacus, also eager to prove the depth of his knowledge, swears that she has all of the Security Headquarters cadres in the palm of her hand because of the favors she extends.

The third star in Number Thirteen is Fire-soldier's 'Build-an-Army' Gao. A student at the 24th High School, her parents are mid-rank army cadres. She is quintessentially northern in appearance, with a plump, round face and a tall, lithe body that makes her seem pure and sexy at the same time. But the woman of Fire-soldier's dreams has nothing to do with sex: he ignores the vulgarities of the pickpockets and their endless discussions about women. Like Fire-soldier, 'Build-an-Army' is a member of Red Angry Fire charged with murder.

She was with him at the August Eighth Sacrifice when he finished off the dying Rebels, he tells me solemnly; and what's more, she and another girl had once used machine guns to cover the retreat of the wounded Changsha Tertiary Education Command. Fire-soldier says with pride, 'Don't think she's one of those fragile types! She fights—she's tougher than a man.' Once the two of them had led a Rebel to the Xiangtan Bridge in Xiangtan, bound him tightly, and tossed him into the waters below where they had watched him writhe violently until he drowned. I think to myself, how unlucky that man had been, to die at the hands of such a beautiful woman. He wouldn't rest easy even when he was a ghost.

Like Fire-soldier, 'Build-an-Army' Gao must have believed she was carrying out a sacred mission, defending the Red cause. The movies portraying the Civil War and the battle against 'American imperialism' glorified acts of revenge against 'class enemies'; the violence and the killing were extolled as great deeds and acts of justice. Her head would have been filled with the political propaganda that steeped these movies and the many memoirs of the Revolution of 1949. I had grown up with the same propaganda. Had my family not been persecuted as counterrevolutionaries by the local authorities, I might easily have acted the same way she did.

Detention has tempered some of Fire-soldier's innocence and fanaticism. From time to time he even expresses bewilderment at the seemingly arbitrary shifts in power. And little wonder: this man who did not flinch at sacrificing himself for the preservation of the 'red rivers and mountains' now sits in a jail house run by the dictatorship of the proletariat. The political realities are much more complicated than the black-and-white image that had been in his mind.

'Build-an-Army' Gao and Fire-soldier Mao, however, are luckier than the Rebels who have taken lives. As the political situation stabilizes, their lots quickly improve. I remain in Number Twenty-three, waiting to go to labor reform, whereas all of the Red Angry Fire members are transferred to another, more comfortable facility. When order is finally restored, they are released without any sentencing at all. The Communist Party has come through for them, just as Fire-soldier predicted.

I do not begrudge Fire-soldier his good fortune, however. We are more than just prison buddies; there is a deeper bond between us. In 1968 and 1969 he and I both watched the 'orthodox' Rebels backed by the authorities crush Conservatives like Fire-soldier with the right hand while, with the left, they smashed 'independent' Rebels like me. He and I are united in our opposition to this kind of persecution and in upholding the rights of the minority.

A bittersweet friendship, it is based on disillusionment. Fire-soldier risked his life defending red power only to end up sitting in a red jail, and one of the prices he paid was the loss of his Conservative ideals. That is something I understand very well: when the great carnival of people's revolution failed to fulfill its promise I lost my own ideals and much more.

7

Doppelgänger

▼

The faces of the accused are gaunt and pale; their bluish shaved heads glisten. 'Hungry prison ghosts,' my grandparents' generation called them, and small wonder: they hardly seemed human. I know better now. Late at night, the 'years of unrest' come back to me, the rows of photos on the Changsha walls. It is the eyes that I remember most clearly.

If you were to flip through Changsha's municipal household register, you might think that half the city's population was related. The pages are filled with literally thousands of Chens and Zhangs—the Smiths and Joneses of China—and with Lis, Lins, and Lius. When you turned to the page listing the Sus meaning 'grain,' however, you would discover only a handful, for it is an uncommon surname that even Chinese can't always pronounce at first glance. The odds of finding two of these Sus, with the exact three-character name are about as slim as finding a needle in the sea. Yet at one time the Changsha register did contain two Su Yibangs. I know, because it was during the Cultural Revolution, and I knew them both.

The name 'Yibang' is a bit out of the ordinary, certainly a far cry from the 'Strengthen-the-Nations' and 'Brighten Chinas' typically given to sons and grandsons in turbulent times. Chinese tradition has long held that a person will eventually become his or her name, but the name can tell you as much or more about the father. One is tempted to look at the eras into which these two 'strangers' were born (one during the Japanese occupation, the other about the time of Liberation), and speculate about the exotic pasts of the fathers or the futures envisioned for the baby boys and draw comparisons. But speculation is cheap.

Were this 'coincidence' limited to their names, there would be no need for me to go on. Sadly, however, the two lives mirrored each other even more closely, taunting and compelling me to record their pasts. Each man found his way into Zuojiatang in the year 1969; each became trapped in the time warp of the Cultural Revolution. One is dead; one might as well be.

The younger Su Yibang was known to virtually everyone at Changsha First High School; he had a reputation for being 'strange.' And if he was a little odd, he was smart—very smart. I respected him and even felt myself to be like him, since I too had a dangerous habit of tossing around unorthodox opinions. Thus, despite our ideological differences, I made a point of keeping track of his activities.

One day in October 1967 I ran into him outside our dorm room. He was about to shower down after jogging. 'How come you spend so much time exercising?' I asked.

'Our generation will suffer a great disaster of at least ten years. I'm getting ready,' he warned.

Two months before I wrote 'Whither China?' this Su Yibang had put up a large poster with the heading 'Down with Lin Biao,' denouncing not only Lin, but the likes of Jiang Qing and Chen Boda as well. In less than a week he was locked up in Zuojiatang. Such 'malicious attacks on the highest leaders' were considered very serious. He was subsequently sentenced to ten years for 'viciously slandering Vice Chairman Lin' and 'bombarding the proletarian command,' and left the detention center shortly before my arrival in February 1968. To my great regret, we had just missed each other. Certainly I never expected the shadow of his tall, thin frame to remain behind.

At Changsha First High School he had been the kind of guy who appeared to be always in thought; he was one of those deep, grinding minds that found himself surrounded by students eager to debate hot political topics. Between classes, they would press him with questions, try to bait him. His answers were deceptively simple.

'What kind of person is Jiang Qing?' someone fired out.

'Empress Lü.'

'You're not allowed to attack Comrade Jiang Qing!' came the response. It was generally accepted that Empress Lü of the Han Dynasty had been an evil, manipulative woman.

'What kind of person is Jiang Qing?' asked yet another student, who apparently did not know his history.

'Jiang Qing is Chairman Mao's *airen*,' Su would parlay. Literally 'love person,' *airen* is the usual expression for 'wife,' but also means 'lover.' In Yan'an *airen* had been applied to the women involved in socially ambiguous relationships formed in the throes of revolutionary ardor.

Perhaps because I felt that we were flip sides of a political coin, or perhaps because we were both student jailbirds, I thought about Su Yibang often, picturing him always as I had seen him last—in the corridor or classroom, matching wits with some of the best young minds in Changsha. Not until 1978, some ten years after both his and my sentencing, did I see this Su Yibang again. I had been home from labor camp only a few days when his mother rang my doorbell. She had brought him to see me, she said.

His eyes dull and white, Su Yibang stared ahead without recognition. There was something wrong with the way he talked, his words were out of place—'the cow's head didn't line up with the horse's mouth.'

It happened at camp, his mother explained. The cadres beat his head and spine, severely damaging his central nervous system.

'Yes, the cadres were good to me,' interrupted Su Yibang. 'When they saw I was hurt, they didn't make me go out and work in the fields anymore.' His eyeballs rolled round and round, his words strung together in a monotone.

After Lin Biao had fallen, the charge of 'vicious slander' had been dropped; still Su had to serve out the remainder of his term. As his mother spun out her sorrows, I listened anxiously, not knowing what to do or say, gazing upon her son, a man of twenty-eight, maybe twenty-nine. Nothing, no spark, remained of his former brilliance. I tried to shut out his mother's trembling, high-pitched voice; it reverberated in my head. I felt my temples throbbing; my senses blurred. Finally, all that I could see was the bloody flesh of the changed and older Su Yibang.

◆

The other Su Yibang is my neighbor to the east, in Number Eight. The day I come to Zuojiatang, he knocks on the wall and calls out 'Yang Xiguang!' I lean up close to the window to listen; it is my first 'call.' He introduces himself politely, then tells me that he knows about my essay. 'Very impressive work,' he says. Our conversation ends there.

That night an inmate in Nine who is connected with Su's case fills me in.

This Su Yibang was born the son of a high-level Nationalist official, who, despite the hardships of war in the late forties, had enjoyed a privileged childhood before Liberation. I could easily imagine the kind of affluent surroundings to which he had been accustomed. In 1958 my own family had lived in the Hunan Provincial Committee compound that had formerly been occupied by a Nationalist of a stature equal to Su's father. There were spacious courtyards in the front and back totalling two or three thousand square feet. And the house itself was huge, containing a great hall that was big enough to be a ballroom, with lights recessed into the ceiling. Never in the homes of top-ranking Communist cadres had I seen such an opulent interior.

In 1950, when Yibang was about eight years old, his father was executed by the Communists during the Campaign to Suppress Counterrevolutionaries. A 'bastard child of an historical counterrevolutionary' would never get beyond junior high school, for even in the fifties, anyone whose parents had been among those 'executed, imprisoned, under surveillance, or in flight' was categorically denied the privilege of higher education. Instead, Su was assigned to a metalworking factory. He was a quick learner, and in about a year's time, had mastered all the basic lathing techniques required to become a master. But every apprentice was required to serve a full three years, regardless of what skills had been learned. Su became frustrated. When the call went forth to 'Let a hundred flowers bloom' in 1956, Su Yibang proposed that the apprenticeship period become a flexible one. In the ensuing Anti-Rightist Campaign, he was added to the growing list of Changsha's Rightists and tracked down. Having expressed 'dissatisfaction with the socialist system,' he was considered to be a 'bad element' requiring re-education through labor. Su's arrival at the labor farm in 1959 coincided with the first of the Three Bitter Years, when China was one big empty stomach.

And so, my cellmate continues, a few of the men at the labor farm began to meet secretly, and had formed a small underground ring called the 'Democratic Party.' In 1966, on the eve of the Cultural Revolution, their activities were uncovered, and Su Yibang and his three friends were sent to Zuojiatang Detention Center.

Before I am able to elicit all the details, a verdict on the Democratic Party case comes down. Late one night in April 1968, there is the sound of a jangling lock and then silence. One by one we crawl quietly up to the windows to see what is happening. 'Su Yibang!' a voice shouts out. In each of the *haozi*, the lights burn twenty-four hours a day for 'security reasons,' and in the dim light, we watch a group of officers and rifle-bearing privates from the Military Control Commission, some seven or eight men in all. They lead Su Yibang down the corridor to the other end of the compound, between Eleven and Twelve, to a little room used alternatively as a makeshift office and prison barber shop.

One of the officers can be seen taking out a big stack of papers, announcing loudly, 'Counterrevolutionary Su Yibang, on behalf of the Changsha Municipal Public Security Organs Headquarters' Military Control Commission, I hereby pronounce your sentence.' We can just barely hear the officer's voice and strain to catch his every word.

'Su Yibang has been a leader of a counterrevolutionary organization. His father was suppressed by the People's Government. When he himself attacked the socialist system, he was given a chance to be re-educated through labor. But Su Yibang hates our Party and our people from the bottom of his heart. At labor camp, he established the so-called 'Democratic Party' and functioned as its head, plotting to overthrow the dictatorship of the proletariat and to restore capitalism. In accordance with the Six Regulations of the Central Committee and the State Council, counterrevolutionary organization leader Su Yibang is hereby sentenced to death, effective immediately.' A brief pause, followed by an angry shout. 'Do you have anything more to say, Su Yibang?'

Su's reply is as swift as it is unforgettable: 'What I hate is the Communist Party; I do not hate the people. And the very reason I oppose the Party *is* the people—the people hate you!'

'Shut your filthy bastard mouth!' the officer snaps. 'Put the death shackles on him!'

Chains clanging, then the hammering of rivets. Brittle and sobering, the metallic sounds pierce the night, echoing across the courtyard. Suddenly we see Su Yibang walk out, faltering. His hands are cuffed, his feet weighted down by the shackles. The darkness of the corridor hides his face, but we can hear his voice, calm and steady as always. Then it fades away. Back in the various *haozi*, prisoners begin to whisper among themselves. 'Those damn shackles won't be taken off until just before the execution, when they tie the death knot,' Spartacus mutters.

Though my eyes are shut tightly, I do not sleep for many hours.

For some reason, only death sentences seem to be announced within the prison proper; other types of sentences are read to inmates in the pre-interrogation room in another building. I have heard two other men sentenced to death for heading up 'counterrevolutionary organizations.' In both cases the defendants had either loudly denied the existence of an organization at all or had refused to confess to a leadership role. Su Yibang is the first person I have ever known who has not tried to defend himself and who, on the contrary, has attacked his accusers.

I lie on my bunk, trying to sort it all out.

The night he leaves Number Eight, he makes one last call to me. 'Goodbye, Yang Xiguang. Take care of yourself.' He seems calm.

He is transferred to the Provincial Public Security Department Model Prison. Xiao Fuxiang explains to me that this is because there aren't any big political campaigns going on at the moment, but that when the right time comes, the Communists will gather all the death row 'chickens' together and slaughter them to intimidate the 'monkeys.' Through the network we hear that he is being held in Solitary and under observation by another inmate.

Executions are not new to me; I know about the executions of countless political prisoners implicated in political organizations. I have been forced to watch many of these. Though I have known only one such man personally—Nine Dragons Zhang—I am beginning to get the impression that the majority of these organizations were started up during the Three Bitter Years and not uncovered till the Cultural Revolution. A subsequent chance meeting persuades me that I am on the right track.

I am sitting by the window when I notice somebody across the courtyard tracing characters in the air, over and over. Checking first to see if any guards are coming, I watch closely and finally realize that he is writing 'Xiao—kai—I—am—Xue—meng.' It is my cousin. 'Xiaokai' is my childhood nickname.

We begin to communicate regularly and I learn that Xuemeng has only recently been sentenced to fifteen years for his involvement in the Great Harmony Party. Not long after this, Number Nine receives a copy of his sentencing bulletin. We study each paper meticulously to determine how many years will be meted out for a given 'crime,' for information of this sort is extremely valuable to us. This is how we learn the 'law,' which is to say, the Six Regulations. Through these 'interpretations' and 'precedents,' we are able to get a pretty good idea of the political climate on the outside—for instance, if any political movements are brewing. Xuemeng's bulletin lists over a dozen charges.

In 1961 criminal Yang Xuemeng took advantage of the three years'
economic hardship caused by the natural disaster to organize a
counterrevolutionary clique, the Great Harmony Party, in a plot
to overthrow the dictatorship of the proletariat. During the
Campaign to Purify the Class Ranks, the organization was
exposed by the organs of our dictatorship of the proletariat.

Later, Xuemeng himself tells me that the only reason he
wasn't sentenced to death was that the group disbanded when
the economic situation improved in 1963. Our Grandfather Yang
had been a landlord who was educated both in the traditional
fashion and in the modern, Western-style schools that had
become fashionable at the end of the Qing Dynasty. He made
sure all the children of my father's generation were also trained
in the Four Books and Five Classics. Xuemeng's father, a high
school math teacher, had continued this pedagogical tradition,
instilling Confucian values in his seven children. Thus it doesn't
surprise me much that Xuemeng, who was the oldest and
worked in a bank, had named his party after Confucius'
philosophy of world harmony. What is mind-boggling is that this
particular cousin—a mild, unassuming sort of guy—would ever
have the drive to start up a political party. How blind I have been
to the world around me!

About a year later, in September of 1969, not long before I am
to be sentenced, we get a 'telephone message' that Su Yibang is
back, this time catty-corner from us, in Number Fifteen. Several
months pass. Then, one warm winter day in late November, on
one of those rare occasions when anyone is released 'out into the
open,' the strident sound of chains grating against one another
causes the inmates at the windows to glance quickly out into
the courtyard, where a small inmate walks slowly.

'Su Yibang!' Spartacus calls out softly.

His face is grey, his sockets sunken. Much of the flesh on his
nose has been eaten away, leaving only two large holes, which
tilt upwards. 'Su Yibang,' I whisper to myself, feeling very cold.
He is a devil returned from hell.

Were it not for the fact that I already knew Su was in Fifteen,
I would not accept Spartacus' judgment about the frightening
person in the courtyard. He is much shorter than he had been
a year earlier, and so thin that he looks like a fourteen-year-
old boy. Bits of cotton fluff poke out of his quilted jacket; at
first glance, it seems to be torn. But the jacket has been cut
intentionally and hangs loosely around his body in long, raveling
strips, perhaps to enable the other inmates to dress him. I watch

him pace back and forth deliberately, the death shackles jingling with each step.

His mouth is moving—he is talking, but to whom? His eyes sparkle and dance, oddly, aimlessly. You can tell he is concentrating very hard on expressing his thoughts. He doesn't seem crazy, but he is changed.

Then I suddenly remember an expression for the madness that had come to China about the time Khrushchev was taking Stalin to task: persecution complex.

Whiskers stands by all the while, monitoring the inmates in the yard. Some are exercising; some, observing the weeds in the sandy soil. Most simply wander about. When it is time for the next *haozi* to take its turn, Whiskers walks over to Su Yibang and barks at him, ordering him back inside ahead of schedule. Su drags his shackled feet back in the direction of Number Fifteen. I never see him again.

After I am sentenced, I am transferred to the transit cell where I hook up with several inmates from my own case. One of these is a local playwright, Song Shaowen, who was held in Fifteen, together with Su Yibang.

'What's happening with Su? It's really a miracle that he's still around.'

The topic is dangerous, and at first Song only shakes his head. At length he sighs, saying, 'He looks like a little kid. Nobody in this place gets enough to eat, but Su, he must have given half his rations away every day. And despite the fact he ate next to nothing, he was full of energy. He lectured us all for hours, cursing the authorities from morning till night. We all knew he was a goner. So thin, you could have picked him up just like that. But as long as no one interrupted him, he just kept on attacking things.'

I remember how he had been speaking to himself in the courtyard. 'What exactly did he attack?'

'Oh, well, you know, he said that we lived under a fascist regime. Whenever we listened to broadcasts about the Sino-Soviet border clashes, he said the Communists were trying to whip up war hysteria again. Whatever the newspapers said—you name it—he denounced it.' Song's words come out in fits and starts, as if he is embarrassed by what he is saying. I can tell he isn't comfortable and decide not to push him anymore. Then, when he sees I've dropped the topic, he adds, as if in spite of himself, 'Remarkable, really. He had to be a spirit, living on thin air like that!'

Before the Cultural Revolution, there had been a lot of

propaganda about how the old society 'turned people into ghosts', the revolutionary movie 'White-haired Girl' being the classic example. In it, a slave girl is persecuted by a landlord and the local officials, and flees into the mountains where she disguises herself as a supernatural spirit to exact revenge. These days, only old people and the country folk believe in such things. But not even a staunch materialist like myself can deny that the Communist authorities had transformed Su Yibang into a ghost.

◆

Su Yibang's sentence was carried out summarily that December, several days before I left Zuojiatang. But I am unable to learn about the specific circumstances surrounding his death until several months later, after I get settled into labor camp. At Reconstruction Farm, I encounter a man named Du who was among those accused at the mass sentencing meeting at East Wind Square—the meeting at which Su Yibang died. Work unit leaders routinely ask their employees to attend in response to the call from 'above'; no one refuses such a request. On that day, 100,000 Changsha residents showed up.

'What was it like?' I ask.

'As the saying goes, "they put the horse's halter on the cow." That day things got out of control,' Little Du answers, remembering the occasion with a visible shudder. 'What Su Yibang did was completely unexpected. He didn't even wait for the proceedings to be over, just started shouting, "Down with Communism! Down with Mao Zedong!" We'd barely caught on to what was happening when the "grain-eaters" rushed him. I was standing right next to him in the line-up, and I still didn't know what was going on for a few minutes. The death knot was tied around his neck—he could hardly raise his head—but he kept on struggling anyway, and trying to shout out more slogans. That's when the "grain-eaters" took their guns and bashed in his head. But he kept on calling out slogans. So one of them finally took his bayonet and stabbed him in the mouth. Blood was squirting up in the air, and Su Yibang just kept on struggling and struggling. So they stabbed him in the mouth again. You could hear the metal ripping and twisting between his teeth and his cheeks. The meeting wasn't half over, but there he was, lying there dead in a pool of blood. By evening, the whole city knew about the incident.'

My hands are cold.

It had been the campaign calling the masses to 'Prepare for war.'

In April 1974, Little Du and I are working out in the fields of the Third Brigade of Reconstruction Farm when the heavens suddenly open. We run for the nearest shelter, a chicken coop belonging to another brigade, and stand under the eaves. Inside an old man is tossing handfuls of grain to the birds.
'Know who that guy is?' Little Du whispers.
I shake my head.
'A KGB. Su Yibang died 'cause of him.'
Breathlessly, I press him for details.
Little Du looks around, shooting a final glance at the old man. 'It was while Su was doing a stretch at the labor re-education farm. The cadres noticed that he seemed to be especially tight with several of the inmates and gave them all plenty of opportunities to be together. Then they planted the old man in the same team. He started acting even more 'reactionary' than Su Yibang; you know, always speaking out. So that they thought he was an insider. Nobody knew he was a Public Security KGB. The cadres promised that if he'd help them break this counterrevolutionary organization, he'd get at least two years knocked off his term.'
I can imagine the rest. The Public Security Bureau would have learned everything there was to know about Su's organization. But there is something which doesn't fit. 'So how come the old guy's still doing labor?'
Du laughs noiselessly. 'He got his. When he gave his final report back to the cadres, his account of Su's political views was so compelling they were convinced that, deep down inside, the guy must have had the same opinions. They'd told him to use any means he could to gain Su's trust—in fact, the reason Su trusted him in the first place was that the old guy had been sent up for complaining about Communism. Brown mud in the pants might as well be shit! Well, after he turned Su in, every single man in the organization insisted to the authorities that this old guy was a bonafide member of the Democratic Party. So guess what? The cadres not only didn't *reward* him, they gave him five more years. And know what the official charge was?' Little Du smiles devilishly. 'Joining a counterrevolutionary organization!'
The old man, who has finished feeding the chickens, slouches down on a bench.
'And though the cadres had in fact asked him to get Su, nobody ever brought up the deal that they had cut. I mean, really, after all that happened during the Three Bitter Years, when so many people starved to death—everybody had to agree with Su Yibang. The old guy. Even the cadres—mutes who swallowed an herbal tonic—they couldn't speak of the bitterness. Yup,

the minute somebody accused you of supporting Su's opinion,
everyone would automatically assume that you *were* guilty,
because, deep down inside, *that* person would agree!'
  The rain is easing up. As we walk back out into the fields, I
find myself reflecting on what Little Du has said. Speaking out
has always been risky. But to be damned, not for your actions,
not even for your words, but for what are assumed to be your
thoughts—rational thoughts—is worse. It leaves the accused no
escape. Was this how people became afflicted with Stalin's
'persecution madness?'
  I still do not know Su Yibang's political opinions or the
ideological bent of his Democratic Party. But the image of his
bloody shadow visits me more often than that of the first Su
Yibang, more often than I would like.

8
Red Blood

▼

It is new to all of us, this game called 'Twenty Questions.' Cheng Deming says he learned it from a United Action friend in Beijing.

The trick to the game, I discover, is to narrow down the possibilities by eliminating entire categories of famous people. In Number Nine, Nine Dragons and I are the best. While we each have our preferred strategies, my first question is almost always 'Foreigner?' 'Dead person?' is usually my follow-up. I've gotten to the point where I can usually guess the person in seventeen tries.

Cheng Deming can't usually stump me, but he can explain why I keep on winning. Elementary, he tells me; the Shannon theorem holds that the maximum information is obtained by assigning equal probabilities to all states in a system. It makes perfect stochastic sense: life and death have aleatoric parity.

Cheng's subjects are often unexpected.

'Foreigner?' I begin, true to form.

'No.'

'Dead?'

'No.'

'Male?'

'Yes!'

Now I have to start using my brain. 'Someone who became famous after 1949?'

'Yes!'

'Southerner?'

'Yes!'

'Famous before the Cultural Revolution?'

'No.'

'From the Hu-guang area?'[1]

'Yes!'

---

[1] Hunan, Hubei, Guangdong, and Guangxi provinces.

'The two Hu's?'

'Yes!'

'Hubei?'

'No.'

'Still in office?'

'No.'

'Conservative?'

'No.'

'College student?'

'No.'

'Still free?'

'No.'

'Detained by the Public Security organs?'

'Yes!'

'In a provincial detention center?'

'No.'

'In Zuojiatang Detention Center?'

'Yes!'

This limits the possibilities. Relatively well known Rebel students here include Zhou Guohui—the former head of Tertiary Education Storm, a college student; Zhang Yugang—the author of Shengwulian's Manifesto, also a college student; Huang Xingying—a woman, and . . . I think to myself, 'This guy is really sneaky. There's an eighty-percent chance that he's talking about me.'

I can ask a couple more questions to be absolutely sure—'In the north wing?' or 'In Number Nine?' but I calculate I have exactly four more questions left, and there are fewer than four people that match the description. 'Yang Xiguang?'

'Yes!'

'I've guessed it in seventeen tries, but have to protest. 'Yang Xiguang is hardly a "famous person". A scientist or statesman would have been more appropriate.'

'Not so,' intones Cheng. 'I have seen several publications recently where your name comes up as the exemplification of the reactionary thoughts of the bourgeoisie. Besides, if it's true that "Whither China?" has been translated into English and distributed all around the world, doesn't that make you a "famous reactionary"?'

My stomach sinks.

Like the first Su Yibang, Cheng Deming was a celebrated political thinker at Changsha First High School. He didn't join any organizations, but most students took it for granted that his ideas were almost indistinguishable from the extreme

Conservative position of the 'United Action,' or as it was formally called, the Capital Red Guard United Action Committee. The members of United Action tended to be children of the highest ranking cadres in Beijing, ministers and vice-ministers and the like. Among the earliest Red Guards, United Action students enraged Jiang Qing by speaking out against her and her Central Cultural Revolution Group. As a result they are now considered a 'reactionary organization.' The rumor mill at Changsha First had it that Cheng Deming was a 'United Action element,' and being an 'element' was never good.

When the lock sounds and he walks in, we're both overjoyed. Though he is a Conservative thinker and I a Rebel, I love his total disregard for authority. As I show him where to stow his belongings, I press him for details about what has been happening at Changsha First since I left. He winces.

Now that the school is completely under the control of workers and military propaganda teams, the two student factions have lost all their power. Conservatives and Rebels alike hate the new teams, for they're as bad as the work teams, which provoked the rebellion in the first place. In many ways they are worse, Cheng reports, because as workers and soldiers they have no inkling of what education is all about. The students who are forced up into the mountains and out into the countryside quickly lose interest in politics. With classes canceled indefinitely, there isn't much to do but assemble radios and make sweaters. It is the 'era of soldering men and knitting women.'

Faced with such tedium, even honor-roll students and political dynamos are fooling around, he reports with disgust. Lurid gossip about various 'peach-colored' affairs float about the school.

'Do you remember?' Cheng asks me. 'When we were in our first year of high school, how if the school found out that a guy had gotten a girl in trouble and he was kicked out of school, everybody got all embarrassed? Now it happens all the time, and nobody thinks anything about it.' He hesitates for a moment. 'Oh, by the way—you don't have a girlfriend, do you?'

I shake my head.

'There sure are a lot of stories going around. People are saying that you led a mass protest against the prison military officials. And that there is always a certain girl hanging around outside the gate asking to see you. Unless she can prove she's your relative, the authorities won't give her a pass.'

Just as I am telling him I have no idea who this woman might be, it occurs to me that I once received some toilet articles and a note from someone I didn't know. Perhaps that was the person, I suggest. Cheng Deming isn't convinced, but he doesn't push the issue, just grins at me knowingly, indicating that my secret is safe with him. Then he gets down to business. 'You've been in here for almost a year—tell me, what have you been doing with all your time?'

'I'm taking English and mechanical engineering. I'm reading *A General History of the World*, *Das Kapital*, *Long Live Mao Zedong Thought*, and another book with Mao's post-1949 confidential talks and memoranda. And there are people in here who can recite the 300 Tang poems and retell each of the 120 chapters in the *Romance of the Three Kingdoms*. Are you interested in long poems? There are inmates who've memorized Fan Zhongyan's "Yueyang Pavilion" and Zhu Geliang's "Chronology of Great Generals."' I pause for a moment to glance at the motley crew housed in Number Nine. 'Right now I'm working on finding a math teacher; I'm determined to finish high school and college math while I'm in here. During the Cultural Revolution there was never any time to study. Now's my chance.'

Immediately he demands to see each of my books. The first one he wants to borrow is Mao Zedong's *Critique of Political Economics*. His choice amazes me, and I ask him why a Conservative like him would want a book like that.

'I always have wanted to understand more about how Mao's ultraleftist ideas were formed,' he says, chuckling. He is as defiant and heretical as ever.

Cheng Deming sets up a study plan of his own. English and the principles of electricity we tackle together. Most of his individual study time, though, is devoted to the thought of Mao Zedong.

What to do for a desk, he wonders. I tell him how when I first arrived, I put a bed plank on a water bucket for my chair and used the edge of the lower bunk for a table, but the cardplayers ended up with my 'chairs' more often than I did. I finally resorted to resting the board on my lap and sitting on the bed. Cheng Deming scouts out another loose board and follows suit.

Finding a good teacher in Zuojiatang is easier than finding furniture, for each *haozi* is a repository of engineers, professors, and other intellectuals.

Teacher Zhu, our electrical engineering instructor, has cataracts and a large nose, making him appear solid and trustworthy. Though he is fluent in the Changsha dialect, he stutters slightly, tripping over his words whenever he is overly excited. He tells us he was born into an extremely wealthy family before Liberation and sent down for labor re-education as a Rightist in 1957. When he couldn't find a job after his release, he remained at home for a while before starting up a little neighborhood shop repairing underwater pumps with a sealant he had invented himself. Since nobody else in Changsha was able to fix this kind of pump, his services were in great demand. But his status as a Rightist meant that no matter how much the shop took in, he could only keep 50 yuan a month. In fact the only real advantage he derived from working there was that his sons were allowed to become workers in the same plant. During the Cultural Revolution he was overheard criticizing the 'new Empress Dowager' (Jiang Qing)[2] and was sent back to prison as an 'ex-con counterrevolutionary.'

Cheng thinks highly of Teacher Zhu, as I do.

With our diverse backgrounds, one never knows what will happen in class, or where our discussions will lead us. When we are learning about electrical name plates on devices, for example, Teacher Zhu surprises us by announcing that there are two different systems used throughout China: one represents horsepower, phase, and frequency with English symbols, and another uses the Soviet symbols.

'Which is better?' As a supporter of the 'Soviet revisionist line,' Cheng often asks such sensitive questions. But his teacher's response is not what he expects or likes to hear.

'Why, the English, of co-co-course! After Liberation the universities made all the English teachers take Russian so they could teach it. All the industrial standards switched over to the Soviet system, and, we-well—we've always had a hard time getting used to it.' Wide-eyed, Cheng and I nod in response.

The following day Teacher Zhu finds a quiet moment to ask me, 'What's Little Cheng in for?'

'Same as you. Said that a perfectly good country was being ruined by the new Empress Dowager.'

Teacher Zhu smiles. Just then Cheng Deming, who has been watching, walks over to see what is so amusing.

'Do you know why the Empress Dowager decided to support the Boxers?' Teacher Zhu asks him, still smiling.

'Not offhand,' Cheng replies, somewhat puzzled by this reference to the old secret society.

Teacher Zhu lifts his cloudy eyes knowingly and slowly

---

[2] Many people criticial of Mao's wife compared her with the Empress Dowager Ci Xi, who ruled for half a century and excelled in the political manipulation of the Qing court. Her misrule directly contributed to the fall of the dynasty.

explains, 'When Emperor Guangxu's reforms failed and he was deposed, the Empress Dowager knew that if she ruled behind the bamboo screen in place of the emperor, she would most certainly be considered illegitimate. She decided to groom a new emperor whom she called "Big Brother." When word leaked out, all hell broke loose in China and abroad, for the Western ambassadors sympathized with Guangxu's reforms. Rumor had it that the Westerners would resist the installation of the puppet emperor. Meanwhile, in Beijing and Tianjin, conflicts between the Boxers and the foreigners were always erupting. The Empress Dowager had heard that the Boxers had all sorts of magical powers and were invulnerable to weapons, that they supported the Qing Dynasty, and most importantly, that they wanted to destroy the foreigners. She was determined to make use of them. Putting Big Brother on the throne became her ob-obsession.

'One day a southern governor-general seized a letter written by one of the ambassadors, in which he intimated that if the Empress Dowager forced the installation of Big Brother, the foreigners would intervene and return Guangxu to power. This news hit her where she was most vulnerable. She had been wrong, she knew, and she was totally isolated. As time passed she became irrational. One day in a fit of temper she called in her ministers and ordered them to have the Boxers attack each of the foreign embassies. That was what led to the "Chaos of 1900," when the Eight Powers entered Beijing.'

Cheng Deming interrupts. 'When Mao Zedong supported the Red Guards, it was pretty much the same situation; he became irrational, only his sore spot was the Great Leap Forward. It was probably Wu Han's criticism that pushed him to the brink.'[3]

'You c-c-cannot say that! You can't say things like that! You'll ge-get your head chopped off!' Teacher Zhu has a horrified expression on his face, though no one else in the *haozi* has heard. An 'ex-con counterrevolutionary' has to be more careful about what he says than the more recently labeled counter-revolutionaries.

When he isn't reviewing his lessons in English and electrical engineering, Cheng Deming spends most of his time copying out Mao's *Critique of Political Economics*. The entire volume. Mao is the only author allowed in without any questions asked; most

---

[3] Wu Han was the deputy mayor of Beijing and a well-respected historian. In the early 1960s he wrote a play about the outspoken Ming dynasty official Hai Rui who was dismissed from office by an emperor unwilling to entertain criticism. The play was generally viewed as a dimly veiled allegory of Mao's dismissal of Defense Minister Peng Dehuai; in late 1965, Wu Han's work was labeled a 'poisonous weed' by the ultraleftist Yao Wenyuan.

of his works we have already read many times. But we are eager to get our hands on the previously suppressed documents like the *Critique* which only now are being published by mass organizations; many are said to show how history has proved Mao wrong. We believe that works like these can provide us with a fuller picture of the background of the Cultural Revolution. Every month I write to my sister Yang Hui, sending her my new wish list of books. A lot of Marx never gets through. Two out of the five edited volumes of Mao's confidential talks make it in.

' "Expertise first. Then what about politics? The expert line. Then what about the masses?" ' Cheng Deming recites. 'You know, I don't think Mao understood economics at all.'

Poring over the *Critique*, notes made by the Chairman in 1959 as he studied a Soviet political economics textbook, Cheng quietly shares his reactions with me.

'Look at this! He was even opposed to piece-rate wages and material incentives. Now how could he ever think that political encouragement would improve production?'

I nod. What had struck me about the book, I tell him, was the slogans of the Great Leap Forward. I had always assumed that 'Politics take command,' 'Raise the supreme banner of steel,' 'Surpass England and catch up with America,' and 'The nation's economy should be controlled like a chess game' were generated by the Communist organs or local governments at the grass roots. Suddenly, I saw that each and every one could be traced to Mao.

Cheng moves on to the post-1949 confidential talks that are collected in *Long Live Mao Zedong Thought!* We continue to zero in on different things. Cheng is interested in the origins of Mao's leftist economic and cultural policies; I look for potential motivations behind Mao's ordering the Communist Party to stop all other organizational activities just prior to the January Storm in 1967, and his support for the Rebels. Neither of us is disappointed.

In reading about the period before the Hundred Flowers Campaign I can trace Mao's search for a suitable form of socialist democracy as he tried to avoid walking down the same path Stalin had. So! He really did want liberalization and wasn't 'merely casting a long fishing line' as he later claimed. Perhaps this was the Chairman's attempt to avoid ridicule after his experiment in liberalization failed to receive the support of the Party power holders.

Page after page of revelations. In 1959 Mao had written that a high-salaried stratum was forming in China; in 1963 he referred to a 'privileged stratum of bureaucrats'; in 1964 he cited the peasants' resentment of the cadre stratum as the 'major contradiction' of rural society. I am looking for evidence to support my hypothesis that Mao's support of the rebelling masses during the Cultural Revolution was an indirect result of the anti-Stalinist movement of 1956. Without this twist in Soviet affairs, Mao, in 1966, would undoubtedly have commanded the Party apparatus to purge his political enemies in the same way as Stalin did in the thirties, instead of encouraging the common people to form organizations that would stand up against Communist officialdom.

Of course, Cheng and I have different perspectives: I am a Rebel, he is a Conservative. I want to prove irrefutably that rebellion is justified; he is doing everything he can to find logical flaws in Mao's economic and political lines. But we are in complete agreement about Mao's boasts of 1959. Cheng laughs out loud when he gets to Mao's 'satellite' speech encouraging the peasants to produce 20,000 pounds of wheat per *mu* (about 6000 square feet).

I show him other instances where the Chairman made even more extravagant promises. Mao made all of these ridiculous claims at the same time he was ridiculing Peng Dehuai and his 'bourgeois animals.'[4]

Cheng tells me that he thinks Mao's mistake in 1959 caused the economic collapse, a mistake for which he refused to accept responsibility, even when he was criticized. He launched the Cultural Revolution to purge the 'political enemies' who had levied the attacks against his economic policies. It is the first time I have heard this opinion and I am impressed at his insight, since the official propaganda has been telling us that the conflict was a 'protracted revolution led by the dictatorship of the proletariat against the bourgeois restoration and a struggle between the proletarian command and the bourgeois command.' Cheng Deming's explanation is certainly more convincing. And yet I have my own ideas about the Cultural Revolution.

'Sure, Mao was wrong in 1959. But by rehabilitating those labeled as "Counterrevolutionary Rebels" during the Cultural Revolution, he really did win the support of the Rebels.'

---

[4] In 1959, Peng Dehuai privately communicated to Mao his concerns about the negative impact of the Great Leap Forward policies first championed in late 1957. Peng was subsequently purged and a nationwide campaign opposing 'right-wing opportunists' was begun against any Communist Party member who had criticized the Great Leap.

I pause. 'If, right now, the authorities capped you as a counterrevolutionary, and Mao Zedong came in and exonerated you, would you side with him or with the authorities?'

'But I'm not a counterrevolutionary!'

'Show me one man who's been labeled a counterrevolutionary and who admits to being one. All Rebels support the man who rehabilitates them.'

Staring at his feet, he finally nods quiet assent. 'Of course,' he mutters, pacing the narrow space between the beds, 'The masses aren't rebelling for nothing.'

As our discussion continues, my thoughts wander. I think back to the autumn of 1959 when I was still very small. My father had picked me up one day and carried me over to the window. 'When cadres have been at the top of an organization for a while, they don't understand what the bottom is like,' he said softly. 'So they have to go down there to see for themselves.'

I was looking out at the red leaves and thinking how strange it was for him to be talking that way, acting so nice, because he had been in a foul temper for days and was constantly arguing with my mother. It wasn't until three years later in 1962, when I was fourteen, that I finally learned he had been labeled a 'right-wing opportunist' for being critical of Mao's policies. 1962 was the same year the Party Central rehabilitated him. My father told me that Chairman Mao had formally apologized to the group of 'right-wing opportunists,' conceding that their views of 1959 had in fact been correct.

Indeed, for our family and most others, 1960 and 1961 were dismal years. After my father went down to the countryside, we had to move from the provincial committee compound into a flat belonging to my mother's unit, where living conditions were poor. Like everyone around us, we were hungry. Meat was scarce. The only food you could buy on the streets was expensive hard candy. Everywhere you looked you saw people suffering from edema. Before long, people had so little energy that the government agencies and schools were forced to shorten their hours. I remember seeing glass jars in windows; people were growing a kind of algae called chlorella as a dietary supplement. In our compound, we spent most of their time sifting the broken tiles and stones out of the dirt in the courtyard and trying to plant vegetables. The public toilets had all been closed, so people built primitive latrines to collect excrement for their gardens. There were classes in how to make 'twice-steamed rice' and 'artificial meat.' For the former, about four ounces of rice could be transformed into one pound of cooked rice. 'Artificial meat' was a concoction of chaff and chlorella that stuck in your throat when you swallowed it. But none of these foods really kept the hunger away.

'Hey, look at this,' Cheng calls out, pointing to his book. 'No sooner had Mao admitted the Great Leap was a mistake than he changed his mind at the Tenth Plenum Conference of the Eighth Central Committee! And to think that he's been using political campaigns to refute that work meeting ever since.'

I smile. He's reading Mao's acknowledgement of his error in the recently published collection of confidential documents made available through the efforts of the mass organizations, the proceedings of the 1962 Chinese Communist Work Meeting. My father often spoke of it. This is the closest Cheng and I will ever come to being on the same side of the political fence.

Perhaps because Cheng and I used to be top students, we think back fondly upon our teachers, who often gave us advanced textbooks and extra homework. One afternoon, when we are discussing Mao's conversations with his nephew Yuanxing, Cheng becomes particularly agitated about a famous conversation in which Mao told his nephew that teachers don't really understand anything, but enjoy intimidating their students by dreaming up tricky or irrelevant test questions.

Curious about Cheng's outburst, Zhang Jiulong saunters over and demands to read the offensive passage for himself. 'Mao's argument is not totally unfounded,' he says at length.

'What? You think that cancelling closed-book exams and encouraging students to get C's is reasonable?' Cheng snaps.

'All right,' continues Zhang, unfazed. 'You need a certain amount of discipline to guarantee that students will learn the basic skills. If you don't have tests and if you attack teachers, young people will suffer. But in Soviet-style education, students didn't have enough freedom. I wasn't allowed to select my own classes. You couldn't even choose between English and Russian—the school made all the decisions. If a teacher didn't lecture well, you couldn't leave the classroom or you'd be punished. You couldn't even skip a grade. Mao's idea of letting high school kids skip grades is quite sensible. I was able to finish the three-year curriculum in two years.'

'Yes, but with the freedom of choice that you had in the Cultural Revolution,' Cheng retorts, clearly annoyed. 'Lots of students chose not to go to school at all. When school children think they can go on strike every time classes are about to resume, you've got a problem on your hands.' He looks at Zhang cynically as if to say, 'Go ahead, make your obsequious little remarks about Mao. We all know very well that you and your kind oppose the socialist system—from the right!'

Whenever his companion's voice grows loud or strained, Zhang becomes silent. He begins to tap his fingers on the edge of his bunk, drumming his feelings and his words into oblivion.

Cheng Deming was one of the earliest Rebels in our school, among the first to protest against the work teams sent by the Provincial Committee. Later, he shifted to the extreme conservative position of the United Action. Rebel or no, I enjoy listening to any fellow iconoclast; my classmates used to kid me that I 'loved any viewpoint coming from a person without power.' Cheng has always been an outstanding thinker in my eyes, and I had ignored my classmates' warnings that his rightist views were too 'dangerous.' Moreover, I was intrigued by his conversion over to the 'other side.'

One day I decide to tell Cheng Deming about how practically all of my cousins in Beijing, cousins on both sides of the family, are children of high-ranking cadres who joined United Action in 1966. Every time I went to Beijing to 'exchange revolutionary experiences,' I used to look them up. 'And you,' I continue. 'How did you take up with United Action?'

'My girlfriend. Same way Zhu Chengzhao did, when he met Ye Xiangzhen.' Zhu had headed the Capital Third Headquarters, the largest student Rebel organization in Beijing, but was pulled over to United Action by the daughter of Ye Jianying and ultimately put under house arrest by the Central Cultural Revolution Group.[5]

'I met her the winter of 1966 on a freight train going from Changsha to Beijing. All of the passenger cars were packed. When the train made a stop, the only hope you had to get aboard was to find somebody you knew and have them open a window. I was still a Rebel then, so I had a friend of a Rebel friend save me a place on the caboose.

'There was supposed to be an attendant on the caboose who could look through the front window and observe the entire train to make sure that nothing out of the ordinary occurred, like somebody sneaking on top of a car to steal luggage. But no one was there.

'It was already getting dark when the attendant came back, bringing a tall girl with him. There weren't any lights in the caboose, and I couldn't really see her face, but she had a Beijing

---

[5] At that time Ye Jianying was Vice Chairman of the Central Military Committee of the Chinese Communist Party.

accent. She kept talking and talking—a typical northern girl. When the train finally got going, I realized that sitting back there was a real mistake. We were getting whipped back and forth, and the noise was terrible. If you wanted to be heard, you had to speak directly into the other person's ear. A conversation was out of the question. I figured I might as well go to sleep early and lay down on one of the two seats. The attendant was sitting across from me at one end; the girl sat down at the other end.

'Then, around midnight, while I was sound asleep, I felt someone pushing at me. When I sat up, I saw that the girl was right next to me.

'She pressed her lips to my ear and asked "What school are you from?" I could smell the scent of her hair and my heart started racing a mile a minute. I told her my name and my school, and I remember thinking she seemed kind of strange. But, I thought, this must be the way all those extraverted Beijing girls act.

'Then she said, "The moon is really nice tonight; do you want to go out for a while?" So I followed her outside to the caboose observation platform. We watched the tracks behind us for a little while and then started to exchange stories about the anti-work team organizations in our schools, shouting at the top of our lungs. We had a lot in common.

'Then she suggested that we leave the caboose and find a freight car to sit in. After we had shoved our way through several cars, she whispered, "Last night that creepy porter kept trying to climb on top of me."

'Under the light of one of the stations we passed by, I saw her face for the first time. I was shocked—she was beautiful. And obviously from a good family. Said she was one of the original Red Guards; she belonged to the Western District Pickets. The month before, there had been a campaign in Beijing criticizing the reactionary line of the bourgeoisie; the old Red Guards were out of power, so she and her friends had set out in search of revolutionary experiences. She was pretty depressed.

'But then friends in Beijing wrote that the members of the original Red Guard were planning a new organization, the "Red Guard Committee for United Action." They wanted a final fight-to-the-finish with the Rebel Capital Third Headquarters. She decided to return to Beijing ahead of time.

'After that the train stopped at a freight station and crossed a turntable that looked like a big spider web under the flashing lights. We finally found an empty freight car. But when we crawled in, someone was already inside. It was a couple—students I think—sleeping under a woolen blanket. When we started up again, I saw that there was something funny about the blanket; it kept moving and suddenly started jerking violently. Yang Xiguang, you have no idea how embarrassing this was for me, watching this with a girl next to me. It was extremely awkward, to say the least. I didn't know what to do. But Hongyan leaned up against me, and squeezed my hand tight. My head started to spin. Then I felt her other hand on my shoulder. I didn't know what all of this was supposed to mean. I don't think she knew either, to tell you the truth. Maybe she just wanted to feel safe.

'That's how we became more than everyday friends. Later she invited me to come stay at her house. It was an old-fashioned compound with a courtyard in the old part of Beijing, just outside the Forbidden City, with at least a dozen rooms. Her father had to be a cadre at the ministerial level to be able to live in a place like that. But what really made me nervous was the couplet sandwiching their front door: "If your father's a hero, you're a good man; if your father's a reactionary, you're a bastard." And over the door was worse—"only ghosts will be disturbed when they read this."

'While I was in Beijing, I got to know a lot of Hongyan's cousins and friends. She was always up to something. The pickets from the East, West, and Haidian districts were all involved in organizing the Capital Red Guard United Action Committee. Hongyan took me along with her to the rallies, and I began to understand their political agenda. Their favorite slogan was "Support pre-1957 Mao Zedong Thought."

'They hated the Rebels with a vengeance. Thought they were all a bunch of landlord-capitalists—"bastards"—who were unhappy with the Communist Party. All "Rightists" and "counterrevolutionaries." Another favorite slogan of theirs was "Only leftists are allowed to rebel; rightists may not shake the earth." One time Hongyan gave a such a great speech, one that I'll never forget. It went something like, "If the Cultural Revolution continues, the country will be crippled for twenty years to come. Economic and cultural development will be irreparably damaged. Our fathers sacrificed their blood to establish red power. We can't just forfeit it all to people like Jiang Qing and Kuai Dafu.[6] This nation is our nation; this land is our land. We can't stand idly by and abandon her to traitors."

'The members of the various pickets were already speaking

---

[6] Kuai Dafu was a Qinghua University student who fought against the work teams in 1966. He was labeled as a counterrevolutionary by the wife of Liu Shaoqi, Wang Guangmei, who at the time oversaw the work teams at Qinghua. Mao personally reviewed Kuai's case and rehabilitated him.

disrespectfully of Mao Zedong—they called him "the old man" instead of "Chairman Mao"; and they were even more vicious toward Jiang Qing. As soon as the United Action was established, they immediately went out to Tiananmen Square to put up big-character posters blasting both Jiang Qing and Chen Boda.[7] Some of them got picked up by the Public Security Bureau.

'I took part in one of the United Action operations to smash the Capital Third Headquarters. They were so serious and well-disciplined—stricter than any other mass organization I had ever seen. Don't think they weren't cruel, though. Their discipline was Communist-style—they never held back when they were dealing with "class enemies." When they discovered that the parent of one Rebel student was a landlord—they whipped the little bastard with a leather belt. One guy spit onto the ground and then made a girl get down and lick it up. But when they smashed the Capital Third Headquarters, they respected public property. Nobody stuffed anything into their pockets; nobody moved unless they were commanded to.

'I used to listen to them talk at Hongyan's place about their revolutionary experiences. Once she told me that when you wanted to beat someone, if you used the side of the belt it hurt more and you couldn't hear it. If you beat someone flush with the belt, it made a lot of noise and didn't hurt so much, but it was a good way to scare people. One kid in the Western Pickets whose father was a high-ranking cadre mentioned matter-of-factly that the best way to kill "black ghosts" was not by using a club, but by using boiling water. You could scald somebody to death without even being near him, and there wouldn't be any marks to link you to the body. He had done this at the Western Picket labor reform camp to an old guy who was a third-generation landlord. All the cadres' kids who were sitting around listening were really impressed. Nobody felt sorry for the dead man.

'After a while I completely absorbed the United Action political agenda. The only thing that bothered me was that all of Hongyan's crowd came from high-ranking cadre families. They looked down on me. I was just the son of a technician from the provinces. I could tell they really weren't interested in me, that they were just being polite for Hongyan's sake. I felt lousy.

'Not long afterwards came the "Five Attacks on the Public

---

[7] Chen Boda was a Politburo member and headed up the Central Cultural Revolution Group until he was purged in 1973.

Security Ministry." You probably heard about it, right? I was there. Row after row of students rushed onto Tiananmen Square, demanding that the Public Security release the comrades who had been imprisoned for attacking Jiang Qing and Lin Biao. Everybody in United Action was chanting, "Down with Public Security!", "Down with the Capital Third Headquarters!", "Down with Jiang Qing!", and "Long live Liu Shaoqi!" When the people at the front of the crowd were seized, their places were taken by students at the rear.

'Before I left Beijing I had a serious talk with Hongyan. We were both worried about the future. She told me how angry she had been during the attacks on the Public Security Ministry: "China is being completely ruined by Old Man Mao and Jiang Qing. The Sixteen Point Resolution clearly states that students can't be attacked, but they're seizing students anyway."

'I told her I would be leaving Beijing the next day. It was our last night together, so I asked if I could kiss her. Was I nervous! Her face turned red, and her voice was soft, but her words ripped right through me. "Don't talk like that—let's just be everyday friends," she said.

'It was her way of rejecting me. My background just wasn't good enough for her crowd, I knew. Once before I had overheard her little brother ask her, "Does his father drive a ZIS or a ZIM?" She was embarrassed and changed the topic. A couple of days later I found out that ZIS and ZIM were names of classy Russian sedans used by vice ministers and on up the line. When I think about that time, I think, boy, was I stupid! Hongyan's world was too far from my own. I'll bet I never was welcome in that old compound.'

Cheng Deming's pride has obviously been wounded. He had been completely suckered in, except for the bit about the blood line. Though he is able to boast he comes from one of the five red family origins (workers, peasants, soldiers, revolutionary cadres, and revolutionary martyrs), that wasn't enough to be accepted by the peers of the person he loved. In a way, I'm glad he is able to rationalize his failure. Better to be rejected for one's social status than for not being attractive to a beautiful woman.

Because so many of my aunts and uncles on my father's side are high-ranking cadres, I am very well aware of the kind of superior attitude Cheng was up against. I have no patience with such snobbery. By the time the Conservative Red Guards were established, my parents had already been labeled counterrevolutionary revisionist elements by the Hunan Provincial Committee, so in the Changsha First debates on the validity of 'If your father's a hero, you're a good man; if your father's a reactionary, you're a bastard,' I argued on the 'against' side, along with the Rebels. But when I tell him this, he is skeptical.

'Really,' I continue. 'When I first heard about the formation of the Conservative Red Guards, I got scared. It was like being a Jew and hearing that the Brown Shirts were being organized. I knew they weren't going to let a kid like me join the Red Guards. I knew from the start they were going to persecute me.'

Cheng Deming corresponded with Hongyan for a short while after he left Beijing. In late February 1967 she wrote a long, newsy letter: Chairman Mao had ordered Jiang Qing and the Public Security Ministry to release all the members of United Action, and was going to permit them to publish their own newspaper on the condition that the local Public Security organs release all the Rebel students captured in early February, assuring their 'Four Big Freedoms'—big speech, big exchanges of revolutionary experiences, big-character posters, and big criticism. Hongyan wrote that 'Auntie Jiang Qing' had met with the newly released United Action members and requested that they change their reactionary views, to which they responded by breaking out in a rousing chorus of 'The Butterfly Loves the Flower,' a poem written by Mao in memory of his former wife Yang Kaihui and put to music during the Cultural Revolution. Their 'Auntie Jiang Qing' was so enraged she could scarcely speak.

Through this letter Cheng Deming became the first person in our school to hear the news that the Rebel students were about to be released. In early February 1967 approximately 100,000 people had been confined in Hunan by the local authorities and the Conservative Red Guards for participating in Rebel organizations. The incensed residents protested in every way they could, including petitioning the authorities in Beijing. In Changsha, the Conservatives of the same political persuasion as United Action routinely led the military and the Public Security Bureau on raids to round up Rebels; Beijing was the only place where Conservatives were being jailed. Still, by the end of early March, all the Rebel students had been set free. Among those held captive, I too had been released suddenly for no apparent reason.

Cheng eventually received from Hongyan a copy of the small, lead-type newspaper *Xiang River Commentary* put out by United Action, a name borrowed from the paper published by Mao in the 1920s when he was living in Changsha with Yang

Kaihui. The United Action paper often printed articles indirectly criticizing Jiang Qing.

What is unfortunate, Cheng tells me, is that because United Action has persisted with its policy of the blood line, insisting that the original Red Guards are the only orthodox revolutionary organization and that all subsequent Rebel groups are counterrevolutionary, it has become isolated from the residents of Beijing. Whereas several months ago, they were readily able to organize mass assemblies and had won the right to publish a newspaper, they now have practically no political influence at all.

Most of the inmates in Number Nine are aware of the clause in the programmatic Sixteen Point Resolution that prohibits persecuting students on any grounds. The authorities have to 'protect the minority,' and so it is generally assumed that no matter whether an inmate is a Conservative like Cheng or a Rebel like me, as long as we are students, we will eventually be released.

Not long afterwards, in December of 1968, a new inmate brings us interesting information. The man's name is Zhao, and because he used to be a Party branch secretary in a small snack bar—even snack bars are completely controlled by the Party these days—everybody calls him Secretary Zhao. He is short and fat, and since there is a trace of a Beijing accent in his Changsha dialect, we know right away he is a cadre. Secretary Zhao tells me the Party Central has passed down a document saying that all Rebel and Conservative student prisoners will be put into Mao Zedong Thought Classes, where they will be able to admit their mistakes and earn their freedom. 'There's hope for all you students!' he says enviously.

At first we avoid him—he might be KGB. But after a while we drop our guard. He is thoroughly guileless and is in jail, in fact, precisely because he was a little too blunt, denouncing the Communists when they supported the North Vietnamese policy. Although Secretary Zhao is a Party member, he takes pleasure in critiquing official policies that don't make sense to him.

'Little Yang, you might not know this, but whenever you give people aid with "no strings attached," or say you're "protecting" somebody, it's always because you want them to capitulate to you. Take the "unselfish help" the Soviet Union offered us in the fifties. In fact the price was high enough! You have to do whatever they say, or risk breaching the relationship. Look at the unconditional aid China gave to North Vietnam—it's going to be the same story. We try to steal a chicken and failing, lose the rice we gave out as bait. Is it worth it? Let the two Vietnams fight it out; China's better off watching from the sidelines!'

As much as I love listening to Secretary Zhao and his independent political views, I feel I must warn him. 'Don't discuss decisions that you're not in a position to make. Besides, you know the old saying, "When you hold your tongue, nobody's going to accuse you of being a mute." '

'You! You!' hoots Secretary Zhao. 'You sure learned your lesson! You're not worried about "Whither China?" any more!'

His prediction about the imminent release of students proves only partially accurate. On a bright, sunny day in early autumn, a pre-interrogation officer comes with Whiskers to open the Number Nine lock. Sitting on the edge of our beds, we watch the doorway in silence.

'Cheng Deming, come out here!' cries the officer. There is a general sigh of relief from the rest of us. 'Bring your clothes and blanket.'

At this last command, Cheng becomes so excited he drops his tea mug on the floor, where it shatters. Nobody else moves. Now we know he is getting out. Nine out of ten inmates who are called out to roll up their quilts before being prosecuted are set free; moreover, we all know Cheng's views are shared by the Public Security Organ Headquarters cadres, every single one of them Conservatives who oppose Jiang Qing. Later we hear that he has been 'released for education.' Rebel students are not so lucky.

But Cheng Deming continues to believe that I too will be released. He writes to tell me what it feels like to be on the outside again. How he wandered around the streets of Changsha for two days; everything was new and interesting. Heaven must be like this, he says. Cheng has forgotten our pledge to visit all the fancy restaurants: he no longer craves food. But he keeps his promise to send me a bundle of mass organization newspapers with all the unofficial news. He even gets me a toothbrush and a coveted tube of 'Zuojiatang toothpaste'—lard! The last postcard I receive is filled with warm words of encouragement and the firm expectation that I will soon be out. He is in constant communication with my family, he says; as soon as he gets the word he will bring them to meet me at the gate.

'Just relax and keep studying,' he writes. 'Stay fit. We know that you'll soon be returning to the arms of the people.'

In a few months, I am sentenced.

9

Gentlemen

▼

Revolutions turn things upside-down. That is the point of the exercise. This was true in 1949 and it was true during the Cultural Revolution, when some of the finest members of the old society suddenly found themselves branded 'politicals' or 'counterrevolutionary criminals,' and cast into the pits of China's penal system. In times of extreme chaos, politicals end up together with common criminals, the men who have broken one or another of society's laws, be it rape or murder. However serious, these crimes are nevertheless considered 'internal problems,' and their perpetrators still belong among the ranks of the people.

Counterrevolutionaries do not. According to whether the individual is a prisoner of conscience, an historical counterrevolutionary, a leftist, a rightist, or an 'organization criminal,' he is relegated to a correspondingly outcast position.

Coming from what was, at least in my own mind, a respectable family, I expect the politicals in Number Nine to comport themselves according to higher moral standards than the common prisoners. But I am disappointed.

The paradigm has changed. What drives the ethics of our little society is deprivation, conditions not so different from the ones the pickpockets and the thieves were accustomed to on the outside. Men like Bandit Xiang know about survival and the group instinct. Politicals like Blindman Lu, on the other hand, who tend to come from the middle or upper classes and who are used to living independently, rarely give up what is 'theirs.' In this hotel for cow-ghosts and serpent-spirits, I, too, fear for my survival and am on constant guard to protect my own interests, a mentality that is chipping away at my old moral standards. Fortunately I am young and impressionable, and I am gradually pulled over to the culture of the lower classes, where I learn to share the bitter and the sweet. But as Spartacus puts it, 'Among the politicals, there aren't many mules who understand "flavor.'" He means the 'flavor' of human kindness. Li Anxiang and Professor Chen are the exceptions.

LI ANXIANG

Though everybody calls him 'Preacher,' Li Anxiang isn't a priest. He is, however, a pious Roman Catholic and has been for twenty out of his thirty years. The church he used to attend lies in the northern section of Changsha and was once sponsored by the Americans along with an adjoining hospital, which became Changsha Municipal Hospital Number Two after Liberation. I was often treated there as a child and can still remember a series of pictures in a display case with a message underneath informing patients how the church and hospital had been the strongholds of American imperialism. During the purge of 1954, the foreign priest was seized and deported and the Chinese priests incarcerated permanently.

Since early chidhood, Li had attended mass with his mother. When the church was boarded up, they began to worship at home. Weekends he would even visit the homes of friends, relatives, and neighbors to 'spread the good word.' By the time the Cultural Revolution erupted, true believers had dwindled, and people like Li Anxiang who openly practiced their faith were almost unheard of. Certainly in my circles nobody was the least bit religious. Li Anxiang is the first messenger of God I have ever met.

At the sight of this strange man on his knees at his bedside, I assume he is mentally ill. There are a lot of crazies in Zuojiatang; two of them are locked up in Number Ten. Whiskers calls them 'counterrevolutionary fakers.' If he is right and they are faking it, they're doing a pretty good job of it, because their piercing screams can be heard regularly throughout the day. When I see Li Anxiang kneeling and mumbling, I don't doubt for a minute that he is touched.

Making the sign of the cross on one's chest before each meal and praying mornings and evenings remain bizarre behavior to me, but I find out soon enough that Li Anxiang is not crazy at all. Li is always the one who dumps the latrine bucket or fetches the water. Any task that is remotely taxing or distasteful becomes his. A few days after I arrive, he pulls out a big rag, proceeds to where the cardplayers are sitting and asks them to get up on the beds, announcing, 'Today is floor-washing day.'

I walk across the room. 'Want some help?'

'No, no,' he replies warmly. 'You just go over there with the others; I can handle it. God will help me.'

I sit back down and watch him ladle clean water into an old wooden bucket. 'He is a "Christian,"' whispers Spartacus. 'Every time anyone volunteers to help or tells him not to be too hard on himself, he always says, "God wants me to suffer for all of mankind in order to save my soul. To save the world."'

Scrubbing the Zuojiatang 'three-way mix' floors, composed of sand, clay, and lime, is not an easy task. One cannot always tell where the dirt ends and the floor begins. Many buckets full of water must be used to loosen the dust, which he must mop up; after that the dirty water must be wrung out into the latrine bucket. The entire procedure needs to be repeated at least three times before the black, pasty floor becomes red, shiny, and dry. Li Anxiang stoops and squats for close to two hours as the rest of us look on. When he is done, the whole room seems much brighter. Even the air improves some. In these times when nobody seems to care very much about sanitary living conditions, Preacher Li stands out as a man who strives for perfection. Thus, though I have never had any respect for religion, I wonder if perhaps I can see in him the workings of God.

'What case brought you in here?' I am sitting on his bed, watching him mend Spartacus' shirt. His thin, angular face shows the trace of a smile; he seems pleased to be interrupted by this potentially sensitive question.

'I put up a wall poster. God sent the White Horse General down to earth, calling me to put it up. I told the masses that the Cultural Revolution could be compared to Emperor Qin Shihuang's burning the books and burying the Confucian scholars; it would leave a stench in history for ten thousand years.'

This is curious indeed, that Qin Shihuang would have anything to do with a Christian general. I nod and innocently inquire, 'Preacher Li, why was God so favorably disposed toward Chinese scholars? Did he know all about Emperor Qin?'

'Of course, of course. My father told me that the earliest Westerners who came to China as missionaries studied Confucianism. Some expressed great respect for Confucius, you see, and Confucianism has always tolerated other ideologies: "The benevolent man loves others." This doctrine is simply another expression of God's love.'

Li Anxiang shows me a picture of his wife and little daughter. Although he had been practicing his faith all along, he tells me that he was only imprisoned after he denounced the Cultural Revolution. Before that he made a living as a mechanic in a Changsha automobile electric parts factory.

He is quite handy. For his comrades who are in need of clothing, Li Anxiang 'invents' a kind of spinning machine, a board nailed to the bottom of a wooden pole, that can make yarn out of the cotton from old quilts. Twisting a strand of yarn in his hand, he attaches it to the bottom of his machine, then begins to spin, his right hand reaching for cotton as needed, pulling and twisting at the strand. The pole is kept turning by pushes from his left hand and by the tautness of the yarn above. With each revolution, the yarn becomes longer and thinner, and when the strand is as tall as Li, he loosens it from the pole, wraps it around the bottom, and begins to spin the next length. A few days' work yields many skeins, which can either be made into twine, or woven into large towel-like squares, which in turn are pieced together to make clothes. After he displays his first little 'blanket,' everybody gets very excited and starts making their own spinners; spinning machines can be found in Number Nine for a long time after Li Anxiang is gone.

I marvel over the fact that anyone can be so consistently selfless. His family sends him a quilt stuffed with dried shredded pork. He divides it up into many little portions, which he solemnly distributes to everyone in the *haozi*. 'They are gifts from God,' he says.

In early spring, his morning prayers completed, Li proclaims: 'Last night God sent the White Horse General down again. He told me that God will soon send me to the most miserable place in the world to truly know suffering so that I can save all mankind.' We are quiet. 'And he told me that when I leave here this time, it will be for ten years. This will be an important mission for me.' His rugged face is glowing.

Over in the corner, Spartacus snorts. 'Was the "White Horse General" dressed like a foreigner or like Guan Gong?' Guan Gong is the legendary military hero who over the years has come to occupy the premier position in the traditional pantheon of Chinese gods.

Li Anxiang doesn't object to this sarcasm. He explains seriously, 'The White Horse General wears a white helmet and white armor, and he rides a white horse. In his hand he carries a scroll containing God's decrees. He appears and vanishes without warning, and is sent directly by God.'

Several days after his vision, Li Anxiang is sentenced to ten years of labor reform, causing the pickpockets to rumble excitedly among themselves. Having packed his bags, Li stands in the doorway with closed eyes, and, making the sign of the cross, gives a final benediction:

'This mission will certainly meet God's expectations. I will do my best to suffer for mankind; I will use this body of flesh and blood to save the souls of God's children.'

Directly behind him in the corridor a cadre is waiting impatiently. 'Don't tell me you're *still* spouting superstitious propaganda! Pick up your bags and get a move on!' he barks.

This is the last I hear of Preacher Li.

CHEN GUANGDI

Professor Chen Guangdi doesn't believe in God, but he is a 'gentleman' in the Confucian sense of the word—a 'moral prince' who takes his ethics very seriously. He is housed five cells down in Number Four, but we all know of him, his reputation having spread throughout Zuojiatang as its guests check in and out of the various *haozi*. Pickpockets, politicals—even the guards— seem to hold this scholarly man in great esteem.

In the winter of 1968, two individuals from the provincial branch of the People's Protection Group (PPG) come to interrogate me. Organized by Kang Sheng during the Cultural Revolution as a political police force, the PPG resembles the Cheka that emerged in Russia in 1917 in that its basic charge seems to be the oppression of the authorities' political enemies. Although my case is being handled by the 'Yang Xiguang Special Investigation Team,' a subgroup of the Shengwulian Special Investigation Group also run by the PPG, these two men are unfamiliar to me. I assume that they are here to question me about someone else's case.

Interrogations take place in a one-story building to the side of the detention center *haozi*. Its rooms are primitive, each containing little more than a table and a couple of chairs for the officers. A wicker *chaise longue* or a wooden bench is placed opposite the table for the prisoner to sit on.

One man asks the questions; the other records the answers. My name, age, and unit are all written down. The person doing all the questioning has a sallow, withered face and seems to be experienced. He pulls a mimeographed document from a file folder, stares at me for a moment, then nods at the document, scolding, 'You probably already know about Comrade Kang Sheng's directive concerning Shengwulian. But I'm going to read it to you anyway, because I want you to answer every question with this directive in mind.'

Kang Sheng was at this time a member of the Standing Committee of the Politburo.

'On January 24th, Comrade Kang Sheng said: "The Shengwulian documents", and by these he is referring to "Whither China?", "Our Outline" and "A Resolution Regarding the Present Political Situation", "could not have been written by high school students, not even by college students. There is clearly an evil black hand at work behind the scenes. We must ferret out teachers, no matter whether their names are Zhang, Li, or Chen, teachers who wave their goosefeather fans in an attempt to manipulate the students."[1] Now, answer all questions in the spirit of this directive.'

He subsequently asks me how I came to write 'Whither China?' Who, for example, had been involved in the process? Who had carried out discussions with me; who had provided suggestions or otherwise influenced my thoughts? Since my capture in Wuhan, I have been asked these questions hundreds of times, and the answer is always the same:

'No one else took part in the writing of this essay.'

Without warning my interrogator pounds on the table, shouting, 'You're not being straight with me! Are you still refusing to admit that you were manipulated by a black hand?'

I answer him with silence, thinking to myself, 'All this talk about black hands is precisely what drove my mother to kill herself. What nerve—you're lucky I haven't come to settle that score with you!'

My mother's surname had also been Chen. It was after Kang Sheng's directive was passed down to Changsha, that she was taken out on the streets for criticism many times, and accused of being the guiding force behind my essay. I remember with bitterness how, when she could take no more of the public humiliation and abuse, she had hung herself from the rafters.

The silence continues for what seems like a very long time. Changing his tone, the interrogator asks softly, 'Do you know any professors at Hunan University?'

'No,' I answer.

'Don't you know any of the instructors in the math department there?'

'No.'

By now I have figured out that they are asking about Professor Chen, but experience has taught me to say 'no' whenever I can.

---

[1] 'Zhang, Li, or Chen' is an expression equivalent in meaning to the English phrase 'Tom, Dick, and Harry.'

The minute you say 'yes' you are in trouble, for then the nagging and screaming begins in full force. Furthermore, since I only heard of Professor Chen after coming to Zuojiatang, it is not untrue to state that I have never 'known' him.

Another slap on the table. 'There you go, lying again! You mean to say you don't know Chen Guangdi, the Chen who got mixed up in the Tertiary Education Storm Rebel group?' He pauses. 'Come now; you were intimate with Zhou Guohui; you knew Hong Dou. How could you possibly fail to know Chen Guangdi? They were always together!'

I am still quiet, waiting for him to slowly get to the point and tell me just what information they expect me to come up with. He pounds on the table several more times before I make the connection: Professor Chen is suspected of supporting the radical student group Tertiary Education Storm and of being at least one of the black hands alluded to in the directive. Moreover, from the interrogator's tone, Professor Chen seems to be a very important black hand indeed.

Finally the sallow-faced man changes the topic. 'Do you know a person who is missing an arm?'

'No.'

'Yang Xiguang, are you going to try and buck authority all day today?' He is snapping at me again.

'A person with just one arm?'

The young recorder turns to me. 'You don't know Liu Fengxiang? Some people call him "The Helmsman." He's a good writer.'

The interrogator cuts in, 'Could you have written "Whither China?" without the help of Liu Fengxiang?' He stares at me and continues, 'Did you read his essay?'

'What essay?'

'The one about Khrushchev.'

'I don't know anything about an essay,' I answer stonily.

They carry on in this fashion for more than an hour, cross-examining me over and over again. I sense that Liu Fengxiang is politically involved and more mysterious and dangerous than Professor Chen. And I am somewhat piqued, for they don't seem to be taking me very seriously. Don't they think I'm capable of writing 'Whither China?' all by myself?

As soon as I get back to Number Nine, I relay the news about the session through Eight, Seven, Six, and Five, all way down to Teacher Chen. Though it is true that I do not know him personally, I respect him, for I have heard from a pickpocket recently transferred from Number Four that the professor still studies English and math every day. Of all the intellectuals in Zuojiatang, there are many who know as much as he does, but he seems to be the only one still advancing his learning. He owns the four-volume English translation of Mao's collected works, which he reads aloud each morning. It is also Chen who eventually supplies Blindman Lu and me with the long-desired three-volume set of *Das Kapital*. For months the efforts of my sister Yang Hui to send me Marx have met with failure; the cadres have heard that the Shengwulian leaders excel at 'using Marxism to refute Mao Zedong thought.' 'Stick to the works of Mao!' Yang Hui writes on her postcard, repeating what the authorities have told her.

In the fall of 1969, during an inspection of Hunan Province, Mao Zedong issues a directive specifically addressing the Shengwulian case. As soon as the Hunan Provincial Revolutionary Committee receives their copy of this directive, the provincial PPG hold a meeting, and announce in October that I will no longer be 'detained,' but instead placed under arrest along with Zhou Guohui, Chen Guangdi, and the other major Shengwulian leaders. Just as I am wondering what in the world is going on outside Zuojiatang walls to cause these developments, I receive another postcard from Yang Hui:

> When Chairman Mao inspected Hunan Province, he sentenced Shengwulian to death. It would appear he has already read 'Whither China?'; he has stated that the Shengwulian masses are good but that the thoughts of its leaders are reactionary.

The man who takes the worst heat is Chen Benwang, the head of the Golden Monkey Regiment of the Xiang River Storm, a workers' organization affiliated with Shengwulian. He is immediately executed as a 'counterrevolutionary murderer,' on the charge that he was responsible for ordering his subordinates to kill a Public Security Organs Headquarters cadre. Everyone else implicated in the Shengwulian case gets from five to twenty years. I get ten.

Before the sentencing meeting, we are transferred to the transit cell, Number Twenty-three, until there are enough of us to be shipped off to a labor reform camp or another prison. It is a cold, bitter day in November, and a bleak time for the Rebel camp. Mao, it seems, has finally committed himself to joining with Zhou Enlai and the Conservative faction in suppressing all the Rebels. Communist Central announcements are broadcast regularly over the loudspeakers in the courtyard: more news about Sino-Soviet border clashes, which continue to be used as excuses to disband all Rebel political organizations. Organizations that do not comply will be suppressed as counterrevolutionary. Mao Zedong's little charade of using the Rebels' quasi-political parties to counter the Communist bureaucrats is over. I sigh to myself, and promptly throw away any remaining illusions that I have about the Chairman.

Professor Chen also comes to Number Twenty-three. Compared with the rest of us, his sentence is relatively light—five years of 'compulsory labor' reform, which is a little worse than labor re-education, but a little better than what is simply called 'labor reform.'

Though only about thirty years old, the professor wears very thick glasses, and his eyes are large and owl-like. His is the face of the classical scholar, the refined, over-educated look that is known as a 'little white face.' His words are measured, his demeanor courteous; his attitude, positive and sympathetic. But his inner core is tough.

These days the official propaganda is directed against the 'white specialization line' that prioritizes education and professional expertise. Intellectuals are called upon to do manual labor and learn from workers and peasants. The anti-expert propaganda drones on and on from the radio; it assaults you in the newspapers, on the wall posters; it's written into the school curricula. People are not only afraid to openly criticize the message, they are afraid to doubt it. But Professor Chen does not hesitate to express those same dissident opinions that had gotten him into trouble in the first place.

'If students don't receive solid basic training, they will never be able to learn well. Knowledge forms incrementally; it is the gradual accumulation of facts. It requires the mastery of interrelated problems. Now with the emphasis on practice, they are saying that the fundamentals are dispensable. How can we expect to continue to produce good graduates?'

I nod.

'The secret to amassing knowledge lies in specialization; through specialization you can increase efficiency, and produce experts. Without knowing calculus, how can we ever learn the theory of probability? And yet Mao Zedong says he wants students to learn everything—industry, agriculture, military science, and business—and he's opposed to the "expert line." If we go on this way, how in the world will we avoid reverting to a primitive society?'

Gradually I come to see that Professor Chen opposes all of Mao's policies on culture and education—a rightist stance. Still, he had supported the ultraleftist, radical students and at times even calls himself a Rebel. Curious, I ask him about the extent of his involvement in the Rebel movement.

'In your indictment, did they cite any evidence to support the claim that you were a black hand?'

'You know, the university branch of Tertiary Education Storm joined Shengwulian, and I'd been working closely with several students who were members. But I never officially joined any organization. The only reason they picked me up was because my name was Chen; you know, all that stuff that Kang Sheng said about "every Chen, Zhang, and Li." When they came for me, I didn't think that I'd done anything wrong, so I was more than willing to share my opinions with the officer. I told him—straight out—I didn't agree with many of the current official lines on education. I had already told my students, who were mostly Rebels: "Mind you, you can go ahead and rebel against the authorities to get them to implement more rational policies, but now isn't the best time because you're bound to be crushed. You should build up a power base to prepare for the *next* cultural revolution, when you'll have a real possibility for success." That's what I told the officer. How could I foresee that all of this would be used as evidence to convict me? The indictment said I was a "deeply rooted class enemy" who was "plotting to overthrow the dictatorship of the proletariat in the next cultural revolution."' He smiles wanly.

Several days later Zhou Guohui tells me that up until the professor's sentencing, he had been a Party member and a 'model teacher' at Hunan University with an impressive record in the area of mathematical research. It was second nature for him to place his trust in the Communist system and the truth. Had Chen not revealed his opinions directly to the cadres, there would have been no 'evidence' at all.

Professor Chen, however, is not especially concerned about his personal welfare. He anguishes, rather, over the fate of the nation. In order to change this irrational regime, he explains to me, one needs both theory and organization. From the fire in his eyes, I know that he hasn't yet given up the idea of a second cultural revolution. I quietly confide to him how determined I am to finish college calculus within the next two years, wondering if he could recommend the best calculus text he knew. He suggests Fan Yingchuang's *Analytical Mathematics*, and I immediately write to Yang Hui.

The tales about Professor Chen's virtues have not been exaggerated. He rises each day at dawn, bathes himself in the icy water, then sweeps the *haozi* floor. Like Preacher Li, he regularly carries the containers of vegetables and rice to and from the door. He has become skilled at mending, and is always ready to patch the clothes of any inmate who asks him. When I look at him sitting on a bunk, sewing somebody's dirty old work pants, his kind face wrinkled in a smile, I think to myself, 'Even a man like this has not been spared.'

One month later he is transferred to the Pingtang New Life Cement Factory. According to Liu Dongyang, a 'bad element' acquaintance sentenced in 1957, the New Life Cement Factory is a compulsory labor unit just outside Changsha that mines lime and processes cement. Liu was in Zuojiatang as a Shengwulian black hand, but had previously done labor re-education at the factory.

There is no further news. I don't hear any more about Professor Chen until 1978.

In 1978, I meet Zhang Yugang, a great admirer of the professor's. During the Socialist Education Campaign in 1964, Zhang had been put on the secret list of the 'Insider Rightists,' students who had bad backgrounds or had been seen kowtowing to Western bourgeois culture. Zhang took advantage of the chaos of the Cultural Revolution debilitating the entire campus, retrieved the damaging 'black dossier materials,' torching them in a public bonfire. As author of one of the key Shengwulian documents, 'Our Outline,' he was handed a sentence of five years.

Not long after his release, Zhang had seen Professor Chen once in the New China Bookstore on May First Road. Hunan University would not permit him to return to the faculty. Forced to take a job as a guard at the cement factory, the professor was nevertheless pursuing his research. He spoke of writing a book.

But in 1976, after the fall of the Gang of Four, Teacher Chen suddenly dropped out of sight. Discreetly, Zhang began to investigate, systematically visiting everyone who had been close to Chen. The workers at the cement factory all remembered this professor who had, without fail, struck a 'gong' made of an iron rail to indicate when the prisoners should wake, work, and eat. He had already completed a very thick treatise on mathematics and a translation of an English-language math textbook. Yes, they said; every weekend he went to the foreign languages section of the New China Bookstore and came back with an armful of English-language journals or books.

Zhang took a bus down to May First Road and found a clerk who knew the professor. For months the professor had arrived like clockwork, always on the weekend, and browsed through the shelves for an hour or so, but he had stopped coming some time in November. That was all the clerk could say. Then in 1978 Zhang picked up another thread, from a New Life Cement Factory political criminal who had just got out. Before the fall of the Gang of Four, Teacher Chen had told this friend that when Mao died, Jiang Qing's group would be certain to clash with the Conservative bureaucrats within the Party. If the radicals were successful, China would finally have a chance to thoroughly change the Communist system; a full-fledged revolution might even break out. However, should the Conservatives gain the upper hand, China would return to the Soviet system and there would be no opportunity for change for a long time.

Zhang Yugang and I reflect at length on how this information might be related to Professor Chen's disappearance. Having placed all his hopes for change on a coup within the Communist regime to be led by Jiang Qing and the radicals, perhaps he had fled in despair when the ultraleftists fell from power. He might have tried to cross the border into Hong Kong. Maybe he roamed the country aimlessly. Somewhere along the line, though, he must have died, or he would have undoubtedly resurfaced when the political tide turned.

In the winter of 1978, Zhang and I attend a 'posthumous' rehabilitation ceremony held for Professor Chen at the university, where we meet his younger sister. This beautiful, traditional-looking young woman begs us to relate everything we know about the brother she so clearly worships. She, too, has chosen mathematics as her profession—she already has a post at a university in Shanghai. During the 1950s, she says, one third of his lungs were cut out when he contracted tuberculosis; but even while he was ill, he had studied hard and had placed into the Fudan University math department immediately after his release from the hospital. Inspired by our stories of Professor Chen and his aspirations, she sets out to search for him and his manuscript.

In 1983, as I prepare to leave China, there is still no news of his whereabouts.

10
Helmsman

▼

Something is brewing. Gathered in Number Twenty-three are the 'ringleaders' of the Hunan Provincial Proletarian Great Alliance Committee, the umbrella organization more simply known as 'Shengwulian.' Zhang Jiazheng, 'Commander' of Xiang River Storm. Zhou Guohui of Tertiary Education Storm. Bi Jian of the Red Banner Army. And the 'cultural czar,' Director Song Shaowen. All here, waiting . . . waiting.

More than twenty Rebel associations had thrown their support to Shengwulian after it was formed in November 1967: the university faculty and students of Tertiary Education Storm; the demobilized military veterans of the Red Banner Army; the high school students of the Red High School Committee; the writers and artists of the Cultural Red Rebel Troupe; the primary and secondary teachers of the Teachers Federation. In all, some two to three million diverse people drawn together by their very exclusion from the newly created Revolutionary Committee Preparatory Group.

Many of these Rebel faces are familiar. 'Commander' Zhang Jiazheng, once notorious for his flashy political maneuvers, has been working on several art projects, the most recent of which is binding a volume of the calligraphy Director Song Shaowen has created since his incarceration. Whenever Whiskers needs an oil portrait or plaster bust of Mao, the 'Commander' is there to lend a hand. Of course, it would take real courage to pass up an opportunity for a decent meal.

I try to remember the first time I met the 'Commander.' Summer of 1967?

'Commander' Zhang's father was a Nationalist official who was killed in the purge of 1951, and so at the very outset of the Cultural Revolution, Zhang was labeled a counterrevolutionary. Joining forces with other intellectual and worker 'counterrevolutionaries,' Zhang had, in response, pulled together the quasi-political party called Xiang River Storm, a cross-sector organization which reached out to all professions and expressed as its goal the rehabilitation of its membership. Then, in the 1967 winter campaign launched by the authorities to suppress the Rebels—later referred to by the Rebel faction as the 'February Countercurrent'—the Xiang River Storm was decreed to be a 'counterrevolutionary organization,' and the 'Commander' was arrested and imprisoned. Unbelievably, by summer of that same year, Mao Zedong reversed his decision and voiced support for the rehabilitation of Xiang River Storm. Zhang was released, and he immediately helped to orchestrate the Rebels' armed confrontations with the Conservative Red Guards. I happened to encounter him and another key Storm leader in the Seamen's Club overlooking the Xiang River at the very time they were planning a battle against the Conservative Red Guards. Rumor had it that Zhang possessed proof positive that Zhou Enlai was conspiring against Mao. There were whispers of a mysterious matter known as the '007 Affair.' But by February 1968 'Commander' Zhang was back in the detention center, seized along with the other Shengwulian leaders. His charge this time round is 'directing violent warfare' and, more seriously, 'opposing Zhou Enlai.'

Zhou Guohui, the Hunan University student leader of Tertiary Education Storm, is also here. Because of his bold initiative in dedicating himself to the Rebel cause without regard for his personal safety, he is especially popular among his fellow students. He is looking well, and I think back in anger to the scene I witnessed from across the courtyard when he was beaten last summer. It is he who represented Shengwulian at critical negotiations and who, on more than one occasion, has met with Zhou Enlai in Beijing.

I silently watch Zhou Guohui move about the *haozi*. A statesman fallen from power, he is unbowed. Unlike the 'Commander,' Zhou continues to express dangerously dissident opinions.

We continue to wait nervously for news of what will happen next. On the third morning, a warm day in late November 1969, the *haozi* door opens and closes, sending in a steady stream of odd-looking people that I do not recognize as Shengwulian leaders. A fat little elementary school teacher from Changsha woefully tells us that, as a member of the Teachers Federation, he too has been seized as a Shengwulian 'black hand.' When I ask him about his case, he explains:

'I criticized Liu Shaoqi in '57, so the hard-liners figured I must be a Rightist.'

Chen Sancai, tall and skinny with triangular catlike eyes, is another Rightist who joins us. And the toothless Zhang Bolun, who makes me think of Chamberlain and who must be over seventy, is said to have collaborated with the Nationalists. Like Chen Sancai, he jumped onto the Shengwulian bandwagon in the hopes of blotting out the counterrevolutionary mark in his file. He, too, is accused of being a manipulative black hand.

'There's something wrong with every one of these types,' Zhou Guohui whispers into my ear. 'Nationalists, Rightists—I'll bet you anything the authorities intend to link up Shengwulian with the politically unclean so they can hammer the nail into the coffin.'

The entrance of one dark-skinned newcomer with thick lips and a padded cotton jacket catches my attention. His right arm is missing. He spends every minute exchanging information with the other recent arrivals. A right-wing reporter named Xiao Qian is moved to Twenty-three temporarily, where he must wait several hours before moving on to another cell. When Xiao appears in the doorway, the dark-skinned man hurries over, raising his empty sleeve without a trace of self-consciousness.

'How is the military situation?' I overhear him say.

My eyes widen. When he speaks, it is always very softly, his Mandarin heavily accented with the dialects of both Yueyang and Changsha. But it is not until the following morning that I place his name—Liu Fengxiang—with the legendary figure described for me by my People's Protection Group interrogator.

Reflecting on that conversation, I smile to myself. This swarthy man doesn't seem all that impressive. Nevertheless, I must admit I am curious, and I approach him.

'What happened to your arm?'

'I was an editor at the *Hunan Daily* till they called me a 'Rightist.' They sent me down to a factory for reform and it got caught in a machine.'

Yet another Rightist. 'How did you get labeled?' I press.

'I guess you could say we were the earliest Rebels. As early as 1957 we were denouncing the old Provincial Committee as "capitalist roaders." So they denounced us as Rightists.' He smiles and turns away.

After several hours the door ceases to open any more and it finally dawns on me: we are about to be sentenced, along with this bunch of shady individuals who seem to have little to do with Shengwulian. A quick poll reveals that each man has recently had his status changed by the PPG from 'detainment' to 'arrest.'

Aware that the hour of reckoning is near, the prisoners of Number Twenty-three waste no time in assembling the various paraphernalia necessary for recreation, bringing out once again strips of paper and grains of rice. Liu Fengxiang's game of choice is Chinese chess. Evidently he enjoys playing with me, for he keeps coming back.

'I've had the privilege of reading your "Whither China?"' he says cordially during one match. 'I thought it was wonderful.'

'Thanks,' I mutter somewhat impatiently, 'but it wasn't all that good. And anyway, my politics have completely changed. I was incredibly idealistic then. I used to think that a democratic body had to be elected by the people, or it violated the basic principles of democracy and needed to be overturned. But I was really wrong. Now I know that one's values should be based on changing historical conditions and that the course of history is more important than one individual's ideals.'

Liu listens quietly. In his already wrinkled face, I see his black eyes sparkle with interest and understanding, and so I continue.

'I used to ask myself, "What's good?" and "What's bad?" or "How should the world be?" But now I just ask, "What will happen?" And what's really sad is that the blackest moment in history may be happening right now, during my lifetime. Any kind of moral or subjective judgment is meaningless. The only thing that matters is for me to find a way to adapt to the environment so that I can survive.'

Liu Fengxiang nods in return.

After supper the others go back to chess and poker, or talk among themselves in hushed tones. Liu Fengxiang comes over to my bunk and sits down.

'Today's realities are brutal,' he begins. 'There's no denying it. And so, sure, a lot of intellectuals have taken up a kind of pure objectivism—saying that there's no right or wrong, no good or evil. But the Cultural Revolution was really evil, and one day history will recognize it as such.[1] Yang Xiguang, this is an objective truth, and not some arbitrary, subjective judgment.'

His tone is like a missionary's, so filled with conviction that

---

[1] The 'Cultural Revolution,' as far as we were concerned in 1969, referred to the years 1966–7, the earliest 'revolutionary' phase. The following eight years of domestic political instability, now included by the term, were an unfolding chapter.

for a moment I am caught off guard. Moreover, I realize that his politics are the very opposite of what he let on in front of the others, when he said he was one of the original Rebels. Why, he totally rejects the basic premise of the Cultural Revolution. Our conversations become increasingly frequent. Sometimes Zhou Guohui joins us. But Director Song and 'Commander' Zhang, who are patently wary of Rightists, stay clear. Even inside a prison cell, they refuse to accept their own counterrevolutionary status and feel superior to the Rightists and to the counterrevolutionaries who have been involved in anti-Communist political organizations. I, on the other hand, embrace the damning label out of pure spite: I have begun to loathe the society which has put me here. If for nothing else, my unorthodox opinions and my hatred for the powers-that-be qualify me as 'counterrevolutionary.'

It is less obvious to me why Liu Fengxiang takes noticeable pains to stay away from 'Commander' Zhang. When I allude circumspectly to this tendency on Liu's part, he tells me that over the many years he has spent in labor reform, he has become a seasoned observer of the complex, dark side of human relations so that he is able to predict accurately whether or not a person can be trusted. The 'Commander', he assures me, is a potential snitch. A 'KGB.'

'Way back in the summer of 1967 I conducted a little survey of the rising stars on the scene, and I said then as I say now: Zhang is not a political animal. His repertoire consists of a few petty little power games.'

I am continually surprised by Liu's self-confidence. He sounds like a professional political commentator.

'Look how easily he adapts to his surroundings. It won't be any problem at all for him to perceive the cadres' burning need for information and to overcome any moral qualms. Oh, he'll squeal all right.'

◆

The sky is clear the day the guests of Twenty-three are cuffed and packed on a truck bound for East Wind Square. I start at the sight of Chen Benwang, who has been held in a different *haozi*, and is now wearing death shackles. Placards with our crimes and our terms are hung around our necks: Mine says, 'Practicing Counterrevolutionary, 10 Years.' Zhang Jiazheng and Zhou Guohui are accused of the same crime. The 'Commander' gets twenty; Zhou seven. Like those of the other 'black hands,' Liu Fengxiang's placard reads 'Rightist,' 'Practicing Counterrevolutionary,' and '15 Years.'

During the Cultural Revolution, political organizations representing every conceivable faction used East Wind Square as a place to assemble. The authorities use it for both general assemblies and sentencings. At least 50,000 people, all hostile to Shengwulian, have been mobilized by the newly established Revolutionary Committee Preparatory Group to bear witness as the thirty of us are sentenced. Everyone from Number Twenty-three is here, plus about ten common criminals who have nothing to do with the Shengwulian case, thrown in for good measure. We are escorted to the front of the platform, where we are made to kneel, each inmate flanked by two soldiers who kick us or bash at us with the butts of their rifles if we move even a little.

When my own sentence is read, I try to listen with detachment. The cadre not only cites 'Whither China?', he presents 'evidence' that I have 'always hated the Party':

'His father was labeled a right-wing opportunist in 1959; his brother and his uncle were labeled Rightists in 1957. His mother committed suicide during the Cultural Revolution to escape punishment.'

At these words I abandon every remaining shred of trust. I need no further proof that this is a society that revolves around hatred, discrimination, and persecution.

Two hours later we are divided up into small groups, put on trucks again, and paraded down Zhongshan Road, May Fifth Road, and Huangxing Road, according to protocol. People cry out, 'So very young!' and 'Ten years—what bad luck!' I realize that the residents of Changsha continue to sympathize with the Rebel cause. But what really gets to me is the sight of my high school classmates following behind the truck for the duration of the parade in affirmation of their silent support.

Back at Twenty-three, I focus on my future. I won't take this lying down. Perhaps I can join a secret anti-communist organization and help overthrow this wretched regime. But then I calm down. No, that's too unrealistic. I'll think of a way to escape from the labor reform brigade. If I make it out of here, I'll have to learn how to steal to survive. Like Bandit. Late that night I confide my plan to Liu Fengxiang.

'Look, this is the second time for me to be sentenced,' he says calmly. 'In 1957 when I was really down, my reaction was just as violent as yours is now. But think about it: the idea of "escape" or a "sentence" is totally meaningless for a political criminal. If the overall political situation doesn't change, it doesn't matter whether you run away or finish out your term; your own situation won't improve at all. And when we've finished our stretch at the farm, do you think the oppression and discrimination will lighten up? Hardly. On the other hand, if the overall political situation improves, even a twenty-year term will magically disappear.'

I realize that in these deliberate words is the crystallization of many years of thought. The timbre of his voice, steady and deep, is as mesmerizing as his message.

'Most important, though . . .' He pauses. 'Your reaction may in fact reflect your lack of hope and loss of confidence in the political situation. You know, I'm sure, Khrushchev's denunciation of Stalin. Droves of intellectuals came forward in almost hysterical support for the campaign, especially those who had been persecuted during the thirties. I believe there'll be a day like that in China. Don't you? If you're confident that there will be such a day, you don't need to think about escape.'

From this day on I stand in complete awe of this man, whom I begin to call 'Old Liu.' I admire him, I love him as a brother. Later that evening he comes to my bunk again. This time he speaks of the events leading to the many charges for which he has been sentenced: 'manipulating the Shengwulian organization, drumming up support for Shengwulian, persuading the Shengwulian leaders to take up the policy of mountain strongholdism with the intent of overthrowing the dictatorship of the proletariat, and seeking to rehabilitate Rightists through nationwide exchanges.' 'Mountain strongholdism' and 'banditry' are the standard terms used to refer to acts of guerilla warfare.

Old Liu tells me that in October 1967, he traveled eastward across China in an attempt to organize groups of Rightists to work to get their sentences overturned. When he got to Beijing, he searched for other Rebels who were critical of Liu Shaoqi, Deng Xiaoping, and Peng Zhen. In the process he stumbled upon several confidential documents that proved that the Communist Party had persecuted the Rightists in 1957. With the help of some friends, he wrote up the information in the form of posters, which were reproduced and distributed widely. They went on to mobilize Rightists in several large Hunan cities to seek rehabilitation. The ideological bent of Shengwulian was, they decided, the one that was closest to their own.

Throughout 1969 Old Liu sought out Zhang Yugang, the author of Shengwulian's 'Manifesto', trying to persuade him to come over to his views. He reminded Zhang to be on the lookout for the possibility of armed confrontation, hence the charge of 'mountain strongholdism.' Using the pretext of a 'negative example' which should never be followed, Old Liu copied onto a large wall poster the 10,000-word 'letter of opinion' that Peng Dehuai had drafted in 1959, criticizing Mao Zedong. Near the end of 1967 the Rightists gradually began to take control of the Rebel tabloids, which they used quite successfully. One celebrated example was the case of Yang Meinan, a Rightist teacher who published her appeal for rehabilitation through the Teachers' Federation newsletter.

The next day I feel that he and I know each other much better and we talk again, this time until early morning. It is the most extraordinary seminar in contemporary Chinese history that I have ever attended. Recalling the series of events beginning with the Anti-Rightist Campaign of 1957, he unveils for me his own political vision.

'Many of the tragedies of modern China can be traced back to the Anti-Rightist Campaign, but the events themselves can only be understood against the backdrop of the international Communist movement. The de-Stalinization campaign of '56 in the Soviet Union exposed the ugly side of socialism, and of course that's why Khrushchev began the Socialist Democratic movement. He was not only rehabilitating the people who had been wronged in the thirties, but setting into motion the campaign against bureaucratization. Mao didn't want the Stalinist nightmare to be repeated. So China began a little agenda of its own: the Hundred Flowers wall posters and the various political campaigns. To launch the movements against bureaucratization, sectarianism, and dogmatism, Mao delivered a talk which we now refer to as "On the Correct Handling of Contradictions Among the People." But the original, confidential version of the speech was quite different from the one that was ultimately published. In fact the two were completely opposite in meaning. The cadres who had heard the tape knew that Mao's original focus had been the promotion of socialist democracy so that he could try out one type of "liberalization."

'The success of the first Five-year Plan had brought security and prosperity to China; the praises of the Party could be heard everywhere. But it was empty talk. The older intellectuals remained dissatisfied: the Party used political movements to govern the nation; large-scale purges violated human rights; the Party bureaucracy controlled the entire educational system. The intellectuals had simply never had an opportunity to give vent

1. Yang Xiguang, his sister, Yang Hui (right), and their parents in Changsha, Hunan Province, in 1952.

2. Yang's mother, Chen Su, in the 1960s.

3. The front gate of Zuojiatang Detention Center, where Yang was detained from February 1968 to December 1969. Yang is shown here revisiting the site in 1986.

4. The Third Brigade of Reconstruction Farm, where Yang was imprisoned for eight years (beginning December 1969). Behind the low wall are cadres' office buildings. The prison lies behind the office building, between the two towers. (Photo taken in the early spring of 1989.)

5. Yang at the back door of the Third Brigade prison during a visit to Reconstruction Farm in 1995. To the right is a cell house used for solitary confinement. A soldier mans the tower to prevent escape.

6. The front gate of Model Prison, where Yang was jailed from April 1970 to January 1971. Here Yang revisits the site in 1986.

7. The door to Number 16 at Model Prison, shown here when Yang revisited in 1986. The prison had been converted to residential flats; the warden's peephole is a visible reminder of the room's past life.

8. The Big Dike near the sluice at Reconstruction Farm. Big sentencing meetings were carried out at the grounds here at least once annually; it was the execution and burial site of many of the prisoners of Reconstruction Farm. The water disappears in winter, exposing the bottom of the 'Outer Lake'; it floods over again in spring, completely covering the burial ground and these water willows. (Photo taken in the spring of 1989.)

9. Dongting Lake, in the spring of 1989. A view from the top of Big Dike, near the sluice at Reconstruction Farm.

10. Yang in 1995 in the cotton fields where he did labor near the Third Brigade prison of Reconstruction Farm. Prisoners can be seen laboring in the distance.

11. Yang and fellow inmate Lu Guoan, wearing caps over their shaved heads to disguise their prisoner identities, during their 'escape' to the town of Guangxianzhou in 1976. (See Chapter 22.)

12. A classroom of the Reconstruction Farm High School, where Yang was requisitioned to teach mathematics in 1977. The scene has changed little, except that students did not have bicycles to ride to school during Yang's time there. (Photo taken by Yang's sister in the spring of 1989.)

13. Zhao Jinxiang, Yang's fellow teacher, at the gate of Reconstruction Farm High School; she was still teaching English at the school when this photo was taken in 1989.

14. Yang just after his release from Reconstruction Farm in the spring of 1978. (Photo taken at Lushan.)

15. Yang after his release from labor reform in 1978, with his sister, Yang Hui, his father, stepmother (left), and aunt.

16. Yang at Princeton University upon completion of his doctorate in 1988.

to their feelings. But Mao thought that all the people, including the intellectuals, supported him, forgetting of course that his prestige and authority were based on oppression and force. He was willing to let the intellectuals criticize the Party and help set political policy.

'Supposedly, when Khrushchev got word of Mao's intention to start up all these campaigns, he was fairly discouraging, saying that he didn't think a socialist system could withstand Western-style democratization and liberalization, and that if Mao gave the intellectuals free reign to criticize the government, all hell would break out. But Mao wouldn't listen. So he went ahead with the Hundred Flowers Campaign, and sure enough, just as Khrushchev had predicted, in a very short time it was clear to all that the intellectuals not only refused to actively support Mao, but that they thoroughly despised him. Then Mao spun around 180 degrees and made preparations to suppress the liberalization movements. Once again Khrushchev voiced his disapproval, stating that since Mao had already allowed the various dissenting views to be aired, he couldn't very well use a political movement as a means to curb the situation. And once again, Mao didn't pay any attention to him and went ahead with his Anti-Rightist Campaign. Never again would anyone dare openly to express a dissenting opinion, for fear of being called a 'Rightist.' Which, of course, led directly to the absurdities of the Great Leap Forward. There in full view was the emperor's bare ass, but everybody kept praising his magnificent new clothes.'

Throughout his discourse on Mao, Old Liu sounds like he is scolding an errant child, his irreverence leaving me speechless. Almost no one dares to doubt Mao, even privately. Liu's cool defiance is bewitching.

'By 1959 an economic crisis had already surfaced,' he continues. 'Faced with little choice, Peng Dehuai submitted a report to Mao, citing many concrete investigations and expressing the hope that Mao would be able to admit the error of the Great Leap Forward. Peng promptly found himself labeled an instigator of an anti-Party clique. So the economic crisis was allowed to continue and worsen, ultimately leading to the collapse of '60 and '61. And at the Central Work Conference of 1962 Mao had no course but to admit that from '58 through '62 his work had been in error. His active supporters—Liu Shaoqi, Zhou Enlai, and Deng Xiaoping—now all tended to support the views of Peng Dehuai. But though Mao had publicly admitted his guilt, privately he harbored a deep grudge against Liu Shaoqi for 'betraying' him, and kept looking for a chance to turn the situation around. At the Tenth Plenum of the Eighth Central Committee, Mao advocated class struggle as the key policy; the calls to "Learn From the People's Liberation Army," to "Revolutionize," and to carry out "Socialist Education" quickly followed. All of these were targeted at Liu Shaoqi and Deng Xiaoping in an effort to weaken them. The Cultural Revolution was simply the continuation of these efforts.'

It is almost light, and everybody else is still sleeping, though a few inmates turn and twitch in restless dreams. Old Liu and I sit curled up opposite each other on a corner bunk, his voice almost inaudible. For me, night has indeed turned into day.

In this dark year of 1969, a year characterized by mindless fanaticism, the numbness of the persecuted, and a general dearth of intelligence—a year when politics threatens the well-being of every Chinese, Old Liu has fed my spirit. I understand now why his Rightist friends call him 'Helmsman.'[2]

Before long I find that I don't feel the need to talk politics with Director Song, Bi Jian, and 'Commander' Zhang anymore. Although they had been heroes in the Cultural Revolution, compared to Liu they are bystanders who happened to have been sucked into the political maelstrom, people who have no inkling of the driving force behind the Cultural Revolution. Once imprisoned, they seem to have lost all awareness of issues and ideas. I watch them spend their time shuffling about boxes and readying their belongings in resigned preparation for labor camp.

During these last days, family members arrive at Zuojiatang, one by one. Director Song's aging mother comes to see him, bearing a large metal pot. He has written her repeatedly, each time asking her for a cooked chicken. His once bulging belly is now concave, as are his eyes. But Whiskers refuses to let the bird pass, so Song has to watch in anguish as his mother leaves, knowing that the mouth-watering fowl is headed back out the detention center gate. Worse, she has left him with bad news. His wife Liang Qi has filed for divorce and taken with her their entire life savings totalling upwards of 6,000 yuan.

Liang Qi is a famous Changsha actress who is said to be one of Mao Zedong's favorite dancing partners when he is in town. The first time Song rebelled, Liang Qi stood by him, but now that he is facing a sentence of fifteen years, she has decided to break it off. He can understand her wanting the divorce, he tells me, but never dreamed she would take his money. There

---

[2] In the Changsha dialect, the pronunciation of the term for 'helmsman' (literally 'steering hand') is very close to that of 'cut-off hand.' 'Helmsman' was also the epithet used for Mao.

isn't much he can do about it, though. The property of
counterrevolutionaries is not protected under law, and the
government not only encourages the divorce of their spouses,
it calls for their children to distance themselves and 'draw
lines,' both politically and economically, between themselves
and their parents. Inmate after inmate who goes to the reception
room to meet with family is hit with stories of this sort. Many
come back to Twenty-three with red, teary eyes.

My father cannot come because he is being confined to a
Mao Zedong Thought Study Class. Old Liu must read the
disappointment in my face. He knows of my father, having
supported his denunciation of the Great Leap in 1959. But I am
quick to tell him that my political views have always been quite
different from those of my parents, especially during the
Cultural Revolution. In early 1967, when Mao backed the Rebel
attack on the Communist bureaucrats, I had personally
witnessed the Changsha residents lash out at the Hunan
Provincial officials in the compound where we lived. I described
to Old Liu how puzzled I had been to discover that even our
family's nanny considered government officials to be the
oppressors.

One evening Old Liu and I are·sitting on the corner bunk
playing Chinese chess when he says suddenly, 'A son will never
really oppose his father.'

'Are you saying that about the father-son relationship in
China or in general?'

He doesn't answer directly, but stops playing for a moment,
and stares at me. 'The problem is, your father's politics were
right for him, just as it was right for you to rebel.'

I have no idea what he is talking about.

'During the Cultural Revolution Mao Zedong very cleverly
used to his advantage the inherent conflicts among the Rightists,
the "right-wing opportunists," the "capitalist roaders," and the
common people. Then, in October 1966, Mao and Lin Biao got
the masses to criticize the "reactionary line of the bourgeoisie,"
and supported the people with "bad" origins and backgrounds,
as well as the intellectuals who had been persecuted, as part of
a power play against officials like Liu Shaoqi and Deng Xiaoping.
Many of these underdogs pretended to criticize Liu, Deng, and
Zhou Enlai just so that they could rebel, which forced the
Conservatives who were in power to prove themselves by
suppressing the so-called Rightists. That's what brought about
the violent clashes. On the one hand, you had the in-power
Rightists pretending to go along with Mao's Anti-Rightist

Campaign to persecute the minority Rightist camp, while on the other hand you had the old Rightists pretending to rebel against the capitalist roaders in order to regain their footing. By using this "historical misunderstanding" between the two Rightist camps, Mao was able to seize control of the government once again.'

Though Old Liu has done labor re-education in a variety of places, most recently he has worked at the New Life Electric Switch Company in Changsha where he served a three-year stint as a librarian and then stayed on. From the first days of the Cultural Revolution, he and his Rightist friends argued incessantly about whether they should side with the Rebels or the Conservatives. When it came to economic and political policies, they all favored Zhou Enlai; but when they remembered the oppression against them, they identified with the Rebels, hoping to reverse the verdicts against them and to weaken the officials in power.

'From 1966 until 1967, we didn't touch the revolution. We stayed out of it until late July, when we saw that the military was going to get involved, and that the conflict was not so much between Mao and Liu, as between Zhou Enlai and Lin Biao. Then, when Liu Shaoqi fell, it really looked like the interests of Mao and Lin Biao were at odds with one another.' He stops and smiles. 'Zhou Enlai is definitely not the type of guy to start a coup. He's like the old Duke of Zhou—even if he had a chance, he wouldn't seize power.[3] But Lin Biao is just the opposite; he likes to be the man in charge. Liu Shaoqi is out of the picture, and you know the old saying: "Once the wily rabbit is dead, the hunting dog gets cooked; once the enemy state is destroyed, the plotting vassal perishes."[4] Mao put Lin in place to get rid of Liu, but now that Liu is safely out of the way, well, Mao's greatest danger now comes from Lin Biao himself.'

Once again I find myself listening in amazement. Lin Biao is Mao Zedong's successor; this is an undisputed fact documented in the Party Constitution of the Ninth Plenum. The preface to Mao's Little Red Book (*Quotations*), found in every corner of China, contains Lin Biao's signature. An open break between the two is unthinkable. But Liu's confident air quickly and completely brushes away any doubts that I have.

[3] The Duke of Zhou was Premier during the Western Zhou Dynasty (11th century–771 BC). He remained loyal to the dynasty even when he had a chance to seize power during a popular rebellion of the people.

[4] An allusion to the career of Han Xin, an ambitious political strategist recorded in Sima Qian's *Record of the Historian* (ca. 100 BC).

'It was exactly because I had predicted the possibility of conflict between Mao and Lin that I believed that the Cultural Revolution could bring about massive political upheaval, and that's why we decided to throw our weight behind the Rebels.'

Several weeks pass. In mid-December, another Big Sentencing Meeting is scheduled in Changsha. Early that morning we press our faces to the windows to identify the prisoners who are lined up in the courtyard. After they are led away, Whiskers distributes to each *haozi* a copy of the sentencing bulletin. Chen Sancai begins to read out the verdicts in a loud voice, but I move up close to see for myself. The first name is Zhang Jiulong: 'Counterrevolutionary clique criminal, death penalty, two-year suspension.'

Another day or so goes by. We are at the chessboard once again, though neither of us are concentrating very much on the game. Old Liu begins to murmur.

'If I could explain my ideas at about the same rate as I have to you, in ten years I could persuade a thousand people, tops. But when you're up against the Communist Party, that's too slow. They control the radio, the papers, the publishers. . . . If it weren't for the Cultural Revolution, when the Rebels were able to take possession of some of the media, we'd never have been able to pull enough of the masses into the movement.'

'Then,' I whisper, 'do you think there is any possibility of taking up arms against the current regime?'

'If Mao and Lin Biao don't go at each other's throats, armed conflict is out of the question. Mainly because when soldiers are transported by rail, the authorities are better able to concentrate their troops within a short time. When the Nationalists planned to attack the mainland in 1962, for example, the Communists were able to concentrate a large military force along the coastal area in just a few days. That kind of speed rules out any possibility of a sudden military outburst like the Wuchang uprising of 1911.'[5]

When Old Liu finds out that I know Nine Dragons Zhang, he asks me about his case. He is especially hungry for details about Guevarist guerrilla tactics and Zhang's experience with underground parties. 'Well then, will there ever be an opportunity for underground activities like Zhang's to succeed?'

---

[5] The Wuchang Uprising of October 10, 1991, constituted the beginning of the successful actions by the Revolutionary forces against the Manchu dynasty. This sudden insurrection was backed by wealthy and influential citizens of Hubei Province, who were unwilling to surrender their interest in private railways to the government.

Filled with despair, I am obsessed with the idea of active political resistance.

Liu Fengxiang shakes his head. One of his pawns has crossed the river, and now he moves it to the left.[6] 'These days it's impossible for an underground party to operate very long in China without being uncovered.'

Another prisoner strolls over to watch us play, ending our conversation. By sundown the following day, we have been deposited on a tiny stretch of land in the middle of Dongting Lake.

---

[6] In Chinese chess, once a pawn has crossed the middle line, or 'the river,' thus moving into enemy territory, it is allowed to move both forward and sideways.

Part II

Reconstruction Farm

DECEMBER 1969–APRIL 1970

▼

11

Reconstruction Farm

▼

Cuffed in pairs, we are marched to the train station. Thirty of us in two files, our belongings piled high on our backs. Escorting us are one prison guard, who carries the keys to our handcuffs, and a military squad of seven, who will watch for any attempt to escape. All along the way, crowds or townspeople press forward and stare at our bony bodies. We stare back at their bright clothing and clear skin. Reflected in the eyes of the pretty young women is unconcealed scorn, cutting deeply into those of us who by rights should be out finding girlfriends now.

Liu Fengxiang and I are linked by simple, 'native' handcuffs; they are not adjustable and hurt more than the foreign variety. As we board the slow train that will transport us to Yueyang, Old Liu whispers, 'The revolution is dead; long live the revolution!' quoting Marx's article on the failure of the Paris Commune.

Old Liu dreams of a cultural revolution very different from the one touted by the authorities, one that can be turned around to oppose anyone and anything, even the line of Mao Zedong. It is a revolution in which he has never once lost faith.

At Yueyang, we are led to the ferry landing where once again we stand and wait. The soldiers grow bored; they scoop up handfuls of pebbles to pelt any prisoner who looks at them the wrong way. The stones hit our heads and the soldiers laugh. When we shift our weight, they bark at us to stand still.

'The proud army is bound to fall; the army burning with righteous indignation is bound to be victorious,' I hear Old Liu mutter, this time quoting Sunzi's *Art of War*. Is this his answer to my question about the possibility of armed resistance? As we march, I can't help watching for a chance to escape, despite my promise.

We are surrounded by silver-grey water.

One   hundred   miles   to   the   north   of   Changsha   is

Reconstruction Farm, built on a narrow islet that rises up out of the great waters of Dongting Lake. Soon after we step off the ferry, we see on the distant horizon the scattered figures of labor reform convicts, their clothes loose and tattered. There are no trees or buildings anywhere.

We march forward. Over the sound of shuffling feet and jingling chains, I hear Old Liu's somber voice: 'Mao Zedong is leading us to our deaths!' As always, he is alluding to the larger panorama of Chinese politics.

Thirty minutes later, our destination appears before us, a row of temporary log shelters with thatched roofs. The Tenth Brigade camp is deserted; most of the prisoners are out working on the dike. The few men that remain are wearing black jackets on which 'labor reform' has been painted in large yellow characters. A cadre with black plastic rain boots and a club strides over to receive us, his eyes vicious and threatening.

I shudder, realizing that this is the slave society I have read about since childhood.

By the time we report to our barracks inside the hundred-foot shed, it is midmorning on the second day of our journey. Each of us has been assigned a place along the two rows of wooden double-decker bunks. Our bags must go in the middle, so there is scarcely room to put down one's feet. Even in the daytime it is dark inside, for there are no windows, a few open doors providing the only light. Mercifully, Zhou Guohui, Bi Jian, Song Shaowen, Liu Fengxiang, and I end up in the same work group.

The lines of prisoners return to camp at dusk, winding along the barren shore like a grey dragon. Overhead, a flock of wild ducks blots out a patch of sky, honking furiously as if in pain. Then the birds fade into the twilight. Though night has fallen, some prisoners are still out. Far away, I recognize the familiar silhouette of one man beating another man with a club.

Somewhat later that evening I learn that we are at Reconstruction Farm's 'Outer Lake.' Even in the past this 'outer lake' had in fact been a lake only in summertime; in winter, the water gradually receded to expose a sliver of arable land. Thus up until very recently the inhabitants of the farm had been confined to the 'Inner Lake,' the area containing the first seven brigades. Faced with the dramatic increase in prisoners, now the authorities are constructing a massive dike before the onset of the spring floods, creating a piece of permanent dry land for three new labor brigades—the Eighth, the Ninth, and our own, the

Tenth, each numbering one or two thousand men.[1] The prisoners from the other nine brigades have been ordered here to help build 'Big Dike,' and they are temporarily housed next to us. All the real muscle of the farm is concentrated here in Outer Lake.

It is still black outside when we hear a banging on an iron rail, the signal to rise. A few gas lamps are lit, revealing only the flickering of shadows as the men bend to pull on their clothes. Half past four.

'Your mother sells cunt!'

'I've had dog-shit luck today!'

'Why the fuck does this always happen to me?'

The angry shouts seem to be coming from the neighboring shed.

'What's going on?' I ask, turning to a white-haired man, trying to make myself understood above the clanging of enamel dishes.

'Some selfish bastard keeps sneaking over to the kitchen when it's still dark and stealing one of the rices,' he replies in a thick Hengyang accent. Every day one inmate out of each work group is designated to pick up the food and water at the mess kitchen doorstep, he explains. Individual portions of rice are steamed in small aluminum containers; along with the bucket of vegetables, they are placed in each team's basket just outside the kitchen door. After the food is brought back to the groups, the inmates are supposed to put their mess kits on the floor, and wait for vegetables to be distributed.

Just then the prisoner-on-duty brings back a bucket of hot water and there is a blur of bodies. Though we newcomers delay only an instant, it is too late; the bucket is already empty when we get there. Instead of washing my face, I must be content to wipe it with a dry towel.

The vegetable bucket lid crashes to the ground. More curses. The air is close with the stench of cigarettes and sweat, and I wince. Old Liu whispers, 'I can see you've never lived with the lower classes. During the Great Leap, all of rural China was this way. In fact,' he smiles, 'it was worse.'

Of course. I am comparing conditions in labor camp to my previous privileged existence within the walls of the Provincial Party compound, forgetting to compare these conditions with those of the peasants.

[1] The size of a brigade fluctuated greatly, so that, depending on the times, a brigade could contain anywhere between 700 and 2,000 men. Each brigade might include three or four detachments; each detachment, sixteen to twenty groups. Groups usually numbered from sixteen to twenty-five men.

The first rays of the grey, December sunlight find us hard at work. In the distance I can just make out the shimmer of water and the vague outline of an embankment, the opposite shore of Dongting Lake. Our job is to haul dirt to the new dike using shoulder poles and scoop-shaped bamboo baskets. As the embankment gradually grows in height, we must move the piles of dirt closer and closer to its base. When the dirt is about a yard higher than the dike, a regularly employed laborer runs over it with a caterpillar tractor.

Within each detachment, work groups are formed according to productivity expectations. Prisoners in Group A can transport more than 140 cubic feet of dirt daily; Team B prisoners are given a daily quota of 105. Team C, the place for old or relatively weak prisoners—people like us who have been pent up in the detention center—must each carry 70.

Our detachment is headed up by a short little cadre with a club. He sticks close to the new arrivals and seems to know some of the Rightists.

He looks Old Liu up and down. 'This is your second time in the palace, isn't it?' he asks icily, making my heart race. I suspect immediately that Old Liu and Chen Sancai were under his command during their confinement in 1957.

But later Old Liu tells me that the Public Security organs had dealt with Rightists in a straightforward manner back in those days and that the cadres had no bones to pick with them. It was only when the Rightists joined the Rebel camp and the Public Security Organs Headquarters threw their support to the Conservatives that the personal interests of the two groups had clashed head on. The summer of 1967 was particularly nasty, for the Conservatives were down and many of the Rebel Rightists were out to settle old scores. I think back to the Three-haired Kid.

'Don't just stand there like a street sign; go get some dirt!'

Liu Fengxiang casually flaps his hollow right sleeve at the red-faced cadre, indicating that there is no way he can carry out the order. The cadre walks over, lifts his club above Liu's head, and brings it smashing down. Old Liu parries the blow effortlessly with his left arm.

Commanding a nearby prisoner to fill a basket with dirt, the cadre sets the pole on Liu's armless shoulder. Liu allows the burden to rest on his shoulder for a split second then lets it slide off onto the ground. The smell of musty earth fills the air. Overhead, a single wild duck cries out hoarsely and flies away. Human relations have degenerated to this extent. Have we returned to the barbaric times of Emperor Qin Shihuang and the building of the Great Wall?

Finally the cadre gives in. 'Get out of here,' he orders. 'Go repair baskets.'

On the days when we do not complete our quotas we are made to work until sundown. We push hard to finish early, and many of the ranks can be seen returning to the sheds along with us at about four o'clock.

It is only on this first trip home from labor that I have a clear view of the island terrain, fields of reeds through which two narrow paths have been worn, fields that only last summer were completely submerged. At all times I look to Old Liu as a respected guide and counselor. As we walk back to camp, he lectures. He is determined to teach me how to analyze a communist economy.

'The benefit of the socialist system is most apparent in the investment in large-scale construction. So whenever you look at this type of economy, you should first see how the large-scale investments are progressing. During the first Five-year Plan, 156 major large industrial projects were completed on schedule, eventually forming an industrial base. Then, during the period from 1958 to 1960, most of these projects were abandoned, which threw the country into a severe economic crisis.'

We are allowed to read the *Hunan Daily*, and our copies are only a couple of days old. Old Liu often scoffs at the headlines— 'Let traditional methods take precedence: implement design, construction, and production at the same time! Oppose the "large," the "foreign," and the "complete"!'

He explains to me how Mao's refusal to fund construction using large-scale, foreign technology and plans which take into consideration both design and equipment have caused many projects to end up so poorly that the engineers often have to start over. The technology is primitive, the scale of operations small, and cost of investment high; a lot of materials and manpower have been wasted.

On another occasion, Old Liu lashes out against the policy which encourages each province to establish a self-sufficient industrial system. What folly, he snorts; to expect each province, and even each county, to build its own chemical fertilizer plant, its own steel plant, and its own machinery plants, which will then supply only that local area.

'That's the advantage of the Soviet's planned economy: specialization and comprehensive planning. They design a few, large-scale key enterprises which are able to supply specialized products to the entire country. Mao's notion of "self-sufficiency" is absolutely feudalistic.'

◆

Because it is less tiring to fill baskets with a hoe than it is to transport the heavy baskets, prisoners take turns loading and carrying. As I dig, I survey the line of prisoners slowly mounting the dike, their baskets overflowing; to their right and left, at a slightly quicker pace, prisoners with empty baskets head back for more dirt. Someone pounds a gong. Three men are parading atop Big Dike: a cadre; the prisoner-on-duty, whose job it is to beat the gong; and a bound prisoner with a placard on his back reading, 'Escapee X X X.'

'Another unlucky ghost!' whispers the man who is digging at my side.

'He's the guy who tried to escape when he was going back to pick up food,' our group leader announces loudly.

Each day at noon we all climb up onto Big Dike, the western perimeter of the farm. The winter wind whips up and cuts though our cotton jackets. We are cold and hungry; it is not a pleasant spot to have one's lunch. But, I reflect, eating here might have its advantages if you are the one who is sent back alone for the food. One could slip away.

While we are collecting our tools that day, getting ready to head back to the sheds, Old Liu tells me that when the thaw of Khrushchev's socialist democratization moved southward in 1957, life at the reform and re-education farms improved considerably. The practice of shaving heads was abolished, as was the printing of 'labor reform' characters on uniforms. Prisoners began to receive a monthly allowance of two yuan. But some time during the Cultural Revolution two yuan became one and a half. Not only were the shaved heads and inscriptions revived, brutal beatings became commonplace.

'No wonder the old-timers are always talking about the good times under Liu Shaoqi,' I muse.

I have heard many such reports, including one story from an old fishery expert who had been allowed to manage several ponds when he was first sent down to Reconstruction Farm. In 1967, though, he was suddenly forced to start doing heavy manual labor, and now he carries dirt along with the rest of us.

'What do you mean "good" times?' whispers Old Liu, shaking his head. 'Liu Shaoqi, Zhou Enlai, and Deng Xiaoping all did their share of damage in the fifties. During the Anti-Rightist

Campaign in 1957, Zhou and Deng were as left as left could be. They called out for every Party member to serve as a docile tool. That feeling—that stifling of creativity . . . It was even worse than the oppressive atmosphere of the Cultural Revolution.' He pauses and sighs. 'It's only because Mao has been so bad recently that people sympathize with Liu Shaoqi. He's the lesser of two evils.'

This latest assertion of my new mentor stuns me, for up to now all of the criticisms he has leveled against Mao have suggested that he feels positively toward Liu Shaoqi. Moreover he has on several occasions spoken quite favorably about Zhou and Deng. 'The lesser of two evils!' I didn't expect to hear this.

No sooner are we back at the shed than the prisoner-on-duty calls Old Liu over and tells him the cadre wants to see him. At suppertime Liu reappears with a package under his arm, which he unwraps in an inconspicuous corner of the bunk, beckoning his Shengwulian friends to come and join him. We feast upon can after can of fish and meat, gifts from his wife, 'Iron Soldier' Zhang, Zhang Tiejun. That night he begins to tell me about her.

Zhang Tiejun was the attending physician overseeing the continued treatment of his injured arm in 1960. She was impressed by his strong will, his native intelligence, and his dogged search for the truth; before long, he tells me with a grin, she was in love with him.

Whenever they were together, Old Liu discussed politics with her. As he had done for me, he explained to Zhang Tiejun the background of the Anti-Rightist Campaign and the Great Leap. Impressed particularly by what he had to say about Mao Zedong, she had quickly adopted his views as her own. When, during the Cultural Revolution, she was denounced as a 'black ghost' and a 'bourgeois intellectual,' and placed under house arrest, Old Liu found a way for a friend to travel to Beijing and petition on her behalf. The documents were passed along to Chen Boda, then the head of the Central Cultural Revolution Group, who happened to be busily implementing Mao's latest policy in defense of all the newly capped Rebel 'counterrevolutionaries.' Chen handled her case personally, requesting in writing that the local officials rehabilitate her. To the Changsha intellectuals and workers whose futures had been previously snuffed out, his endorsement was welcomed as a very promising sign.

After Zhang Tiejun regained her freedom, she began actively to assist her boyfriend. Soon, though, Old Liu became aware that his movements had caught the attention of the Public Security Organs Headquarters, and he warned Zhang that he might at any time be taken into custody. He must go with her to register for a marriage license, she had insisted; otherwise she would have no way of legally communicating with him once he was in prison. Old Liu consented.

He was picked up the very next day.

During the almost two years that Liu was confined to Changsha's Model Prison, Zhang Tiejun took advantage of her status as a wife to send him packages and information. She had moved in with Liu's mother, who lived closer to Yueyang, as soon as she learned of his sentencing. Laden with provisions, she lost no time in coming to the camp for the first of her allotted annual visits.

As I crouch on the bunk listening to his tale, I can't help but think of Director Song and the many other instances of 'revolutionary' women who, upon hearing of their husbands' sentencing, have lost no time in filing for divorce. The pressure to 'draw the line' is so very great that, as the days pass, the story of Zhang Tiejun becomes a legend at Reconstruction Farm. Among the politicals she is revered as a saint.

'Yang Xiguang is one of us,' Old Liu has confided to her. She beamed in response, he assured me, and asked him to send me her warmest regards. I am flattered and not a little surprised at the importance he seems to assign to my friendship.

I have joined the ranks of men in black jackets who stumble home every evening too tired to move. Old Liu tells me that heavy manual labor is the cadres' favorite method of neutralizing criminals, especially politicals, who are not supposed to have any energy to think about serious topics. Each winter, during the agricultural rest period, the cadres rack their brains to come up with additional taxing jobs—such as dike-building. But Old Liu and I never stop talking. By taking advantage of the fifteen-minute walk along the paths or the moments allowed for gathering up our equipment, we are able to discuss many, many issues.

One afternoon I ask Old Liu what he would do if he could stay at home without having to work.

'Oh, I'd write a little piece on *The Romance of the Three Kingdoms*; if you know this book backwards and forwards, you basically know Chinese politics.' He talks about the famous chapter, 'Warming Wine and Evaluating Heroes,' where Cao Cao invites Liu Bei to come and have a drink. Pretending to be drunk, Cao Cao boasts that they are 'the two heroes of the world.' But Liu Bei is canny enough to use the tactics of concealment, and he pretends to be content with his subordinate position. It is only then that Cao Cao decides not to harm him.

'In China,' Old Liu cautions me, 'the people who have an opportunity to get involved in politics cannot possibly have enlightened outlooks. As soon as a man sees what's really going on, he doesn't want to be a politician anymore. So the secret to gaining power in China is to act very tolerant and to hide successfully any ability that you might have. And that's a tough call, because if you don't come out into the open and clash swords with the opposition from time to time, all your political faculties will atrophy.'

Old Liu is particularly sensitive to the passing of time. Sooner or later they will split us up, he warns me. Before the Cultural Revolution, the only time politicals implicated in the same case were allowed to stay in the same brigade was when the farm authorities intended to plant a KGB in their midst.

Indeed I have been carrying baskets of dirt back and forth at the Tenth Brigade of the Outer Lake for only about a month when the cadres announce that we are to be transferred. Just as Old Liu has predicted, politicals involved in the same case will be dispersed to different brigades. In this action Zhou Guohui will go to the First, Bi Jian to the Fifth, Song Shaowen to the Seventh, and I to the Third. Old Liu stays on at the Tenth.

Several months later, on a bright, sunny morning in April I am ordered to report to the farm office. Two military officers wait there, claiming to be from the Provincial Cultural Revolution Committee's PPG. In light of the Strike One–Oppose Three Campaign, the Shengwulian case is to be reopened; my presence is urgently wanted in Changsha. In these times of extreme chaos, it is no secret that this campaign is aimed at political enemies of all stripes. This trip home does not bode well.

The two cadres accompany me onto the ferry all the way to Yueyang, where we are scheduled to spend the night. A jeep is waiting at the landing. As we drive from the dock to the Yueyang Municipal Public Security Bureau Detention Center, I peer out, trying to read as much as I can on the walls. They are plastered with slogans, all demanding that the authorities 'execute the counterrevolutionaries who have earned the bitter wrath of the people.' Suddenly the names of Liu Fengxiang and Lei Techao leap out at me. Lei served as a cadre at the Provincial Public Security Department and, like Old Liu, was labeled a Rightist in 1957. Old Liu has told me how the two of them did labor re-education at the same camp and were apprehended together in 1968.

By the time we finally arrive at the Yueyang detention center I am tense and cranky. Where is Old Liu? Once again, I find myself sharing a tiny cell, four or five yards long and three yards wide, with some thirty others who are sitting or lying on the thin reed mats covering every inch of the floor. Many of my fellow inmates have only recently been sentenced and are waiting to be sent on to prison or labor camp.

Despite my persistent questioning, no one seems to know anything about Old Liu. I encounter a young worker in his early twenties, only a year or so older than I am, who tells me in a voice choked with desperate rage that this latest mass suppression is an exercise in revenge: the Conservatives and the military have joined forces to rout the Rebels once and for all. Though he once made his living pedaling a two-wheeled cart, his class origin is bad; moreover, during the Cultural Revolution he had rebelled against the cadres at the subdistrict police station, singling out the men who had repeatedly discriminated against his family. The station cadres, all Conservatives at the time, waited for the tide to turn, and as soon as Strike One–Oppose Three came along, had struck back. In just one night's time they were able to produce enough 'evidence' to prove the young worker had 'attacked and slandered Chairman Mao and Vice-chairman Lin,' and with the help of the Military Control Commission not only completed all the paperwork necessary for his arrest, but sentenced him to twenty years. The efficiency with which the Conservatives handled these types of cases was unprecedented.

The young worker also tells me that the power to execute criminals has already been transferred from the Central Committee's Supreme Court down to the provincial level—the Military Control Commission and the People's Protection Group. The sentences have been heavier than usual, terms as long as fifteen or twenty years. Many of the accused have already been shot.

From the sound of things, we seem to be encountering the ripples from a major political upheaval. Mao and Lin have shifted their support back to the Conservatives, and are now actively suppressing all Rebels. My heart sinks. I am finished. I wonder grimly if this is how the betrayed radicals felt when the Nationalists purged the Communists in Shanghai in 1927.

At length I am able to find a prisoner who knows something about Lei Techao and Old Liu. Both men are already dead.

'But what was the charge?'

'Guilty of heading up the Chinese Labor Party; inciting mountain strongholdism and banditry; plotting to overthrow the dictatorship of the proletariat.'

Like bolts of lightning, his words surge through my body, and I go limp. Despite all my premonitions, I am unable to absorb this news, overcome by sadness. How can it be possible for such an excellent man to end this way? Again and again, my country is cannibalizing her best children. But outside the detention center his absence will go unnoticed. It is as if the authorities have assassinated him in a covert operation: the vast majority of the people who will see his name on the wall posters will have no inkling of what his ideas were; they won't even know who he is.

And yet do I? For all the time I spent with Old Liu, never once did I hear the words 'Labor Party' pass his lips. To be sure, there existed between us an intense chemistry, an unspoken understanding, as if we were both quietly toying with the idea of an opposition party. But he was inconsistent—sometimes his remarks suggested he supported guerrilla warfare; at others, he seemed very much against any tangible form of underground organization.

I think back to the Tenth Brigade and an exchange on the path leading to Big Dike. 'Yang Xiguang,' he told me, 'the ruling regime is able to use the passing of each generation to wipe from history all traces of its political enemies. Take, for instance, the transition of power from the Nationalists to the Communists. Young people, who have come of age hating the Nationalists, don't really knowing what a "Nationalist" is. These young people have grown up in a vacuum, and their consciousness and interactions have not been been shaped by the presence of a second party. The Nationalist Party automatically becomes an object of contempt. And as everyone knows, despite the fact that the Rightists were totally correct in 1957, the new generation was taught to be "anti-rightist," so that they were ultimately able to deny the very possibility of a right wing. That is why any hope of political change lies completely in the conflicts that might arise *within* the ranks of the Communist Party.'

I sift through many such conversations in my mind, and still I cannot determine whether Old Liu truly joined an underground party early on, or whether the charge has been trumped up. If the former is indeed the case, then in the two months I knew Old Liu, he was slowly but surely priming me for induction into his 'Chinese Labor Party.' The thought that I may be on the fringes of such a group knocks about inside my head. I begin to panic.

What was the truth?

Was Old Liu really an opposition leader? If so, then who had betrayed him? At Zuojiatang I had regarded Nine Dragons Zhang from a painful, but safe distance. But this time is different. Never before have I been this close to death, close enough to be a part of it. Was I? What were the words of the PPG interrogator? And hadn't Old Liu once announced: 'Yang Xiguang is one of *us*.'

Was I, or was I not?

Night falls, and the newly sentenced inmates sleep, yet I am scarcely aware of their intermittent grunts and coughs. Though my thoughts still race, I mourn. Old Liu, Old Liu, you were my father, you were my brother. I weep and think of my own family.

My older brother Yang Shuguang, a Rightist, who was labeled at the same time as Old Liu—for having loved the daughter of a successful entrepreneur in Tianjin. In the 1950s a member of the Communist Youth League needed approval before becoming romantically involved, and the Tianjin Hospital Party organization refused even to consider such a match. When during the Hundred Flowers Campaign in 1957, he put up a wall poster denouncing the system which denied the 'freedom to love,' he was cast into the 'right wing.'

My uncle, a high-ranking Communist cadre, whose situation was similar to that of Old Liu. Chen Sancai told me that he and my uncle were good friends in labor re-education camp. As soon as my uncle's term was up, he came to visit us, talking politics as always, telling my mother that the Communists had fallen into 'left-wing opportunism.'

And my father, who in 1957 had disagreed with my uncle, but who was himself labeled a 'right-wing opportunist' two years later for denouncing the Great Leap Forward. My mother pleaded and pleaded with him to change his views. But by 1962 she, too, believed that the policies of 1959 had strayed too far to the left, which meant that during the Cultural Revolution she would, along with my father, be pronounced guilty of 'counterrevolutionary revisionism.' Like Old Liu, she was gone forever.

Wave after wave of grief washes over me until I am almost numb to the pain. And then it hits me, the realization that Old Liu has all along been supplying the threads that connect my fate to the fate of my family. Suddenly I see how each of their actions was as valid as my own 'rebellion' during the Cultural Revolution. By outlining the subtle misunderstanding between the Rightists in power and the Rightists out of power, Old Liu has pulled us together, making explicit the links between three generations in Chinese politics. And so it has become my turn to be persecuted, and the turn of yet more and more people, people who just months earlier were persecuting others.

Daily we hear stories of how the standard of living is sinking. Despite the campaigns to suppress the violence, political clashes continue unbroken throughout the nation. Perhaps it is true, what Old Liu said about Mao leading us to our deaths.

Aboard the train to Changsha, I imagine for one horrible instant what Old Liu must have felt before he was shot. I think of his mother and the Iron Soldier collecting his body.

No matter how long it takes, I need to find out the truth about this man's past.

12

Fugitives

▼

Upon my transfer to the Third Brigade I am abruptly returned to the twentieth century in the back of an open truck. Accompanied by a group of other politicals, I bask in the hazy winter sun, northbound on the bumpy, muddy road that cuts over to Inner Lake. For forty minutes there is nothing but marsh grass. Then suddenly squat brick and wood structures can be seen beyond the grey embankment. This is the desolate 'Reed Store,' a small, sleepy village, which is the site of Reconstruction Farm Headquarters.

During the past month I have heard so many negative things from Old Liu about Mao's radical, ultraleftist policies, and so many positive things about Liu Shaoqi and Zhou Enlai and their right-wing policies, that my mind has begun to play tricks on me. Can it be a coincidence that the moment I placed my trust in Premier Zhou, believing him to be the only rational individual left in power, I was taken out of the slave society of Outer Lake? There must be some force, invisible and all-powerful, prodding this turn of events, arranging my fate. Is it Zhou Enlai, I wonder? Deep down I know that such speculation is absurd. But a person who has lost all control over his life and who craves the warmth of reason cannot resist illusion.

'You're Yang Xiguang?' the Farm Headquarters cadre asks in disbelief.

I assure him I am.

'In any province only a few people can be leaders, but every organization wants to be in command; now how can we have that?' From his tone, it is clear he means to lecture me, but he also seems to want to explain away the political clashes of the Cultural Revolution, and the fact that overnight so many organizations had been labeled counterrevolutionary.

I find his remarks disturbing, for they imply that all political conflicts can be reduced to a struggle for power. I cannot accept this premise, since in my opinion my problem with the authorities was a result of my ideas. No matter, it is a relief to hear a fresh explanation for my status as a counterrevolutionary. Here at least is one man who is trying to make sense out of the political situation in a calm and rational way. This man does not treat me with contempt.

I remember a bit of information Zhou Guohui picked up at the Tenth Brigade from an old prisoner, that the cadres at Reconstruction Farm had split into two major factions during the Cultural Revolution: one that supported the Public Security organs and one that supported Xiang River Storm. It does not surprise me that more than a few farm officials ended up sympathizing with the Rebels—labor farm cadres are at the bottom of the cadre hierarchy. Nor is it a surprise that the cadres who got sucked into the factional maelstrom of the Cultural Revolution tend to be the cadres who are most understanding of my own predicament.

As we near the Third Brigade camp, its massive wall looms in the foreground. Over 12 feet tall, the top is wrapped with barbed wire. A soldier holding a rifle looks down at us from the watchtower in the corner.

It is exactly midday as I am formally handed over to the vicious little man named Ji who heads the Third Detachment of the Third Brigade. When he speaks, it is always through clenched teeth. From his accent, I guess that he must be from north China.

'Your crime?'

'The Shengwulian matter.'

His face darkens. '*Matter*? You didn't commit a *crime*?' he hisses. 'While you're here, you had better settle down and submit to the law. You're all the same a bunch of untrustworthy malcontents. You can't accept your lot in life, and so, with your inflated individualism, you think you can rebel against the dictatorship of the proletariat. You Cultural Revolution Rebels are just like the Rightists of '57—you're simply not satisfied with the Communist Party!'

I don't dare argue, but think to myself, how different his attitude is from that of the cadre back at Farm Headquarters. He takes from me the slip of paper issued by the Changsha Municipal Public Security Bureau which combines verdict and enforcement orders. I never see it again.

FU ZIGENG

Most of the prisoners in the Third Brigade, some two thousand of them, are temporarily stationed at the Outer Lake area, working on the dikes. But every detachment has left one group behind at Inner Lake—the 'Old and Weak Group'. From the Third Detachment, there are seven of us who are told to stay back.

Prisoners are housed in blocks of cells running east and west within the Third Brigade walls. The Third Detachment is sandwiched between the blocks containing the First and the Second Detachments. In the center there is a narrow courtyard where we assemble each morning before going out to labor. To the extreme south lie the mess kitchen and an auditorium for meetings. Each group has two authority figures, a study leader who guides the evening political study class and who reports our thoughts and actions to the cadres, and a production leader who supervises our work.

Our study leader is a man named Wu. He has white hair and a little white goatee. In conversation, he is slow to respond—an old bookworm. Wu is a former Nationalist official who after Liberation went to the countryside to teach school. When the brunt of the famine hit the rural areas in 1959, some of his students decided to start up an opposition party. One evening a group of them stopped by to ask his advice. Wu responded by quoting the writer Lu Xun, 'The world did not come equipped with roads; roads are made by many people walking.' The students' organization was eventually uncovered by the Communists, and Wu, I learned, was sentenced to fifteen years as a 'counterrevolutionary black hand.'

On our first morning, Detachment Leader Ji strides over to the cells with his hands clasped behind his back, stopping directly in front of the assembled Third Detachment. He scowls at us briefly. 'Some of you don't seem to know your places,' he bursts out. 'Just who do you think you are, enquiring into other people's cases the minute you get off the truck? Still tempted to toy with counterrevolution, perhaps? Don't even think about it! You have come to a place where dragons crawl and tigers kneel.' At this point he fixes gaze on me. 'You had better conform,' he snorts, continuing, 'I've seen it all before—cold-blooded robbers, Changsha hoodlums, Nationalist generals. Makes no difference to me. Whoever comes here toes the line.'

Somebody has been informing on me. It is my first time to be railed at in front of the others, and I feel angry and humiliated. I glance over at the 'old and weak prisoners' who stand on either side of me; their heads are lowered. My companions would indeed seem to be 'crawling dragons and kneeling tigers.'

With the exception of Fu Zigeng. It is Fu Zigeng who keeps

me going. Almost childlike, with his round face and short stature, he can't be more than twenty years old. His shackled feet jingle and jangle wherever he walks, for he 'harbors the desire to escape.' Fu has been placed with the Old and Weak Group. I assume this is because the cadres can more easily control this kind of group, a 'control' with which I am already painfully familiar. Fu and I are the only members who aren't enfeebled.

One day, having just learned who I am, Fu approaches me while we are out cutting hemp, and offers to teach me the ins and outs of the Third Brigade. First lesson: I must always remember that the camp relies on common criminals to monitor politicals and on 'historical counterrevolutionaries,' those people who became political enemies before 1949, to monitor 'practicing counterrevolutionaries,' the post-1949 dissidents. The two group leaders communicate to Detachment Leader Ji twice a day: in the morning, before prisoners leave their cells, and in the evening, before political study class.

Pointing to an old man, Fu says quietly, 'See that guy? That's Grandpa Liu. Old Man Wu used to get a kick out of baiting him by asking him to explain the political situation. Grandpa Liu answered in all honesty, never suspecting that he was being set up. He told Wu that things were so bad the Communist dynasty might collapse at any moment. Just like that!' Fu turned his palm over suddenly. 'Wu kept nodding, as if he agreed. But very shortly afterwards Wu repeated the entire conversation to Detachment Leader Ji. Fortunately, Grandpa Liu didn't care. He never had made a point of hiding his opinions.'

As Fu talks, I look closely at Grandpa Liu. His uniform is in sorry condition and he keeps a ratty gunnysack tied around his belly. Over time the frames of his thick glasses have grown layer upon layer of adhesive tape, which are crusty with dirt and grease. A timid, soft-spoken man with a heavy Changsha accent, he seems at once vulnerable and dignified. But though he is a loner and keeps his distance from the rest of us, I eventually find a chance to strike up a conversation.

To my surprise I learn that he not only had been a county magistrate under the Nationalists, he had even served as Chiang Kai-shek's secretary. The change in power did not sway him from his anti-communist views. He assures me he had only expressed his opinions to the Communist cadres directly, in personal conversations, and had never been involved in resistance activities.

His son, who was well-educated and had become a senior

official in the government in Beijing, distanced himself from his father as required by the Four Purifications Campaign of 1964. At the age of seventy, Grandpa Liu was abandoned, politically and economically. The old man had subsisted on the small stipend that the Party issued each month, finally becoming so feeble that he wasn't even able to carry a sack of rice home from the store. He was still denouncing communism publicly when the Cultural Revolution erupted. This time the Public Security Bureau declared him guilty of 'stubbornness in reactionary thought' and sentenced him to seven years labor reform. A proverbial 'diehard of the last dynasty,' he seems frozen in time.

My new mentor points to another of our crew, Yuan Sheng, a muddle-headed old man from Hengyang, who used to be a cobbler. Though he had worked himself to the bone, Yuan couldn't support his family. Then he learned that each prisoner in labor camp got 40 pounds of rice a month, more than he could ever get on the outside, so he wrote a slogan advocating the overthrow of the Party and was soon sent to the Public Security Bureau where he was sentenced to five years. Yuan Sheng is a regular subject at our nightly political study sessions, for he is constantly muttering that it was only because he couldn't make ends meet that he had put up an anti-communist slogan in the first place. Study Leader Wu pounces on him vigorously, never missing a chance to denounce a prisoner for not taking responsibility for his own crime.

I learn that the reason Fu trusts me to the extent he does is that the prisoner who had escaped with him had read about me in the papers and thus considered me to be someone who dared to challenge the authorities. Over time, Fu fills me in on the story of his life. Like Bandit Xiang, Fu Zigeng began to steal in the early sixties along with the masses of other Hunan peasants who fled to the cities. Initially his term had only been for five years. He tried to escape twice, failed twice, and got slapped with an additional ten years. Not long before my arrival at the Third Brigade, he tried a third time and was tossed into the solitary confinement of the little *haozi*.

I have already seen the little *haozi* of the Third Brigade; there are four of them in a row, situated just within the walls of the northeastern corner. Whereas our cell doors are always left open and are roomy enough to house over a dozen men, the little *haozi* hold only one prisoner at a time and the doors remain shut. Conditions are even worse there than they were at Zuojiatang, and the rice ration is only about 26 pounds a month (well short of the 30-some pounds an adult would expect to eat on the

outside, *in addition* to similar amounts of meat and vegetables).
Anybody who breaks a farm rule inevitably finds himself in the
little *haozi* for some length of time. Fu Zigeng stayed in Solitary
for half a year, before a friend slipped him a small iron shovel
with his meal. This he used to dig a thirteen-foot tunnel to the
other side of the outer wall, fleeing the Third Brigade camp some
time after dawn. When it was discovered that he was missing,
the guards hopped on a truck in pursuit. They had little trouble
locating him in the northern section of Reconstruction Farm, he
reminisces with a laugh.

In spite of Fu's stories and my own resolutions, I daydream,
perhaps only in the recesses of my consciousness, about ways to
escape. The finality of sentencing has hit me hard and the daily
routine is so much worse than I ever expected that the logic of
Old Liu's argument against escape gradually pales.

The milk vetch is sprouting; winter is drawing to an end. The
water in the rice paddies is completely drained and now we must
clean the irrigation ditches. We have to shovel dirt into the ditch,
jump in on top of it, and then scoop the dirt and any garbage or
other unwanted foreign matter back out onto the top of the bank,
deepening the furrow in the process.

Up on the bank, Study Leader Wu beckons. It is time for a
cigarette break.

'What lies to the north of the Third Brigade camp?' I ask him
casually.

'The Second Brigade, and further on, the First', he answers.

'And then?'

'That would be Moneygrain Lake Farm.'

'How far is that from us?'

'Uh, well, I'm not really sure . . .'

On the main road I can make out an oxcart with wooden
wheels inching slowly forward. Never have I seen such a
primitive vehicle. 'What's that used for?' I ask.

Study Leader Wu frowns impatiently, 'That's the fertilizer
cart. Driver's a free prisoner.'

'*Free* prisoner?'

'He's allowed to work alone, without any supervision. Most
free prisoners are in for just short stretches: Their cases are fairly
unimportant, and their behavior's been good.'

'But we don't have a cadre supervising us, either.'

'Who in this crowd is going to run for it?' He looks at me
oddly, pausing for a moment, then continues. 'When all of the
troops come back from the dikes, you'll move on to one of the
able groups. There you'll have a cadre out with you every single

day. Why, last year at this time, we had an armed guard *and* a cadre watching.'

Suddenly I hear the sound of an engine running and turn my head to see a tiny truck on the distant gravel road that cuts through the fields of the Third Brigade. 'Where does that road go?' I ask.

'From Huarong County on over to Yueyang County.'

As the cloud of dust fades away, I memorize the shape of the truck. It might be possible to sneak into the back while the driver isn't looking.

But at assembly the next morning Detachment Leader Ji focuses his gaze on me once again. 'Some fellows just won't give up the idea of running away and think they can spend their days making inquiries about escape routes. I want those counterrevolutionary elements who are actively plotting escape to regard the shackles on Fu Zigeng's feet. These are what you will get for your efforts.'

I am completely surprised. Wu has obviously communicated my 'intentions' to Detachment Leader Ji in the form of a little report. Soon there is always someone around whose job it is to watch my every move. Overnight I have become a maximum security prisoner.

By late February the work out on the dikes is complete. The Third Brigade compound comes alive. The barracks that previously housed only the twenty-odd men of the three Old and Weak groups now overflow with the vigorous laborers returned from Outer Lake. They bring with them the specter of hunger: seven or eight mouths have joined our little group. At mealtime they hold their bowls in anticipation, hovering behind the old men with small appetites. Some jockey to wash the dishes and vegetable containers, hoping to scoop up small particles of food.

It is time to fertilize the fields. Every day the able groups must haul about twenty baskets of cow and pig manure. For ten miles, all along the road, one can see prisoners who have put down their bamboo baskets and are standing in the middle of the fields pulling up young rape shoots to eat.

Ever since the men have come back from Outer Lake, I have noticed that the jangling sound within the Third Brigade walls continues almost unbroken. Each pair of foot-shackles bears testimony to a failed escape attempt. But one of my white-haired companions informs me quietly that there are ten prisoners from our detachment who are still at large.

By March, Fu Zigeng is back in Solitary again. When it is my turn to go to the mess kitchen or to fetch hot water, I make it a point to walk by his little *haozi*. He waves to me through the hole in the door, whispering things like, 'Oh man! I'm dying in here—the floor in this place is all cement!'

STRIKE ONE–OPPOSE THREE

The milk vetch and rape fields are lush and green, the brown soil nearly covered. Along the bank, the twisted water willows are shrouded in pale yellow clouds that will soon turn into leaves. The air is heavy, humid; it is springtime in the countryside of south China.

It is a beautiful morning, fresh and warm. A big sentencing meeting has been called for all the men. According to protocol, it will take place on the shore just outside the Big Dike sluice, the major gateway through which the waters of Dongting Lake flow on their way to farms of the Seven Brigades.

An old prisoner tells me that such sentencing meetings have been held every year in late February or early March, just before the strenuous spring planting, while the ground was still above water. Two or three prisoners will be executed to keep the rest in line—'slaughtering chickens to frighten the monkeys.' Outside the newspapers are calling to 'push revolution in order to promote production.' The cadres have erected a stage, which they have decorated with the red-paper slogans of the new campaign, urging the masses to 'Kill, kill, kill until a bright red world emerges!'

Nightfall finds the entire ranks of the Seven Brigades assembled on the beach. More than ten thousand men sit noiselessly in the darkness, surrounded by armed soldiers. Thirty feet away is a mounted machine gun, pointing at the densest part of the crowd. Groups of cadres stand behind each of the brigades, looking on with undisguised hatred. I wonder who the chickens will be. I think again of my uncle and brother, and of Liu Fengxiang.

Suddenly the farm cadres representing the Military Control Commission order that the two criminals be brought forward, and to everyone's surprise, Fu Zigeng is among them. He and the other man, who is in his mid-twenties, are pushed up onto the platform. They are already wearing the death knot. Hung upon Fu's back is a placard reading 'Counterrevolutionary Fugitive'; the other man's says 'Counterrevolutionary Recidivist.' I have never heard of either charge before.

According to the verdict read by the cadre, while in prison Fu has attempted to escape three times, disseminated counterrevolutionary ideas, and criticized the Communist Party.

The other man is said to have denounced Mao Zedong and the Party. Both are to be shot immediately.

And so I again have occasion to witness a person I know well sentenced to death; moreover, the sentence seems to be based entirely on the individuals' unorthodox thoughts and speech.

It is clear to all that Fu's death penalty has been imposed in response to the frequent escape attempts during the preceding weeks. Before the Cultural Revolution no one had ever heard of re-sentencing a prisoner because of an escape attempt; after being captured, one simply finished up one's term. Only those people who committed another crime after their escape had been sentenced again in the courts. Fu is scared out of his wits.

Shortly after this meeting I am transferred to an able workers' group. On the first morning, just before we go out to work, the icy-faced Ji orders one of the prisoners to step out of the ranks.

'Kneel down in front of me.'

'But I haven't done anything,' the man replies in a voice barely audible.

'Just what do you think you're doing? Trying to organize an escape—did you really think I wouldn't find out?' Ji hisses derisively. 'Get some rope.'

A couple of the group leaders promptly obey, pushing the man on his back while they tie the rope around him. Ji has the prisoner's quilt and clothing brought out and commands the prisoner-on-duty to paint 'labor reform' in bright yellow on each.

'Strike One–Oppose Three' has arrived in full force at Reconstruction Farm.

Nightly at our study meetings we hear the sounds of struggle sessions echoing in the neighboring cells, cries of condemnation and cries of pain, as prisoners club their fellow prisoners. New posters have been hung up on the walls of the cells, the mess kitchen, everywhere:

CONFESS YOUR DESIRE TO ESCAPE!
CONFESS YOUR REACTIONARY THREE LONGINGS!
CONFESS YOUR RESIDUAL CRIMES!
ADMIT YOUR GUILT AND SUBMIT TO THE LAW!

To launch the campaign formally, a man named Counselor Liu delivers the mobilization speech at a meeting held for all the brigades.

'Among you are those who bitterly hate the Communist Government and long for three things: the restoration of the Chiang Kai-shek gang, the restoration of American imperialism, and the restoration of Soviet revisionism. Some of you simply will not give up your wicked designs and are plotting your escape even as we speak, in hopes that you can return to society and stir up more trouble. Now, in this movement, you must take all of these thoughts, thoughts of the three longings, thoughts of escape, and of any other new criminal activities which you may be hiding in your heart and confess them.'

In my new group, two individuals are routinely struggled against. One, a seventeen-year-old peasant, grew up hearing his parents and his grandfather—poor peasants—say that the rural folk fared better under the Nationalists, especially during the years following the Great Leap Forward. From his family's stories he developed such a favorable impression of the Nationalist Party that he started carving the emblem of the blue sky and white sun on wooden posts. When this pastime was discovered, he got a ten-year sentence and was sent to Reconstruction Farm, where he continued to carve the Nationalist symbol on the prison pillars. As an 'element who resists molding,' he is a natural target for criticism.

The other scapegoat is a tall peasant not yet thirty years old, Liu Guinong from Chaling County. He appears very traditional; he wears a towel wrapped around his shaved head, and he never says very much. He seems upright, unassuming, and a bit slow. But there is a Chinese saying that 'honest-looking men do surprising things, and men of great wisdom may look foolish.'

Desperately seeking to win the cadres' trust, our new study leader, a primary school teacher from Shaoyang, hurries to struggle against the prisoners and dash off reports. One evening, Detachment Leader Ji suddenly appears in our doorway and announces ominously, 'Two years ago Liu Guinong ran away for more than seven months, committing even more crimes. Since he was apprehended he has never really accounted for his criminal behavior; in fact his attitude has been extremely uncooperative. Your group has been much too lax in struggling against him. Is it, perhaps, that somebody here feels sorry for him?'

After offering these remarks Ji goes out to investigate the situation in another block, leaving the remainder of the struggle meeting under the supervision of the study leader. He does not need to say much, because everyone understands what Ji meant; today we are supposed to take up arms against Liu Guinong.

'Come forward, Liu Guinong, and get down on your knees.' As the study leader begins to shout, I look upon this man Liu with increasing respect. 'Don't think you can squeak by without confessing tonight,' the study leader continues.

Liu does not protest, simply kneels quietly on the floor and begins his narrative. In the previous year he had fled the camp, stealing 120 yuan in cash and grain coupons worth 50 pounds of rice. Over his recitation can be heard shrill screams and the cracks of shoulder poles coming down on people's heads next door.

One member of the group suddenly leaps up, shouting, 'Liu Guinong, this is all old stuff to us—don't think you can put us off this time with the same old stories.'

The study leader also rises. 'If we don't let him know we mean business, he's never going to confess completely.'

Liu Guinong does not say a word. Finding some rope, the study leader ties him tightly, muttering, 'Today you're not going to shed any tears until you see your coffin, are you? Holding out to the very end. Allow me to give you a chance to experience "hanging a side of pork" firsthand.'

Within minutes Liu's left hand and foot have been strung from the rafters. When the two group leaders pull on the ends of the ropes, Liu dangles in midair, screaming out like a pig being slaughtered.

'I'll confess, I'll confess!' Scarcely a minute has passed.

That evening Liu's account of his booty escalates to 1000 yuan and several hundred pounds of rice. On the following morning Detachment Leader Ji commands him to remain in the cells to put down everything in writing.

'I don't know how to read or write,' say Liu, wincing.

The assignment of recording his confession is given to me.

But the cagey man is not illiterate at all; he simply wishes to avoid providing the authorities with evidence in his own hand. I listen to his stories for an entire day, scribbling furiously all the time he is speaking.

He was just an ordinary peasant in the beginning, he relates, but gradually branched out into business, carrying out transactions for his production brigade. It didn't take long for him to learn how to counterfeit the bills of lading which could be exchanged for goods at state factories. Eventually he mastered the basics of theft as well. But at Reconstruction Farm he had a good track record, for he was known to work hard and keep his mouth shut. The cadres made him production leader.

In 1968, when the fall cotton was at its highest and ready to be harvested, he crept through the fields and out of the camp. Because he had always picked away quietly, collecting more and better quality cotton than just about anyone, and because, after all, he was production leader, nobody ever considered the possibility that he might have escaped; they thought he had gone back to the cells. Only after dark was the truth discovered and a search party sent out.

Liu tells me that he had lived by stealing. He proudly details each of his thefts for my report. On one occasion while he was 'fishing' at the train station, he noticed a young woman preoccupied with a large bundle. Snatching her pocketbook, he slipped into the men's room to tally up his booty. When he came back out, he saw that the woman had already discovered her money was gone and was as distraught as an ant on a hot wok. A wave of compassion swept over him. He walked over to ask what the trouble was, and helped her search for her purse. After some time, he magnanimously opened his wallet and presented her with a token of his affection—most, but not all of what he had just taken from her. Then, pretending to be heading in the same direction, he boarded the train with her. By the time they reached the city of their destination, the two of them were on very good terms indeed, 'sticking to each other like glue and lacquer.' Only after spending several pleasurable nights together did they reluctantly part company.

As Liu was a firm believer in the principle that 'a rabbit should never eat the grass at the edge of his hole,' he was good to his own and, whenever he got hold of a fair amount of money, he went home and showered his friends and neighbors with largesse. Because the people of his village all thought well of him, he never had any trouble with the local authorities.

At the end of the day, I have finished recording Liu's 'complete' confession and know quite a bit about the man. But it is only later I learn that, in addition to his considerable understated talents in other areas, he knows a thing about politics as well. Just about one week after Liu was strung up like a slab of pork, Detachment Leader Ji once again graces our group's morning assembly. This time, however, he orders the study leader to step forward. 'You counterrevolutionary, you!' he screams. 'Did you think you could keep my trust without deserving it? You've only been study leader a few short days and already you're resisting reform. A man doesn't know when he's ugly; a horse doesn't know when he has a long face!' The study leader is dismissed from his post in view of everyone present.

It is from the deposed leader I learn that Liu Guinong quietly 'informed' the cadres that the study leader was constantly 'complaining of not getting enough to eat.' I listen and smile.

Never again do I hear this man—at Reconstruction Farm for fifteen years because he ostensibly led a counterrevolutionary clique—criticize his fellow prisoners with his previous enthusiasm. Liu Guinong, on the other hand, is the same as always: slow-moving and generous, seemingly quiet, yet remarkably effective in doing what needs to be done.

Part III

Model Prison

APRIL 1970–JANUARY 1971

▼

13

Master Bin

▼

The jeep is already parked out in front of the train station, waiting to take me to the Provincial Public Security Department Detention Center at Liudongli, located out near the North Station. In 'Model Prison,' as the inmates call it—under the Nationalists it had been touted as the perfect prison—I will be interrogated as the Shengwulian case reopens.[1]

'Kill, kill, kill! Kill until the world is all red!'

Party members and Conservatives are marching on the streets, demanding that the People's Government 'suppress' all counterrevolutionaries. By now I know too well what is meant by the term.

As we drive from the station to Model Prison, I peer out the window trying to read the walls. Suddenly, the names 'Zhang Jiazheng' and 'Yang Xiguang' leap out at me. The slogan demands that the authorities execute the two counterrevolutionaries who have earned the bitter wrath of the people. My body turns cold.

It is not my first visit to Model Prison. I was taken there during the February Countercurrent of 1967 when the members of Xiang River Storm were seized by the Conservatives. My spirits sink even lower at the thought that I have come full circle. As we pull up in front of the gate, I remember how my Rebel comrades and I fasted for days, demanding to be allowed to negotiate with the authorities. We had been set free in less than a month.

This time, however, the Storm's 'Commander' Zhang Jiazheng and I have been singled out as enemies of the people at the precise moment that Lin Biao and Zhou Enlai are joining forces to suppress the Rebels. 'Strike One–Oppose Three' is escalating.

---

[1] After the Gang of Four fell from power, Model Prison became a public housing complex. It was probably situated too close to the downtown area to be considered secure.

'Kill, kill, kill until a bright, red world emerges!'

The call of the masses will be answered swiftly and decisively; those who have 'incurred the bitter wrath of the people' should be executed without delay. Old Liu is already dead.

Along the dark corridor I hear the familiar sound of death shackles from behind the closed doors, the others who are waiting. I am brought to Number Thirteen, where a white-haired prisoner sits atop a rolled quilt, leaning against the window.

He has got to be a plant, this odd little man with the decadent but rather elegant name of Bin Lanting, *Lanting* meaning 'orchid pavilion.' My days are numbered. It is common knowledge that prison authorities isolate prisoners with death sentences. A trustworthy individual is always assigned to monitor the individual so that no 'accidents' happen.

Only when Bin Lanting stands up do I realize how very short he is. His face is long and homely. He wears that wooden expression brought to a fine art by the worldly-wise Chinese. A look of utter stupidity, underlaid by a tense wariness. Bin's clothing resembles neither those of a worker nor cadre. Perhaps he is a prosperous urbanite; no doubt the kind with a particularly complicated background.

I spread my quilt on the outer half of the bunk, which can sleep about three people and which takes up half the cell, and lie down, exhausted. Pleasant pictures, memories of my childhood come back to me, one after the other, fragments of songs and smells of flowers. The world is a wonderful place; I want more than anything to keep on living. Everything in my short life, even the pain, deserves to be remembered and savored.

I drift back to a warm spring evening in 1966. My parents, my brother and sister, and I are rocking gently back and forth. In a boat in the middle of the lake, we are talking about 'Drafting Able-bodied Men,' the new movie set in Sichuan on the eve of the Communist takeover. The powerful, evil landlords are contrasted with the ignorant, small landlords. But the papers have begun to criticize the film, saying that all landowners are reactionary. As the sun dips behind the pale-green willows, I assume a knowing tone. 'You know, Papa, you've been influenced by this kind of class compromise, too. You said once that Grandfather was a fair landlord, without any power, that whenever there was a famine he would help them fight the drought.' My father smiles mysteriously. Perhaps there is a trace of unspoken encouragement there; perhaps I only wish there were.

The next day Chen Lingmei, head of the Shengwulian Special

Investigation Team of the Provincial PPG, interrogates me with the help of two other old cadres.

'We've brought you back again so that you can account for your past. To let you make a clean breast of the crimes perpetrated by your whole gang.' He pauses. 'I presume you know Liu Fengxiang?'

I do not respond.

'*He* was a counterrevolutionary Shengwulian black hand and we've *killed* him!'

'So it was you,' I think. Looking into his gloating face, I am suddenly filled with hatred and a desperate desire for revenge.

'Starting today, you will not be able to communicate directly with your relatives,' Chen continues. 'If you need anything, tell us—we'll pass the information along.'

The situation is bad. At labor camp I was informed that my family could visit me once a year and that I could send and receive one letter each month. And at Zuojiatang, for the longest time, I had received one parcel a month. But here I am completely cut off, not only from my family, but from other prisoners. The gnomelike 'Elegant Orchid' will monitor my behavior, and after the authorities have gathered the information they need, they will execute me. I have seen many prisoners with 'crimes' lighter than my own be put to death and I have even become aware of the arbitrariness of the sentences. For the same act, you could die or you could walk out scot-free. When the political situation is unstable, as it is now, political 'chickens' have to be slaughtered. There is no doubt in my mind that someone like me, who has not been at all shy about challenging the current regime, has qualified for a death sentence.

I begin to consider in earnest how to deal with the crisis at hand. My first impulse is to flee before they have a chance to put the death shackles on me. But even after careful inspection of the surrounding area I can't come up with a decent plan. Each time I am taken to the office to be interrogated, I look for a way out along the way. I consider bending or filing the iron bar on the window, but can't find a suitable tool. Finally I decide to punch a hole through the ceiling. If I can scale the rear cell wall and stand on the window, then I can crawl through the ceiling up onto the roof and out into the courtyard. I still need to think of a way to get over the yard wall. The only real obstacle to this plan is Bin Lanting.

What I need is a drug that will knock him out for a few hours while I work. If I have to beat him to death, the noise might alert the guards. I remember that certain plastics are toxic; perhaps I can pulverize a piece of plastic and poison him.

In the last week or so the Changsha authorities have held two mass killing meetings, sentencing almost a hundred people to death each time. Half of these have been politicals—including Old Liu. From the loudspeakers of the nearby units—an automobile parts factory, a gymnasium, and the New Life Silk Factory, we hear intermittent broadcasts notifying city residents that tomorrow there is to be yet another sentencing meeting at East Wind Square where some sixty 'counterrevolutionaries'—more politicals—will be sentenced to death. I must act. I must act quickly.

But when I wake early the next morning I hear only silence. In the past, whenever there was to be a sentencing meeting, there was a steady clanging of metal as the guards exchanged the shackles for the death knot. In fact, everything seems a little strange.

Finally at about nine o'clock the speakers announce that the sentencing meeting has been cancelled. Soon thereafter an inmate who was supposed to have been executed today 'phones' me from the back window, saying that his sentence has been commuted to fifteen years.

At the beginning of Strike One–Oppose Three, Party Central gave the power of execution to the provincial authorities. Local Conservatives have wasted no time in working with the authorities to eliminate as many politicals as they could. But now, on the eve of this most recent sentencing meeting, Party Central in Beijing has reclaimed its exclusive right to declare the death penalty. Most likely the local authorities have been killing too many chickens, too fast.

For now, at least, the danger of death has passed. I look at Bin Lanting with new eyes, and realize sheepishly that this little man hasn't been sent to spy on me; he just happens to be locked up in the same cell.

Bin Lanting comes from another era and has a lot of old-fashioned habits which are bothersome. He feels obliged to belch some twenty times a day; on top of this he must do at least one set of *qigong*, 'breathing kung fu,' during which he produces more obnoxious noises. His cheeks puff out, and after the longest time, he emits out a loud mouthful of stomach gas. Sometimes it sounds as if he is going to spill his guts out. I have been trying to figure out whether this is part of his routine or some sort of gastric disorder.

And he is continually passing gas. I suppose the fact that he

is approaching sixty is the reason for this flatulence. After every
blast, he gently taps his behind to facilitate the escape of the
imprisoned air.

We do calisthenics together twice a day, once in the morning,
once after our noon rest. I do the modern kind; he sticks to his
breathing kung fu.

After I make him a chess set out of paper and rice, Chinese
chess becomes our primary form of recreation. He rarely beats
me; still, he is patient and usually a good sport about losing.
Every once in a while, though, when he makes a wrong move
and I eat up one of his important men, he will snatch the piece
back, saying, 'I didn't want to move there.' His brows knit and
he becomes argumentative, like a sullen child.

But Bin is a knowledgeable student of history, especially of
the relatively modern Ming and Qing dynasties; he has read
countless volumes of official and non-official accounts. He also
enjoys filling in my educational gaps with stories of the ancient
periods of the Spring and Autumn and the Warring States.[2]

The Qin State, he tells me, was a culturally backward nation
in western China, but the king was very humble and often
solicited people from foreign countries to counsel him. One day
the Qin ruler asked a scholar from another state to visit his court
and expound on his philosophy of government. This scholar
began to speak of 'the way kings rule with benevolence and
righteousness.' He advised the king how to love and protect his
citizens. 'The lord is lesser than his people; the people are the
foundation of the nation and food is all-important to the people.'
The king lost interest, however, and began to doze. When the
scholar looked over and saw the king nodding, he was secretly
delighted and immediately began talking about the 'way of
dictators'—the Chinese equivalent of Machiavelli's The Prince.
He began emphasizing that commoners did not understand the
political maneuvering required to rule a country, that the public
was often in favor of policies that were not good for the nation.
The king, therefore, was by necessity required to make use of
unscrupulous political methods. A king had to know how to lie
and how to scheme; and he had to 'threaten the people with
regulations,' cruelly punishing dissenters. On the other hand,
'the man who obeyed the regulations would know mercy.'
Hearing this, the Qin king was overjoyed and immediately
appointed the scholar prime minister.

[2] The Spring and Autumn period lasted from 770–476 BC; the Warring States from 475–221
BC.

Some months passed. One of the prime minister's advisers warned him that his life would soon end. The prime minister was stupefied. The adviser then asked him to tell him how each of the previous prime ministers of Qin had died. The premier related the story of how each had offended the conservative nobility with his successful reforms. As soon as the king died, the conservatives forced the heir to kill the prime minister. The premier finished his account, visibly rattled. He paused, and then asked, 'What should I do?'

'Retire now, at the peak of your career,' was the reply. He should withdraw from the court altogether and give his power to someone else, someone who would agree to continue his policies. The premier relinquished his title to the adviser and retired to the countryside to enjoy the life of a recluse.

But the lesson of quitting while one was ahead was lost on Han Xin, one of the founders of the Han Dynasty. Bin Lanting paces back and forth in the narrow cell, his hands clasped behind his back and delivers the moral of his tale: 'Once the wily rabbit is dead, the hunting dog gets cooked.'

It is late May, and Lin Biao is more powerful than ever. Bin's meaning could not be more clear.

'This opera called the Cultural Revolution is a real kick,' he chuckles. 'The only problem is that, for the audience, the price of tickets is a bit steep.'

Though I don't know exactly why Bin Lanting has been imprisoned, it's hard to imagine that he was ever directly involved in any organization. Based on the many allegories he has told me, however, I speculate he is in on a charge related to this untoward political commentary. I smile to myself, remembering the Chinese character for prison: 'speech' surrounded by two dogs.

One day Bin tells me the story of how he first became interested in politics. In the days before Liberation, he ran a small watch repair shop that was patronized by many well-to-do merchants and top Nationalist officials.

'Back then the Communists had hardly any influence in the cities; nobody even felt their existence. Then, in 1949, they occupied Changsha and my customers started disappearing. As the old saying goes, "Men can perform deeds, but heaven determines if they succeed."'

It wasn't until he saw the official bulletins a few months later that he realized that many of his patrons, among them many close friends, had been purged.

'The bulletins contained no evidence, no facts related to

a crime, just the job titles the people had held under the Nationalists. Dozens of these things were posted every day—it was horrible—each with a big red 'X' on it. And, Little Yang, what we're seeing now is just like what it was then—this is what it's like at the changing of a dynasty!'

When I think back on my trip from the station, the roadside crowds and placards, and the hysterical cries to kill, I know what he means. Revolution. Before the Cultural Revolution, the mental picture I had always painted of the Revolution of 1949 was beautiful, even sacred. My entire family had profited from the war: we were so full of the self-righteousness of conquerors that we were blind to the side of revolution that was brutal, dehumanizing, irrational. The victory had been built upon the blood and bones of ten million people, people who had always been invisible to me.

I am silent for a moment, then mutter, 'So what is the best way for political change to occur, do you think?'

He answers my question with a question: 'Do you know the strategy Sima Yi used against the Shu State?'

A military general of the Wei State during the Three Kingdoms period, Sima Yi was an excellent swordsman, but his intelligence was inferior to Zhuge Liang, the celebrated premier advisor for the Shu. I try to come up with the strategy Bin is referring to.

Pushing his glasses up on his nose, Bin continues, 'Sima Yi knew he couldn't beat Zhuge Liang, so he decided to stall. Zhuge Liang was in poor health, that much was clear, and was bound to die before Sima. This tactic enabled him to conquer the Shu.'

He is speaking in parables again. Though I am not certain exactly which contemporary political figure he is alluding to, I don't care. I will use this strategy with Mao Zedong. The day of Mao's death will be the day of my emancipation.

'The Communist Party and the Nationalist Party are so very different . . .' Bin Lanting speaks as if he is a thousand miles away. After pausing briefly, he suddenly asks, 'Do you know the old way to write the Chinese character for political "party"?'

'A "still" on top; a "black" below.'

'Correct! "Still black" could only be—a "party"!'

I laugh aloud. He is right, of course. It doesn't matter which party you are talking about, it is bound to have a dark and seamy side. Chinese characters are wonderful.

It is autumn. The rain drizzles down outside my window, bringing with it melancholy, resignation, and a thousand different memories. On days like these, Master Bin, as I now call him in deference to his status as a petty proprietor, thinks back to his life before Liberation.

He was born into the Hunan rural gentry. Every time he came home to the countryside from Changsha, where he was attending high school, his paternal relatives gave a banquet in his honor to 'rinse off the dust.' All the ranking clan members and local gentry would attend. Master Bin is partial to the idea of a formal clan hierarchy and tries to persuade me that a powerful gentry is a good thing.

'Throughout the history of China,' he lectures, 'informal organizations like these have served as a kind of buffer, neutralizing the power of the government and allowing the villages a certain degree of autonomy.' He stops short, but the point is made: by destroying the buffer, the Communist Party had placed the localities completely under their control.

Rarely does Master Bin directly state his dissatisfaction with communism. But one day he sees an item in the *Hunan Daily* raving about the bumper crop of tea oil in the eastern portion of the province.

In outrage, he throws down the paper. 'Before Liberation our home town produced 800,000 catties of tea oil a year. After Liberation we didn't even get a third of what we used to before. Everybody knows that if you give the tea trees over to individuals to handle, you can increase production, but no one dares to say so. Even if you did say it, it wouldn't do any good.'

Another time Master Bin comes across an article on the new kind of doctors that are being sent out into the countryside. 'Of course they need barefoot doctors!' he blurts out. 'All the real doctors have already been driven out of their homes. That, or beaten to death.'

Not surprisingly, Master Bin thinks back favorably upon the Nationalist military. On more than one occasion he mentions one Nationalist major he encountered when he was in high school who could speak excellent English and who was exceedingly polite to him. He emphasizes to me that most of the Communist officers he met could barely read Chinese.

But for all of this, he often praises the abilities of Mao Zedong. Telling me about a chapter in Ming history, he remarks that Zhu Yuanzhang, the founder of the dynasty, wiped out the local gentry of the preceding dynasty and installed his own officials. But, he adds, 'a dynasty like the Nationalists' tends to be extremely unstable.'

'How is that?' I ask.

As if he is opening the lid of a secret box, he confides to me with a hoarse whisper, 'Because it kept the foundation of the old dynasty intact; it didn't start from scratch the way the Communists did. Mao Zedong is amazing. He replaced his enemies to a man. He destroyed the entire social foundation of the Nationalists.' He fixes me in the eyes as if to say, 'The stability and longevity of the current regime are hallmarks, not of enlightenment, but of despotism.'

In 1956 Master Bin was compelled to convert his watch repair shop to joint state–private ownership. The first floor of his property on May First Road was seized by the government for a state-run bookstore, and he was allowed to retain the second as his private dwelling. He whispers to me about another petty proprietor with a similar background, who went up against the authorities by insisting on starting a privately run children's clothing store, but who was driven out into the streets during the Cultural Revolution when his building was confiscated. The man was ultimately found dead in a back alley.

In spite of the fact that he lives in mortal fear of the Communist regime, Master Bin is not free from the cynical resignation so common in his generation. 'As long as a country doesn't get involved in any major wars for twenty years or so, the economy will develop eventually. Chinese are always quick to react to a shift in power. You know the saying, "Better to be a dog in peace than a man in war."'

I mention to him that while I was at the labor farm, I ran into a lot of prisoners who had been sent there because they had criticized Mao.

'Oh, well, when you've been head of a family for a couple of years, even the dogs resent you,' he responds evasively, nervously eyeing the pen in his hand.

Though Master Bin is just an observer of the political arena, he can sound like a player. One day while he is reading through an article denouncing Liu Shaoqi, he sighs and mutters to himself as if he is having trouble holding onto the lever in one of his watches. 'It will take more than a couple of years to root out the Liu Shaoqi line; and then there are the new opposition forces that have come out of the Cultural Revolution.' He talks as if he is sitting in the general's tent on the eve of battle, laying out strategy.

From April to October 1970, the papers champion the achievements of Lin Biao, pronouncing him the natural successor to Mao. One morning Master Bin looks at Lin Biao's picture in the newspaper and makes a wry face.

'Little Yang, do you know the story of how Emperor Kang Xi

passed down his crown? Kang Xi had a lot of sons, but he liked the fourteenth prince the best; the boy was upright and capable. He also liked the fourth prince, who was equally bright but more subtle; that is to say, he knew how to hide his intentions. But because this son was mean and vindictive, the emperor did not feel comfortable about letting him reign.'

Behind his thick glasses, Master Bin blinks. His eyes, which seldom reveal his true feelings, radiate the inner peace of an old man who has no quarrel with the world.

'In his will, Kang Xi wrote in classical Chinese, "The fourteenth prince shall take the throne." When he died and the document was opened, however, the words that appeared were "The throne shall go to the fourth prince." Someone had secretly added one stroke to the character for "ten," effectively transforming it into a "go to." As soon as the fourth prince was in power, he put all his brothers under house arrest and subsequently devised ways to kill them off, one by one.'

I listen with great pleasure. Nobody, not even Mao Zedong can control his court after his death. Once again, Master Bin blinks contentedly, as if to say, 'Now you understand what Mao's passing his throne to Lin Biao is really about!'

For fourteen months we share our tiny cell. Strike One–Oppose Three has pretty much blown over and the country is preparing for the Spring Festival. I am to be shipped back to Reconstruction Farm. Master Bin and I are friends.

In 1978 I visit his repair shop and invite him over to our house for dinner. He never has been sentenced, simply released after the Lin Biao incident without explanation. A man with skills like his is in great demand, and he has resumed his former occupation. On the surface it appears that Master Bin's life has returned to normal. When he comes to see me, he shrouds himself in the formal etiquette of the Nationalists—greeting my father, he bows deeply from the waist, a gesture of great respect I have rarely seen in my lifetime.

I run into him again in 1980, and learn that the Communists have decided to return all property that was previously privately owned.

'Are you going to open up your shop again? If you're still interested in doing business, this storefront location is perfect!' I am enthusiastic.

Shaking his head, he tells me he has already decided to move away from May First Road in the downtown business area, where he will give up his two-story townhouse to the government in exchange for two apartment units on the outskirts of town. His son will soon be married and needs a place of his own.

I am speechless. Master Bin is one of those resourceful people who always has a trick or two up his sleeve. I know how much he values real estate, technical expertise, and his career. And now, just when the authorities are about to implement an enlightened policy, he is unwilling to take advantage of it. He has chosen to forget about property and business. I remember the expression in his eyes when he told me the story of Han Xin: I know this man cannot have made his decision in haste. Borrowing from the ancient to reflect upon the modern, Master Bin must have thought a great deal about how the Communist dynasty would evolve.

It would appear that he has lost all faith in the government. And he doesn't even care.

14

Chief Engineer Yu

▼

Master Bin is doing his silly exercises again, the ones he learned at the traditional middle school he attended in the 1930s. His routine is incredibly simple: he bends; he stands up; he extends his arms forward; he brings them back to his side. When he has finished, he sits on the bunk, closes his eyes, and takes up his noisy breathing kung fu. Time for me to jump down and do my pushups. I am on 'two' when Master Bin opens his owl-like eyes widely and whispers, 'Someone's coming!'

The lock rattles. Warden Lu appears with a fat little man of about forty-five who is staggering under a mountain of quilts and books. The door closes behind him. Gasping, the little man drops his load on the bunk, and quickly turns to hammer on the door. Soon Warden Lu is back and our new cellmate exits. Moments later he returns, clasping still more books.

With his light skin and wisp of a mustache, the owner of all these things looks just like the entrepreneurs—the villains—you see in the movies. His stomach puffs out so much that he resembles a large penguin when he walks, yet his eyes sparkle with intelligence. Corpulent physiques like his are a rare sight these days, especially in jail. Either this man is a high-ranking cadre or he is a well-connected 'big-skull'; in any case, no one who should be in Model Prison.

We look on as he pulls out bottles of various shapes and sizes from one of his bags. 'Mind if I sleep next to the wall?' he asks. Without waiting for a response, he begins to stow his books and containers on the ledge, chatting with us all the while. His voice is soft and full, and he speaks the Changsha dialect. Several days later, he reveals to us the contents of his bottles—lard, glucose, and royal jelly—and his name—Yu Yuyi.

Like Scheherazade, Old Yu tells us a new tale every evening.

'I was minding my own business, just having a bowl of noodles,' he begins the first night. 'Sitting next to me, were two

Red Guards wearing the usual uniforms and red armbands, who were quite obviously from Beijing. I heard them ask for noodles in hot and sour soup. But when the order came, they told the waiter they wanted noodles with shredded pork instead, so he went to prepare this. When they finished, they walked toward the door. The waiter demanded that they pay the bill. One of the Red Guards, who was very tall, snapped his fingers at the waiter and said, "What bill?"

' "The bill for the noodles with shredded pork."

' "Noodles with shredded pork? Huh? We just changed our order from hot and sour soup to shredded pork."

' "But you didn't pay for the hot-and-sour soup noodles either!"

' "If we didn't eat hot and sour soup noodles, why should we have to pay for it?"

'The waiter was so upset he began to curse, "You arrogant shits! Your fathers must be tossing in their graves."

'The tall Red Guard became violent. "This whole country was brought to its knees by my old man. Back when he was fighting Chiang Kai-shek and his bandits, I doubt very much whether you had even been conceived!" After that, those two high-ranking cadre kids wiped their mouths and ran. The waiter knew from the way they talked that they were original Red Guard Pickets! Too bad that the Changsha Rebels hadn't mustered full strength then, or they would have put those kids in their place.'

Though Old Yu speaks deliberately and without emotion, I note silently that he sympathizes with the Rebels. Later that evening he tells us of the bitter years of famine (1959–61).

'Back then there were shortages of everything. Everyday items like shoes and tea mugs just weren't available; you had to line up for every single thing you wanted to buy. A bowl of saccharine water containing a few grains of rice cost fifteen *fen* (cents). We engineers were considered the intellectual elite and commanded top salaries, but if there's nothing to buy with your money, you still go hungry. That's why every month when we got paid I gave a lot of cash to my son and my daughter, and told them to wait in any line they could on their way to and from school. One day they would come home with a mug; the next day it would be a couple of pounds of fruit candy. One afternoon when my son got home, he handed me a train ticket. I asked him what it was for, and he says to me, "The line was really long, Dad, so I had to wait for two hours and I still only came up with just one ticket for the whole family."

'I was absolutely furious. "We're not going anywhere," I said. "What in the world did you buy a train ticket for?"

"But Dad, didn't you say that as long as I saw a long line, no matter what it was, I should get as much as I could of it, even if I had to spend every last *fen*?"

Master Bin and I are laughing even before he finishes. Soon I realize that Old Yu's humor is almost always political in nature. His tales are less anecdotes of real people or real events, I suspect, than allegories of our times; he concocts them passionately to make his points.

His story about the Red Guards, for example, cannot possibly be true. There were no waiters during the Cultural Revolution. When you went to a restaurant, you paid before you sat down to eat. Another humorous tale concerned a high-level official who, not long after Liberation, became outraged when he attended his first basketball game and promptly commanded that the game be halted. The individual in charge of recreation was rebuked and instructed to go out immediately and acquire several hundred basketballs. 'This is simply not acceptable,' the official reprimanded; 'Ten people fighting over one ball, as if our socialism can't provide a ball for every player. Now I want you to go out and buy balls for *everyone* so they can have a good time and understand the superiority of our system.' I heard a different version of this joke at Zuojiatang, in which the hero was not a high-level cadre but Han Fuqu, the governor of the Nationalist provincial government during the 1930s.

Grinning broadly, Old Yu continues. When the Communists took over the administration of Changsha, he tells me, one cadre became extremely distressed upon learning that traffic regulations stipulated that cars and pedestrians keep to the right.

'We can't have this! If everyone stays on the right-hand side, who's going to walk on the left?' A bystander explained to the government cadre that an oncoming pedestrian keeping to the right would in fact be on his left. But after the cadre finally absorbed the situation, he frowned again. 'The Communist Party is a left-wing party; how can we let the people walk on the right? No, we must change it—from now on all pedestrians will walk on the left!'

Story after story, he fills the empty nights of Model Prison. Amidst my laughter, I think to myself: Old Yu's being here most certainly has something to do with his political barbs.

One day he reveals to me he got a Master's Degree in civil engineering from Yale in the 1940s. The War of Resistance against Japan was drawing to a close, a time when every Chinese who had been educated overseas burned with desire to settle down and do something great for the nation. After running with Chiang Kai-shek and losing the presidential election in 1948, Cheng Qian returned to the provincial capital and established the Department of Construction. From the best universities in China and abroad, Cheng recruited a top-notch team of professionals to help him rebuild Changsha's roads, waterworks, and industries. Old Yu was among this group of intellectuals, and recounts the era with a bittersweet pride. 'We were the first,' he adds with a chuckle, 'to wear modern bathing trunks in the municipal swimming pool. The older residents accused us of corrupting the morals of the city's youth.'

Old Yu cannot say enough good things about Cheng Qian. Back in Hunan, the general had wasted no time in carrying out the '3–7 Rent Reduction,' the law which forced landlords to lower their rents from 50 percent to almost 25 percent. Cheng valued and used intellectuals to a much greater extent than did Chiang Kai-shek, who had been more interested in military affairs than engineering projects, giving control of the newly formed Construction Department entirely to the graduates of American colleges.

'In those days there were only four departments in the provincial government: Education, Police, Taxation, and Construction. Compare that to the hundreds of departments we have today, where for industry alone you have the Department of Light Industry, the Department of Heavy Industry, the First Bureau of Light Industry, the Second Bureau of Light Industry . . .'

A man of boundless energy, Cheng Qian was determined to modernize Changsha's traffic system by widening and straightening its main thoroughfares; in the downtown area, he wanted to pave the old cobblestone of the Octagonal Pavilion with asphalt, which meant relocating several stores that stood in the way. The owners tried to buy him off with a gold brick, but he sent it right back, and the roads were completed on schedule.

Then, to everyone's surprise, just when the Communist troops were closing in on the city limits, Hunan's provincial chairman declared an insurrection, surrendering the government to the Communists and volunteering to assist in the peaceful transition of power. Old Yu and the other intellectuals at the Department of Construction loyally followed Cheng Qian out of the Nationalist era and into the next. They were now reporting to the Department of Water Conservancy and Electric Power, where they went on to design many of the large-scale flood control projects built in Hunan during the fifties. No one anticipated that, during the Cultural Revolution, Lin Biao would announce out of the blue, 'Hunan's peaceful liberation was not peaceful—the residual Nationalist bastards still penetrate the province.' Cheng Qian and his staff were suddenly targeted for criticism by the masses.

My generation had always been taught that Cheng Qian was a backward and incompetent bureaucrat. Only in the school of Model Prison was it possible to learn that Cheng had made significant contributions to local public works.

The piles of books and journals stacked neatly around the cell fascinate me, for they are for the most part treatises on hydraulic and civil engineering. I confide to Old Yu that while in prison I hope to finish up high school math and get a start on college math. He seems genuinely pleased and spends several hours designing a curriculum for me. The next morning after breakfast we tackle logarithms, and for the next six months we have two hours of math every day until we part company.

The importance of logical thought cannot be overemphasized, he admonishes me during our first session. A case in point: the invention of the I-beam. A youth, having drawn a sketch of a beam under stress, realized that when the beam was weighted from above, the upper half was compressed, while the lower half was stretched. However, the middle received no stress whatsoever, so that by removing part of this interior section, you could safely reduce the beams' weight. The invention, Old Yu intones, was worked out entirely with pencil and paper; subsequent experiments only confirmed the logic of the concept.

Not surprisingly, the former engineer does not appreciate the 'theory of practice' so popular among students and professionals alike and speaks bitterly about his experiences in the classroom. Upon discovering that Old Yu didn't know how to ride a bicycle, one physics student with poor marks stood up and announced, 'All this gobbledygook about the moment of force, the arm of force, and balance. Why can't you just *show* us balance? As Chairman Mao has said, "True knowledge comes from practice!"'

Old Yu sighs. 'I told him that theory was important precisely because it could predict events that couldn't be enacted. For example, no one can lift the earth, yet we can prove theoretically that, with a long enough lever and a proper pivot, any child could lift the planet. I told him, too, the process by which the I-beam was invented. No experimentation, just deductive reasoning on paper.'

During the day, Old Yu spends much of his time calculating the optimum shape of various types of irrigation pipes and various runoff coefficients. To my amazement I discover calculus can be used to find the extreme values of a function and thus help solve optimization problems in engineering technology. Our society's focus on politics is total: virtually everybody has forgotten about the applications of science. The once popular adage, 'Armed with physics, chem, and math, there'll be nothing in your path', is ridiculed from kindergarten to college.

Old Yu has a thick looseleaf notebook in which he continually scribbles. For days I pester him to tell me what he is doing. Finally he shows me. It is a book he began before the Cultural Revolution and completed in his previous cell, containing a design for a gravimeter that can measure solids. To determine an object's ratio of weight to volume, one has only to deposit it in the graduated container, a liquid-bearing vessel in the shape of a logarithmic curve. I am impressed.

Lecturing on runoff coefficients, Old Yu uses the following illustration:

'The Dazhai Brigade, the model for our nation's agriculture, repaired the dam there three times, but not once did they bother to calculate the maximum runoff. As a result, the dam was washed away by a landslide in the first heavy rain. And still they insist that all of China should learn from these mindless and unscientific methods.'

Master Bin blinks and clears his throat.

Without warning, there is a violent clatter at the door.

'Out! Quick!' The voice is loud and brittle. 'Leave all your belongings inside!'

Prisoners line the corridors of both blocks. An unarmed soldier stands by each of the cells. Soldiers with rifles guard both ends of the corridor. Several disappear into Number Thirteen, followed by a loud uproar. 'It's an unannounced search,' croaks Master Bin, who is unusually pale. An hour later we are allowed back inside.

The *haozi* looks as if it had been vandalized by thieves. Clothes and quilts are strewn across the cement floor. The bottles on the ledge have disappeared. Master Bin explains that cadres carry out such searches once every year or so to ferret out forbidden goods. With politicals like us, this is an opportunity for them to discover dissident writings which can be used as criminal evidence.

'My book!'

Old Yu rushes to the door and begins to pound with both fists.

A soldier flips up the wooden cover of the round window. 'What's the problem?' he bellows.

'One of my manuscripts is missing—there's years of research in there. It's just a technical work. Nothing but hydraulic engineering!'

The guard laughs. 'Why do you insist on taking the road of "white expertise" and "technology first"? Pack it up once and for all. Make an honest attempt to reform your reactionary outlook on life! If you have free time, you should use it to study the writings of Chairman Mao and to reflect upon your own reactionary thoughts. All that capitalist intellectual stuff is completely useless! To society and to you!'

The wooden cover slams shut.

'When a scholar meets a soldier, even a good argument is made in vain,' quotes Master Bin softly.

◆

Neither of my cellmates has any idea what labor camp is like, so that they relish the stories I tell of my three months at Reconstruction Farm. They ask questions about everything: what the farm looked like, the number of prisoners, the kind of work we did, what we ate. I mention to them that I met quite a few prisoners who longed for the days of Liu Shaoqi because life had been easier for them then. Every brigade had set up its own canteen. But in 1966, when the canteens were closed, they were compelled to buy things through the cadres.

'Liu Shaoqi? What's so good about Liu Shaoqi?' Old Yu interrupts. 'He certainly wasn't shy about attacking the Rightists in '57 and didn't have a clue about how to run the government. And he had some nerve saying that mechanization wasn't suitable for the "Chinese style" of agriculture. Even though the level of mechanization of agriculture hasn't been all that extensive, you can still see that the more they mechanize, the poorer the peasants become. If they would just let individuals in the villages handle things, mechanization would take care of itself in most cases.'

'So you got hit in '57, too?'

'Oh, I was labeled an *ultra*-rightist. Why, you ask? Because I'd been following what was going on in Taiwan. When their National Assembly met, I asked some friends overseas to send a telegram of congratulations.'

After 1957 he had never uttered the word 'Taiwan' in public again.

Old Yu then tells me about how he and several other friends who had studied in the United States got together after the Japanese were defeated in the War of Resistance. They were worried about how quickly the Communist camp had been developing since the close of World War II. 'I told them, "If the Japanese had collaborated closely with the Germans and had attacked Russia instead of China, the Germans would have fought their way east instead of west, the Soviets would have been destroyed, and the world would never again have been threatened by Communism." '

I start, in spite of myself, for his unspoken assertion is chilling: Better a world dominated by Hitler than threatened by international Communism.

'Twenty years ago many people were saying how terrible the Red Peril was,' he continues. 'But the way things look now, it's much worse than anyone ever expected.' He pauses. 'Why even if we had gone along with Stalin's crazy notion of splitting the Heavenly Kingdom along the lines of the Yangtze River, with the Nationalists and the Communists each taking half, we still would be better off than we are right now!'

I glance over at Master Bin. Behind the lenses of his glasses, his eyes show no emotion, so that I am unable to tell whether he agrees with what Yu is saying or not. With several months of labor camp experience now under my belt, I find some of Old Yu's ideas almost palatable. Had I heard such radically anti-communist statements in Zuojiatang, I would have rejected them out of hand.

Old Yu is clearly not one of those engineers who is interested solely in engineering. Like many other intellectuals I've met in prison, he spends a lot of time talking about history and books, including *The Romance of the Three Kingdoms*, the classical historical novel that tells of China's second-century heroes and their diplomatic and political strategies. This book, he tells me, is 'required reading for anyone who wants to understand politics.'

'So, who do you think is to blame for the loss of Jieting?' 'Losing Jieting' is his favorite chapter.

'Ma Su, of course,' I respond. 'He disobeyed the order to set up camp at the foot of the mountain, insisting instead that they go up to the top, and that was how the Wei kingdom forces were able to set fire to the entire mountainside.'

Old Yu smiles. 'No, you're mistaken. It was not Ma Su's fault. The entire responsibility lay with his superior, Zhuge Liang. In the next chapter, "Wiping Away Tears as Ma Su is Beheaded,"

Zhuge Liang quickly shifts the blame to Ma Su in order to pacify the troops. The same thing happened when Cao Cao killed the provisions officer during the grain shortage, accusing him of graft. Why, that officer never stole any grain! Cao Cao just needed a head to sacrifice as part of his political games. Zhuge Liang was actually much better at playing this kind of game than Cao Cao; he *never* showed his hand.' Old Yu looks up briefly, then mutters, 'The same thing is going on right now— everybody's attributing all the problems with Communism to Liu Shaoqi.'

I'm not so sure I can swallow all of this, but the comparison of Mao and Zhuge Liang is interesting. Old Yu believed that, during the Cultural Revolution, Mao pushed the blame for the mistakes made by the Communist Party onto Liu Shaoqi. Mao hadn't directly faulted Liu Shaoqi and Deng Xiaoping for the 1959 error, but he *had* taken full advantage of the fact that Liu and Deng were persecuting people who opposed the Communist Party, inciting the persecuted to rebel. Unaware of behind-the-scenes political tensions, Old Yu thinks Mao, Liu, and Deng are equally accountable.

Sometimes Old Yu's pedantry gets to be a bit much. He obsesses endlessly about isolated phenomena. He investigates whether or not mosquitoes are able to track people by following their footsteps. After days of close observation, he announces solemnly: 'My experimentation has led me to believe that mosquitoes are able to locate humans only by following the smell of the human body.'

Master Bin and I burst out laughing.

But Old Yu can tell a good love story. For three nights he keeps us spellbound with a tale about a romantic encounter at the New Life Silk Factory. The silk factory was a labor reform institution to the rear of Model Prison housing mainly women prisoners, though men with long, twenty-year terms were occasionally sent there as well.

'I heard this one when I was still in the big cell,' he begins. 'From a political with a death sentence. The hero of the story was a man by the name of Liu Jiajin, a member of the underground "Chinese Democracy Party," in for twenty years. Before they grabbed him, he was working as a mechanic; so he was brought to the silk factory to do maintenance work on the looms.'

Old Yu nods soberly. 'The heroine of this story is White Orchid, a singer who used to perform for underground salons during the early fifties. After Liberation, Changsha didn't have much of a night life to speak of, so the kids of the old Nationalist upper crust got together to sing and dance. Tunes like "Good Flowers Don't Bloom for Long; the Good Times Don't Last" and dances like the rumba and the tango were officially banned. Before too long, their evening parties were declared "black society gatherings." Many of the participants got prison sentences.

'Well, White Orchid was no exception. She got five years, which is how she came to the New Life Silk Factory to be a weaver. Of course, at a place like New Life, there were lots of women prisoners, whereas men were exceedingly scarce. A debonair young prisoner like Liu Jiajin was bound to catch the ladies' attention in short order.'

I think back to the mornings when I've gone out to dump the latrine bucket, fetch water, or scrub a pot in the rear of the prison, and looked across the courtyard to see a host of women inmates crowded at the window, peering down at us men prisoners. They must be the women from New Life Silk Factory. Despite the fact that I have virtually no experience with women, when those women look at me, the fire of desire in their eyes is enough to make my heart race.

'Back in the mid-fifties they were still using the "jailer system," in which a few well-behaved individuals were made honorary "jailers" over the rest of the inmates. That way, the cadres had only to keep track of the jailers. The woman serving as jailer in White Orchid's group was doing time for murder— she and her lover had killed her husband. She was supposed to get the death penalty, but somehow had gotten her term commuted to twenty years. Because her last name was Sun, everybody called her "Mistress Sun."'

Master Bin and I nod appreciatively. 'Second Mistress Sun' was the name of the conniving, cannibalistic innkeeper that we both know from the classical novel *Tales of the Marshes*.

'At meals, or before the lights went out at night, all the women in their work group would sit around and talk about Liu Jiajin. Some said he was a "sappy ghost" who was immune to women. And some said, "Don't be fooled by that sweet white face; once you get him into bed, he's probably not all that great!" Only two women refrained from joining in the conversation— White Orchid, who had a crush on him and wasn't about to let anyone know, and the jailer, Mistress Sun, who naturally had to maintain a certain decorum.

'Back then, grain rations were slim, so that while the women prisoners could usually get enough to eat, the men were always hungry. Early on, White Orchid noticed how Jiajin wolfed down his rice, scraping up each grain with his spoon, so she decided that she would start saving part of her own rice ration, which she wrapped in paper and dropped into his toolbox when nobody was looking. After many days had gone by, Jiajin finally discovered who the 'fox spirit' was.[1]

'When White Orchid became ill and didn't show up at the looms for two days, Jiajin got so upset he ran around like an ant on a hot wok. His behavior did not escape the attention of Mistress Sun. The next day she called him aside. "White Orchid is sick on account of you," she scolded. "Don't you think you should visit her?"

' "How am I going to get into her cell?" he asked.

' "I'll put her in my *haozi* for an hour tomorrow, and you can go and see her,' replied Mistress Sun sympathetically. As she was a "free criminal," she had a cell to herself, located outside the workshop.

'And so, the following day Jiajin pretended he needed to inspect some machinery and wandered over in the direction of Mistress Sun's *haozi*. When no one was looking, he pushed open the door. Sure enough, there was White Orchid. They melted into each other's arms in a frenzy of ecstasy and decided that White Orchid would begin to be sick once a month. The day after they made love for the first time, Mistress Sun stalked up to Jiajin and demanded to know why the machines seemed to be having so many problems.

' "There aren't any problems," he assured her quickly.

'Then all of a sudden she started shouting at him in a voice so loud it could be heard over the machinery. "You'd better change your attitude and concentrate on your work. Don't be letting your mind wander!" All the women prisoners stopped what they were doing to see what was wrong.

'The next morning White Orchid failed to show up for work again. Poor Jiajin didn't know what was going on, and he wasn't about to ask. Then, when it was almost lunchtime, Mistress Sun came up to him and whispered into his ear, "Go to my *haozi* at two this afternoon; White Orchid will be waiting."

'Jiajin agonized for a long time about what all of this might mean. "Mistress Sun was pretty hostile to me yesterday, but today she's back to her old self again; probably everything is all

---

[1] In the popular fiction of the Ming Dynasty, such as is found in *Strange Stories from a Chinese Studio*, 'fox spirits' enamored of mortal men appeared in human form as very kind and beautiful women.

right now," he told himself. "Unless White Orchid skipped her period. But it wouldn't be this quick." He considered all the possibilities over and over. Lunchtime came and went, but he had no appetite for food. Even before two o'clock, he was standing outside Mistress Sun's *haozi*. But when he pushed open the door this time, he found Mistress Sun sitting there on the bed, flushed and laughing slyly.

' "What's wrong?" Jiajin asked.

' "Nothing," she said. "I thought you might show *me* a good time for once." Then she slipped one arm around him and started to take off his clothes.'

Master Bin and I look at each other and grin. It is the final evening of the story, and I await the ending with both impatience and regret.

'But Jiajin rejected her advances. "This is no good," he said.

' "What do you mean, no good? If it's all right for you and White Orchid, why isn't it all right for you and me? And you had better not breathe a word to anyone. If this gets out, believe me, it won't do you one bit of good. And in case you're thinking about just going through the motions, don't, or you'll never see White Orchid here again." ' Old Yu renders Mistress Sun's conversation in a loud, shrill voice, making us laugh.

'Well, by now Jiajin realized he had been set up, but he was like a mute who has swallowed an herbal tonic; there was little he could do but pull himself together and satisfy her. From that time on, Jiajin had to go to Mistress Sun's *haozi* twice a month. His heart ached with guilt, but he couldn't do anything about it. And he didn't dare tell White Orchid what was happening.

'It was only when White Orchid told him that she had become pregnant that he finally broke down and told her the truth. When he asked her what they should do, she gave the matter a lot of thought, but couldn't come up with any way to deal with the situation and avoid disgrace. If Jiajin refused Mistress Sun, that would put an end to his trysts with White Orchid; on the other hand, he couldn't continue to sleep with Mistress Sun. That was no good either.

'Finally White Orchid told him that in three days' time she would let him know her decision. Several evenings later they were discovered on the wall of the New Life Silk Factory, hanging from the electric fence. Their bodies were drenched, for the rain was pounding down and the wind was whipping about the courtyard. Inside the woman's womb was a fetus about one-month old.

'Is this a true story?' I have to ask.

'You know, I'm not sure. I asked the same thing when I heard it, but no one seems to know. But one thing is true: in the late fifties the jailer system was abolished.'

It is January 1971, time for me to leave Liudongli and return to Reconstruction Farm. Old Yu remains in Number Thirteen. I never see him again, so I don't know if he is sentenced or freed. Like Master Bin, he has been secretive about his legal affairs. But what he did share has served me well. Sometimes late at night, when I have to use the log tables or look up a trigonometric function, I hear echoes of his sonorous voice; fragments of the tales he spun come back to me, causing me to pause and reflect.

Part IV

Back to the Farm

JANUARY 1971–MAY 1978

▼

15

The Remolding of Liu Zhenyu

▼

'The following prisoners will remain at camp today,' announces Supervisor Yang one June morning at assembly.

My name is among the seven on the list from my own detachment.

The early rice is planted and the pace has slowed, but I am glad to miss work. The other inmates shuffle off with considerable envy in their eyes.

Supervisor Yang orders the twenty-seven fortunates to gather around him. 'The government has arranged for you to participate in a five-day "Confess Your Guilt and Submit to the Law" class, beginning today. Most of you have yet to confess. Some of you even persist in appealing your cases. Our government—magnanimously setting aside this time for you to learn—has spared no cost in fulfilling its promise to mold you into new men.'

We are commanded to take our stools to a newly constructed room behind the block of little *haozi*. From where he sits at a simple desk in the corner, Supervisor Yang asks the prisoner-on-duty to pass out blank paper to each of us. Our assignment is to write one essay detailing our crimes and another essay acknowledging our guilt. I am not really sure what to write and so, in 'The Facts About My Crime,' I explain that though I had been raised by the Communist Government, during the Cultural Revolution I had forgotten what the Party had taught me:

'My sense of individualism became inflated, and I walked down the path of crime.'

Self-criticism had always gone something like this. The assumption is that, as long as you align yourself with the Communist Party and are willing to repent and reform, you deserve to be forgiven.

Supervisor Yang sits and reads our confessions, one by one. When he finishes with mine, he throws it on the table and barks,

'Yang Xiguang, you're determined not to confess, aren't you? Your case is scarcely one of "a little individualism." You have political ambitions! You are a counterrevolutionary! You must admit that you long for the overthrow of the dictatorship of the proletariat.'

His words confound me. The purpose of this exercise, it seems, is not to seek forgiveness. The evident premise is that we are evil and our crimes unforgivable; we deserve punishment. This sort of brainwashing is hard to take, but not to be resisted. The authorities will continue to badger me until I produce a suitable confession.

Supervisor Yang turns to a diminutive man with thick glasses, a grade school teacher who seems rather submissive. 'So, you're telling me you wrote a counterrevolutionary slogan because you were sick that day, that your hands were shaking so much that you wrote the wrong characters? How could that be? You despise the Communist Party and Chairman Mao! Sonner or later, your counterrevolutionary nature will expose itself. Perhaps you were ill—but illness was only an external cause. Your hatred of the Party and of the Chairman are the internal causes. Without these internal causes, the external causes could never have come into play. That is the philosophy of Chairman Mao. You must read Chairman Mao's 'On Contradictions', again and again—do you hear me? Then you can come to understand the relationship of external and internal causes.'

Evenings we are back at the rehabilitation room. In the dim light we are told to reflect on our bad attitudes. The grade school teacher at length announces in his high, effeminate voice that he harbors an all-consuming hatred for the Chairman and the Party because he was labeled a Rightist in 1957. It was his deep-rooted counterrevolutionary nature that made him write the words 'Communist reactionaries' instead of 'Nationalist reactionaries' when he was quoting from the *Quotations of Chairman Mao*. The fact that the Party and the people's government sentenced him to seven years was entirely justified, he admits solemnly; he had got what was coming to him.

This statement is pronounced acceptable by Supervisor Yang, and the teacher becomes the first among us to pass the confession test.

When I hear this primary school teacher rebuke himself in this way, I cannot help thinking of Old Liu's categorization of the 'Rightists.' He had said that there were five kinds. First, those who favored the Nationalists. Second, those who belonged to a middle faction, and stood somewhere between the

Nationalist and Communist parties. Then, he said there was another large group of Rightists consisting of primary school teachers. According to Old Liu, their social status was low, their dependency on the government high, and since they were not in a position to act independently, they acted the most subservient inside the camps. This was in stark comparison to the college students and liberal intellectuals who were labeled Rightists, individuals who were the most stubborn and the most unwilling to acknowledge any guilt. Finally, in the period following the Anti-Rightist Campaign, there were also 'Rightists' identified from within the Communist Party ranks as well as 'Rightists' identified as 'bad elements' from within the ranks of the workers.

For some reason, we reconvene the following morning in the auditorium. Supervisor Yang directs the proceedings as Liu Zhenyu is ordered to make a clean breast of his crime. A little man in his fifties, Liu can be found wearing a quilted jacket even on a hot May day in southern China.

Prisoners are issued a set of new clothing two times a year: when fall turns to winter, we get blue quilted jackets and pants, printed with 'Labor Reform' in yellow; when spring turns to summer, white cotton shirts and pants, with 'Labor Reform' in red. Anyone who wears the quilted jacket on the warm days of fall, winter, and spring either has no family at all, or has a family unwilling or unable to send any clothes.

Liu's jacket is a patched survivor but still neat and clean. Clearly he is not one of those slickies who let their clothes fall apart so they can be sure to obtain new ones each fall. He seems an unlikely candidate for our group of hard-core impenitents.

Standing before us, Liu cuts a modestly elegant figure. He addresses the supervisor without a trace of nervousness. His words are carefully enunciated, each phrase laced with the elongated 'uh's' and 'ah's' that distinguish the speech of officials.

'My major problem, uh, was the 1957 Rightist problem.'

I note immediately that he has neglected to use the word 'crime.'

'My 1957 Rightist problem, uh, was basically that I made a few erroneous statements. This oratorical aberration was, ahhh, was examined by the responsible authorities, uh, in 1957. During, ahhh, the Cultural Revolution, a uh, personal diary of mine was, ahhh, seized, seized by the Red Guards, and became the basis for the, ahhh, charge against me.'

'That's utter nonsense!' interrupts Supervisor Yang, reaching for a file on his desk and flipping it open. 'Your Rightist speeches can hardly be considered a "problem," nor is this counter-revolutionary manifesto a typical diary. Let's see—let's just see what kind of "personal matters" are recorded here:

> January 1957. Today I read in *Confidential Reference* a condensation of Khrushchev's secret report criticizing Stalin. This report is truly gratifying to the masses for it exposes the cruelty of Stalin's tyranny, his lust for persecution, as well as the dark side of socialist government. China should follow the Soviet example and clear away the soil left by Stalin.

Joseph Stalin was a great—a *great*—Marxist! Are you aware of this fact, Liu Zhenyu? You, accusing a great Marxist of being a sadist and a tyrant, even going so far as to say that China has "Stalinist soil" on it—aren't you in fact making a thinly veiled reference to our beloved Chairman Mao? Yes? And in denouncing "the dark side of socialist government," aren't you in fact—aren't you brazenly opposing both socialism and the Party?'

Supervisor Yang is becoming increasingly agitated; the veins pop out on his temples and his eyes are vicious.

'You call this a "personal diary"?' he shrieks, flinging the dossier into the air. 'You are an ultrarightist, anti-communist, anti-socialist, anti-Chairman Mao, counterrevolutionary snake! Of course you should have been sentenced to fifteen years!'

Sulking, Liu Zhenyu lowers his head, as Supervisor Yang leafs through the papers once again and sneers, 'You're hardly a paragon of virtue. Look at this filth!

> November 2, 1956. I've been on the road for two weeks already. I truly cannot understand why people have to abide by hypocritical moral standards. If a husband and wife are stationed in different places, and the wife finds a male companion and the husband a female, why can't they both indulge themselves once in a while? It certainly won't keep the two from living happily together again once they are reunited.

Liu Zhenyu, you are despicable!'

I am shocked. Really shocked. I would never have thought that this passive little man with his wispy, billy-goat beard, hunched over like an old peasant, could harbor such radical ideas. It is not uncommon for people with views like this to get twenty years or more; some have even been executed. Certainly Liu's sentence cannot be considered heavy. Still his unwillingness to repent is understandable. After all, he wrote these words in '57, not '67. In the fifties such an attitude would not have jarred so sharply with the official line.

Supervisor Yang is ranting again. 'Look what a contemptible specimen we have here! On the surface he appears to be a perfect gentleman, but his heart is verminous. Make no mistake! Make no mistake.'

Actually, the candid entry in Liu Zhenyu's diary is embarrassing to many of us. During the Cultural Revolution, proof of illicit relations was the most powerful salvo one could fire against political enemies. I think back to one socially active Rebel leader who was made to stand together with twelve of her past lovers during a struggle session. These 'struggle escorts' were later paraded behind her through the streets of Changsha, forced to pound gongs and cry out, 'I am the first adulterer of X'; 'I am the second adulterer of X . . .'

'Liu Zhenyu, we have ways to make you confess your guilt and submit to the law. Tonight the entire brigade will criticize you. We will struggle against you. Think long and hard about your guilt; honestly accept our criticism.'

In the afternoon we all meet again in the auditorium. Gao Zhiming is next. Tall and lanky, he has large eyes like a deer.

'I was still in high school when the Cultural Revolution began. At first I wasn't very active in the revolution, but spent all my time reading the works Marx, Engels, and Lenin. A few of us got together and organized a little Marxist research group. Because my thoughts were counterrevolutionary, I wrote an article in which I foolishly tried to prove that Leninism was incompatible with Marxism. If my thoughts hadn't been counterrevolutionary, I never would have realized that many of Lenin's writings ran counter to those of Marx. . . .'

Gao's delivery is quiet and unemotional, but Supervisor Yang loses no time in stopping him. 'No more poison! Don't spread your counterrevolutionary ideas here! There's no need to expose the corrupt and erroneous *details* of your counter-revolutionary opinions; you need to expose your crime! Your counterrevolutionary crime!' He pauses a moment, then continues, this time adopting a more dignified tone. 'What is there to *research* about Marxism, anyway? The Communists' own Chairman Mao took care of all research long ago; all you need to do is read what he has written. The fact that you think there's a need to do research means you don't trust the Party, that you don't trust Chairman Mao, that you want to come up with something different. When you pit Marx against Lenin, you're raising the red banner to oppose the red banner! The core of Leninism is the dictatorship of the proletariat—and you hate the dictatorship of the proletariat! Gao Zhiming, you were born into a landlord bourgeois family. Ever since you were a young child, you've hated the fact that your parents were suppressed by the dictatorship of the proletariat. *That* is the source of your crime!'

As night falls, the 800 prisoners of the Third Brigade gather to witness the criticism of the man who refuses to confess his crime and submit to the law. Standing on the platform with his bowed head, poor Liu Zhenyu appears even shorter than usual. According to protocol everyone is to follow the prisoner-on-duty's lead in shouting out lines adapted from the *Quotations of Chairman Mao*:

'Liu Zhenyu [the original text says "the enemy"] will not surrender, so we will see him destroyed!'

'A counterrevolutionary will never fall unless he is beaten.'

Hundreds of voices chant in unison. Following the liturgy, several prisoners make speeches of denunciation. When it is all over two or three hours later, Liu's face is whitish-yellow and drenched in sweat.

A week passes before I see him again. At another general meeting held to mobilize the 'double rushes'—harvesting the early rice crop and planting the late one—the brigade leader praises Liu Zhenyu for having made great progress. He enjoins the members of the audience to follow Liu's example, for Liu has not only confessed his crime and submitted to the law, he has agreed never to appeal his case again. Liu is to be rewarded by being sent to a melon patch, where he will serve the rest of his time as a free prisoner. Some free prisoners look after melons, some after greens, but all live independently in the thatched huts in the fields, far away from the prison yard.

I wonder how Liu Zhenyu has managed to gain the complete trust of the cadres. Perhaps because he has never tried to escape and has obeyed prison regulations, the cadres seem to feel comfortable about allowing him to come and go as he pleases. Or maybe they trust him because he served as a Communist cadre in the early days.

Whatever the reason, as a free criminal, Liu has attained the highest rank possible for a labor camp prisoner. Ever accommodating and self-deprecating, he lowers his eyes when he meets anyone in camp.

16
Weeds
▼

A warm breeze heavy with the fragrance of milk vetch and rape blossoms sweeps over the courtyard. The work days have grown longer, the prisoners restless. Boundless energy courses through the musty air, intoxicating and full of promise. The spring of 1972 and the restoration of social order have arrived.

My mind wanders to my first few months at the farm, to the stillborn spring of 1970 and Strike One–Oppose Three, when the sky was leaden and the earth a sea of mud. The death in the air was palpable, spring came and went almost unnoticed amidst the chorus of 'Kill, kill, kill!' and the execution bulletins that seemed to paper every public wall. And though there must have been some nascent signs that life would be returned to us last year, in the spring of 1971, I can remember none—only a few lingering cries for class war and a gnawing dampness.

Now at last I feel refreshed.

Ever since the disappearance of Lin Biao in September, the political situation has been undergoing a subtle transformation. Many of the ousted cadres have resumed their former positions; erstwhile capitalist roader and Foreign Minister Chen Yi is on the front pages again. Money is trickling down, even to the labor camps. Our monthly allowance has been adjusted—increased to two yuan from the one-and-a-half we've been getting since 1969—and the Third Brigade reading room has been reopened. On one of the tables we find a catalog previewing dozens of periodicals that are about to resume publication. Any prisoner may subscribe. I can barely afford toilet paper and toothpaste, even with my new raise, but my father wires me money for three journals. After weeks of reflection, I have chosen *Science and Technology Abroad*, *Chinese Science*, and *Learning and Criticism*.

The warm winds carry Political Director Liu far away. Taking his place in the Third Brigade is a man named Guan, a recently rehabilitated capitalist roader. He speaks a *putonghua* heavily seasoned with the accent of northeast China; as soon as you hear him, you know he was one of the elite troop of cadres who came down to Hunan in 1949 as part of the southern march.

Political Director Guan guarantees us that things around camp are going to improve. Once a month a pig will be slaughtered and one film shown so that prisoners will settle down and work. 'We haven't seen any movies since 1966,' one old prisoner tells me in a hushed voice. In fact there have been no new movies anywhere in China; the Cultural Revolution brought the film industry to a standstill. No one even considers complaining about having to see 'old' movies. A couple of days before the show, many prisoners can scarcely contain their nervous excitement. The day after, there is talk of little else.

Certainly no one asks the cadres why such perks are no longer regarded as 'the revisionist line of material incentives.'

We scrutinize the *Hunan Daily*. The faces of leftists like Jiang Qing and Zhang Chunqiao seldom appear these days; increasingly Zhou Enlai is making his presence felt, confident in the knowledge that the nation is placing their hopes in him. I think back to Liu Fengxiang's prediction about the Cultural Revolution, that it would be 'a victory not for Mao, but for Zhou. As things get back to normal, Zhou will gain the upper hand, and Mao will become increasingly passive.'

Most striking is the change in propaganda, which seems to have reverted to the oxymoronic style of 1962 doublespeak— every aphorism is saddled with a contradictory rider:

We must put politics first—*but* we must also excel in our professional work.

We must follow the mass line—*but* we must also allow specialists to do their part.

We must make sure that education serves the politics of the proletariat—*but* we must also stress the quality of education.

That same year I graduated from elementary school. The nation was just getting back on its feet after the turmoil of the Great Leap and the famine that followed. Everything around me seemed to be moving toward the right.

Villages were implementing the household production responsibility system; factories had the '60 Industrial Provisions,' calling for 'profits,' 'material incentives,' and the 'expert line.' Educational policies were shifting as well.

Previously, if your background was bad, there was no way you could hope to get into a decent school. But in 1962 the government began to use test scores as their primary admissions criterion.

Changsha First High School became one of China's new keypoint schools. Many of the kids who lived alongside me in the Provincial Committee compound didn't make it in; in fact, I was the only kid in my class who had been 'born red' as the majority of my classmates were the sons and daughters of engineers, doctors, and teachers.

My instructors in math, biology, and foreign languages were all returnee Rightists, retrieved from labor re-education camp by the school authorities. On the first day, our teacher privately told us that the quality of the education was much worse than it had been in the fifties and that education in the fifties was not as good as it had been before Liberation. With renewed emphasis on the quality of instruction, the authorities hoped that Changsha First would regain its pre-Leap admission rate of 97 percent of its graduates into college, most of which were top-notch institutions like Beijing University and Qinghua University.

It is almost uncanny how much the smells, the color of the sky—everything—reminds me of the way things were in 1962, of the grand, Western-style structure with its banyan gardens and the life my family lived ten years ago. Insulated from the world by the walls of the Provincial Party Committee compound, I was bored with my surroundings, and fantasized about how I would one day roam about China just as Gorky had traveled about Russia, leading the exhilarating life of the lower classes. I never appreciated what I had. Only after my months of detainment at Zuojiatang did I finally abandon my conviction that material comforts were odious conveyers of lethargy and spiritual emptiness.

I shut my eyes and try to picture my own room. When I open them again, I am just another tattered black jacket marching across the wasteland, returning to the barracks. Here I will sleep twelve-abreast with the other hungry prison ghosts in a large bed reeking of sweat and cheap cigarettes. At night I dream troubled dreams of rage and indignation. Mornings I awaken and mourn.

Now the restoration smiles on me like sunshine after the rain.

Like other children of the old aristocracy who have participated in revolution, now that order and reason have returned I am profoundly embarrassed for my past revolutionary fanaticism. But I also feel anger and grief at the fact that my parents and other relatives have been toppled from their seats of power.

In the darkness of the Third Brigade auditorium, the faded images of high-ranking cadre children dance upon the screen, the 'Sons and Daughters of Heroes' who are answering their country's call to fight in North Korea. It takes us back to a place we have not been for many years, to a time before the Cultural Revolution, when veteran Communist cadres were not yet portrayed as capitalist roaders.

From a friend I get my hands on some contraband translations of Shakespeare. I like *Macbeth* and *Hamlet* the best. Over and over again I read the scene after the coup, where the Prince of Denmark laments his fall. Now I understand the prince's sentiments, for I have watched the ruin of my own family during the Cultural Revolution: my mother driven to suicide; my father dispatched to a Mao Zedong Study Class; my brothers and sisters sent to the countryside to labor.

Political Director Guan does little to discourage my feelings of resentment; in fact, he seems to be giving me special treatment. He transfers me out of the Intensive Labor Group and lets me do easier work, like planting cotton and rice. After that, he moves me back to the Construction Group, where the work is even lighter and where I can learn how to design and build houses.

Despite his warmth, I find I am unable to revert to my former self. No longer am I a cocky, high-ranking official's kid; I have been transformed into a bonafide 'counterrevolutionary.' Somehow I have never considered myself to be essentially any different from the others who have been labeled. Guan's class line troubles me, for I know full well that the 'goodwill' he demonstrates toward prisoners with 'good backgrounds' is a reflection not of his largesse, but of the fact that Zhou Enlai has gained ascendancy. Like the United Action's 'discipline' in implementing the 'blood line,' Zhou's new 'order' further suppresses those who are already oppressed.

Quite a few prisoners in the Third Brigade benefit from these right-wing policies. One, 'Rambling Zhou,' was sent here several years ago when he was still a junior high school student because he had expressed dissatisfaction with the 'Rebel faction' of his village:

'They're not Rebels at all, just good-for-nothings who sit around all day waiting to be fed, always looking to pick a fight with the brigade production team. But, because the Cultural Revolution was a time for troublemakers, they got to be big heroes. They came around to our commune, beat up the brigade leader and party secretary, and sent them to the village to work. But when it came to managing production, it was only the old cadres who knew what they were doing!'

As a Rebel, I feel uncomfortable listening to Rambling Zhou's numerous tales about how the old Conservative cadres had been more decent and more competent than the new Rebel cadres. From his examples, though, I have to admit that the peasants probably had not sided with the Conservatives out of blind partisanship.

Rambling Zhou has never made a secret of his opinions: he has refused to confess, gotten into fights with the labor camp cadres, and been criticized as a resister who will not be molded. Today, when the cadre orders him to step outside, everyone winces. Certainly no one expects him to come back and start gathering up his belongings. 'I've been cleared,' he announces loudly. Rambling Zhou, a man who traces his lineage back through three generations of lower middle peasants, a good laboring-class background, is going home.

From our work group alone, two men are released unconditionally, their charges of attacking Chairman Mao and Vice Chairman Lin Biao dropped. Both come from good class backgrounds.

Most of the politicals think Guan is a kind-hearted man because of his many magnanimous gestures, like dropping by the cells during meals to see if we have any complaints about the food. But I detect a vicious side to him as well, especially when it comes to 'poisonous weeds' threatening the social order.

Thundergun is shooting off at the mouth again.

Though his surname is Lei, or 'Thunder,' the rest of his name bears no relation to a 'gun.' His nickname has evolved because he spends his days railing against the Communist Party, his real name forgotten. Thundergun is a short, slight man. The first time I notice him, during an early-morning broadcast, he is standing in the hallway, pointing at a loudspeaker and providing a running commentary. I listen to the dialogue as I eat my breakfast.

'What are you going on about?! Show me the top Communist cadres with any education at all and they'll have been trained in Nationalist schools!'

Odd as his little diatribe seems to me, his thoughts are remarkably clear. But he is very nervous and seems oblivious to the people around him, shouting at times, whispering at others.

'Colonialism is all you know! The labor camps you've built,

the Mao Zedong Thought Study Classes: nothing but colonialism! You've turned China into a colonized slave society. It's one big cell! Every single Chinese is serving a prison term!'

Each morning at six o'clock, Thundergun points at the loudspeaker and shouts out a rebuttal to the broadcast. Late one night he denounces the Communist Party with such vehemence that he is overheard by the watchtower guard. In short order Guan enters the cell, fuming. As soon as the lock is opened, he commands loudly, 'Prisoner-on-duty, get me some rope. I want him tied up.'

Thundergun offers no resistance to the deathknot, but continues to call out: 'Communists don't bat an eye at slaughtering innocent men . . .'

Political Director Guan forms two loops, slipping one over each wrist, then pushes Thundergun so hard that he crumples onto the floor like a little chick, his two wings pressed against his back and the ends of the rope tucked through the noose around his neck. Guan's face is twisted with contempt as pulls the rope, jerking Thundergun's arms up to the nape of his neck. The curses cease instantly.

Guan's excessive malice and loss of control are appalling. What motivates him to act against a defenseless man with such intensity? Can he be feigning hostility in order to display the 'strength of his resolve' and his 'unambiguous loyalty to the dictatorship of the proletariat'? I consider the possibility for a moment, until the sparks of malice in his eyes persuade me otherwise. This is hatred, pure and simple, a hatred that defies all reason.

Thundergun has not gone out to work with us for several days. Rumor has it that the cadres are keeping him for all-night interrogation sessions. A couple of prisoners on sick leave report to us that Thundergun never stops talking. We are told he has Nationalist roots.

Rumor has it that his father, like many officials of the old dynasty, was killed during the early 1950s in the Campaign to Suppress Counterrevolutionaries. Years later, in the turmoil of the Cultural Revolution, the Conservative faction in the city of Chengzhou, fearful that the descendants of the 'suppressed' would take advantage of the chaos to strike out against the Communist Party members, quickly created a Poor and Lower-Middle Peasants' Court and began to eliminate anyone they felt would be a threat. Thundergun's elder brother tipped off all the young people with bad backgrounds so that they were able to flee. But as soon as the violence of the revolution subsided and order was restored, the brother was arrested for involvement in a counterrevolutionary organization and summarily executed. The news of his brother's death greatly affected Thundergun: hitherto politically silent, he suddenly began his incessant tirades against the Communist Party, which eventually landed him fifteen years of labor reform.

Several days pass. It is the March sentencing meeting, the point being, as always, to scare us so that we will work harder at the upcoming spring planting. High upon the platform, Thundergun is held fast by the death knot, but his face shows no fear, and his mouth never stops moving.

Sure enough, the pronouncement of guilt alludes to Thundergun's family lineage: 'Lei's father was a reactionary official in the Nationalist Party who was suppressed by our people's government. His brother was suppressed by our people's government. . . . Lei hates our Party and our People's Government with the enmity of a man who seeks to avenge the death of his father and brother.' The cadres' unabashed public acknowledgement of the need to 'cut the weeds and pull the roots' of the descendants of the former enemies of the Communists terrifies and angers me at the same time.

The official documents refer to the massacre in which Thundergun's family had been killed as the 'Chengzhou Dao County Incident.' There are four or five eyewitnesses to the massacre among the Third Brigade; one of them, a peasant named He, is a member of my group. The man greets everyone with a vacant smile and a subservient nod. His body is unnaturally stiff, and everyone calls him 'Dumbbell He.' I am told that Dumbbell's family—labeled 'class enemies' because the patriarch was a petty landlord—were also victims of the Poor and Lower-Middle Peasants Court in the fifties. The militia forced his parents at rifle-point to dig a ditch and bury alive his younger brothers and sister, one by one. The youngest was five years old. Then his parents were commanded to dig their own graves and jump in. The militia shoveled earth over them.

The Dao County Massacre took place in August and September of 1967, just after the Conservatives had lost their political advantage in the cities. According to official statistics, approximately 3,000 lost their lives in that rural county. Of all his extended family, only Dumbbell escaped alive. Since that time he has had an outburst every couple of months.

On my way to the latrine one night I hear someone, intoning loudly, like a Buddhist monk chanting sutras for the dead. I can barely see in the dark.

It is Dumbbell, waving a wooden pole, droning, pacing back and forth in front of the rows of urinals. His eyes are ferocious.

'Oh Great Way, Heaven, do not kill, do not betray. Heaven has eyes, perpetuate the Way, return to the Way.'

I step in and whisper, 'You'd better get some sleep, Dumbbell.'

Dumbbell continues his chanting and waving, oblivious of my presence. I go for some help, but I am told to leave him alone, in a couple of hours he will be all right.

The following morning Dumbbell is back to his pleasant and self-effacing self. It occurs to me that the 'counterrevolutionary statement' for which he was imprisoned must have been made during just such an episode.

Baby Qiu was not only a witness of the Dao County Incident, he was one of the executioners.

Late one evening, an old landlord tells the story of Baby Qiu, this solid-looking man in his twenties. A third-generation poor peasant, he fell in love with a landlord's daughter. But the girl's family had suffered at the hands of people with good class backgrounds and swore she would never marry any of them. By the time she turned eighteen, she was incredibly beautiful, and many sons of poor and lower-middle peasants proposed to her. True to her promise, she refused them all, insisting that she would never marry anyone who wasn't the son of a former landlord.

Then, during the Dao County incident, some of the poor peasant boys she had rejected broke into the landlord's house, gang-raped the young woman in full view of her parents, and then murdered the entire family. When order was restored after the Cultural Revolution, the killers were seized and sentenced to terms ranging from three to five years. Baby Qiu was among them. Had the victims not been the progeny of a landlord, Baby Qiu would most certainly have received a life sentence or the death penalty.

When this story comes to an end, many of the men in my group sigh. One bearded landlord mutters, 'Yes, that's the "class orientation" of Communist law: 'The law serves the interests of the ruling class—it's at the disposal of the proletariat!'

Stability shines on China. From nowhere, pork appears in our bowls, and books in our libraries, and we rejoice. Yet out in the newly plowed fields of Reconstruction Farm, the warm earth underneath our feet is rank and smells faintly of blood.

17
Director Song

▼

It is odd how Song Shaowen and I seem to travel in tandem through the channels of the Chinese gulag. From the transit cell of Zuojiatang to the wasteland of Outer Lake. With the new 'Separate Handling' policy, designed to keep politicals from associating with common prisoners, the ten brigades are now reduced to five. Thus, though politicals implicated in the same case are technically not to be assigned to the same work group, the director and I find ourselves together once again, laboring in the rice paddies of the Third Brigade.

True to his part, Song Shaowen has become the spitting image of a labor reform criminal since I last saw him three years ago at Zuojiatang. No more elitist classical allusions; instead he tosses off colloquialisms of the lower classes. Once fair and clean cut, he is now swarthy and rough. It is hard to imagine that this is the same man who was a playwright, director, and actor, a highly paid intellectual who in 1965 took home 300 yuan each month, as much as a Provincial Committee Party secretary. This, along with the other perks such as a house, a car, and other intangibles that came with his job, clearly placed him in China's privileged class. Out of respect for his past, many of the inmates call him Director Song.

Rumors from the Second Detachment suggest that Director Song is a collaborator. I can't be sure. A friend informs me that the political study leaders have been approaching many prisoners, trying to worm out details. Director Song's own study leader subsequently reported to his superior: 'When Song was out in the fields picking cotton, he pointed to the cottonless branches and said, "They're all bare-stalk commanders now." '

'He's probably sulking about the fact that the Communists have "picked off" all his soldiers and turned *him* into a bare-stalk commander,' the detachment leader had replied.

Is Song's submissiveness feigned? Though the director's status diminished somewhat in my eyes when I met Liu Fengxiang in the Transit Brigade, another window into his past leads me to believe that he is an independent thinker.

The very first time I saw Director Song was right after the January Storm of 1967. A group of us had gathered in a classroom at Changsha First High School which was commandeered by a Rebel student group, and was being used as both an office and dormitory. Director Song was on the run and in desperate need of shelter. As he reported the beatings he had experienced at the hands of the Conservatives, I stared at his expensive jacket and the stunning woman beside him, his wife Liang Qi.

As he recounted, 'Our Hunan Theater Troupe was just like Changsha First—a key experimental unit of the Provincial Committee, but you know the saying, "A strong evil wind blows through a little temple; many demons are submerged in a shallow pond." ' Song Shaowen had smiled at the circle of admiring students surrounding him and paused dramatically. Silent, he appeared soft and even effeminate, but when he spoke, he radiated passion and self-confidence. 'Things are never simple. We were called the Sixth Brigade of Performing Arts under the Nationalists' Ministry of Culture. And while those of us in charge had a lot of contacts in the Nationalist Party, we secretly belonged to the Communist underground. Back during the War of Resistance, you see, I had joined up with the Nationalist Youth Corps to fight the Japanese in Yunnan and Burma.'

'Is that how you got labeled a "black ghost," Teacher Song?' asked one student breathlessly.

'Yes, the Nationalist connection was part of it. But I also once wrote a screenplay called *Underground Fire*, in which Liu Shaoqi was the hero. Later on, in October 1966, after Mao and the Central Cultural Revolution Group came out for Rebel rehabilitation, we organized the Red Rebel Troupe of the Arts, joined forces with Xiang River Storm, and demanded the black counterrevolutionary 'caps' be removed. One day the Conservatives came for me, and that was that. It was a long time before I was able to get away. I've been moving to a new hideout every couple of days.' He glanced around nervously, as if the enemy might be lurking outside the classroom door. Each of us hoped that we would be the one to provide sanctuary for this handsome couple.

That night Director Song told us he felt sure that the Conservatives were actively plotting revenge and would, with the help of the military, soon be in a position to have the Rebels formally pronounced counterrevolutionaries.

I was impressed; it seemed that Director Song and I saw eye-to-eye on politics. For weeks my friends and I had been putting up big-character posters warning the townspeople that the interests of the military and the Conservatives were the same. For the moment, it seemed the Rebels had the upper hand, but renewed military support for the Conservative cause would quickly tip the scales.

Sure enough, several days later the mass suppression had begun in full force. Across the nation, Rebel organizations were stripped of their political rights. In Changsha alone, tens of thousands of Rebels were seized. Many of the workers, students, and intellectuals of the Xiang River Storm found themselves in prison. Even then, Director Song and I were together.

On February 4, 1967, we were thrown into the Provincial Public Security Detention Center—the 'model prison' where I would later meet Master Bin and Chief Engineer Yu. It was my first experience behind bars. The other students and I fasted in protest. We were released in mid-March. Director Song probably got out in June or July, when Mao decreed a general rehabilitation. According to witnesses, the director showed extreme bravery during that period, fasting for three days, after which he was force-fed by the guards.

As soon as he was released, he was on the streets again, marching. This time he joined the ranks of the radical Rebel students faction who were denouncing Zhou Enlai as the principal force behind the Conservative cause. Zhou, it was clear, had personally directed the military suppression of the Rebels the preceding February. Before long, Director Song was picked up again. And though he personally never served as a Shengwulian officer, his Cultural Red Rebel Troupe had been part of the Shengwulian coalition; moreover, he had been observed at anti-Zhou activities. In 1969 he was pronounced a 'black hand' and sentenced to fifteen years.

It is the height of the restoration, a rainy day during the 1972 winter agricultural rest. I decide to go to Director Song's *haozi*. Climbing up to the top bunk, I find him alone. The others are below playing cards.

'Old Song, have you noticed how gloomy Jiang Qing's face has been recently?' I ask, keeping my voice low, so that no one else can hear. 'And how Zhou Enlai—the man who once criticized the ultraleftists—once again basks in public support? It's as if he doesn't have a care in the world.'

'Mmm,' he grunts. His eyes are dull.

'I've just finished reading Fan Wenlang's *General History of China*,' I whisper. 'And Mao Zedong's new power play reminds me of a maneuver the emperors used—playing the "dowager faction" against the "court officials' faction." '

Director Song blinks, and I detect a glimmer of the old fire. Certainly he must understand that by the 'dowager faction' I mean Jiang Qing, Yao Wenyuan, and Zhang Chunqiao, the original members of the Central Cultural Revolution Group, and by the 'court officials faction'—the supporters of the prime minister—Zhou Enlai.

Vaguely encouraged, I go on. 'So there sits Mao Zedong, right between the 'dowager' and the 'court officials,' waiting to see which way the wind will blow. If the dowager proves too powerful, Mao will back the officials; if the officials become too strong, he'll support the dowager. Right now my bet is that Mao will go with the dowager against the officials.'

I am aware that during the Cultural Revolution Director Song was pro-Mao and anti-Zhou. By not referring to Mao as 'Chairman,' I have taken a risk. How will this fellow inmate of mine respond to this expression of defiance? It should be all right, I decide—an educated Chinese knows history. My comments have been neutral enough—an objective analysis; he will surely keep things in perspective.

Suddenly, Director Song props himself up on an elbow. 'So, will Jiang Qing and the others counterattack?' Now he's awake.

'In the past,' I hurry to explain, much relieved, 'when Jiang Qing was on the move, she hardly ever appeared in public. She has to be up to something. But now I think the best political card that she and Mao can play is the matter of the 'May Sixteenth conspiracy.' Zhou Enlai was pretty zealous in his purge of the May Sixteenth elements—so much so, that when Lin Biao fell, a lot of Rebels went down with him.'

'Mmmmm. Last year a huge number of people came up from Changsha to question me—all trying to tie the Rebels in with the May Sixteenth Group.'

It seems that Director Song has been the object of many external investigations. I sigh softly. I want to share with him more of my thoughts about this possible strategy of Jiang Qing's, and my apprehension. I have tasted the sweetness of restoration, and I am tired of political revolution. I will even concede that there is a place in society for a conservative faction. Still, I doubt that Director Song will appreciate a lengthy political exegesis. I try to frame my ideas in more philosophical and historical terms:

'And yet the situation isn't exactly the same as "the dowager and court officials" model, because both factions are emotionally involved in the rehabilitation of the Rebels. Rather an issue of human rights than of power politics. The Rebels were like the Third Estate in the French Revolution or the Whigs in England after the revolution there—and Zhou Enlai's Conservatives, *they* were like the Roundheads. In order for a situation like this to stabilize, the two factions have to arrive at some equilibrium. Whenever one faction crushes the other, the seed of turmoil is planted.'

'Yang Xiguang, how is your family doing?' Director Song interrupts abruptly, apparently bored.

I tell him that with my mother's suicide and my father's continued detention at a Mao Zedong Thought Study Class, my two sisters have become homeless. One has been sent to the mountainous, western region of Hunan; the other has fled to Shanxi, where we have relatives. My elder brother has been laboring in the countryside since his dismissal.

Director Song nods sympathetically. He confides that his mother became increasingly distraught and died not long ago. Liang Qi has divorced him. One of his daughters was given to him; custody of the other went to her mother.

A week passes. The cadres are looking at me strangely, even Political Director Guan, who in the past has always been kind to me. Though I would like to believe otherwise, I can only think of one reason. Someone has been informing. It can only be Director Song.

Two days later, in the middle of the night, my detachment leader orders me into the office. Guan is waiting.

'Yang Xiguang, have you any resistant behavior to confess to the government?'

'I go out to work every day. I haven't been resisting.'

Guan's eyes flash cruelly. 'Yang Xiguang, you're not being straight with me. Do you think we're not aware that you've been spreading counterrevolutionary ideas among the prisoners, using the old to discredit the new, attacking the Party Central proletarian command, and attacking Chairman Mao?'

I try to disguise my panic. It seems that there is very little that Guan doesn't know. 'Goddamn you, Song Shaowen!' I scream inside my head. If substantiated, these charges will make additional sentencing a very simple matter. I have seen many cases where seven to ten years have been tacked on to the sentences of men who uttered sentiments less offensive than my own. But I am relatively sure that Director Song is the only one who could have heard me that day. If I deny everything, and they can't come up with another witness, I have a chance.

In the minutes that follow, I insist repeatedly that I never

attacked the proletarian command or Chairman Mao. Though
Political Director Guan rails at me viciously for over an hour, I
get the impression that he isn't trying very hard to solicit
additional evidence. At length, the detachment leader
admonishes me to 'reflect on my evil ways by wearing
handcuffs.' I try to console myself that at least I have been spared
foot shackles or solitary confinement in the little *haozi*.

There are two types of 'reflection.' In one, both wrists are
cuffed behind one's back; in the other, in front. The first is much
worse, because you can't eat by yourself, and sleeping is difficult.
But the second kind, which is what I get, is bad when you squat
in the latrine, since someone always has to be there to keep you
from falling and to clean you up afterwards. 'Reflection in cuffs'
is clearly an assault on the spirit. To political prisoners, already
acutely sensitive to any form of persecution, the mere sight of
my hands brings fear into their eyes. I watch in agony as my
comrades shrink from me and lower their glances. In all the
times I was dragged out into the streets for criticism at
Zuojiatang, I have never felt moral or psychological pressure like
this. And during the Cultural Revolution so many people were
being criticized that one rarely felt alone. Now, in this time of
relative law and order, when the authorities seem somewhat
more rational, it is difficult to throw off the burden of guilt.

To my great relief, my fellow workers in the Construction
Group do not ignore me. Each morning they take turns washing
my face; they help me at mealtime and in the latrine. On the
third day of my punishment, the entire brigade assembles to
struggle against me. Instructor Yang steps forward to announce
my crime.

'Counterrevolutionary Yang Xiguang was born into a
reactionary, landlord-bourgeois family. His father was a right-
wing opportunist; his mother killed herself to escape
punishment during the Cultural Revolution. His older brother
and his uncle were anti-Party, anti-socialist Rightists.
Counterrevolutionary Yang Xiguang detests our Party and the
socialist system, having vehemently attacked the proletarian
command and the old generation of proletarian revolutionaries.
He wrote the reactionary article 'Whither China?' in which he
communicated his plot to overthrow the dictatorship of the
proletariat, to establish a new party, a new nation, and a new
military . . .'

Anger washes over me in waves. I stand on the edge of the
platform, still in cuffs, looking down on row after row of dark
faces, and think of Thundergun. As in all struggle sessions, the

members of the Third Brigade have become zombies. They shout and raise their arms on cue: 'Down with counterrevolutionary Yang Xiguang!'

Seeing that I have not lowered my head, the prisoner-on-duty walks over and pushes it down viciously. I wish I had a gun; I would not hesitate to silence the man who is directing my fellow prisoners to struggle against me.

Isolated like this, it is easy to become disoriented. But as the days and weeks go by, my ability to endure such criticism grows. As my fellow inmates gradually learn why I was targeted, they lose their detached numbness. In fact, when my handcuffs are finally removed, everyone is convinced that I'm not KGB, and many men begin to share their secrets. Thus, though I have suffered for my policy of relative openness, I have no regrets. But I know I have been lucky.

Director Song is rewarded for his behavior by being named the new prisoner-on-duty of the Second Detachment, which means he is exempted from working in the fields. Instead, he lingers in the cells to supervise the men on sick leave. When the cadres are out of the building, Director Song is the man in charge. He takes his job very seriously, applying to his new calling the passion which he formerly reserved for the Nationalist Youth Corps and the Xiang River Storm. Early mornings and evenings after political study class, he can always be found sniffing around.

Life in the Second Detachment soon becomes unbearable. Whereas the more lenient prisoners-on-duty shut one eye when we cook our stolen vegetables or eggs on homemade kerosene burners, Director Song gives us no slack. Rules must be followed to the letter. He confiscates any and all burners and turns them in to the cadres.

◆

By 1974 all the newspapers are noisily criticizing Confucianism and extolling the totalitarian Legalist philosophy of the ancient past which tolerated no authority but that of the ruler. As a result the prisoners throughout the camp have begun to refer to Director Song as the 'damned Legalist.' One man complains bitterly to me that Old Song can fake any political position: 'He's a pathological performer.'

No, I argue; Director Song is not pretending. His is a compulsive personality type that is eminently susceptible to the euphoria of revolution.

After some time, Director Song is further rewarded for his activism with a two-year reduction in his sentence. By now, however, he has antagonized so many prisoners that he is in serious trouble. The members of the Second Detachment band together, accusing him of feigning compliance with prison regulations. The cadres, who hope to pacify the majority of prisoners, decide to sacrifice him. They revoke his title, then quickly call a struggle meeting. And while prison protocol dictates that prisoners merely go through the motions of beating the person who is being criticized, this evening is an exception. United in their loathing for him, the prisoners and the cadres do not hold back.

Though I never communicate with Director Song again, stories of him follow me. After many years, I learn that he was released following the fall of the Gang of Four, and that with the rehabilitation of the Sixth Brigade of Performing Arts, Director Song's 'black ghost' cap was officially removed. And then there is the story of how he got involved in the student democracy movement of 1979. Liang Heng tells me that when he and the other Changsha students were demonstrating and fasting for the right to hold elections to the People's Congress, Director Song sought him out to suggest a few tactics for political warfare.[1] He is rehabilitated and given a large sum by the government in compensation for his imprisonment. After suffering a series of personal losses, he throws his heart and soul into another activity—gambling, ultimately succumbing to it.

Throughout his life this man was propelled forward, pressed towards risk and drama, and even heroism. Perhaps every kind of revolution in society and every kind of extremist social movement can be traced to personalities like Director Song.

---

[1] Liang Heng is the author of the Red Guard memoir *Son of the Revolution* (New York: Random House, 1983).

18

Red Schemers, Black Schemers

▼

Summer harvest lasts from mid-July to August 6, after which there is a period of short, but greatly anticipated rest. Even now, the oppressive heat does not let up; at noon the water in the fields will burn the feet. The shoots we planted just days ago have turned a deep green.

In the series of transfers comprising Separate Handling, the Third Brigade is being transformed into a group limited to 'practicing counterrevolutionaries' as politicals from the Seventh are gradually swapped with the common criminals of the Third. New faces appear daily.

Three of the these new practicing counterrevolutionaries from the Seventh join me in Group Six. We are an interesting mix. 'Donkey' is a little fellow who can shoulder more than two hundred pounds; Cao, a lanky, taciturn man who rejects with contempt the jackets and quilts issued in winter. He absolutely refuses to do any heavy labor, squatting instead on the sidelines where he watches the rest of us weed, or, if he is in the mood, repairs a basket or two. Both Donkey and Cao are charged with having written counterrevolutionary slogans.

The third, 'Baby Yao,' is the son of a top Nationalist leader by his third concubine and is in for 'counterrevolutionary slander.' Before coming to camp he was a machinist drifter who contracted with the type of underground industries described to me by Nine Dragons Zhang. The owner of a little plastic set of Chinese chess, he is constantly on the lookout for partners. One of his regular competitors lives next door in the Group Five barrack—Huang Wenzhe, another of the practicing counterrevolutionaries newly arrived from the Seventh. I know Huang only by sight: a tall, thin man who seems to know his way around the system.

Counselor Tang holds a detachment meeting in late August, soon after our regrouping.

'As part of "Separate Handling,"' he begins, his eyes bulging with intensity, 'many prisoners have changed locations. This can be a fresh start for you. No matter what you've done in the past, you can build a new life by reaching out to the government and performing deeds of merit. And by atoning for your crimes, you will be able to have your sentences lightened.'

By 'reaching out,' of course, he means informing. Though KGB's are universally despised, even by the cadres, the practice continues, for the incentive is high. Just who is 'snitching' is not obvious to the labor camp initiate. Only after weeks of tutelage by the old-timers do we learn to see how, when a cadre comes into the cells, or monitors prisoners in the fields, there will always be someone lingering nearby, waiting till no one is around to approach the cadre and slip him the note. Even when we do see the hand-off, there's no way of knowing what it says. Has it got your name on it? Only time will tell.

By September, the seeds that Counselor Tang tossed into the wind have borne fruit. He calls another meeting. 'It seems that there are a few individuals in Group Five whose heads are swollen with counterrevolutionary arrogance,' he barks sternly into the microphone. 'One of these—Yang Guochang—is a die-hard counterrevolutionary element who to this day longs for Soviet revisionism, longs for Chiang Kai-shek, and longs for a capitalist restoration. Some of the other members of the group are spreading the poison of feudalism by retelling the *Myths of Gods and Heroes* and *Journey to the West* to their fellow prisoners, creating havoc throughout Group Five. Why, even our group leader has been collaborating with the resisters, secretly dispersing an extra pot of rice stolen from the mess kitchen. What a hell of a lot of nerve!'

As we sit quietly in the yard, listening to this tirade, I wonder which nameless bastard is trying to shorten his term.

The following evening we hear the clamor of voices in the barracks next door. We can make out the Huarong accent of our group leader: 'Tonight we will struggle against the resister, Yang Guochang. Yang Guochang, come forward!'

I think of Yang's round face. Not yet thirty years old, he is a wiry, outspoken peasant who can't be bought. Pretending to listen to the words of our political study leader, we strain to hear what Yang is saying. He seems determined not to admit to 'the three longings.'

In our own class, meanwhile, the study leader continues to drone on, reading aloud a *Hunan Daily* article which accuses

Lin Biao of being an adventurist, a schemer, and a counterrevolutionary. It seems like only yesterday that the shouts of 'Vice Commander Lin Biao is Chairman Mao's successor' echoed in our ears. Since Lin Biao's disappearance, Mao has been trying quell the people's resentment toward the Cultural Revolution by placing all responsibility for the chaos on the former Vice Commander.

Counselor Tang is watching this evening's events from a chair planted in the open doorway of the Group Five *haozi*. 'Yang Guochang's resistance tonight is particularly outrageous; why hasn't anyone put him in his place? Where are all the people who should be reaching out to the government?' he presses, his face enigmatic. Then, as is his custom, he rises from his chair and leaves the barracks, indicating he is shutting his eyes to all that will follow.

We hear punches and kicks. Somebody shouts, 'Kneel down.' Still, we can tell that the blows aren't as bad as they could be. A man like Yang Guochang, who never fawns upon the cadres, is not disliked by his fellow inmates.

The next day a rumor is circulated by the prisoners of the Fourth Detachment that the KGB was Huang Wenzhe. I try to remember the last time I saw him playing chess with Baby Yao and can't. 'Just what kind of guy is this Huang?' I ask in a whisper.

'Oh, he's a good man,' insists Baby Yao. 'He never informed on anybody when we were at the Seventh. As a matter of fact he had a reputation as a resister and was always getting the stick himself—you know, one of those frozen bean curds.'

'Then how come he's turned KGB now?'

'Who knows what kind of "new man" the Communists have turned him into. They can do it, you know—change someone so much that even his closest friends won't know him any more.' Grabbing the back of his head as if he has run into trouble on the chessboard, he scowls, squinching his eyes and nose together. Baby Yao looks stupid at times, but he is usually three steps ahead of the rest of us.

'So what's he in for?' I ask.

'He was a member of the underground Democracy Party. Got ten. Could be he thinks the time has come for him to try a new strategy.'

In the days that follow we hold meeting after meeting, where we must listen to the cadres sing the praises of Huang Wenzhe. We are told he is an industrious worker, that the quantity and quality of the cotton he picks is outstanding, that by reaching out to the government he has been able to leave behind the evil ways he once practiced at the Seventh Brigade.

By now there is no one in Group Five who does not utterly despise him.

It is almost October, time to pick cotton. In the rich soil of the islets the plants have grown quickly and are now as tall as the prisoners.

Picking can be grueling work or it can be easygoing. If you are pushing for 70, 80, or even 100 pounds a day and want to keep the leaves out, you need to use both your hands at the same time, picking fast and carefully. Your feet have to keep moving, too. Branches scratch at you, tearing your clothing and bruising your skin, but there is no stopping if you want to make top quota. After a day like that, a prisoner is dead on his feet. If, on the other hand, you don't care about quotas and take your time, harvesting cotton isn't bad at all.

Huang Wenzhe picks like a man possessed. You can hear him snapping off branches from a long way off; he grabs furiously at the balls with both hands, barreling down each row at such a clip that he disappears behind the foliage in no time.

And at quitting time, when we have to go to the drying field for weighing, Huang Wenzhe is inevitably one of the top three pickers, his quality either grade two or three.

One night, as a part of our political studies, Huang Wenzhe is to explain to the Third Brigade how the writings of Mao Zedong inspired him to reform his reactionary views. The prisoners, who have been instructed to bring their little wooden stools, wait in the darkness, peering vacantly at Huang, who is holding his manuscript under the light of a hanging lamp. When he begins his tale, however, his candid and incisive analysis of past political events takes my breath away.

'In 1962 the Indian reactionaries were at the Sino-Indian border, inciting armed conflicts. Chiang Kai-shek's gang of bandits was clamoring to counterattack the Mainland, while the Soviet revisionists, having broken all their promises, were making a mockery of our treaties by withdrawing their experts and halting all aid. Being a counterrevolutionary, I thought it was the perfect chance for a capitalist restoration and joined a counterrevolutionary organization. I hoped to take advantage of the troubles brought upon the Party and the people by the three-year natural disaster and plotted the overthrow of the dictatorship of the proletariat . . .'

He continues like this for an hour, during which time I am

increasingly impressed. I think back to Baby Yao's comment—
'This man has a great head for politics'—and it suddenly occurs
to me that Huang might be up to something. Otherwise, how
could the cadres make a man like this reveal his inner thoughts
this way?

Soon thereafter comes startling news from Group Five. Their
study leader no long wishes to serve in this role. Everyone in his
group is now actively resisting reform; the only one still reaching
out to the government is Huang Wenzhe. Most of the men have
turned in notes accusing Huang of having reactionary thoughts.

Huang Wenzhe has been completely ostracized.

Thus, at a meeting held by the First Detachment several days
later, he is singled out again. 'There exists in Group Five a
counterrevolutionary troublemaker who is trying to cause a lot
of trouble. Huang Wenzhe accuses the other members of his
group of refusing to be reformed, saying that he alone is good,
when actually he is the worst kind of resister.'

Late the next day Group Five holds a struggle session against
Huang Wenzhe. This time, there is no need for any invitation
from the cadres. We are told afterwards that Yang Guochang took
the lead by seizing a club, whereupon everyone else who had
been squealed on—no small number of men—rushed forward
and struck him until his head began to bleed.

Huang Wenzhe is a changed man. Now he is one of the last
to go out, and he doesn't do much in the fields. He has stopped
washing his face and brushing his teeth. His clothing is dirty and
disheveled.

'What's the matter, Huang Wenzhe?' the cadres ask him. They
repeat the question several times before he finally responds.

'I just don't get it.' Huang tilts his head.

Four days after the struggle session, we are woken by a
chilling scream in the night. There is a long pause, then a voice
crying out, 'My god, a man's been hacked to death!'

When we press into the Group Five doorway, there is Yang
Guochang lying atop a blood-spattered bed. In the grey light we
can see brains and congealed blood protruding through a hole in
his skull. The cadres and soldiers are called in, and Yang
Guochang is carried to the clinic. But he is beyond help. Though
nobody asks who it was who has done such a thing, we all have
our suspicions.

Before sunup the next morning, Counselor Tang saunters into
the *haozi* to blow the assembly whistle and the study leader
immediately reports the incident.

'Who did this?' The counselor's voice shakes with anger.

'Me!' Sure enough, it is the tall shadow of Huang Wenzhe that steps forward.

'What did you hit him with?'

Huang stoops down and pulls out a large pick from under the bunk. He is put into solitary.

The incident particularly unnerves Baby Yao, who still thinks of Huang as a friend. On the pretext of taking him some clothes, he asks to accompany the prisoner-on-duty to the little *haozi* at mealtime. When he gets back, Baby Yao tells me that Huang has reverted to the way he used to act in the Seventh Brigade. Despite urgings to the contrary, Huang keeps on shouting, 'There are indications everywhere that the Communist government is in danger. Chinese history will negate Mao Zedong and the Cultural Revolution: Baby Yao, just sit back and be patient! It won't be too long now.'

Baby Yao had looked at Huang's emaciated body and shackled feet one last time before calling out, 'Take good care of yourself, you hear?'

A month goes by. At a general brigade meeting Counselor Tang divulges the fate of Huang Wenzhe: 'Since he has been in the little *haozi* he has continued to write reactionary slogans on his blanket and his clothes, attacking our great leader Chairman Mao and the Chinese Communist Party. This man is obviously tired of living; it won't be long before he'll be out at the sluice chewing on the lawn.'

The execution is planned for the next biannual sentencing meeting, when Huang, wrapped in the death knot, is pushed up onto the stage by armed police. Hung across his back is a long, narrow white placard with the black characters 'Counterrevolutionary Killer-criminal, Huang Wenzhe,' overlaid by a bright red 'X.'

A heavy-set cadre reads the formal pronouncement of guilt, finishing, 'To be carried out immediately.' His words reverberate across the fields of milk vetch, bouncing off the cement wall at the lake's edge. We must look on as Huang Wenzhe is led away behind the platform, where he is made to kneel before an open grave dug this morning. Two dull shots ring out. His thin body tumbles forward, and disappears.

19
Spectacles
▼

Spectacles doesn't bum cigarettes, quibble about the assignments or tools he is handed, or fuss about much of anything, for that matter. He lives peaceably amidst the sometimes violent frays of the Third Brigade, untouched by the crossfire of the KGBs, who think only of shortening their terms, and the hard-core, practicing counterrevolutionaries, who will do anything to defy the authorities and their instruments of deceit. Much like a Taoist priest, Spectacles Huang seems to transcend it all.

But he is not totally free of desire. He is passionate, even compulsive, about writing. He lives and breathes for the characters of his books. For weeks I thought he was suffering from a serious health problem, so often is he absent from the fields. Only after I was retained for interrogation and spotted him atop the clinic bunk did I realize what he was up to. There he was, scribbling furiously in a world of his own, his rough, thin face pressed against a notebook.

Spectacles' near-sightedness must be extreme indeed. The plastic lenses of his glasses are greasy and cracked, and the frames don't fit right, despite the fact that he has wrapped them with strips of adhesive from the clinic. They fall off so much that when he works in the fields, he ties them to his head with a piece of hemp. I guess that he must be in his mid-fifties, with his little white beard and short salt-and-pepper hair that is thinning rapidly. Perhaps because his jaw hangs open so often, he seems rather thick. Every so often, especially when he gets worked up, saliva trickles down from the corners of his thick lips. When he calms down again, he notices his drooling and quickly wipes his mouth on his sleeve.

It is essential that Spectacles write several pages every single evening. He frequently stays up all night, huddled under a kerosene lamp, scribbling, scribbling. Instead of buying soap and toilet paper, Spectacles' monthly allowance goes for paper, pens, and ink. A few of his comrades help him bind the blank sheets of paper into elegant notebooks in which he writes his masterpieces; faithful readers make secret copies. I soon discover that there are always two or three volumes of each work circulating around the underground library of the Third Brigade.

The first that I am able to get my hands on is his novel about a student at United Southwest University in Chongqing who falls in love with a prostitute during the War of Resistance Against Japan. The plot is so involved and the narrative so rich in detail that I find I cannot put it down. In many ways it is reminiscent of Zhang Henshui and his romantic 'mandarin duck and butterfly' fiction, the Chinese answer to Maugham and Zola. I have been following the intrigue, page by page, through Chapter Eight when the cadres confiscate it.

In a general meeting Instructor Yang warns that 'a certain prisoner is continuing to write pornography, even in prison.' Spectacles is not struggled against, presumably because there is nothing politically exceptionable in his pages. Soon he resolves to rewrite the book and for weeks stays up night and day. After three frenzied months, he is finished. By this time the cadres are convinced he is suffering from a nervous condition, and this compulsive behavior, added to the fact that his books are relatively innocuous, prompts the cadres to shut one eye to his habit for the rest of his term.

Spectacles also writes magical screenplays that are entirely different from his novels, including one called *Truth, Goodness, and Beauty*. It is my first encounter with Chinese literature of this sort, for though I have been reading novels since grade school, these have all been works of revolutionary realism. His screenplays, many of which are set in Scandinavia around the Second World War, with their highly symbolic lines peppered with bawdy curses and jests, remind me of what I have read in Shakespeare's comedies. I find myself drawn to this writing, in which the romantic, the fantastic, and the abstract ring truer than reality itself. In prison, the notion of embracing creatures 'half-angel and half-demon' does not seem so absurd.

The rumor around camp is that Spectacles has been sent here because he committed a political error during a nervous outburst. Apart from his drooling, however, he seems quite normal. I have been watching carefully, and still have not seen any evidence that he is incapable of monitoring his tongue.

One morning in late October of 1972, the cadres convene the entire camp in order to announce a directive from the very top.

Lin Biao has attempted to assassinate Chairman Mao and has vanished on his way to the Soviet Union. We are to be given a brief holiday from the fields so that we can destroy any printed matter referring to the man who up to now has been considered Mao's successor.

Our primary mission is to ferret out all copies of the ubiquitous Little Red Book harboring Lin Biao's preface. This task alone takes most of the morning. Then we pore through all of the other books and papers which might contain the characters 'Lin Biao' or his picture. The offending pages are turned over to the cadres who wait somberly in the yard. Other guards march in and out of the *haozi*, scouring our bags for any materials we might have overlooked.

Several of the politicals in the Third Brigade who have been imprisoned for 'expressing opposition' to both Mao Zedong and Lin Biao decide to approach the cadres with their sentencing documents hoping to have the phrase 'oppose Vice Commander Lin' deleted. They are dismissed with a curse: 'Your crime is opposing Chairman Mao and the Communist Party. Don't think you can use the Lin Biao incident to weasel out of your sentence!'

That evening, as some of the bunks hum with quiet excitement in celebration of the downfall of Mao's revolutionary successor, Spectacles begins to brood. While heartened by Lin's bold act of defiance, he is inconsolable about the fact that the attempt has ended in failure.

It is business as usual the following morning: we must go back to work. Inside the *haozi* walls, the three detachments form and wait for roll call to begin. Now we must march single-file through the narrow door and shout our numbers to the cadre-on-duty, responsible for the daily count.

But when it is Spectacles' turn, he storms out the door without stopping, frantically rushing past the other prisoners in the yard. 'Hey', he calls to them, 'Lin Biao rose up to kill Mao Zedong! Now it is our turn to rebel! If we don't act now, we'll never get another chance. Rise! Rise up to help Lin Biao kill Mao Zedong!'

Mortified, the cadres order Spectacles to be tied up, whereupon a couple of lackeys rush to fetch some rope and secure him to the flagpole in the yard. Atop it flies a little iron flag with peeling red paint, raised every day at sundown to signal the men in the fields that it is time to return.

Spectacles remains there the entire morning. Whenever his fellow prisoners walk by, he cries out, 'Rise, rise up and rebel!

Answer Lin Biao's call to kill Mao!' To the cadres, however, he hisses, 'Maoist running dogs! Claws of Mao Zedong, come to your senses; forget about Mao! Look at Lin Biao who has already rebelled! Don't be deceived any more!'

By noon his mind has cleared, and he is somewhat calmer. The cadres call for the prisoner doctor to come and check his condition, and the doctor, who is a man of conscience, reports that Spectacles is suffering from a mental disorder and 'has no control over what he says and does.' He does so at great personal risk, for in the past the authorities have often viewed 'making excuses for counterrevolutionaries' as a punishable criminal act.

But the cadres, who are themselves having trouble adjusting to this unexpected political development, feel no enmity toward the drooling, foolish-looking man in the yard and release him. Spectacles is not further detained.

I have no opportunity to talk with him for several weeks, until one day, when I am alone in the *haozi* 'reflecting in handcuffs,' Spectacles comes to visit. As he plunks down beside me on my bunk, he flashes a rare smile.

'Yang Xiguang, you probably can't imagine how much ambition I have. I think of myself as a modern-day Cao Xueqin. He was destitute and forgotten most of his life, but after his death, he became famous for having written *Dream of the Red Chamber*. No, I don't seek fame during my own lifetime; I only ask that people remember my name.' His dark eyes brighten, and for once he doesn't seem quite so dense.

It is the first time I have heard anything about his 'ambition.' Evidently he hasn't given up hope.

'Don't judge me by the way I look now,' he repeats earnestly, No doubt he has read the skepticism on my face. 'Both my father and grandfather were prominent figures at the end of the Qing and in the early days of the Republic. But say, Yang Xiguang, you should record *your* family's story when you get a chance.'

'Maybe when I get these damned things off,' I confide to him, shaking my cuffs. 'But right now the most important thing for me to do is to keep up my desire to create—like you do.'[1]

He wipes the saliva from his mouth. 'Yes,' Spectacles continues, 'a fellow like me has done just about everything. I've been a buyer for a factory, a train conductor—done all sorts of odd jobs. I liked those jobs because I had a chance to observe

[1] As time went by, my conversations with Spectacles and my recollections of *Doctor Zhivago* and *The Gulag Archipelago* convinced me that literature can be a powerful political tool. Spectacles acted as both mentor and critic, and our ongoing exchanges of personal writings cemented our friendship.

society up close. But my real job is writing. In 1959 I wrote a novel about a girl from a good family who fell on hard times and ended up as a prostitute. I submitted it to a publishing house, and it was even scheduled for publication. Then the Cultural Revolution broke out. Not only was its publication canceled, I was labeled a "little Deng Tuo of the artistic black line."' Deng Tuo was a former member of the Secretariat of the Beijing Municipal Party of the Communist Party who was attacked for his 'Evening Chats at Yanshan,' which were said to 'promote peaceful evolution' instead of 'revolution.'

'Some folks said to me: "Your writings are your life, and your life is water." Worthless. And they were right. When I heard my novel wasn't going to press, I felt as if I had been struck by lightning. I stayed awake for days and nights on end, trying to make sense of things. It wasn't until I was interrogated that I finally learned what it was I had done to get locked up. Apparently while I was out on the streets reading big-character posters, I started shouting: 'Listen! Mao Zedong is a great villain! Mao Zedong is a modern-day Emperor Qin Shihuang—in fact, he's even worse than the Qin Emperor. Mao Zedong will die! Hurry up, Mao—hurry up and die!'

'Of course I was taken to the Public Security Bureau in short order. Not too long after that, the Rebels gained the upper hand and rehabilitated everyone labeled as evil in the early phase of the Cultural Revolution, including me. I joined the Rebels as soon as I got out of the detention center. Then, when the authorities regained control, they came for me again, and I got sentenced to fifteen years.'

A classmate of mine had behaved similarly in 1964; it seemed at that time people everywhere were developing the same symptoms—losing control in the factories, the government agencies, and the armed forces, and the stories of such outbursts had become even more prevalent during the Cultural Revolution.

'When I was in ninth grade,' I tell Spectacles, 'there was a boy named Shen Shouda who came from the petty bourgeoisie. He always got top grades and was sure to get into a good college. Then came the announcement about the change in admissions criterion to class background. He knew then he would never get into college. One morning he woke up, his face puffed out, and he started babbling. They took him to the hospital and pronounced him schizophrenic. After a year, though, he was all right again.

'But there was more. During the Cultural Revolution, the

Conservative Red Guards discovered his background and beat him to a pulp. Since the Rebels had gained some power, he had the courage to fight back. He took his bloody clothes all the way to Beijing and filed a petition with the Central Cultural Revolution Group. In return, he was given a paper authorizing him to criticize the blood line and to demand compensation from the local government.'

Spectacles sits on the bed, staring into space.

'There must be as many cases of people who have become "schizophrenic" for political reasons since 1964 as there have been cases of people who got edema after the Great Leap Forward,' I add pensively.

'Whenever I look at the picture of Mao in the Little Red Book, I think of Lenin,' announces Spectacles suddenly. It is not unusual for him to change topics like this, and I try to keep up with him.

'You know Big-head Sun next door?' I ask, referring to the intellectual next door who once sang star roles in a Peking Opera troupe and made a whopping 200 yuan a month.

'Mmmm,' Spectacles grunts.

'My apprentice-brother Lu Guoan asked him, "How come you couldn't be content living the good life?" Big-head Sun started singing as if he were on stage, "It's a lo-o-ng sto-ry. . . ."' Apparently they hadn't been doing all that well for some time, and when the Cultural Revolution began they were sent out into the countryside. Their salary shrank and they weren't allowed to sing. Instead they carried hoes around on their shoulders to turn the earth. Big-head said he cursed Old Chairman Mao every time he opened his mouth. When Strike One–Oppose Three started up and the man from the Military Propaganda Team asked him why he was attacking the Chairman, Big-head said it was like soybeans being dumped out of a bamboo vase. He spilled out everything—how, if he ever ran into him, he'd pluck his eyes out! Big-head Sun was grinding his teeth, reaching his arms out, and clawing at the air.'

'Heh, heh, heh,' Spectacles chuckles softly.

Judging from the enormous number of laborers who are in for 'viciously attacking Chairman Mao,' it would seem that this kind of passion is quite prevalent. Certainly people like me, who had been at the very top of society before the Cultural Revolution and are now imprisoned, are not well-disposed toward Mao. My family was ruined; in fact, all of China seems to have been plunged into a great abyss, all at Mao's hands. Whenever I see Mao's portrait, it is as if I am looking at a murderous devil, signified by his tall forehead and evil stare. In fact, the portrait isn't anything like my image; it is because I see him through the anger of the persecuted.

Outside the rain pours to earth, beating down mercilessly on the thatched roof overhead. We rejoice. Labor camp prisoners love more than anything the rain and snow that falls in late January and February, for there is almost nothing productive left for us to do. On clear winter days we can slog out to the dikes, but when it rains, the mud becomes utterly intractable.

Moreover, since the Spring Festival coincides with the rainy season in southern China, from time to time we are able to stay in the *haozi* for three or four days straight, and sometimes even a week. Except for mornings, which are devoted to political study, the day is ours to spend as we wish: mending clothing, playing poker or chess, and reading. Or storytelling.

Two very different breeds of raconteurs inhabit Reconstruction Farm—the illiterates and the intellectuals. The former know hundreds of folk tales, having spent much of their pre-prison lives in teahouses, where for only a few pennies they could listen to professional storytellers recount the adventures of itinerant swordsmen, or episodes from the serial novels of the Ming and Qing—*Journey to the West*, *Three Knights and Five Cavaliers*, and *Burning Red Lotus Temple*. The intellectual, on the other hand, offers a more exotic repertoire: Chinese and Western novels of the twentieth century. Spectacles, who belongs to this latter category, is particularly fond of telling Zhang Henshui's *A Marriage of Tears and Laughter*, and, from the West, *Laughing Boy*, *Tale of Two Cities*, and *Uncle Tom's Cabin*.

Tonight there has been a special request for *Camille*.[2] As usual, Spectacles is hunched up on the bottom bunk, surrounded by eight or nine prisoners; some leaning back against the wall, some on their stomachs, propped up on their elbows.

Every so often Spectacles pauses, takes off his crusty glasses, and wipes them on his grey handkerchief before resuming. As I watch his beard dance about, it occurs to me that the plot is somewhat different from the one I remember; as usual, he seems to be adding touches of his own.

'And so Camille fell deeply in love. The two lived together for some time, kneeling under the moonlight to swear that if they could not live together, they would die together. The young lord

---

[2] Alexandre Dumas' 1849 play, *La Dame aux Camelias* on which Verdi's opera *La Traviata* is based.

abandoned his studies. Eventually, worried by his son's silence, the father rushed from the provinces to Camille's opulent dwelling in the capital city, demanding to see his son. Camille turned him away several times before he finally induced her to persuade his son to return to school. Breaking off her relationship with him, she announced that she was going to marry a lord who had been pursuing her for many years. Crushed by the news, the young man came to the wedding ceremony, bringing a pistol. Just as the couple was about to exchange vows, the boy fired, first at the groom and then at himself. When Camille saw her lover lying in a pool of blood, she hastened home, and after leaving a note explaining her reasons for marrying, poisoned herself. She was determined to honor her vow.

'No one knew that he was not really dead—he had only been wounded and lay recuperating at his father's home in the provinces. But when he heard about Camille's death, he hurried to her graveside, wrote a letter asking to buried together with her, and shot himself again, dying upon her tomb.'

The little audience on the bunk seems very touched, and some of the older prisoners sigh out loud. Overhead the sound of falling rain continues, broken occasionally by a low rumble of thunder.

Though I have never read the book *Camille*, I saw the play in 1962 when I was in junior high. Not long after the opening, *People's Daily* had run a critique denouncing the work as a 'bourgeois poisonous weed preaching the supremacy of love,' and the title had disappeared from the bookstores. In retrospect, however, I think I prefer Spectacles' rendition, with something of *Romeo and Juliet* thrown in, to what I remember of the play.

Spectacles' pen never stops moving. While he is with the Third Brigade he finishes at least three screenplays and three novels which are quickly circulated. For me, the most memorable is a love story set in the fifties and early sixties, entitled *Qin Yan and Wang Jun*.

The hero Wang Jun is a young officer in the Hunan provincial military command who falls in love with a high school girl named Qin Yan. The two decide to marry. But according to the regulations of that time, Wang Jun's superior must examine the girl's files before he can sanction the match. When he discovers that her father is an historical counterrevolutionary still serving in a labor camp, he immediately orders the young officer to break off all ties with her and introduces him instead to a more suitable girl—a member of the Communist Party. Pressured with stern threats on the one hand and sweet promises on the other, Wang

Jun agrees at length to wed. Qin Yan remains at home and for
months tries to find a job. Finally she has no recourse but to
marry someone whom she does not love, a minor cadre from
Changsha. She does not want her children to grow up with bad
family backgrounds.

Then, in 1959 Wang Jun is suddenly pronounced a member of
a Peng Dehuai anti-Party clique and is dishonorably discharged,
and soon after that, his wife divorces him. With no income, he
has little choice but to return with his six-year-old son to his
parent's home in Shandong Province, and on the way, decides to
stop over in Changsha for a few days. There, in a chance
encounter with Qin Yan, he is able to talk with his former lover
about what has befallen each of them over the past few years,
and they are overcome with a sense of great loss. The evening
before Wang Jun is scheduled to leave, Qin Yan asks him if she
can keep the boy, who bears a striking resemblance to his father,
at her home overnight. Wang Jun agrees, taking a room in a hotel.
The next day when Qin Yan goes to the station to see them off,
she presents Wang Jun with a vest she has knit during the night.
As the train begins to pull away from the platform, Wang Jun
tells his son to say 'Goodbye, Auntie,' but, strangely, the boy
refuses.

'She won't let me call her "Auntie,"' the boy explains after
the train starts to move.

'Why not?' asks Wang Jun, puzzled.

'She told me I should call her "Mama."'

The son proceeds to take out an envelope from this 'Mama'
which contains a bundle of cash and grain coupons, of immense
value to a man who is jobless and heading into the countryside
during a time of widespread famine. Grasping the packet in his
hand, Wang Jun looks at Qin Yan in the distance and begins to
weep silently.

'So did you call her "Mama?"' he asks.

'Yes.'

'Then what happened?'

'She hugged me and started to cry. She said I was a good boy.'

'Did she say anything else?'

'No, she just kept hugging and kissing me.'

During the final scene of the novel, Wang Jun pulls the boy
close to him and passionately kisses the small face which has
been planted so many times with his lover's kisses.

In marked contrast to the novels which have been published
outside over the past dozen years, the emotions of the main
characters are richly portrayed, and the tone throughout dark and

poignant. By the time I put down the soiled, hand-copied notebook, I myself am weeping, something which I have not done very often during the eight years I have spent in prison.

This manuscript, I learn, experiences a fairly wide circulation at Reconstruction Farm. At the time of my release two years later, I run into several inmates from other parts of the camp, who inform me they have all read the book. Moreover, they tell me, whenever it rained or snowed, the tale of Wang Jun and Qin Yan was a favorite of the resident storytellers of their own brigades.

Spectacles and I never give up our iron belief that a relatively tolerant 'Khrushchev era' will come one day to China, bringing with it a cultural renaissance. Even during China's darkest hour, Spectacles fiercely maintains his creative impulse, documenting the world around him in underground works that he hopes will serve as source material—precious jewels waiting to be mined in the inevitable renaissance.

Technically, Spectacles' term is not up till 1983, but he is sent home in late 1978, two years after Mao's death. The authorities explain that he had not been wrongly imprisoned since he had, in fact, committed an error, but that fifteen years was too excessive a punishment. I am told that, upon regaining his freedom, Spectacles requested to be legally rehabilitated and to be reassigned to his old factory. Whether these requests were granted or not, I never heard.

Though Spectacles was not a political man, and did not write about politics, in the years that I have browsed through the shelves of the bookstores, I have yet to see familiar-looking titles or names. Nevertheless, if he is still alive, I am sure that he is scribbling, scribbling, for there will be characters within him, growing, waiting to be born.

20

Soothsayers, Barristers, and Boddhisattvas

▼

LAWYER LONG

The 'death knell' sounded minutes ago, but here I lie on my bunk, unwilling to face the fact that I must get up. The thought of another scorching, backbreaking day makes my head pound. From the neighboring barracks, I hear the footsteps of prisoners carrying buckets of rice and water; from the front of the mess kitchen, hostile shouts. The sun is just rising.

Breakfast will be ten ounces of rice with vile, briny, pickled vegetables that stick in your throat and just won't go down. Today, however, some of us decide to deposit these black pickles in a large pile in the yard where the cadres usually stand during assembly. We are working on our rice when Counselor Li makes his rounds.

'Who dumped these vegetables on the ground? Who did this? Somebody have a gripe about the dictatorship of the proletariat?'

Nobody answers. Hopping mad, Counselor Li steams up and walks over to where we are squatting. We quickly finish up and assemble in the courtyard. Before the ranks are complete, a young man named Wang Baiqiu marches up to Counselor Li.

'Cadre, sir, I can't go out to work today.'

'Why not?' the counselor asks, glaring.

'I just got my period.'

'You come from a dog's cunt? Since when do men have periods?' he snaps, allowing himself a faint smile. Counselor Li knows that Wang is frozen bean curd material.

'Communism tells us that men and women are equal, and women have periods, so why not men?'

Many of the prisoners burst out laughing.

'You're just like a turtle wacking off—I hear a shell clacking like crazy, but I can't *see* anything,' whispers Baby Yao.

Counselor Li squints his narrow eyes, this time stifling his smile. 'Listen here, you son of a bitch: Your father and mother certainly wasted a night's work on you. Now get the hell out to the fields.'

Counselor Li lacks refinement, but we infinitely prefer him to the relatively well educated Brigade Leader Ji and Political Instructor Yang. Because Li can make out only a few characters and has trouble understanding the KGBs' bulletins, he ends up being more of a general supervisor for work than a political monitor. And when we joke around with him, he usually lets it pass.

The ranks of the Third Detachment are now in place. 'Some of you guys just won't submit to the discipline of the government,' Counselor Li bellows. 'You're not satisfied with the dictatorship of the proletariat. And now you're dumping your vegetables on the ground and throwing around your rice bowls in open defiance of the dictatorship of the proletariat! When you go out to the fields, you slack off. But when you want to steal eggs and other produce, you're full of pep! I hear some of you guys have been sewing big pouches in your jackets to hold your booty. Well, today we're going to check that rumor out. Prisoner-on-duty! Proceed to the septic tank and fetch me a bucket of shit!'

Counselor Li has us open our jackets, one by one, and soon enough finds what he is looking for. When the prisoner-on-duty returns with the stinking bucket, Counselor Li commands him to scoop a ladleful of feces into each pouch. Then, using his bare hand, he squashes down on the jackets and scrubs vigorously, so that the manure oozes through to the skin. 'Now we'll see if you steal vegetables again.'

Probably a dozen or so of the men are punished in this way. I predict they will steal even more in the future. One of our Reconstruction Farm mottoes is, 'Stealing vegetables is the sacred right of all prisoners.'

Suddenly, a short, old man streaks from a *haozi* door into the courtyard. He is holding a club in his right hand, with which he beats a basin that he holds in his left hand.

Gong, gong. 'The tiger is the king of beasts; Mao Zedong is the king of men,' he chants, then beats the basin several times again. 'If you want justice, you won't get it unless you defeat this king of men. If you want justice to be done, you have to be able to defeat many men—you have to defeat the king of men; the man who is able to defeat all the other men won't be fair!' *Gong, gong.*

Counselor Li orders the prisoner-on-duty to take the old man away.

'That's Long Caizao,' the prisoner next to me explains. 'He was a lawyer before the Revolution. When he speaks, poetry comes out of his mouth. He's loony.'

Long is still reciting as he is dragged off. 'Under the Nationalists, you have freedom, but no equality; under the Communists you have equality, but no freedom!' *Gong, gong, gong.*

His voice trails off, and the political prisoners smile at each other knowingly.

By now the courtyard is almost empty, which means it is time for those of us in the Construction Group to begin work. It has been decided that the three detachments will be separated by brick walls, which we must build ourselves. But as I reach for my trowel, I notice Long Caizao slowly emerging from his *haozi*. He is gazing soberly at the sky completely lost in thought, his hands clasped behind his back. The few long, wispy hairs of his beard jiggle every time his chin moves. With his face spotted and wrinkled with age, he is rather homely. Nor does the newly applied plaster on his right temple help his appearance. He looks like one of the old gentry who has fallen on hard times.

I wave to him from where I stand atop the scaffold, but he doesn't respond. My fellow apprentice, Lu Guoan, busily laying bricks beside me, mutters, 'What in the world do you want him over here for? There's trouble every time he opens his mouth!'

I tap slowly on the scaffold with my trowel, waiting with some impatience for the assistant to bring more bricks and mortar. 'I'm dying to hear one of his speeches,' I whisper.

Lu Guoan winces. 'All right, all right. All you have to do to get him to come over is call him Lawyer Long.'

'Lawyer Long!' I shout out cheerfully.

Slowly, the old man turns his head in our direction.

'Lawyer Long, I'd love to hear your speeches. Come here so I can listen to you while I work on the wall.'

He walks toward me, but just before he reaches the scaffold, leaps back with a start. 'Don't hit me! I'm meat on a chopping block! Cut me up any way you want, horizontally, vertically. Sooner or later, I'll be at your mercy.'

This man has been beaten many times. 'Lawyer Long, I'm not going to hit you; I would like to be your student and listen to your lectures.'

He nods vaguely. 'Little Yang, can you believe that after 1949

China had no business law or civil law—law that had been in existence for some twenty years? With neither business nor civil law, there are no standards for doing anything, no rules. The Nationalists may not have been able to defeat the Communists, but by the twentieth year of the Republic, they already had civil law, business law, and corporate law. And we still have no law— and no heaven! No law and no heaven!'

I listen silently, laying bricks all the while he talks. It seems that the minute he gets onto the topic of law (which indeed seems to happen every time someone addresses him as Lawyer Long), his behavior becomes perfectly normal.

'Little Yang, you must know about the jury system? English common law and continental Roman law both make use of the jury system.'

'No, tell me about the jury system,' I call down to him.

'Well, when two people get into an altercation, there should be a mediator who is unrelated to both of them if the dispute's going to be dealt with fairly. The jury is unrelated to the plaintiff and the defendant; the decision is made by the jury. Sometimes they ask people who happen to be walking on the street.'

I let the trowel in my hand rest. 'What? They just grab people off the street for a jury?' I can't believe it.

In point of fact, I have read something about juries and know, for example, that at the beginning of the nineteenth century one way in which the French legal system was superior to the Prussian was that it has a jury system. I knew that China had juries for years, juries made up of government officials. The courts, the members of the jury, the Procurate Department, and the Public Security Bureau were all controlled by the Communist Party. After the Great Leap Forward, juries disappeared. So did lawyers, for that matter. During the Cultural Revolution prisoners were punished merely for filing appeals. Lawyer Long's talk of juries composed of ordinary people seems like a story from heaven—too good to be true; wondrous and exhilarating!

He paces about, orating loudly, bubbles forming in the corners of his mouth. After a while he starts acting oddly again. His eyes roll upwards. Pointing to the sky as if he were cursing someone, he shouts:

'The mouth that has two flaps of skin,
Can speak of thick and speak of thin.
The mouth that has two shiny blades,
Cuts until the blood cascades.'

He rolls his reproachful eyes once again, then gazes at me and cries out in a raspy voice, 'The tiger is the king of beasts; Mao is the king of men. If you want justice, you have to beat Mao.' For a split second he pauses, then screams at the top of his lungs:

'When men raise a man up, he becomes a priceless treasure,
When a man vies with other men, he is angered to death,
When men trample upon a man, they trample him to death.
Mao Zedong, today everyone puts you up on a pedestal,
Tomorrow everyone will trample you,
And only then will you remember Han Xin's words,
"The water that carries a boat
Is the same water that overturns it.'

Lu Guoan and I look at each other, worried. These rantings are going to get Long killed. 'Lawyer Long.' I whisper, 'don't get all excited; come over here and lecture to us *quietly*.'

'We're the only ones who need to hear you,' Lu adds.

But Long Caizao has stopped listening. Casting a suspicious look at us, he chants loudly in a sing-song voice. 'Mencius said, "Secure ownership leads to constant effort;" but you Communists won't allow people to have "secure ownership." Look at you—crabs, crawling sideways like this. How long can you last?' His head thrashes about wildly.

Unable to silence him, we knock our trowels loudly against the bricks so that the watchtower sentinel cannot hear.

But the following morning we cannot resist asking Lawyer Long to lecture to us again. He is much more cautious than yesterday. 'Little Yang,' he whispers mysteriously into my ear, 'you may not tell anyone else, do you understand? You must give me your word you won't spread this around.'

I crouch down beside him and nod; anything to hear his secrets. He presses his mouth to my ear, his foul breath sweeping across my face, and in a voice as soft as the hum of a mosquito, begins, 'Little Yang, Peng Dehuai is a good man; don't believe the bad things Mao Zedong says about him. You know, if we had gone along with Peng Dehuai, fewer people would have starved to death in 1959.'

I can't help but laugh out loud, for what he is saying is so outrageously and blasphemously truthful. No one I know has the nerve to say such things.

Lawyer Long has no idea why I am laughing. Wrinkling his brow, he gets a terrified look in his eyes, thinking most likely that I am a collaborator or KGB.

'You are a great person, you are a great person with integrity.'
I reassure him.

On hearing such praise, he becomes very shy, acting much like a child.

For three days Lawyer Long lectures us in the courtyard. Sometimes he is normal; sometimes he is crazy. When he is rational, we hear ideas we have never heard before. When he loses control, he curses violently, but hidden within his wild words is always a profound message. At the end of the third day, Counselor Li informs him he has to go back out to the fields. The counselor is not overly concerned with prisoners' thoughts; all he cares about is that we slave away and stay away from the vegetable garden. Long Caizao is better off under his command than he would be anywhere else.

The next morning, after Lawyer Long has shuffled out to work, I feel his absence.

Late that afternoon when the iron gate swings open, we look for Lawyer Long in the crowd of returning laborers. There is a commotion as the teams file into the *haozi* with peals of laughter. Some time passes before they are able to catch their breaths and answer our questions.

They tell us that Counselor Li had been standing outside the gate to observe the incoming prisoners count off. As Cadre Liu, the cadre-on-duty, busied himself with the tally, the counselor noticed Wang Baiqiu's bulging shirt.

'Wang Baiqiu, what's that lump underneath your shirt?' Counselor Li had demanded imperiously. 'Take it out and show me.'

'It's nothing much; really nothing at all.'

Wang turned to go, but the sly look on his face had not escaped Counselor Li. Grabbing Wang's collar, he had sneered, 'If there's "nothing much" here, why don't you want me to take a little peek?'

Wang Baiqiu crossed his arms tightly over his chest. The Counselor yanked at Wang's shirt, revealing a brown-paper package, which he snatched triumphantly.

'Again you have been plundering the vegetable garden! Stealing! And smuggling!'

Wang Baiqiu cooed softly, 'No, no, that's just something I'm taking to the lab. Better not to open it, sir.'

Counselor Li had placed the packet on Cadre Liu's table and slowly unwrapped it beneath the gaze of many prisoners. Under the first layer of paper Counselor Li discovered a second, and inside that—a pile of fresh, golden human feces, stinking to high heaven.

'I told you it wasn't vegetables and you wouldn't believe me,' Wang admonished. 'This morning the cadre told us to take a stool sample to the clinic for a blood fluke test, and this is my sample. I *told* you not to open it, but you didn't believe that either!'

The prisoners had become hysterical. Counselor Li looked at the pile on the table. 'Wang Baiqiu, you son of a bitch, you son of a bitch!'

Hastening to the gate, Cadre Liu tried to restore order, shouting to the prisoners to count off one more time. He commanded the prisoner-on-duty to remove the offensive packet while the rest of the team rushed wildly inside. For once, Cadre Liu did not insist on getting an accurate tally. Wang Baiqiu and many others in our ranks gloat about this successful act of revenge for days.

YANG TAONIAN

At the end of the week yet another orator joins us in the courtyard—a sober little man by the name of Yang Taonian. Despite his relatively glum demeanor, we enjoy having him around, for he has a habit of periodically announcing he will not go out to the fields, his way of protesting that the government has no 'legal system.' On each of these occasions he lounges around the *haozi* for three or four days. Should a cadre come in to roust him out of his bunk, Yang Taonian engages him in a long debate on the subject of his vision of law—a mishmash of Buddhism, Confucianism, and, of course, his 'legal system.' Nobody quite knows what this system might be; his theories are generally rather abstruse. Yang is famous throughout Reconstruction Farm for never having lost a debate, though I have never been sure what 'winning' means. Perhaps it is his self-assurance and stentorian voice that enables him to hold his own against the cadres. Pushed to their wits' end, they lock him in the little *haozi* and hold struggle sessions, but it is no use. He continues to do and say whatever he likes.

After the cadres disappear, Lu Guoan and I call Yang over to the scaffold and ask him to address us. We are still working on the cursed wall.

Yang is both peasant and intellectual. Though he comes from rustic stock, his father's generation was educated gentry in the 'old society.'

He stares us straight in the eye, sounding at times as if he is reciting classical poetry or intoning a sutra. One minute he talks about the essays of ultraleftists, Qi Benyu and Wang Li of the Central Cultural Revolution Group, saying that their essays demonstrate the chaos that prevails and how the Communists have disrupted the 'legal system.' Then he tells us that, while Premier Zhou Enlai is the man who best understands this system, his policies have been ruined by the bad cadres who serve under him. I listen for a long time before I realize that by 'system' he refers not to law, but to the social mores and ethics enshrined in Buddhist and Taoist writings.

He offers us practical rules to live by. Of all the ties that bind people together in political circles, those based on a person's ideology are the weakest; the only stable bonds are personal relationships. He cites a passage from the *Three Kingdoms*, in which strategist Zhuge Liang evaluates the political performance of the Shu State ruler, Liu Biao, and counsels his King, Liu Bei.

> Favor the people with titles, for when there are no titles, disaster descends; reward the people, for when there are no benefits, they will rebel. . . .

> Limit the number of dukedoms, so that an elevated rank will give them a sense of honor;

> Punish them with law, for when law is enforced, kindness will be appreciated.

He lectures, shaking his head back and forth, and I suddenly realize that he believes he himself has the ability to rule China.

'How will you be able to fulfill your duties without any power?' I ask mischievously.

'Mencius once said, "Objects do not become infested unless they are decayed; men will not be humiliated by others unless they have humiliated themselves; a nation will not be assaulted by other nations unless it has assaulted itself with internal strife. The man who respects other men will always have their respect; the man who loves other people will always have their love." Members of the Communist Party brutally kill each other—they neither respect nor love the people. They keep fooling with class struggles. It won't be too many more years before they stumble, and then the real heroes will be able to show their stuff.'

'What do you think will happen when Mao dies?'

My question delights him. 'After Mao dies, China will once more be governed by the "legal system" of Buddhism and Taoism. I've rubbed my fingers to get a reading on China's horoscope: After Mao, there will be a transitional political figure, and after that, a man by the name of Zhao will take control.'

'But there are so many people in the world named Zhao—do you know *which* Zhao it will be?'

'This is something I've thought about for many a night. Very likely it will be Zhao Puchu, head of the Chinese Buddhist Association!'

How disappointing. Zhao Puchu writes excellent classical poetry, to be sure, but he is hardly a political animal.

In a few days the Third Detachment is ordered to struggle against Yang Taonian. The major charges: he refuses to work and he has written a letter to Premier Zhou Enlai accusing the lower-level cadres of bringing chaos to the 'legal system' and of failing to implement the Premier's policies.

High upon the platform, Yang never once lowers his head or weakens. The minute he is attacked, he delivers a crisp rebuttal, citing his 'system' to indict the cadres. I marvel at his bravery.

Yang Taonian serves seven years in this fashion, eight years fewer than Lawyer Long. He finishes up before I do.

Much later, after Zhao Ziyang has been premier for a while, I suddenly remember Yang's 'prediction.' I cannot help but wonder whether his 'legal system' is at work.

SHEN ZIYING, THE TRUTHTELLER

'How's life treating you?'

Removing his straw hat, one of the peasants on the bank looks up from where he has been cutting grass to answer Lu Guoan. 'Oh, we're getting by—'bout the same as you folks.'

No walls or fences surround the fields of Reconstruction Farm, nothing to bar the occasional peasant from Huarong County who is traveling south from Thousand Red Mountains Farm, or north from Junshan Farm to cut through camp. The cadres don't miss a chance to rough up these 'trespassers' who use the farm roads and chop down firewood, so that the local peasants tend to sympathize with the prisoners.

'Are you under the impression that only cow-ghosts and serpent-spirits are kept here?' I ask, smiling.

'We know well enough who you are. As far as we're concerned, you politicals are better men than most.'

There is much laughter among the 'counterrevolutionary criminals' as we go back to work. Though there are eight work groups out today, they are scattered around the farm, and only two cadres are out, both of whom are very far away.

The peasant's words echo in my ears. I doubt that I am worthy of such deference, though there is one man in our group who certainly is—Shen Ziying. There is nothing he won't do for his comrades. Our daily ration for boiled water is a single mugful, but Shen always gives his away, drinking instead from the stagnant, parasite-ridden pond.

Admittedly, Shen can be a pain. Outlasting both Lawyer Long and Yang Taonian, Shen is capable of delivering political sermons twelve hours a day. At first he jabbers away in his bunk, all night long. Finally somebody squalls at him, demanding that he go outside to talk. Shen dresses and leaves wordlessly. Now he always delivers his speeches under the stars.

One night, I get up to go to the latrine and I see Shen's small frame pacing about the yard, his tiny eyes and shaved head reflecting the moonlight. He seems totally unaware of my presence. Though his voice is passionate, his face is calm.

'Even though the 1954 state monopoly for purchase and marketing is said to have been implemented because the government lacked sufficient grain to develop industry, the real reason was because you Communists, in your campaign of the Three Antis and Five Antis of 1952, wanted to label grain merchants as bourgeois profiteers when property was nationalized. Then the state monopoly brought on a *real* grain shortage, and the peasants starved.'

I am flabbergasted. Normally his muttering is indecipherable, but the ideas I am hearing tonight are clear and well-organized.

What is most surprising, Shen Ziying's account of the state monopoly policy is completely contrary to the propaganda with which I have group up. I recall someone having mentioned that Shen had been forced to sell his grain at an abnormally low price to the government in 1954. With his entire family on the verge of starvation, Shen had sneaked into a granary, and was sentenced to four years when he was discovered. I had always assumed he was a typical peasant who knew next to nothing about the outside world.

As he begins to babble again, I glance around.

'In 1962, Liu Shaoqi started his "Three Liberalization" policies and "Contract System."[1] The peasants rejoiced. You, Mao Zedong, were the only one who wasn't happy. You wanted to denounce it and overthrow Liu Shaoqi. You are the Qin Emperor who has been cursed for centuries; the evil you create manifests itself in a thousand ways. You will die a horrible death!'

His voice is now loud and shrill; his face twisted with rage.

[1] These reforms advocated free markets, individual responsibility for an enterprise's profits and losses, private land plots, and a contract system with fixed farm output quotas for families.

Pointing to the watchtower in the corner of the compound, he rails, 'You Communists have perpetrated every sort of evil, but you won't allow anyone to criticize you. How can you expect to get away with that? I will curse you anyway; curse you! Unless you take down this vile Communist signboard!'

Enough! All I need is to be charged with having listened to a speech that 'vilifies and slanders Chairman Mao' without reporting it to the cadres, and I will be in serious trouble.

At a sentencing meeting soon afterwards, it is announced that Shen Ziying's term is to be extended to twenty-four years. I keep thinking of Shen's remarks about Mao and Liu Shaoqi during the Cultural Revolution—how could a peasant who has been locked up in labor camp for twenty years be so well informed?

On the way back from the sluice, Shen's face is ashen. Fear and hatred flash in his eyes, marbled with cataracts. He is muttering again.

'In 1958 you sentenced me again and tied me up; in 1961 you added more time and put me in handcuffs for two days; in 1964, you sentenced me again and cuffed me for a week. In 1966 you sentenced me yet again, and you Red Guards came to work me over. For days at a time I couldn't get out of bed. If you Communists want to kill me in prison, just do it! Don't carve my flesh off piece by piece! The day before yesterday Instructor Yang threatened me again—oh, you know very well I'm a coward. You know that if I keep talking like that I will get myself killed. You're afraid that I'll talk, and if I tell the truth, you'll have to kill me. But if you're so afraid of people telling the truth, then stop doing so many despicable things! You're set on doing evil, and yet you won't allow anyone to criticize you.'

He rattles on, making my heart soar. No doubt there are many Chinese who agree with him—people who are unwilling to be silent, unwilling to 'call a deer a horse.' They cannot be heard in Chinese society, because they are put in jail as soon as they speak out.

◆

Though the Spring Festival is passed uneventfully, the Year of the Tiger slinks in anyway, renewing the ten thousand living creatures. Almost overnight the fields have turned from brown to bright green. Whereas in the past we have always planted in early May, this year Reconstruction Farm is popularizing a new method, 'transplanting shoots.' And so at the end of March we trudge back to the fields with the most primitive of tools, the ox-driven plow. The weeds are turned under, and the surface is tamped down with an iron harrow. Manure from the ox and pig sheds is to be carried up on shoulder poles. Only then can we begin to bury the roots of the young rice plants in the mud.

Oddly enough, while those of us from Changsha are generally despised by the cadres—in their minds, we are too educated for our own good, talking up a storm and always up to something— come planting and harvesting time, we cityfolk are often more efficient than the peasants. In the Third Brigade, Lu Guoan and I are the fastest. Once we get going, our hands become a blur of motion; we can finish over a tenth of an acre in a single day.

After a while, though, it becomes apparent that Lu Guoan and I are always given the heavy assignments, whereas the laggards get lighter work. As soon as we learn this lesson in labor camp economics, we ease off.

But Shen Ziying is slower than slow. Afraid that he will injure the little plants, he picks up one shoot at a time and then bends down to plant it. Every so often he straightens up to look at his rows, muttering. I try to listen, whenever I am working near him. One of his speeches is an analysis of Chairman Mao's 'Serve the People.'

' "Everything we do is for the benefit of the people," ' Shen recites, passing a shoot from his left hand to his right and slipping it into the mud. The essay is one of three written by Mao that prisoners are required to memorize, the other two being 'In Commemoration of Bethune'[2] and 'The Foolish Old Man Who Moved the Mountain.'

'One must be particularly cautious when talking to people who say such beautiful things.' Shen stands rigidly at attention and addresses the young shoots, his face void of emotion. 'If someone who wants to do business with you *admits* that he is selfishly motivated, feel free to carry out the transaction; he won't hurt someone else to benefit himself. However, the person who says he is not selfishly motivated, saying that he wants to serve the people from the bottom of his heart—*he* will most certainly take advantage of you!'

Though I would like to linger, Shen is just too slow, and I leave him far behind. When I catch up with him again on my next round, two other prisoners are between us. He is still talking to his plants.

'Listen, you; this is my speech to the United Nations.

---

[2] Norman Bethune was the Canadian doctor held up as a socialist hero for assisting the Chinese Communist Revolution.

Representatives of the United Nations, I tell you that China is going to be divided into many, many districts, and every district will follow my plan. All houses will face the south, have two stories and sinks with running water, and each district will have a centrally located cooperative. In every cooperative there will be a bakery. Mechanization must be voluntary, not the way the Communists carried it out, so that the more machines you had, the more money you lost.'

I sail down another row before looking over again. Though Shen is still working on his first row, he has moved onto the relationship between workers and peasants.

'As soon as you Communists entered the cities, you forgot all about us peasants. And what happened when they got there? Without us countryfolk, you city people couldn't live for a day. Try and imagine what it would be like without our grain; could you live for a single day? Could you get by without eating? But without you, we can get along just fine, same as we always did before.'

Shen is not a popular man. His poor productivity makes it hard for his work group to meet quotas, meaning that they often get home very late. Nor does his penchant for political speeches win him many friends. He makes a natural target for the cadres, who in this busy agricultural season need to find ways to spur the prisoners to work even harder.

On a rainy spring evening, some seven hundred prisoners crowd into the auditorium and huddle together on the floor. Brigade Leader Yang stands on the stage, a banner draped overhead proclaiming:

PUSH REVOLUTION TO SEIZE PRODUCTION!
GENERAL MEETING TO STRUGGLE AGAINST THE
    RESISTER SHEN ZIYING

'Counterrevolutionary bad element Shen Ziying, male, forty-three years of age, has always hated the Party and the socialist system, having many times viciously attacked our great Chairman Mao and the glorious and correct Chinese Communist Party. Since 1954, when he was first sentenced, he has received from our public security organs sentences totaling twenty-four years. During the demanding spring planting season, criminal Shen Ziying still did not show a willingness to repent and stubbornly maintained his reactionary positions. On the job, he is passive and lazy. Yet when it comes to resisting reform, he is very active. Resister Shen Ziying, come up onto the stage.'

Looking haggard in his black cotton jacket, Shen slowly emerges from the ranks. As he moves forward, I can hear him mumbling, 'You've got it all wrong—my Chinese age is forty-one. I was born in the twenty-first year of the Republic. My attack may have been evil poison, but what I said was all true.' He sounds less confident than usual, even a bit defensive. One can see that his bravery has eroded some under the gaze of so many people.

The individuals who will deliver the criticism are all prisoners, and include our own group study leader and another man who regularly 'reaches out' to the government. The counterrevolutionary utterances that are being 'exposed' we have heard before. Privately, I sympathize with many of these ideas and suspect that most people in the audience feel the same way. After the individuals have completed their denunciations, each prisoner-on-duty leads his group in crying out, 'If Shen Ziying doesn't surrender, destroy him! Thoroughly criticize counterrevolutionary Shen Ziying to the rotten finish!'

Though all the prisoners are required to join in the chanting, there are different levels of engagement. One quarter of the men in the crowd raise their hands and shout loudly; one half shout rather half-heartedly, and the remaining quarter keep both their hands and their voices very low. Still, to the person being struggled against, the 700 voices come together as one.

Shen's eyes droop. Every time the crowd chants a new slogan, he lowers his head a little more. When the shouting finally stops, he raises it slowly, his mouth moving almost imperceptibly. Although I cannot make out what he saying, I am certain he is once again voicing his political commentaries, though he is probably doing more defending than attacking.

Two years later Shen Ziying receives yet another four years, bringing his term to a total of twenty-eight. It now seems likely that the authorities have determined to keep this man in labor camp forever.

Since I first arrived at Reconstruction Farm, I have been plagued by the question, 'Are Chinese naturally submissive?' As the months pass, I have at least a partial answer: your labor reform camps are filled with people whose spirits are still intact, people like Lawyer Long, Yang Taonian, and Shen Ziying, who persist at all costs in shouting out their challenges, refusing to be muzzled.

21
Teacher
▼

He Minhe's health is in a precarious state. Having 'drunk' more ink than virtually everyone else in the Third Brigade, his stomach is full of the black poison—a condition, which in the 1970s, is increasingly viewed as terminal. As Counselor Li is wont to remind us, 'The more books you read, the more foolish and reactionary you become.'

In order to survive, most prisoners learn to assume appropriate defensive postures. Elementary school graduates claim not to recognize a single Chinese character; high school graduates say they have only finished elementary school; university graduates, high school. Poor He Minhe is so blind there is no way he can disguise his educational level. Countless concentric rings surround the rat-like black dots which constitute his eyes. You don't have to have a college diploma to know that the only way a man becomes a 'four-eyed terrier' is to have read books, lots of books, referred to colloquially as 'drinking ink.'

But when He Minhe takes off his glasses, he doesn't seem to be the well-bred, scholarly type. He reports to morning assembly barefoot. The labor reform uniform he wears is so old, it is brown and not black; instead of a belt, he keeps his pants up with hemp. A veritable workhorse out in the field, he can hold his own with anyone. The total absence of refinement is, however, most apparent at mealtime. He is among those who grab for the bucket of dirty dishwater, hoping to be the lucky one who will suck the rice particles into his mouth. More than once have I observed him along the roadside, bolting down live loaches and the tips of rape plants. When we wash, you can see that he was once a large-bellied VIP, for though the fat is gone, the stretch marks remain. He must have had a huge appetite at one time.

Because he is unable, or perhaps unwilling, to conceal the voracious hunger which seems to dominate his life, and never shares his care packages from home, He Minhe is not well regarded by the lower classes. Any prisoner who chooses to forget his pride and the existence of others will have few friends; but when such a man also has a bellyful of ink, he will have none at all.

I continue to use rainy days and the minutes between supper and political study to pore over the lessons in the math textbook Yang Hui has mailed to me. In about a year's time, I have muddled through only one volume, and though I tried the exercises at the back, I haven't been able to get very far with them. For math, it seems, one really needs a teacher. I decide to take my book and seek out He Minhe.

From the moment I enter his *haozi*, calling out 'Teacher He,' he can't stop beaming. The appellation is music to the ears of this pariah, who for months has been abused as a stinking counterrevolutionary intellectual.

Quickly tossing aside his cigarette, Teacher He cradles the textbook in his arm and turns the pages, ever so gently, scanning its contents. In a week or so, I find I am spending my evenings with him, whether on his bunk or my own, working on problems. Our class is not a traditional one. I constantly interrupt him with questions about everything that comes into my head, especially things about how mathematical concepts and theorems evolved; his stomach is full of this type of thing. When I get stuck on differentials and derivatives, always taking the derivatives for the average rate of change, Teacher He draws the distinction between the average rate of change and the marginal rate of change. He tells me stories of Newton, Galileo, and the acceleration of gravity, explaining in vivid terms how differentials were first created. Slowly the concepts fall into place.

As a young man, He Minhe received an education which was typical of the pre-Liberation, Anglo-American tradition. He graduated from Zhongshan University in Guangzhou in 1948, and after Liberation worked as an engineer. The new regime informed him that if he wanted to be rehabilitated he must learn Russian, and so gradually he acquired familiarity with Soviet technical materials. Upon returning to the university for a year of re-education, he was exposed to the Soviet educational system.

Since my math book comes from the Soviet Union, I am curious about how the Soviet texts differ from the American.

His response is so quick that I know he has thought about such things before. There are certain advantages of a standardized, interchangeable technology that outweigh the inevitable sacrifice in flexibility and spontaneity, he begins, then pauses, peering at me through his glasses, wondering perhaps if I will break this confidence. Then, rather abruptly, he resumes. 'The Soviet education system develops experts—who are skilled in one area, but have no ideas of their own. But in Europe and America they develop scholars—with the broad knowledge necessary for independent thinking.'

I am somewhat surprised. It is unusual for Teacher He to express value judgments; he prefers neutral statements of fact. I sense from his comments, however, that he has a more sophisticated understanding of Soviet culture than Chief Engineer Yu did, for he is able to articulate the pros and cons of the Soviet system without ever saying a word about socialism, and I never hear him utter any anti-communist sentiments.

Once he tells me an anecdote about how, after Liberation, the Communists implemented a series of water conservation projects which had given their small group of engineers a chance to show their stuff. At the project site at the Jing River, which was to connect the Yangtze River with Dongting Lake, Teacher He met with Deng Zihui, a Party Politburo member. Deng was subsequently branded a 'right-wing opportunist' in 1956.

'That was the first time I ever saw a high-level national Party leader,' he says with visible nostalgia. 'He wore plain old everyday clothes and didn't put on any airs. Boy, did he know his engineering!'

When Teacher He gets in trouble for his antisocial behavior, I do what I can for him. The 'black language' I picked up in Zuojiatang helps. But I also get a lot of mileage out of bathing in snow. I bet people that if I can wash myself with snow outside, the other person will have to do a turn for me as prisoner-on-duty. If I don't stay out in the snow stark naked for the prescribed period of time, the agreement is that I will do one of their turns. What they do not know is that when I was in high school I swam in the wintertime in order to fortify my revolutionary stamina. Thus I can almost always win these bets and, whenever I can, use the good will that I earn to smooth things over for Teacher He.

One day my sister Yang Hui wires me some money, and I decide to splurge and buy some pork. Since Teacher He has stayed back on sick leave, I ask him if he will chop the meat and stir-fry it for our small group of masons. While we are eating, my fellow apprentice Lu Guoan complains, 'This meat is as dry as a bone; how long was this pig lying around dead?'

Through the cell window, we hear the voice of one of the older prisoners holler over, 'Four-eyes dumped the oil left in the wok into his own oil bottle.'

This revelation incenses Lu Guoan, who rolls up his sleeves and is just about to pop He Minhe in the face. 'I told him to save it so we could use it the next time we fry vegetables,' I lie quickly, but I am privately very unhappy with my teacher.

'He still doesn't have any business putting it into his own bottle!' Lu shouts.

'Does a father need his son to teach him how to make love? Old He is old enough to be your father—lay off him!'

Seeing that I am bent on protecting him, Lu and the others let the matter go, but they do not attempt to hide their contempt for Teacher He during the rest of our meal.

The cadres, too, anger easily at my teacher. One afternoon, while we are standing in the scorching water of the fields inserting rice plants into the mud, Political Director Liu saunters up to the edge of the bank to watch. 'Now you know how tough manual labor is,' he lectures He Minhe while chewing on a piece of watermelon. 'You intellectuals used to live the life of parasites. When the rice was served, you simply opened your mouths. And when the dishes were placed on the table, you reached out your chopsticks. If the Communist Party hadn't sent you here to be reformed, you never would have known where the rice in your bowls comes from!'

Teacher He continues to absorb himself in his work, but I can tell that he is furious. Finally, after a moment he looks up at the director standing on the bank and says defiantly, 'One of my days in the drawing room contributed more to society than a whole month of my time here planting rice!'

Director Liu's face drops. He flings the melon rind down on the bank. 'Another attack on labor reform? Stinking intellectual! A dog just can't help from eating shit.'

Despite my fear that Teacher He will be struggled against at political study class, it doesn't happen, and the director is dispatched to another camp several days later.

Our friendship irks the authorities. One evening when I return from the fields, I discover that my bunk has been ransacked; notebooks, math worksheets, and textbooks are scattered across the bunk. A week later, it happens again. The searches recur—and then suddenly stop. It seems they can't attribute any political danger to differential equations. What does suffer, however, is my study of English, for unfortunately they confiscate everything they find in this language. Though I was required to take Russian in elementary school, and another four more years in junior high, the intellectuals of Zuojiatang persuaded me that English would be infinitely more useful, and I switched over then.

For lessons, I have found a prisoner who was once a high school English teacher; for materials, I rely on translations of Chairman Mao's *Quotations*, the works of Marx and Engels, and an English–Chinese dictionary, all sent to me by my father. Every week I receive a new edition of the English-language *Beijing Review* through the help of a Rightist engineer who works in the compulsory brigade, the unit for prisoners who have finished their sentences. Because prison regulations specifically ban the use of foreign languages within the *haozi*, regular prisoners are not permitted to subscribe to non-Chinese publications, not even official translations.

When everything in English is taken, I go to Brigade Leader Liu's office to protest. He is unsympathetic.

'A labor reform prisoner hardly has any opportunity to fiddle with Chinese words; what the fuck do you want to learn a foreign language for?' he mutters.

'Look, I've been reading things in English like Chairman Mao's *Quotations* and some government publications. Things that can help me reform my thoughts.'

Brigade Leader Liu can recognize only a few characters, but he speaks the language of a Yueyang bureaucrat fluently. Though we are constantly at loggerheads, I must confess I like his bluntness.

'I've never learned any of this English stuff in my whole life,' he continues sarcastically, 'and I'm better off than you are. You can learn as much English as you like, but you'll still be a labor reform prisoner. Now if *I've* never talked to a foreigner, do you really think a labor reform prisoner like you is ever going to have a chance to speak in a foreign tongue to a foreign person?'

'Talking to a wall would be more interesting than talking to you!' I bristle.

'Yang Xiguang, for a counterrevolutionary you're awfully full of yourself. If you don't toe the line, when your time is up I'll plant a counterrevolutionary cap on your head so large that you'll never be rehabilitated. Then we'll see if you speak any foreign tongues. You won't even be allowed to speak Chinese.'

We'll see about that! I watch for an opportunity to approach Farm Director Li. Li visits regularly to observe our work, and several weeks later I get my chance.

'Farm Director Li, sir, there's something that is troubling me,' I begin, when no other cadres are about. I then proceed to tell him how the Third Brigade cadres have continually confiscated my materials.

'Don't prison regulations forbid prisoners from conversing in a foreign language?' he asks stiffly.

'But I haven't been *talking* to anybody. I've been reading these government publications on my own.'

Farm Director Li is silent for a moment. 'Very well. But you must promise never to converse with other people in a foreign language.'

Of course I promise, and from that time on my English materials go undisturbed. My comrades in the Construction Group think I am out of my mind. My own master, Master Wang Jinguo, sees me sitting on the top bunk with a board across my lap solving math problems in the dim light and scoffs, 'Give it a rest, egghead! You're drowning in kerosene and still playing with matches. Get down here and play some chess.'

This kind of running commentary is especially annoying during my apprenticeship with Master Wang; he remains poised to demonstrate the superiority of his practical experience over my fancy formulas.

When master builders Wang Jinguo and Yang Zili team up to design a building, they don't ever use blueprints; the entire building is in their heads. This means that the two of them must personally supervise construction, guiding their underlings every step of the way. I cannot deny that the system works; we have just completed a new dormitory for the cadres in under four months.

'I don't understand any ma-mathe-ematics, and look at me— I can design and construct a building as well as anybody,' Master Wang crows when we are through.

Perhaps it is ungrateful of me to say so, since they are my masters, but the methods they use seem incredibly primitive. Though Yang and Wang are able to calculate tangents, or 'water,' as they call it, whenever they come up against a situation where they need to convert the values of angles and sides, they are lost. They are ignorant of the formulas for trigonometric functions, nor do they know how to use tables. And they certainly don't know how to use differentials to calculate the optimal distribution of stress.

Here, at last, I see my chance.

To design the numerous structures used for irrigation in the Third Brigade, Masters Wang and Yang always use the curve of a cut circle. From my text, I know that the curve of a suspended cable is better able to take stress. But the curve of a suspended cable can't be drawn with a compass, and in order to tailor such a curve to a certain span and weight, you have to use calculus. I tell them this, but it is only after I help the two masters design several suspended ditches and aqueducts in this fashion that they begin to respect the formulae in my head. Patiently I show them all sorts of ways to calculate their 'water,' as well as other trigonometric functions. It is a small but important victory for the intellectuals of the Third Brigade. Thereafter my companions show increasing support for my quantitative endeavors, though they never do stop teasing me about learning English.

◆

One day I am visited by a cadre from Farm Headquarters who notifies me that the leadership wants me to teach the cadres' children at the Farm high school. The school is short of teachers, he tells me, and Farm Director Li needs someone capable of teaching math to the senior class. Additionally, there are several dozen recent graduates who are presently laboring at Reconstruction Farm along with the labor reform criminals, because they haven't passed the college admissions exams and can't find any other work. Farm Director Li has decided that Farm Headquarters will put up some money for a remedial class so that they, too, can sit for the college entrance exam. Part of my teaching responsibilities will be to help them review math. It would seem that prisoners with ink in their bellies are in demand once again. Now that Mao is dead and the Gang arrested, the world is changing.

'I've heard you used mathematics to design some great arch bridges and aqueducts,' the cadre coos.

I nod quietly.

He has me carry my luggage to the Farm Headquarters, to the guest house complex that lies less than half a mile from the high school. The complex consists of a small residence for the remedial students and me, and an auditorium where the class will be held. I am assigned a room with two beds in it, an extraordinarily clean room. Or perhaps it just seems so in comparison to the filth of the *haozi*. The quilt has been recently aired and smells of the sun. Setting down my bags, I lie down, the crisscrossed palm fiber frame of the bed nearly as comfortable as a spring mattress, and I gaze up at the white plaster ceiling. My thoughts race. How many years has it been since I slept in a real bed in a room with no other people? A large window opens out onto the corridor, bathing the room in light. It seems impossible that I, a virtual slave, should be lying here in such luxury. And no one is here to watch me.

That night I write home asking Yang Hui to send me some new clothes. Everything I own has 'labor reform' on it and I am reluctant to wear this label in front of my students. The next morning, however, I realize that all my planning is pointless. When I walk through the classroom door to greet my seniors, they remain seated, instead of standing up and calling out, 'Good morning, teacher,' as convention dictates. How foolish to think I was free. I am half-master, half-slave.

Two days later, when one boy comes to the front of the room to ask about homework, he startles me by addressing me as 'Mister Yang.' No one uses this term any more; the generic address is 'Comrade,' and students call their instructors 'Teacher.' After some time I become aware that this throwback to pre-Liberation days is applied to a variety of social reprobates. In spite of the fact that the 1975 directive from Mao Zedong and Zhou Enlai has freed historical counterrevolutionaries ranked above brigade commander, the authorities are unwilling to dignify us with a revolutionary title like 'Comrade.' Though no longer criminals, we remain enemies, politically and socially, and must be addressed with the distant 'Mister.' My students could not have come up with this subtle form of denigration on their own.

I no longer eat with the other prisoners. Every day I go to the cadres' dining hall at Farm Headquarters, where the food is excellent, and cheap too—about one-quarter of the cost of meals at Reed Store Restaurant. Because all the produce has been grown by local slave labor, prices can be set at will by the cadres.

The principal takes me into a little room next to the auditorium which serves as the office of the regular classroom teacher. 'This is the new math teacher, Mister Yang,' he says, presenting me. 'And this is the teacher in charge of Class One of the junior class, Comrade Zhao Jinxiang.'

With two braids that are neither short nor long, she looks like a bright-eyed doll. Though once again the 'Mister' grates on my ears, Zhao Jinxiang is smiling warmly. She casually pulls a chair over for me to sit in and begins to talk about her two English classes. Her voice is soft and easy to listen to; it melts away any self-consciousness I might feel. No girl has spoken to me so earnestly since my incarceration.

The next day, I come to observe her class. She seems very strict; perhaps because she is so young, she feels she must put up a tough front. I am touched when she formally introduces me, even though she, too, refers to me as 'Mister Yang.' In the senior class, no one bothered to tell the students who I was; I stepped into a room of silence and simply began talking about equations. But here it is obvious that a detailed explanation has preceded my arrival. Before today I never cared about what people said about me behind my back. I scorned their scorn: 'You may look down on me, but I think even less of you. I rely on my own resources to make a living. Advanced culture will always dissolve the lower culture!'

But when Zhao Jinxiang introduces me to her class, I shrink. I wonder how the authorities related my counter-revolutionary crimes to this beautiful girl.

And what do the students think of me? Notorious counterrevolutionary author of 'Whither China?' Privileged city-dweller and son of a high-ranking cadre in Changsha? Easygoing teacher who keeps us on our toes? They seem to be warming up to me.

Soon Teacher He joins me at the complex. Having finished his term, he has been 'authorized' to fill the physics teaching position as a compulsory laborer. Only Farm Director Li may assign prisoners or ex-prisoners to instruct cadres' children—a highly unorthodox arrangement which will cause many parents to raise their eyebrows, given that the primary mission of education is to 'foster revolutionary successors.' He Minhe will teach physics to the same two classes of students I teach.

As a criminal, I am not allowed to wear a watch. Since there are no clocks in the auditorium, to mark the beginning and end or each class Zhao Jinxiang must come into our class and signal us. One day she asks me into her office.

'Yang Xiguang,' she says, startling me by this new form of address. 'I'm leaving you my watch so you can keep track of the time yourself. I have to go into Yueyang today.' Regular teachers travel into the city once a month for in-service courses.

Her gesture is surprisingly generous. Watches are prohibitively expensive; almost nobody loans them to other people. Perhaps she trusts me—perhaps she has even stopped feeling political bias against me. After this I sense a subtle change in our relationship and I invite Teacher He to go with me to visit her office evenings.

Zhao Jinxiang belongs to the generation whose education was interrupted by the Cultural Revolution. During her years in high school and Normal College, the bookstore shelves had been virtually empty. Since Mao's death, all sorts of literary works have begun to appear. She waits anxiously for each issue of *People's Literature* and for other periodicals containing old novels.

When I tell her about *A Tale of Two Cities* and *The Red and the Black*, her eyes sparkle. But she likes most of all to hear the stories by Hugo and Tolstoy told by Teacher He, who has read dozens of the great English and French novels, as well as quite a few modern Soviet works. As Zhao Jinxiang listens, enraptured, I look on, thinking what a strange trio we make.

Suddenly I am at once restless and full of hope. The loudspeaker now plays the soft melodies once criticized as poisonous weeds. Each passing day brings 'new' phenomena. In fact these are bits of culture from the 1950s which, having been banned during the Cultural Revolution, are now gradually reappearing. The culture which was repressed for so many years is coming to its senses. And my term is almost up.

At dusk Teacher He and I take long walks around the compound and talk. Stimulated by the changes around us, we reminisce about the past twenty years, from the Anti-Rightist Movement of 1957, to the Great Leap and the famine of 1959, to the subsequent restoration of 1962, to the Cultural Revolution, to the restoration of 1972, to the rehabilitation of the Rebels in 1974, all the way up to the Tiananmen Square Incident of 1976.

We are particularly excited by Yang Hui's letter, which says that some Communist Party members are actively advocating the rehabilitation of the 1957 Rightists and the 1959 'right-wing opportunists.' That night neither of us can sleep.

Lying in bed, I recall our conversations and am struck by how different Teacher He is from a 'true' Rightist like Yu Yuyi. Teacher He had been a victim of the Hundred Flowers Campaign. When the Party leaders urged him to offer his suggestions, he had racked his brain to come up with ideas: his unit's Party branch secretary always claimed to represent the Party, yet if anyone had a differing opinion, the secretary immediately accused that person of not obeying the Party leadership. Wasn't this behavior too high-handed? And hadn't Hitler once promoted 'national socialism?' What was the difference between his socialism and the Chinese?

When the Anti-Rightist Campaign began, and every unit had a quota to meet, Old He was a natural for labeling. Then, a decade later, during a meeting in 1969, he was caught doodling on a newspaper and it was discovered that he had written the word 'reactionary' on a page with a picture of Chirman Mao on the opposite side. Such an 'attack' on Chairman Mao was reactionary behavior, and this affront, combined with his previous record, brought him seven years of labor reform. Before this afternoon I had never known what crime brought my teacher here. To me it seems that he is innocent of any crime at all.

One afternoon Zhao Jinxiang drops in on me out of the blue, hopping about like a sparrow. She has gotten hold of the record and book for *Nine Hundred English Sentences* and asks me to go to her office. There, the two of us are alone for the first time. As we listen to the exercises, I look at her face, dimpled and flushed with excitement. She seems so young and alive. Do I want to borrow the book? Nodding, I rise to leave.

'How come you spend so much time with He Minhe?' she asks hastily, almost as an afterthought. 'You should keep away from him. Those old Rightists are different from the people like you who were put in jail during the Cultural Revolution.'

I blink in amazement. All along the road back to the guest house, her words keep spinning about in my mind. She knows a lot about us; in fact she very likely knows more about what is in my dossier than I do. If, on the surface, she has been polite to Old He, in her heart, she despises him. And as I remember how kind she has been to me, I realize with horror that this too has been mere politeness, that in her heart she has drawn a line separating her from counterrevolutionaries and from me. By the time I reach the room, Old He is asleep on his bed, breathing heavily. The sight of him makes me feel even more lonely and depressed.

That is when it hits me: I have fallen in love with her. I ache to see her, and shudder at the thought that she might discriminate against me. Not once since I have been sentenced have I been afraid of being discriminated against; in the past, when I faced discrimination from a person, I thought to myself, 'You look down at me—well, I look down on *you*.' The awareness of my new vulnerability disgusts me, but I cannot help it. Moreover, how can I expect to be loved by the daughter of the very people who have crushed me? How can I love someone who discriminates against me? The memory of her disparaging remarks lingers and tortures me.

I have come to understand these old Rightists; I love them.

It is precisely because Teacher He is better educated than I am, and I, better educated than Zhao Jinxiang, that our social positions are ranked in the reverse order. Yes, there's no doubt about it; she is a political idiot. I plop down on my bed and try to come up with other epithets to ease the pain. I don't really love her, I decide.

But I cannot forget her. At school I find myself paying more attention to her movements and to the sound of her voice than ever before. I now spend almost all my free time with Teacher He, taking walks and discussing politics and mathematics. I go out of my way to display my pleasure at being with him. Let her just try to polish my curious political sensibilities. Let her try to understand why I choose to discriminate against political discrimination.

Several weeks pass. Then late one night, when I am alone in the room grading papers, a slim woman suddenly rushes in the open door.

'You're Yang Xiguang?'

I nod, stunned for a moment by the sight of the incredibly beautiful woman standing before me. She can't be more than eighteen or nineteen.

Sitting down on my bed, she begins, 'I'm Little Liu's girlfriend. He's locked up in solitary. And, well, he snuck me a note saying that I should find you and ask you for help.'

Liu Chengning is a man I met two years ago through a friend from the Third Brigade. He works at the Reconstruction Farm machine repair shop and is a tall, good-looking man with a Roman nose, a pair of sharp, penetrating eyes, and a deep, booming voice. He was a Rebel in the New China Printing Factory. During the Cultural Revolution, a car he was driving killed three people, but because the incident was completely unintentional and was not politically motivated, he was put in charge of the labor reform machine repair shop. In only a couple of years, the men at his shop have earned a reputation for excellent work; they can assemble and maintain large agricultural machinery and can even repair cars. The state-run shop in Yueyang can't compete; virtually everyone makes the long trip out to Reconstruction Farm for their repairs.

I ask the woman, whose name is Zhao Jian, but who goes by 'Missy Jian,' to tell me what has happened to her.

Missy Jian works part-time at the shop. She is the daughter of a compulsory laborer there, a former Nationalist officer who wears a counterrevolutionary cap and must therefore stay on permanently. She idolizes Little Liu, and dreams of what life must be like in his hometown of Changsha. Sighing, she confides to me that she has only been to Yueyang a couple of times.

They had been seeing each other for some time when Missy Jian discovered she was pregnant. Little Liu, who often left the farm to test-drive the vehicles he was working on, occasionally traveled as far as Yueyang to pick up parts, always dressed in his tattered clothes that were spattered with grease. On one of these trips, he took Missy Jian to a clinic to get an abortion. Someone found out about the incident, and Liu Chengning was placed in the little *haozi* of the Third Brigade, as neither the repair shop nor Farm Headquarters have facilities for solitary confinement. A representative from the Yueyang court is already investigating the case. Sobbing uncontrollably, Missy Jian tells me she is afraid that the cadres are going to add years onto Little Liu's sentence.

'Are you really serious about him?'

She nods emphatically.

'Your feelings haven't changed?'

When she shakes her head, I tell her, 'Look, as long as you insist that being intimate with Little Liu was *your* idea, you can probably keep him from getting more time.'

Privately I doubt that anything can be done at this point. I have seen so many cases in which men who got involved in unorthodox relationships ended up with prison sentences. One extreme example was a fellow from the Third Brigade's Third Detachment whose father had died young and who was raised by his mother. When the boy turned sixteen, the mother began to seduce him. She slept naked and let her son see her body. Eventually the neighbors got wind of their incestuous relationship and reported the situation to the Public Security Bureau. When the son was arrested, the mother went to the Bureau many times to plead on her son's behalf, trying to prove that she had taken the initiative and was thus responsible, but the son was ultimately sentenced to seven years for 'destroying social mores.'

The law seems to favor women in any sex-related case, and so there is nothing to make me think that Little Liu won't get more time. But with a beautiful woman before me in tears, I can only encourage her to try.

I am walking back from the remedial class to Farm Headquarters several days later when I see a group of women standing in the road, shouting and cursing. When I get closer, I stop, for Missy Jian is in their midst, her silky black hair pulled out of her long braids and hanging down wildly around her shoulders. The others appear to be cadre wives, and they are also attractive women. One of them spits into Missy Jian's face and shouts, 'You shameless, stinking whore—admitting to seducing a stinking labor reform prisoner! Do you have any notion how despicable you are?'

Missy Jian does not falter. 'I don't care what you call me,' she answers softly. 'If Liu Chengning doesn't think I'm a whore, I don't have anything to be ashamed of.'

I feel my eyes get hot and blurry. Unable to watch any longer, I quickly turn toward the guest house. Several minutes later Zhao Jinxiang comes along. Although her face isn't visible to me, I cannot help but sense that she despises Missy Jian. Then it finally hits me: the two of us are from enemy camps. We have completely opposite responses.

The next morning I learn to my surprise that Little Liu had indeed been freed when Missy Jian insisted the affair was her idea. As soon as he got back to the shop, she rushed over to see him, whereupon the two of them, still under careful scrutiny, were immediately seized by the cadres. Liu was tied up and sent right back to the little *haozi*.

The day I leave Reconstruction Farm, I see Zhao Jinxiang again. My sister Yang Hui and I are standing at the Farm Headquarters bus-stop waiting for the bus that seems as if it will never come, when I notice Zhao walking towards us nonchalantly, as if by coincidence, greeting me only with her eyes. But when she sees a cadre coming, she quickly starts in another direction.

In comparison with Missy Jian's love for Liu, the love I feel for Zhao Jinxiang is laughable. I am sure that I have never really loved this person from the enemy camp.

But the events of my life seem to mock me. In Changsha I find myself still haunted by her doll-like face. We start up a passionate correspondence, the kind of overly serious communication that only lovers carry on. In my letters I tell her I love her; in hers, she confides that, from the very beginning, she had been fascinated with everything about me. I had not been imagining things. She admits she loves me, that she has stayed awake several nights thinking about me. She quotes from 'The Vagabond' at times, but she is also careful to warn me: 'I don't have the courage to be a Rita; you know how the people at labor reform camp treat women who associate with prisoners.'

We correspond in this fashion for two years. I realize that because the events of the Cultural Revolution turned out to her advantage, she cannot begin to comprehend how people can criticize Mao Zedong. She doesn't like the Democracy Wall Movement in Beijing and can't imagine why anyone would want to rehabilitate the Rightists. But my family and I have suffered. In my response I use several pages trying to explain how in 1957 and 1959 the Rightists and the 'right-wing opportunists' were correct and how Mao had been in error.

Every time I write letters like this and mail them, I get scared. If I tell her I still believe in the Rebels' anti-persecution stance but like Mao for having once supported the Rebels, and that I disapprove of Deng Xiaoping's persecution of the Rebels but respect and welcome his economic policies—will she see me as a counterrevolutionary? Again, I decide that she and I are too far divided. I don't destroy all her letters, though. I hide them, keeping them as testimony to the kind of bittersweet love that exists between enemies.

After I am released, one letter comes which makes me extremely happy. Zhao Jinxiang has gone to He Minhe's home to visit and learned that his Rightist and counterrevolutionary caps have been removed. His reputation restored, he has resumed his career as an engineer. More than anything, I hope that she has lost all traces of the discrimination she once felt toward Old He. Then she writes again, saying that she went to Changsha to see me, but that I had already moved away. She tells me how much she regrets not having been able to see me.

Eventually I hear that Little Liu is out free. He has married a city girl and is in Changsha. The news stings me, and brings back memories of Missy Jian, sitting on my bed the night she came to me, and the resilience and strength she showed when facing the cadre wives. Having overcome an almost impossible political hurdle in keeping Liu from being re-sentenced, this woman who was exquisite enough to drive any number of men half-crazy, lost him anyway, defeated not by political persecution, not by another woman, but by the household registration system, which keeps people born in the countryside chained there for life.

22

Masters and Apprentices of Revolution

▼

The men closest to me in the Construction Group of the Third Brigade are first-rate masons, and under their tutelage I absorb new skills daily. These same men took part in one of the most amazing demonstrations of quiet bravery in the earliest phase of the Cultural Revolution.

◆

I was eighteen years old in 1966, the same year the Cultural Revolution Work Group of the Hunan Provincial Committee assumed complete control of my school, Changsha First High School. Along with the other students who loudly opposed the work groups, I had been labeled a 'counterrevolutionary student.' On August 17, 1966, a surprising directive descended from China's top leaders, the Sixteen-Point Resolution, which required Communist Party committees at every level to rehabilitate 'counterrevolutionary' students. We were even granted the right to form our own political organizations. The 'Rightist' label was not to be applied to students, and the 'minority' was to be protected.

The next day, on August 18, Chairman Mao appeared before thousands of cheering Red Guards at Tiananmen Square, assuring them of his unqualified support for their revolutionary activities. In Hunan, few of us had any understanding of the political situation in Beijing, and we assumed that the 'Red Guards' were yet another front organization put together by the authorities.[1] The Hunan Communist apparatus immediately organized the Communist Youth League into every sort of 'unofficial mass organization,' in an attempt to retain control of

[1] I did not know then that, in fact, the earliest Red Guard group in China was not an official organization at all, but a grass-roots group that was ultimately labeled 'counterrevolutionary' and illegal.

the local political situation and thus prevent the seeds of 'rebellion' in Beijing from spreading. At Changsha First, the children of the high-ranking Communist cadres organized the conservative Red Guards troops, the 'Red Power Guardian Army'. This group refused membership to any of their classmates with bad political backgrounds, raiding the homes and otherwise persecuting students who weren't of the 'reddest' background.

One month later, on August 19, a grass-roots organization of Hunan University students assembled in front of the Changsha Municipal Committee compound, demanding the abolition of the 'three trusts'—trust in the Hunan Provincial Committee, the Changsha Municipal Committee, and the work groups. They also demanded that the Municipal Committee formally recognize all 'unofficial' student organizations. In conspicuous imitation of Mao's manner and clothing of the previous day, Municipal Secretary Kong Anmin stepped out to meet the students and delivered a message that was, in essence, precisely the opposite of Mao's address: Kong publicly mobilized the conservative Red Power Guardian Army to counterattack the Rebel students. He also called for the Red Guardians, the loyalist organization composed of Communist factory workers, to come and protect the Changsha Municipal Committee compound.

Ever since I could remember, political demonstrations had been organized from the top down and directed against clearly 'external' targets such as the 'running dogs of American imperialists' or the 'corrupt bourgeoisie.' All other public protests were illegal. The Hunan University student demonstration was extremely unusual, and I needed to see for myself what was going on. I took the May First Street bus down the tree-lined avenue, all the way to the five-story Municipal Committee building where I joined the crowd gathered there.

By the time I arrived, the Red Guardian workers had already surrounded the students and were shouting out threats.

'Do you know what's happening in the schools?' cried one student. 'The Cultural Revolution has started! The work groups are restricting our activities. They won't let us demonstrate. This goes against the spirit of the Sixteen-Point Resolution.'

'Don't the work groups represent the Communist Party? If you're against the work groups, you're against the Party!'

'People in the Communist Party make mistakes, too.'

'You're spreading poison! You're attacking the Party! You're a Rightist! You want to change China!' A worker grabbed a student's lapel and ripped off a button.

'No,' the student insisted. 'We're responding to Chairman Mao's call.'

The worker pulled the student's arm into a half nelson and pushed him to the ground.

'What gives you the right to beat people?'

'You Rightists deserve to be beaten.' The worker put his foot on the student's back and gave him a contemptuous little kick. These students who thought they could assault the local Communist organs were like eggs dashing themselves against rocks. The authorities had every aspect of society tightly under control. Convinced more than ever of the utter hopelessness of the situation and of my own impotence, I went home for dinner, where I found a note on the table left by my father. 'Under no circumstance are you to take part in the demonstrations.'

My future was already ruined. 'I've learned my lesson,' I scribbled in response. 'Don't worry; I won't ever get involved in politics again.' Then I went back out on the street to read the walls.

To my amazement, another group of workers had put up anti-work group posters even more militant than those of the students. A burst of adrenalin and of hope. But I was also scared—scared that I might do something stupid.

That evening at dusk a great battalion of somewhat older demonstrators appeared out of nowhere, sweeping wordlessly down May First Street toward the Municipal Committee headquarters. Workers! As each wave approached, I read the banners they carried:

RESOLUTELY SUPPORT THE REBELLION OF THE
    REVOLUTIONARY STUDENTS!
TO REBEL IS JUSTIFIED; REVOLUTION ISN'T A CRIME!
DOWN WITH THE THREE TRUSTS!
DISMISS MUNICIPAL SECRETARY KONG ANMIN!
REPLACE THE MEMBERS OF THE MUNICIPAL
    COMMITTEE!

They wore no armbands; their faces were somber and resolute. Many of them wore work clothes stained with grease—they had come straight from the factories. Only the sound of footsteps could be heard; they dared not cry out slogans for fear of inciting a backlash against the students. Though their ranks were not orderly, they moved steadily forward, as if propelled by the urgency of their mission, completely unlike the wooden official demonstrations. I could feel the blood rush to my head. They seemed so self-confident, so oblivious to their own risk. At home that night, I could not sleep.

The event also left its mark on the residents of Changsha. Incensed by the violent suppression of the students, few of the townspeople had dared to express their outrage. The sight of the workers' spontaneous demonstration of support moved many to tears. No one dreamed that Mao Zedong would continue to endorse the rebelling students and workers, and at the same time encourage the masses to attack the local Communist apparatus.

Rebel and Conservative forces clashed again and again that autumn. Each time the Conservatives gained the upper hand, the Rebels were labeled counterrevolutionaries. When this happened, the Rebels' most pressing political goal was full rehabilitation, the removal of their counterrevolutionary caps.

For years I have sought to understand more about what led the workers of Changsha to rebel that fall, when it seemed that there was no chance for support. Could anyone have anticipated Mao Zedong's subsequent support? Masters Wang Jingo and Yang Zili, two of the highest-ranked masons in our Construction Group, had been there. I am apprenticed to Master Wang when I join the group in 1974. Lu Guoan, my 'apprentice-brother' and my peer, reports to Master Yang.

Master Wang, a handsome man in his late twenties who has been blind in his left eye since he was small, is often respectfully addressed as the 'One-eyed Dragon' by the inmates. He has vast experience as an independent contractor and is quick and dextrous. Furthermore, he is one of those laid-back men known around camp as 'brothers,' men who go about their work without a lot of fuss, as steady as a rock. Master Wang is a natural leader, and during the Cultural Revolution served as the commander of the Red Banner Corps, the Rebel group of construction workers in the Xiang River Storm. Master Yang headed up a squadron in the same Rebel corps.

In the *haozi* after lights out, I find a compelling new apprenticeship. My fellow masons tell me how in 1964, when Mao sent the military out to curb Liu Shaoqi's power, a 'political office' was established at their state-owned construction company. The office was run by newly deployed demobilized soldiers, and Masters Wang and Yang were required to attend weekly political study sessions. Work policies began to change. Piece-rate wages and bonuses were eliminated, effectively lowering salaries by more than one-third. Productivity declined steadily. The workers grew to loathe the military cadres, and when the conservative Red Banner Corps was formed in 1966, the workers sought out the objects of their enmity and dragged them through the streets of Changsha. In 1969, the Military Control Commission authorities banned all unofficial political organizations, but Master Wang refused to dismantle his corps and was sentenced to fifteen years as a counterrevolutionary. Master Yang came to prison after a nasty fist fight with a Military Control Commission man. Like me, he's in for ten years.

Under somewhat different conditions my apprentice-brother Lu Guoan became a counterrevolutionary overnight at the age of fifteen. He was guilty of wishing Chairman Mao, not the customary 'Ten-thousand years with no end!' but 'Ten-thousand smells with none of them good!'

Neither Master Wang nor Master Yang will admit to being counterrevolutionary. Because they believe that I am a Rebel— one of their own kind, unstained by Rightist or Nationalist pedigree—they are candid and caution me not to become too close to the 'real' counterrevolutionaries. As always, I find it repugnant when politicals discriminate against other politicals, but since these men are my masters, it is not appropriate for me to question their beliefs directly. Moreover, I sense their attitudes are not entirely rooted in social snobbery; they think that if they adopt the ideological face of the authorities, they can repudiate the charges against them.

I am determined to show them how unfair their judgments are, and how tenuous their notions of 'revolutionary' and 'counterrevolutionary.' I hope to reveal to them the broader canvas of political history. And so, as the days pass and we build our houses, aqueducts, and brick walls, I tell them stories about the English and French revolutions. Because Master Wang has finished junior high school, I predict he will be more receptive to my ideas; Master Yang has only completed a primary school education and claims not to know how to read or write. And indeed it is Master Wang who finds my tales about the power struggle between the Whigs and the Roundheads particularly intriguing.

'Well, there may have been a Glorious Revolution in England after the Restoration, when the underdog Rebels got a chance to compete as a legal party with the Conservatives,' he sighs. 'But that will never happen in China. Those Conservatives have us under their thumbs. We're like a dick with no balls: We'll never be able to stand up again.'

'And why not?' I insist. 'Why can't China's Rebels have the same kind of chance that the Whigs had? Politics boils down to personal relationships; whenever the relationships change, the political situation changes.' My mentor Liu Fengxiang has never left me; I want my fellow workers, people who I admire for their skill and their courage, to see how social forces at the grass roots level can influence politics.

Master Wang shakes his head. 'China is different. The Communist Party is very tough.'

I press on, convinced that, given a little more historical perspective, his doubts might be dispelled. 'Suppose as a counterrevolutionary Rebel, you were suddenly rehabilitated and could start all over with a clean slate? What would you do?'

'The Communist Party is playing games with us. It doesn't make any difference if they use 'rehabilitation' or some other trick—they can't fool me any more. Just let me out of jail! No matter what those Communists do, I'll go straight up into the mountains and become a monk. I'm going to retreat from the world and never get involved in politics again!'

◆

Three months later, 'Criticize Lin Biao and Confucius' slogans begin to appear in the *Hunan Daily*, as do essays written by Changsha's Rebel leaders. Sleep will not come to me. Every night I replay in my mind the events that have occurred since the spring of 1966 and the launching of the Cultural Revolution. Now as in the past when Mao found himself isolated within the Communist Party, he is playing the Rebel card against those who would threaten his control—predictably, against his conservative adversary, Zhou Enlai. But this time I am not moved by his call for rebellion. I have seen what happens: The collapse of social order. Economic stagnation. Repression. Though it is gratifying to know the Rebels will have another shot at regaining their civil rights, it is clear that the price will be high. What would it take for us to break out of this cycle once and for all, so that the two factions could coexist in a democratic system and compete on an equal basis?

Supper is over and done with. In no mood to go to Teacher He's, I pace up and down the corridor. I have had little luck in altering my masters' beliefs. Can it be that the two factions need to persecute each other equally ruthlessly before each side awakes to the realization that political persecution should be banned? I resolve to weave this idea into a screenplay, which I call *Contemporaries*. In doing so, I am risking another ten years of labor reform.

The plot revolves around a Rebel boy and a Conservative girl who fall in love, only to be torn apart by the social and political conflicts at the heart of the Cultural Revolution. Except for this romance, the plot parallels the story of my life: the boy's father is involved in the persecution of Rightists in 1957; in 1959 when the father discovers that the Rightists' views were in fact justified, he criticized the Great Leap Forward policies and is subsequently labeled a 'right-wing opportunist.'

The boy's mother had initially accepted the Party line and joined with the various local Party organizations in denouncing her husband, but reverses her position in 1962. With the support of Liu Shaoqi, her husband is rehabilitated and the boy's life returns to normal.

When the Cultural Revolution begins, the boy cannot understand why his parents and uncle are opposed to his involvement. He rebels, anyway, against the school authorities' repression of students and against the Conservatives and their unfair treatment of all students with bad class backgrounds. The boy's girlfriend is a member of the Conservative faction, which is actively persecuting the Rebels in an effort to preserve the privileges of its class.

On a personal level, the couple's squabbles seem trivial and absurd, yet their ultimate failure to resolve their differences is symptomatic of the larger social and political conflicts. Conferring with Spectacles, I try to emulate Shakespeare to show the rational and the irrational aspects of both Conservative and Rebel cases, painting a defiantly clear picture of both extremist positions, including the rightist views postulated by Liu Shaoqi and Peng Dehuai, who were openly critical of Mao's post-1957 line.

Lu Guoan is so enthusiastic about *Contemporaries* that, every couple of days, he takes what I have written and hides it beneath the roofboards. Some of the other inmates copy it from cover to cover, so that at one point there are three editions floating about. Other copies are hidden out in the workshop. I also carry a little notebook with me, in which I compulsively jot down anything that comes to mind. Tipped off by the KGB's, the cadres start snooping around. Thanks to the sustained efforts of the politicals around me, however, the manuscript is never found. I subsequently position decoy notebooks filled with English vocabulary lists and calculus problems in conspicuous locations, and at length the authorities abandon their search. Before my term is up this screenplay and other manuscripts safely find their way to the light of day.

◆

Outside Reconstruction Farm, leftists are ripping apart the restoration and 'right-wing revisionism.' By the spring of 1974, utter chaos has descended upon the province of Hunan and all of China once again. Plastered upon the trucks that lumber through the outlying fields we see slogans calling for the ouster of Yang Dayi, the Hunan Provincial Party Secretary and Commander of the Military District. Articles in the *Hunan Daily* accuse him of opposing the Cultural Revolution and advocating restoration. Yang Dayi is notorious for being the man who tried to restore the reputation of capitalist roaders by saying, 'A phoenix is a phoenix; a chicken, a chicken. A phoenix without any feathers may be inferior to a chicken, but as soon as they grow back, the phoenix will be a phoenix, and the chicken, just a chicken!' A 'phoenix,' of course, would be an old Communist cadre; a ' chicken,' one of those Rebels who in 1966 and 1967 had turned the world upside-down.

Master Yang's Rebel wife spends a night at the Third Brigade during one of the few family visits that she is allowed. She meets with her husband twice under the cadres' gaze, but she also finds a way to slip us several back issues of the newly legalized Rebel tabloid *United Workers*. In each is a list of people who have already been rehabilitated. Some articles expose how Rebel members were persecuted by the Military Control Commission and the Conservatives during the campaigns to 'Strike One-Oppose Three' and to 'Purge the May Sixteenth Elements,' which we have experienced here at Reconstruction Farm. I thought the May Sixteenth Purge had been cruel here, but from these documents I learn that elsewhere, thousands upon thousands of inmates were beaten to death or forced to commit suicide. Another article contains the complete text of Zhou Enlai's self-criticism at a Party Central work conference, in which he admits he shared responsibility for these deaths. All over the country, Rebel workers and students are rushing to prison gates to greet their comrades-in-arms.

Soon after this visit, a car is sent from the construction company. My two masters are free. Not since 1949 have released prisoners been escorted home in a sedan. Cadres and prisoners alike are astounded and talk of nothing else.

There are no further confessions. Overnight, 'counter-revolutionaries' have donned the red paper flowers reserved for heroes and are being spirited away in vehicles that the low-ranking reform cadres can only dream of. For a while, the cadres have neither the energy nor the inclination to bother us, and life is good.

Back in Changsha, however, Master Wang breaks his vow and jumps right back into the political maelstrom. He has become the head of the 'Criticize Lin Biao and Confucius' office of his construction company, and is bent on clearing the names of previously labeled Rebels. When I hear this news, I smile bitterly: political rehabilitation is a temptation that no one who has ever been persecuted can ever resist. Once again Mao Zedong has succeeded in roping the Rebels onto his chariot, as he prepares to open fire on the economic and cultural policies of the Conservatives. In their search for dignity, the Rebels are tragically blind to the fact that Zhou Enlai's policies are the more reasonable.

My apprentice-brother Lu Guoan mopes around the *haozi*, not sure what to do with himself. Though he is genuinely pleased for his masters' sake, *he* is still in camp; moreover, this latest campaign has deprived him of one of his most treasured activities, the opportunity to perform on stage. Following the Restoration of 1972, when ideology receded into the background and the arts became acceptable once again, Political Director Guan organized a first-rate performing arts group within the Third Brigade. This was not a difficult task—among politicals, there is inevitably a wealth of talent. Because Lu Guoan plays the bamboo flute extremely well, and isn't bad at drums, he was asked to join. The troupe has toured each of the ten brigades and has even appeared on stage at Farm Headquarters, attracting peasant audiences from miles around: for the first time in five years the repertoire included something other than revolutionary model dramas.

With his deep-set, round eyes, fair skin, and engaging smile, Lu is a good-looking man. On stage he cuts a striking figure in costume, appreciated especially by the opposite sex. Among the inmates, he has quite a reputation for 'shooting glances' at passing women. He commits to memory every detail about the woman's face and the way she moves; and if she indulges him by returning the look, he fixes his eyes on hers and won't let go. He is only about twenty.

Not long after the Farm Headquarters' performance, Lu Guoan suddenly contracts a mysterious disease which keeps him from the fields. According to Doctor Wang, who looks in on him at the barracks, Lu simply lies in bed all day long, lifeless.

'Lu Guoan, do you have a sick pass? How come you're still here?' barks Counselor He when he comes to inspect our *haozi*.

'Counselor He, sir, I don't have a pass, but I sure am sick. You can point a triple-barrel gun at me, and I still won't go out to work.' Groaning, Lu rolls over on his bunk.

'Crossing me again?' Counselor He's eyes widen. He knows Lu Guoan has a reputation for giving lip, but Lu's productivity is unimpeachable, so that while the Counselor's tone is harsh, it is clear that he likes Lu.

'Counselor He, the way I feel today, even if you chopped me to pieces and pulverized my bones, I still couldn't go out!'

The counselor moves a stool over to the bunk and slowly lights a cigarette, determined to talk some reason into him. If Lu isn't going out to work, Counselor He is going to stay and keep him company. But this new tack unnerves Lu, who is the kind of 'tough' man who begins to crumble under a gentle approach.

'Tie me up and drag me out into the fields and I still won't work. You might as well throw a rock up into the air and try to beat the heavens!'

Sighing, the counselor finally gives in and lets Lu have the day off. The minute he is out the door, however, Lu jumps up to find Doctor Wang, asking if he can go along with the doctor when he rides out to the Farm Headquarters pharmacy.

This new illness seems to be chronic; Lu takes a medical leave once every month. It is a strange phenomenon. According to Doctor Wang, Lu was never sickly before. In fact he has always been a picture of health. It is a Third Brigade ritual for Master Yang periodically to waken the lot of us younger prisoners and flip the quilts up off our bunks to see whose dicks are the biggest and the hardest. In these competitions, Lu Guoan always comes in first.

Several months later, Lu startles me by crawling onto my bunk and whispering, 'Apprentice-brother, I'm in a real jam—you've got to help me out.'

When I ask him what is wrong, he pulls from his undershirt pocket a kerchief in which a piece of folded paper has been carefully wrapped.

'Here—this is a letter from my girlfriend. I have to write her back, but I don't know what to say. I haven't drunk enough ink to write a good love letter. You've swallowed lots of ink; writing for you is as easy as bowing is for a hunchback. Don't let me down!'

'Well,' I reply quickly, 'You're going to have to tell me every single detail about you and her. We want to make this sound convincing.'

Reddening, Lu agrees.

It seems that when he performed at Farm Headquarters, the nurse who was stationed there—a cadre's daughter—was spellbound by his charisma and the sound of his flute. The next day, back at the Third Brigade, he received a hand-carried missive from Doctor Wang. The nurse described how impressed she was by his musicality. It so happened that she herself was studying the violin! Could they get to know each other, she wondered. After a few sleepless nights, Lu's illness erupted, a condition requiring continual medical care. Of course, the only one who could truly cure him was the woman at the pharmacy. But since Lu cannot always ask for sick leave or to run errands at Farm Headquarters, by the time he comes to me, he is desperate.

I help him write his letter. Unfortunately, before long, the correspondence, along with a series of 'illegal encounters,' inevitably catches the attention of the cadres, who cannot tolerate the 'decadent seduction of a revolutionary successor by a counterrevolutionary criminal.' In their hands is material evidence, one of the nurse's letters. Fortunately, Lu is never punished, simply singled out at a camp meeting as 'the counterrevolutionary who continually debauched a revolutionary successor.' Lu and I are extremely grateful to the woman, for had she turned over a letter in my handwriting, we both would have been in very hot water. At the very least it would have meant reflecting in handcuffs; at the worst, a visit to solitary.

As 1975 comes to a close, life at the Construction Group is peaceful. All the Nationalist officers—the historical counterrevolutionaries—are released. Deng Xiaoping, now Vice Premier, is promoting relatively moderate policies. A rational government is finally a real possibility. What's more, an increasing number of readable books are appearing in print.

In this new climate, Lu Guoan and I decide to pay a sneak visit to the New China Bookstore in the neighboring town, Guangxianzhou, to see what is happening in the outside world. Lu wants his picture taken. He hasn't had one taken since he was imprisoned seven years ago. After striking an agreement with Master Zhong, our sympathetic counterrevolutionary production leader who is currently supervising us in the building of a warehouse, we begin our preparations. We must cover our shaved, labor reform criminal heads with hats and shed the outer layers of our clothing, so that no traces of the incriminating yellow characters remain. No cadres are scheduled to monitor the Construction Group today. If anyone asks about us, Master Zhong will say we have gone to relieve ourselves.

The road stretches ahead; the sky is a deep blue-green. We are completely alone. Lu and I look at each other and grin. Perhaps because our terms are almost up, we are thought to be unlikely candidates for escape. We cover the seven-mile distance in a couple of hours.

Though actually a small town, Guangxianzhou is much larger than Reed Store Village where Reconstruction Farm Headquarters is based. It is here that runaways often head in hopes of finding a boat, for there is no other way to leave this long, narrow peninsula jutting out into Dongting Lake. After so many years in the wilderness of the farm, the sight of bright clothing and wide streets lined with shops is strange and beautiful. But the announcements blaring from the public broadcast system remind us that here too we are under the tight control of the government, as a voice, critical of Deng Xiaoping, charges the public to 'fight back the right-wing opportunist rehabilitation trend.' Another period of political unrest seems to be imminent.

At the bookstore, I have only a few minutes to select the titles that interest me most: *An Overview of the World*, *A General History of the World*, and several collections of translations published in Shanghai. Then we cross the street to the photographer's studio and have our pictures taken together. We leave Lu Guoan's home address in Changsha with the photographer, along with instructions to mail the photos there. If we are to make it to camp before lunchtime, we had better move. By the time we get back to the construction site, we are sweating like pigs, but everything seems to be normal. With the exception of our supervisor Master Zhong, no one has been aware of our absence.

As the first days of 1976 and the Lunar Year of the Dragon unfold, the smell of gunpowder grows stronger. Soon it is springtime again. At our nightly political study classes we must now go through the motions of criticizing Deng Xiaoping, echoing the articles printed daily in the papers. Lu Guoan and I refuse to make statements. Counselor He, who is not a bad man for a cadre and who usually makes allowances for moderately deviant behavior, seems tougher than usual. This campaign is clearly a big one. Instead of letting me sit in the corner reading my own books during class, he calls out my name and insists that I stand up and make a statement.

'I don't understand these political struggles,' I reply. 'And if I *do* make a statement now, in the future you can't come back and ask me to criticize what I say. You had us write down our support for Lin Biao, and then we had to go find all those essays and tear them up. If I can't keep the politics straight, it's better not to say anything.'

'No, no, that won't do at all,' Counselor He responds quickly. 'Why, every cadre has to make a statement criticizing Deng—so how much more important for you criminals to make statements.'

'No, we're different from you. We're just meat on the chopping block—you can cut us up vertically or horizontally—any way you want. What does it matter if we don't give an opinion?'

But Counselor He continues to insist on my participation.

'All right,' I say at length, holding up a newspaper. 'How about if I read this editorial aloud?'

'That'll be just fine,' he says without hesitation.

One day in early April Lu Guoan and I must stay late at the site to pour the foundation for a courtyard. When we return to camp, we find the main gate locked, so we walk over to the cadres' office and call out for it to be opened. Silence. The cadre-on-duty totally ignores us for a good ten minutes.

'Is everybody dead?' Lu Guoan, shouts finally. He wants his dinner and is quickly losing his temper. 'When I talk to a wall, at least there's an echo. But when I talk to you, there's nothing at all!'

This remark succeeds in vitalizing the cadre-on-duty, who jumps up and shouts. 'It sounds to me like you're answering the call of the counterrevolutionaries at Tiananmen Square to rehabilitate Deng Xiaoping and that you're rising up against the dictatorship of the proletariat!'

It is only later that we discover that the morning editions of the official Communist papers and radio announcements had declared the crowds who had gone to the square to mourn Zhou Enlai's death to be 'counterrevolutionary hoodlums.' Many have been taken into custody.

But the ravenous Lu is in no mood to accept being called a 'counterrevolutionary hoodlum.' 'First you said we were imperialist-revisionist-Nationalist-capitalist dogs,' he screams. 'Then, when Deng Xiaoping came into power, you said we were a gang of Rebels. When he fell, you said we were his black claws. When Lin Biao got into power, you said we were Liu Shaoqi's power base. And when Lin fell, you said we were *his* commandos! Now it's Deng. Really now, don't you think you're giving us too much credit! If I were on such friendly terms with Deng Xiaoping, I sure wouldn't be starving here, begging you to open the jail gate!'

Eventually the cadre strolls out and unlocks the gate. On the following evening, however, a meeting is held to criticize Lu. Having 'responded from afar to the Tiananmen Square incident and called back the spirits of the "dead capitalist roaders" and Deng Xiaoping,' he is ordered to reflect in cuffs.

It seems the cadres waited till we went out to work, then searched Lu's bed. Among his belongings they discovered excerpts copied from Deng Xiaoping's speeches: 'It doesn't matter if a cat is black or white as long as it catches mice.' 'The burden of past troubles is so great that change will not be easy;' 'Cadres shouldn't occupy the latrine if they don't intend to shit!' No matter that the seized excerpts are clearly literacy exercises, they are enough to tie him to Deng Xiaoping. No matter that every reasonable individual with a conscience believes that Deng's ideas are infinitely more practical than the empty platitudes of Jiang Qing and Mao Zedong, the exercise is said to constitute solid evidence that Lu supported the 'Rightist rehabilitation tendency.'

While Lu is in cuffs, I help him at mealtimes and on his vists to the toilet. In the evenings, sitting on a stool next to his bunk, I keep him company and listen to him hum or sing. He has a strong voice and loves to belt out choruses of the 'Volga Boatman' and 'La Paloma.'

After one week, his cuffs are removed.

◆

Spring passes into summer. Then one afternoon in early September there is a blaring of a funeral dirge over the loudspeaker. Master Zhong and Lu Guoan come running from the spot where they have been mixing ash and sand for our bricklaying, so excited they can barely contain themselves.

'Great news!' whispers Master Zhong, beaming.

'Old Mao died!' Lu Guoan is panting.

Even prisoners get a day off. Cadres will wear black armbands fastened with a safety pin and attend a memorial service; criminals aren't fit to do either. We are secretly very happy about this, because having to appear as if we were in mourning would be somewhat problematic.

The story in the *haozi* is that when the cadres heard Mao was gone, they wept uncontrollably, and when I look into their eyes

I see that it must be true. Then, a couple of days later, a new group of peasants joins the Third: all freshly sentenced to five years for expressing joy at Mao's death. One old man tells us they caught him jumping up and down and shouting, 'Now that Old Granddaddy is dead, we should be able to get something in our rice bowls again!'

We sympathize with them, and can't help heaving a sigh of relief that we are still safely tucked inside the *haozi*. Had we been on the outside, we would have certainly said something infelicitous and got ourselves sentenced again. Fortunately, only 'die-hard counterrevolutionaries' witnessed our private celebration, for no one informs on us.

The news about the arrest of the Gang of Four follows soon thereafter, formally communicated by Brigade Leader Liu, who gathers us together and then links us with the fallen faction. Lu gets so angry he curses between his teeth: '*Now* we're the power base of the Gang of Four. Whatever happens out there, abusing and oppressing us will always be correct!'

With the demise of the left wing, the Rebels are in trouble again, and the major leaders of the faction with which Masters Wang and Yang were affiliated find themselves back in prison. We pray that no one we know will get sent back to camp. At length, 'political criminal' Lu Guoan, my apprentice-brother, this warm, practical man who has never been particularly concerned with political ideology, is finally released—judged free of all guilt, just before his ten-year term is up. Now that the Gang of Four has been removed from power, cursing Mao ceases to be a valid 'counterrevolutionary' charge.

After my own release in 1978, I visit Lu Guoan many times in Changsha. He has become a highly skilled master builder, with dozens of homes to his credit. And he has a child, a little boy, whom he has named 'Jinxi' ('Toward Xi'), urging his son to follow in my footsteps. I feel deeply honored.

23

Doctor Wang

▼

Prisoner doctors don't seem to last very long at Reconstruction Farm.

One might think they would take pains to stay on forever, for doctors are relieved from doing heavy labor and are on friendly terms with the cadres and their families. Given a choice, even the reddest of cadres will ask for a prisoner doctor.

Inevitably, however, the prisoners who serve as doctors seem to always end up getting entangled with the cadres' women. Doctor Fan lasted about two years before his relationship with one cadre wife was discovered, and he was sent to our group to become a laborer. The revelation created quite a sensation. Each day, as the gossip spread to the wives in the other brigades, more women would come out to the cotton fields, where we were hoeing. Though they kept their distance, we could see them in twos and threes, pointing and whispering 'That's the one!'—a phenomenon for which Lu Guoan was particularly grateful.

Of all the cadres, labor-farm cadres are at the lowest level, which means that beautiful city women won't even look at them. Still, as cadres they can get free rations of 'national grain' and possess the coveted urban household registrations, so they have their pick of the most beautiful, young peasant women. Both leaders of the Third Brigade have absolutely stunning wives. It is no secret among the inmates that these women don't think very much of their husbands.

The prisoner doctor's greatest power derives from his authority to write sick passes. A sick pass means sleep. And if a prisoner doctor can document that a prisoner is seriously ill, that prisoner is allowed to do less taxing work. Such documentation will often be provided upon presentation of an appropriate quantity of stolen vegetables or a care package from home.

Doctor Zhou, who accepted more than his share of bribes before being caught carrying on with a cadre's wife, lasted about a year and a half. The man who is about to replace him is a prisoner in his early twenties known to those of us in the Construction Group as Little Wang.

Ever since his arrival in camp a few months ago, Little Wang has worked with us in the Construction Group, acting as Lu Guoan's assistant and doing menial tasks for him. I love to listen to him talk. Despite his youth, he knows a lot about women. For people like me who have no idea if a uterus is vertical or horizontal, his stories are riveting and not without a certain educational value. He has some remarkable insights about how the shape of a woman's face and the fineness of her skin are related to other, less conspicuous features.

In the *haozi*, lights go out promptly at ten o'clock, the electric switch being controlled by an armed guard. In the darkness the prisoners talk on and on until we drift off to sleep, especially during the agricultural slack season. When Little Wang first comes to our group, Lu Guoan and I listen to his stories for three nights straight.

'When I was three, my father and mother arranged for me to become engaged to the still unborn child of his good friend, the Party branch secretary of the brigade, providing the baby was a girl.' Little Wang speaks in the Changsha dialect, but it is heavily accented by the pronunciation of the Chengzhou area.

This is the first time I have heard of an arranged marriage occurring after 1949. 'Isn't that against the law?' I ask him.

'Oh, we lived way up in the mountains, where nobody cared anything about matrimonial law. Lots of people got married without any paperwork at all,' Little Wang explains, before continuing his story. 'But before I was sixteen, my prospective father-in-law decided to use some of his pull and go ahead and apply for a formal license. He probably saw that I wasn't too ugly and thought I might wander off.' There is no denying that Little Wang is a very good-looking guy. Though of average height, he has large almond eyes and thick black eyebrows. His nose is small; his cheek-bones high, his chin narrow: the very model of a manly man.

'So tell us what this woman was like,' Lu Guoan presses. Details about things like marriage licenses hold little interest for him.

'If you saw her, you'd want to throw up your breakfast. But at that time I was afraid to go against my parents' wishes—I was just a poor little country boy who had never stepped outside of the county. Once a month I had to indulge my father by visiting this girl's home and paying my respects to her elders. According to our village custom, my bride was supposed to formally 'cross the threshold' when I turned seventeen. Every time I thought about sleeping with that dog I got depressed. Finally, though, I came up with a way to get out of it. I lied about my age and enlisted in the army for three years, promising to marry her as soon as I got back.

'But I had really rotten luck. When I reported to duty, I was assigned to a military medical school in Sichuan Province. About two years after that, our class was sent to various village clinics for internship. Two of us were assigned to one of these clinics, me and a woman we called Little Li. I still didn't have the nerve to cross my father; on the other hand, I sure didn't want to go through with the marriage. I thought, "Well, I might as well take advantage of the little time I've got left."

'The clinic was not very elaborate, just a very small room, divided into two sections by a hanging grass mat. The front served as the office, and that was where I slept. The back part was the pharmacy, and that was where Little Li slept. One cold night when the wind was howling outside, we decided to quit early and, in our separate quarters, prepared for bed. But I couldn't sleep and kept tossing and turning. Finally I called over to her, "Little Li, it's really cold in here. . . . Aren't you cold?"

' "Mmmmm," she said.

'I waited for a while. "Really, it's so cold I can't sleep. It'd be a lot warmer if we put the quilts together."

' "You are bad!"

'I completely ignored her remark, picked up my quilt, walked through the slit in the screen, and started to climb into her bed. She started yelling, "Go away! If you don't go away, I'll scream!"

'I pleaded with her, "Come on, don't scream. I'm not going to do anything; we'll each sleep under our own quilts. I won't touch you. It'll be much warmer this way, you'll see."

Lu Guoan and I look at each other, grinning.

'So then she quieted down. I lay down next to her and we stayed under our individual covers for all of about ten minutes. Then I started tossing and turning all over. "I'm *still* cold," I whispered to her.

' "There you go again," she whispered back.

' "Why don't we just put the quilts on top of each other? I *promise* I won't touch you."

'I snuck in under her cover even though she kept right on scolding—"You're bad, you're bad," but she never pushed me away. How could I have possibly kept my promise not to touch her? By the next morning, you couldn't keep us off each other.

'After that we were together all the time at night. Sometimes, though, Little Li would get intimate during office hours, and a couple of the old villagers must have seen us. They assumed we were man and wife and nobody ever bothered us. But not too long afterwards one of the leaders at the medical school came to observe our work and, upon arriving at the village, asked a peasant for directions to the clinic. "Ahh, that young couple . . ." ' That was all he needed to figure out that we were living together. We got transferred back to the unit straight-away, where the school held a struggle session against us. After that they discharged me and sent me back home.'

Little Wang stops there, despite our loud protests. It is very late, and there is no way that he can finish his story. The day passes very slowly indeed as we wait impatiently for the continuation of his romantic adventures that evening.

'After my discharge, I decided to take every chance I could to look for women. It wasn't hard. Women like me: I must have had a dozen of them.'

Lu Guoan and I gaze at him, wide-eyed. I try to imagine what it must be like to have such vast experience in the world of women.

'The last one was a clerk at the commune food store. She could never get enough. We had already done it two times one night and she still wanted more. It was pretty late, and I told her that she had better get up and get dressed if she wanted to leave the clinic before daybreak. But she wouldn't hear of it. So we started again, when there was a violent pounding on the door.

' "Open up, Little Wang's father-in-law is here."

'The door pushed open, and there they were—my father-in-law and my bride-to-be, just standing there. We were stark naked. Then four or five armed militia came in and paraded us in our underwear all through the village. I wore a big hat that said "Counterrevolutionary Hooligan." My girlfriend's said "Female Hooligan." All along the way, they made her keep beating a gong and shouting, "I am the mistress of the adulterer Wang."

'After being humiliated like this, I was in no mood for a wedding. Then, pretty soon some of the villages started accusing me of making "counterrevolutionary statements," which, when added to my women problems, was enough to get me put up on a charge of being a counterrevolutionary and another crazy charge called "destroying a military marriage." Of course the whole thing had been arranged by my prospective father-in-law. It was when I read the sentencing document that I learned my class origin had suddenly been "upgraded" from lower-middle peasant to rich peasant. But the most serious count I faced was for attacking Chairman Mao. People in the country joked around all the time about "Old Granddaddy Mao," and sometimes I would pitch in and crack a few comments. This kind of stuff usually never leads to anything, but I had offended a powerful cadre and so I was in trouble.'

I have met quite a few men at Reconstruction Farm who are up for 'destroying a military marriage,' but they were all individuals who had entered into illicit relationships with wives or fiancees of military personnel. Normally the sentence ranges from two to seven years. But the situation with Little Li was completely different: he hadn't had sex with anyone's fiancee; he was just an army man who didn't want to go through with his own marriage.

On subsequent nights Little Wang tells us other fascinating stories, many dating from his military past. His military school is not far from Number One Prison, a maximum security facility, housing, for the most part, politicals who spend their time producing machine tools. In 1970 the prisoners secretly manufactured a batch of guns and rioted. Afterward, all the participants were sentenced to death. Some of these men were sent to the medical school where they were kept alive until their bodies were needed for autopsies.

During his army days, Little Wang tells us, he once witnessed an amazing sentencing meeting of a PLA soldier. As part of the campaign calling for the 'prioritization of politics,' the commander of every company was to select one or two troublemakers as examples for criticism. One private had a habit of talking back to the cadres, so he became a natural target in the campaign. As the weeks passed, the private came to despise the commander and, one night, took out his rifle, stormed into the commander's quarters and killed him, as well as some twenty soldiers who were trying to stop him. Eventually the private was wounded and brought into custody, whereupon he was quickly sentenced to death in a military court. But the officers waited until the private had completely recovered to hold the big sentencing meeting in front of all the troops. When the day came, tanks were stationed outside the grounds—you would have thought an entire enemy division was about to be executed.

When our comrade 'Little Wang' formally becomes 'Doctor Wang,' he moves his belongings over to the clinic, and, to my disappointment, evenings in the Construction Group become much quieter. Once in a while he stops by to tell an occasional story about one of his old flames. And he gives us sick passes. Doctor Wang is more self-disciplined than his predecessors, less eager to accept bribes. Sometimes he pretends to go out into the fields and work for a couple of hours, so he never seems to get into trouble. As time goes by, however, and his privileged position becomes known to more prisoners, Doctor Wang seems to take increasing advantage of the 'respect' that others are anxious to show him.

The very last story he tells me, he relates along the road back to the Farm Headquarters clinic where I am to be tested for blood flukes. As we walk along, he finds a topic to relieve his boredom. 'Did you ever see the newspaper article about the "Railroad Heroes?" ' he asks.

I do remember the story; it had been major news. 'Wasn't there a militia battalion commander there and over twenty "Iron Maidens" trapped in a caved-in tunnel?'

'Yup, that's the one. The paper said that when these people were threatened with imminent death, they all studied Chairman Mao's *Quotations*, and ultimately defied death with their indomitable spirit.' Little Wang smiles at me knowingly. 'Talk about calling bull's balls horse's balls! The real story wasn't like that at all.'

I urge him to tell me what really happened.

'After the tunnel collapsed, the battalion commander and the "Iron Maiden Squad" worked inside the tunnel for a while.' Doctor Wang's voice is animated and full of confidence. 'The area where they were trapped had not caved in. According to the battalion commander, it would take the rescuers at least twenty days to dig into the mountain, but they only had enough food to last them two or three days. The girls all started blubbering. They had been crying for an hour or so when one of the older girls said suddenly, 'In twenty days, our bones will be rattling, and I've never had a chance to marry. I don't want to die before I get a taste of what married life is all about.' Nobody said anything for a long time. Then another of the older girls said, 'Look, there are two men here. Let's use the time left by having them take turns making love to us—then we can die in peace.' There was immediate agreement. So the battalion commander and the other male militia soldier began to make the rounds. Only the two youngest girls refused; they squatted over in the corner, covering their faces, saying things like, 'I don't want any part of this; I don't want to mess around.'

Laughing, I interrupt, 'I can't believe that kind of thing would really happen.'

Doctor Wang is wounded. 'Why the hell would I lie to you? I heard this from a guy who was personally involved in the investigation.'

'So how did they ever get to be heroes studying Mao's *Quotations*?'

'Just hold on. After one week, they finally dug through to the tunnel and rescued these people, who were half dead from lack of food and oxygen. The battalion commander was the one who started the lie, but the newspapers kept making it bigger and bigger, so that the story eventually made the front page, saying that while they were trapped, they had sustained themselves by reading the Little Red Book every day, 'pledging never to succumb in the face of adversity, and overcoming all obstacles as they battled with boulders.' The commander and three of the women even got an award at Railroad Militia Headquarters in Beijing.'

I remember seeing the picture of the ceremony in the papers, the commander looking very pious as he received a banner from the head of the Railroad Militia. Nobody would have pegged him as the Casanova type.

'The truth leaked out only after the two young girls who hadn't done anything saw the article about the ceremony and went to the authorities. Needless to say, the prizes had to go back. And the commander was discharged.'

Doctor Wang is a quiet, gentlemanly sort of fiend; with the exception of his few confidants in the Construction Group, he keeps his activities to himself. Most people think he is an upstanding individual, and he remains a prisoner doctor for a long, long time. Although I do not know for sure, I suspect that he has taken a lover from one of the cadre families.

His discretion is a striking contrast to the behavior of other members of the Third Brigade who just won't stop blowing off about their exploits. Some claim to be able to 'move their spirits' four or five times a night, others, seventeen. I can't help but being impressed. Doctor Wang listens to these pretenses with veiled amusement, and when we are alone, reminds me: 'Little Yang, the big talkers aren't usually the big movers.'

Occasionally Lu and I see some of the inmates who have been in action. One night we are awakened by loud shouting and scramble from our bunks. In the early light of dawn, we see a stream of inmates heading toward the area under the watchtower. I jostle my way to the middle of the crowd where two men are tied together, back-to-back. The politicals look on in disgust, muttering amongst themselves. 'What's going on?' I whisper to a friend.

' "Chicken relations," ' he tells me, using the common term for sodomy.

'You're not even human,' shouts out one prisoner angrily, 'you're *animals.*'

'Animals! Animals!' chants the crowd, louder and louder.

As individuals who consider themselves morally superior beings, many of the politicals are bothered by homosexuality and other 'decadent' activities much more than the authorities are. This public display of indignant outrage notwithstanding, incidents like this are not all that uncommon among the ranks of the Third Brigade. And there were even more instances before Separate Handling, since many of the common prisoners were doing time—five to seven years—for precisely this conduct. One inmate confides to me slyly he would 'rather have one tight asshole any day than three virgin spinsters.' And there are disciples of strange religions, for whom sexual acts take on an almost mystical expression, like the man who believes that by eating the sperm of one hundred virgin boys he could live forever. Still, I get the feeling that most of the homosexual behavior is due to the limited supply of women around camp. Workers and peasants have it particularly tough; women just aren't interested in them. The two men who are in for 'destroying social mores,' ugly and rather crude fellows, and who are said to have resorted to venting their passions on sows and cows, probably just couldn't find any willing human partners.

It is late, and sleep eludes me. I am thinking of women, thinking of prison, thinking of how lucky some men are with women—men like Doctor Wang. Sighing, I close my eyes, and prepare myself to face another interminable day of laying bricks.

24

A Cause Betrayed

▼

Hou Xiangfeng may have come to the Third Brigade in 1972, when we were reorganized for Separate Handling. Then again, he may have been sent over individually from a detention center at a later date—I cannot be sure. Whenever it was, I certainly took notice of him very quickly thereafter, for Hou is a good-looking man with a brilliant mind. Nor is he reticent about revealing his intellect.

All across the cottonfield, I can hear Hou expounding on the phenomena of the world. Nixon's visit to China, the international dateline, Robespierre and the French Revolution, or Guanzhong, the fifth-century statesman; no topic lies outside the scope of his tirades. In fact, he seems to favor the esoteric. Occasionally an inmate questions the accuracy of a particular fact and an argument ensues. But the challenger inevitably concedes defeat, for, as the membership of the Third Brigade will testify, Hou 'knows half of what is going on in heaven and everything on earth.'

I place him at about thirty, in spite of the fact his behavior is more reminiscent of someone just out of college, eager to prove himself. Hou's *haozi* is only two down from mine, and whenever I run into him in the hallway, he nods his head in greeting. It would appear that he knows who I am. Outwardly, however, I ignore him. Having been in camp long enough to know the score, I now make it a practice to make delicate inquiries about a case before I approach an unfamiliar prisoner. At length I learn that Hou is at Reconstruction Farm because of a 'political organization problem,' an observation which I decide must be true. The cadres treat him with considerable contempt, monitoring not only him, but any individuals with whom he speaks regularly. But inmates like Hou make friends easily, and his many casual interactions with politicals cannot readily be distinguished from the act of building an underground network.

Eventually I learn from Chen Sancai, the Rightist who had joined Shengwulian and whom I first saw in Number Twenty-three at Zuojiatang, that Hou was implicated in the same case as Liu Fengxiang. Here at last is the thread that will lead me to Old Liu, to the Labor Party, and to clues about what may be written about me in my dossier. Like Director Guan, I too begin to stalk Hou and listen carefully to the gossip.

I bide my time. 'Hou is an *organization criminal*,' I tell myself. I must be patient and discreet. Over and over, I rehearse in my head the questions that I will ask him.

Finally, one early morning when I see him in the corridor before the cadres come in for roll call, I respond to Hou's greeting. The others are busy fetching water, brushing their teeth, eating their breakfasts. Hou seems pleased, and asks, 'Yang Xiguang, are you doing all right?'

I nod. Over the loudspeaker an official radio program is being broadcast loudly, a denunciation of an article written by Lin Biao. 'Did you know Liu Fengxiang?' I hear myself whisper. 'He was a good friend.'

'Way back in 1969 Old Liu said that Mao Zedong would end up killing Lin Biao the same way Liu Bang killed Han Xin—but now the party line is that Lin Biao was plotting to bring down Mao,' I continue tentatively, probing his eyes for any indication of what he might be thinking. 'Who do *you* think initiated the attack?'

'It was Mao who wanted to get rid of Lin, of course,' says Hou without hesitation. 'Old Liu's prediction was quite accurate. Lin Biao wasn't about to be a sitting duck, so he went on the offensive.'

Anyone aspiring to reach out to the government will be taking note of our conversation, so I break off abruptly and disappear into the *haozi*. No, Hou is not KGB. Our brief exchange has convinced me he has maintained both his savvy and his integrity. Not once does he disavow his relationship with Liu Fengxiang; on the contrary he continues to use the intimate form of address, 'Old Liu.'

Soon after the Lin Biao incident, the newspapers begin to fire salvos at Lin's 'ultraleftist' line. Zhou Enlai becomes very active, widening the scope of the political movement he initiated even before Lin's plane plunged to earth, the 'Purge the May Sixteenth Elements Campaign.' 'May Sixteenth,' the name of an internal circular issued by Mao, Lin Biao, and Jiang Qing on that date in 1966, was also the name of a Rebel student organization in

Beijing critical of Zhou Enlai. Now in 1972, the label has become a euphemism for all Rebels. I am included among the thousands targeted for investigation because of my association with the extreme left. Several of the cadres handling the campaign make a trip out to Reconstruction Farm to dig into my past. Once again, I fear for my life.

I am ordered to stay in the *haozi* and wait for interrogation. An officer from the People's Protection Group informs me, 'Chairman Mao recently communicated that, whereas before the Cultural Revolution, the worst counterrevolutionaries were the Nationalists, nowadays the worst are the May Sixteenth Elements. And everyone who assaulted the Party or the government organs during the Cultural Revolution, who took part in smashing or looting, or plotted the overthrow of the dictatorship of the proletariat is "May Sixteenth." '

During this period I am frequently asked to stay back from work. Late one afternoon when I return from interrogation, I notice Hou Xiangfeng in the *haozi*. He is resting on his bunk, reading the *Hunan Daily*. Nobody else seems to be around, not even the prisoner-on-duty.

'You're under external investigation, too?' I ask.

'Cultural Revolution rebellion stuff.'

'One might think Zhou Enlai is the one responsible for persecuting the Rebels, but I'll bet the one behind it all is Old Mao.' I share what I have just learned.

Hou listens quietly.

'Isn't that name just perfect?' I laugh bitterly. 'May 16th' was what launched the revolution; now it's what Old Mao is going to use to persecute the same people he urged to rebel in 1966. He can even use this to appease Zhou Enlai.'

Hou nods. 'Just like when Chiang Kai-shek expressed support for the Communists before the coup of April 12, 1927, only to crush them later on. It's true, this purge is a turning point.'

Only one month later, during the early evening hours, the cadres of the Third Brigade enter the *haozi* and announce that a general meeting will be held to communicate an urgent matter. Unbelievably, Brigade Leader Liu reads aloud a recent directive from Chairman Mao prohibiting 'cursing, beating, and otherwise mistreating prisoners,' and supporting the prisoners' 'protest against fascist treatment.' Such a statement from the highest leadership, publicly sympathizing with prisoners and castigating the labor-reform cadres, is unprecedented.

Hou Xiangfeng and I exchange knowing glances. Zhou Enlai

must have gone too far, incurring so much public outrage that Mao again feels the need to speak out on behalf of the 'oppressed.'

For once, Brigade Leader Liu does not editorialize on Mao's text, and the general meeting is quickly adjourned. The cadres are stunned; obviously they have not been briefed and have no clue why Mao has suddenly stripped them of their authority. There is an awkward moment, then a sudden shuffling of feet as most of the prisoners pick up their stools. Some break into groups and begin to converse in hushed but excited tones; some walk quickly away; others linger, doubtful that a meeting with no punitive action can actually be over. The younger, inexperienced prisoners mill about, their faces revealing unabashed joy. The older men appear more cautious than usual, sensing from the cadres' odd mood that something is seriously wrong.

Suddenly Instructor Yang of the Third Detachment blows his whistle and orders us to assemble. 'Counterrevolutionary Hou Xiangfeng, what are you so smug about?' He must have seen Hou smile at me. 'Don't misjudge the situation, or think that you can ever realize your counterrevolutionary hopes. Prick up your dog ears and listen well: if a big shot like Lin Biao can't find a way to overturn the dictatorship of the proletariat and restore capitalism, little Trotskyites like you don't stand a chance.'

Although the comparison of Hou and Lin Biao seems silly and rather forced, the vindictive gleam in the instructor's eyes alarms me: Hou is really being watched like a hawk. 'Trotskyites' are what the authorities call any of their political enemies within the Communist Party. Before 1957 both Liu Fengxiang and Lei Techao had been high-ranking Communist cadres and had supported a political ideology similar to that of Khrushchev's. The labor reform cadres particularly resent these 'Trotskyites' who, in many instances, are in a better position to understand the complex politics underlying Mao's directive than they are.

I remember something Old Liu once said—'The outcome of political warfare is decided by the superior player.' What moves on China's chessboard would he be contemplating if he were here?

Gradually I acquire indirect confirmation from official sources that Old Liu and Hou are indeed linked. All the unresolved questions come back to me. How was it that the authorities knew absolutely nothing about this 'Labor Party'—if indeed it existed at all—when he was first sentenced? Was it plausible that the authorities would knowingly set free a leader of an underground political party, only to put him to death in the subsequent Strike One–Oppose Three Campaign? I resolve to put these questions to Hou.

One day at dusk, during the few minutes we have after dinner, I spot him sitting alone in the corridor, cradling his zither. He is playing 'The Night of the Spring River and Flower Moon,' a tune which ordinarily doesn't seem sad, but which in his rendering has acquired a mournful quality to it. I turn over a wash bucket and sit down beside him. After a while, I whisper, 'Exactly how many people were sentenced to death with Old Liu?'

'Altogether there were four of them,' he replies, without stopping his music. His eyes are fixed ahead. 'Old Liu. Lei Techao, who worked as a middle-level cadre at the Provincial Department of Public Security before being labeled a Rightist in '57. And two students, who were also Rightists.

'Then when were you sentenced?' I glance out the window behind Hou to make sure no one is in the next *haozi*.

'The first time was not long after Old Liu was killed. I was supposed to get the death penalty, but the sentencing meeting was canceled at the last minute. After that I stayed at Model Prison for a couple of years before being sentenced to fifteen in this place.'

'Since you've escaped from hell's jaws, you're bound to have luck from here on in,' I quip, trying to lighten things up.

He doesn't smile. 'Old Liu got the death shackles put on him right after he was transferred from the farm to Model Prison. He banged and pounded on the door, screaming at them that there was some mistake, but of course nobody paid any attention to him.' Hou's eyes are creased with pain, his music cold and beautiful.

As I listen, I think of the metallic sound of chains I had heard outside my cell in Model Prison that day in 1970, the day of the 'red terror.' 'So how was it that they pulled you in?'

'Do you know Zhang Jiazheng?'

'Of course,' I answer, thinking of how the 'Commander' had strutted about in 1967 when he was directing the various membership groups in Xiang River Storm.

'Lei Techao had already joined Xiang River Storm. We had control over a number of Rebel tabloids by then. But Lei Techao got noticed by the authorities because of Zhang Jiazheng and the 007 Affair.' He grips his bow tighter than ever; the rhythm falters. His gaze shifts to the prisoners' movements in the courtyard, where a cadre has just entered from the main gate of

the outer wall. Political study is about to begin. I jump up and
hurry to my *haozi*, trying to dredge from my memory what this
familiar-sounding event, this 007 Affair, refers to.

Soon afterwards I am transferred to the Insecticide Group.
Because spraying cotton is considerably easier than the other
forms of farm labor, most of the inmates in this work group are
older men. There is only one other young person in the group, a
man named Deng. As 'educated youths,' he and I have been given
responsibility for spreaders with two-cycle engines, which sit
heavy on one's back and cannot be repaired without some
knowledge of mechanics. But since China has only just begun to
mass produce these machines, they always seem to be breaking
down. The cadres decide to organize a two-cycle spreader
maintenance workshop up at the Fifth Brigade so that the
prisoners can learn from each other's experiences. The old men
all use the smaller and lighter manual machines, whose tanks
function like simple bicycle pumps.

Deng and I set off for the workshop, walking unescorted. We
will be free prisoners for three whole days.

At the Fifth Brigade camp, we are told to report to the
auditorium, where our days are spent dismantling gas engines,
oiling parts, and trying to fix broken spreaders. After dark we are
left to ourselves—two glorious nights without political study.
Sleeping next to me is a man who says he is with the Fourth
Brigade and used to be a Rebel Worker in Changsha.

'I've heard a lot about you,' he opens, then confides to me that
he, too, has been imprisoned because of a 'Cultural Revolution
problem.'

'What exactly?' I press.

'Do you—uh—know about the 007 Affair?' he asks
tentatively, catching me off guard.

Having 'worn holes in iron shoes searching in vain,' the
information I have sought so badly is dumped right into my lap.
We talk long into the night.

In late 1966, Mao Zedong commanded the Communist organs
to cease their activities and suddenly allowed everyday citizens
to form their own organizations. The urban residents stormed
the compounds of the Provincial Committee, the Municipal
Committee, and the Military Command in order to seize and
destroy the incriminating black dossier materials. To everyone's
surprise, Mao and the Central Cultural Revolution Group
subsequently came out in public support of these 'Rebels.' My
new friend from the Fourth Brigade somehow perceived that
Zhou Enlai, along with many other veteran cadres, was unhappy

about this turn of events. In late December the most violent clash between Zhou's forces and the Central Cultural Revolution Group took place. The Beijing Rebels held a secret meeting to plan how they would respond to the Conservative threat. The Conservatives and the young members of United Action gathered on the streets of the capital Beijing to demonstrate their support for Liu Shaoqi, who was already calling for the ouster of the Central Cultural Revolution Group and Jiang Qing. A few days later when my new acquaintance was passing by the Hunan Military Command, he claimed to notice a slip of paper fall from the back of a motorcycle headed into the compound gate. He was shocked at what it said: 'A military coup will take place the first day of the year. By the personal command of Zhou Enlai.'

My Rebel friend immediately sought out 'Commander' Zhang Jiazheng, then Deputy Commander of Xiang River Storm, who in turn called an emergency meeting of Storm headquarters to discuss the order, which for some reason they referred to as the '007 Document.' Shortly thereafter, Storm Headquarters responded by issuing a confidential 'Command One document,' appealing to Storm membership to swear that they would defend the command of Chairman Mao and the Central Cultural Revolution Group, and to be ready at any time to smash the counterrevolutionary evil plot of the bourgeois command.

Nothing unusual happened during the first week of January 1967, as Mao continued to back the Rebels in their efforts to seize power from every level of the Communist government. Then, in early February, a right-wing coup really did break out. Encouraged by Zhou Enlai's support, Minister Tan Zhenlin, Marshals Ye Jianying, Chen Yi, and other national military figures joined forces. They attacked Jiang Qing and pressured Mao to apprehend the leaders of all large Rebel organizations in China. Storm 'Commander' Zhang Jiazheng was among those detained. When, in July 1967, Mao authorized the release of every Rebel who had been labeled a counterrevolutionary the preceding February, the first thing Zhang did was to track down my new friend and ask him for the '007 document.' The incriminating paper was, however, never found.

The next evening I resume my questioning: 'Was the document a fake? Did the Provincial Military Command forge the document?'

'It's possible.'

'Did *you* forge it? What would have been in it for you?'

'Uhh . . . They say I was trying to use it to get a chance to travel to Beijing.'

Lights out, and no answers, only questions. If this man did indeed forge the document, then he is a political wizard, for at the end of 1966, no one could have foreseen a right-wing offensive. Still, whether the order was genuine or forged, 'Commander' Zhang must have thought it was real, or else found it very compatible with his game plan. At the very least the exercise would have allowed him to demonstrate his unswerving loyalty to the Central Cultural Revolution Group.

◆

With my newly acquired knowledge about gas engines and palace coups, I return to the Third Brigade, where I devote much of my energy to defending cotton and vegetables against the assault of insects. That winter I am transferred again. The Third Brigade has taken on a series of major construction projects, including the expansion of the barracks and a new system of irrigation pipes.

My assistant is an unskilled laborer named Guo Zhongzhu, a short man with a round face. The characters 'Labor Reform' cover his clothing. His jacket is cinched around the waist with a crude piece of hemp. Because he doesn't own anything else but an undershirt and a pair of pants, he must anchor his jacket like this, or it will become a great wind tunnel in the gusts that sweep across the lake. Guo can't be getting many care packages from home. He works silently through the day, wearing the perpetual smile of humility. Had he not been assigned to work with me in the Construction Group, I would never have been aware of the existence of this simple-minded peasant who seems utterly devoid of ambition.

Guo and I find ourselves alone one afternoon in the corner of the new *haozi*, lost in the rhythm of laying bricks. At length we begin chatting. He is, I discover, quite sociable. Though he knows the Changsha dialect, one can tell at once that he comes from a rural area. But what comes out of his mouth is not peasant talk. After several days I am completely convinced that his ignorant air is an act. This man is an intellectual in disguise and extremely savvy.

Two more weeks of conversations elapse before Guo lets it slip that he was Liu Fengxiang's friend. Another thread. He, too, had been in Model Prison on the day of Old Liu's execution. Guo had originally faced a death sentence himself, but like Hou's, his was rescinded. Later, he was re-sentenced to fifteen years' labor reform.

I continue to heap mortar onto the wall. 'Do you know if Old Liu had any last words?' I ask him.

'I heard from a friend that just before he was transferred from Reconstruction Farm at the beginning of 1970, he gave away all of his belongings to the other men. The People's Protection Group commanded him to take his things with him, but he said, "No need." He seemed to sense that his trip to Changsha was going to lead to a death sentence. Apparently he was very composed. But as soon as he got to Model Prison, the death shackles were clapped on him, and he started to cry out, "I'm innocent!"'

Guo's account brings tears to my eyes. I think back to that bitter day in early spring and the terror I felt the entire trip home to Changsha, during the Strike One–Oppose Three Campaign when it was virtually certain I faced imminent execution.

◆

Early one morning, our little group of masons, apprentices, and assistants gather to prepare for work. According to routine, Guo Zhongzhu carries the buckets over one by one, as I stir. As he dumps a pile of sand into the mortar trough, I ask him straight out what Lei Techao had to do with the 007 Affair.

'Lei was a man of passion,' Guo replies. 'He loved books written by the Russian social democrats who became professional revolutionaries.' Guo takes the last brick from his rack and places it on the pile next to me. Three of the four buckets are full, and he sits down to rest. 'When we debated what strategy to adopt, Lei was the one who came up with the idea of joining the Xiang River Storm and taking over their tabloids.' He pauses. 'That's when he started working on Zhang Jiazheng.' Guo leans on the scaffold, watching me build the wall one brick at a time.

'That doesn't make any sense. Old Liu always used to say Zhang Jiazheng was a man of questionable character, with no sense of politics. Old Liu must have told Lei that.' I focus on my mortar, trying my best to appear indifferent.

'Don't know. Old Liu used to also say that an idea could only become a political reality by being channeled through a large political faction as ideas of the masses. We all believed we had to join a mainstream political group.'

By 'we' I know he means the Rightist intellectuals who

had been in labor re-education. Had they formed a secret organization? I don't dare ask him too suddenly or too obviously. 'In any event, Zhang Jiazheng wouldn't cooperate with us,' Guo continues. 'And during the Xiang River Storm investigation of the 007 Affair, he was informed that a group of Rightists back from labor re-education had "penetrated" Xiang River Storm. To demonstrate that he was a Rebel who was "revolutionary" and not "counterrevolutionary," Zhang secretly authorized a small group of his Storm Rebels to expose this Rightist "counterrevolutionary organization." '

'But how could he know whether there really *was* a "counterrevolutionary organization?" ' I ask quickly. The trowel in my hand lies still.

Guo lifts the empty bucket up onto his shoulder pole and hurries back for more mortar.

I am certain that Old Liu and Lei Techao had become Rebels. Shengwulian and Xiang River Storm would have been the 'mainstream' political bodies that would allow the secret ideas of a few intellectuals to be communicated as agendas of the masses, in organizations functioning much like seedling parties capable of influencing hundreds of millions of people in the Cultural Revolution. But 'Commander' Zhang had been more concerned about weeding out what he considered undesirable 'Rightists' than in broadening the Rebel vision. He had not only sabotaged the old Rightists' plan to seek rehabilitation, he had even seen to it that the activities of Liu Fengxiang— regardless of whether they were part of a formal organization or not—became sufficiently visible to the Public Security Bureau.

I have asked enough questions; more details are unnecessary. One of the slogans of the Strike One–Oppose Three Campaign comes to mind: 'The Cultural Revolution has exposed class enemies; now is the time for us thoroughly to destroy the political blight hiding in our society!' And Nine Dragon Zhang's remark that the Cultural Revolution was Mao Zedong's way of allowing the townspeople to vent their frustrations with communism. Perhaps Mao's strategy of backing the Rebels guaranteed that Old Liu would never be able successfully to use the Rebels for his own purposes. If 'Commander' Zhang could legitimize himself by supporting Mao and opposing Zhou Enlai, why would he still want to identify himself with 'Rightists' or 'counterrevolutionary organizations'? For if Mao had not thrown his support to the Rebels, the Rebels *would* have sympathized with their fellow underdogs, the Rightists. As I reflect on all of this, I mourn for Old Liu as never before. Perhaps his demise had not been the result of a random move on the chessboard. Did a Chinese Labor Party ever exist? Was Old Liu a member? I dare not ask. But based on my many conversations with Old Liu, and his remark that 'political power is in reality based on personal connections and doesn't necessarily require a formal organization,' I can guess the answer. Most likely Old Liu, while actively trying to sway the umbrella Rebel group Shengwulian, had rejected the idea of a bona fide organization, whereas Lei and the others had supported the establishment of a formal 'Labor Party.'

◆

1974: The Year of the Tiger is upon us. Two days of rest, two blessed nights without political study. My sister Yang Hui has brought me a care package with cocoa, coffee, and two little cans of concentrated milk. On a kerosene stove, we heat up a washbasinful each of coffee and cocoa. A couple of the masons and their assistants join Guo Zhongzhu and me. Perched atop a window bunk, we dip our mugs into the basins and raise them in celebration of the new year.

Everyone is eager to taste this exotic fare. But no matter how much sugar I add to the coffee there are still frowns. After one taste, Lu Guoan, whose family grows vegetables on the outskirts of Changsha, begins to make loud clicking sounds with his tongue. 'No wonder the "government" (by this he means the cadres, who routinely refer to themselves as the "government") tell us that life in the Western capitalist countries is "bitter." If you had to drink this stuff every day, life would be hell!'

Guo Zhongzhu, however, savors the hot coffee one sip at a time, his face flushed with pleasure. I am gratified. He leans over and murmurs, 'Old Liu became aware of you very early on. It's true, he didn't think much of Zhang Jiazheng, but he liked you, and he liked Zhang Yugang. He said you were a spiritual leader of your generation. "If we can win over Yang Xiguang," he told me, "we'll be able to get the rest of his generation."'

Unnerved, I glance around, noting with some relief that the others seem to be absorbed in loud conversation. I think back fondly to the first days of 1970 and my intimate exchanges with Old Liu in Number Twenty-three. With a pang of bitter-sweet recognition, I realize that I must have been his mark all along.

25

The Exit Brigade

▼

Director Guan has dropped out of sight. His replacement, Director Zhou, a younger, thinner man with a sullen face, is slow to arrive. Rumor has it that Zhou is being transferred from the city prison to be reunited with his wife, who is rurally registered. At Reconstruction Farm, both of them will be entitled to rations of 'national grain.' If, in his new position, he has to be content with a less comfortable environment, at least he can content himself with the fact that he is still a cut above the locals.

When Zhou finally does show his face, it is without ceremony. But as the months pass, I get the feeling that he is watching me. My suspicions are confirmed suddenly one afternoon when I go to the library and the Rightist elementary school teacher in charge whispers into my ear, 'Director Zhou came to inspect the reading room today and took away everything on Lu Xun. And, Little Yang, he asked about you—if *you* had borrowed anything by Lu Xun.'

Most members of the Third Brigade are fans of this great writer of the 1920s and '30s. They appreciate his defiance in speaking out against the authorities, and his works are often cited by the politicals in their private refutations of the authorities. The vogue for Lu Xun has thus far escaped the attention of the farm cadres, who are not inclined to think too much about ideological subtleties. Director Zhou is a different breed of cadre. A man who has worked in the city prison most certainly has experience in breaking counterrevolutionary organizations, in probing the minds of people like Old Liu and Su Yibang. Now he is sniffing after me.

Ironically, I don't even like Lu Xun's books all that much. I find he makes rather dull reading, and his writing is limited artistically. A naïve radical. But my literary taste is not at issue here.

Several days go by. When I get back to the barracks, I am informed by a friend that while we were out working, Director Zhou rifled through all my belongings, paying special attention to anything that had been scribbled on. This is nerve-racking. Someone has given him information about my conversations with other politicals and he is looking for supporting evidence. Fortunately, on the days he looks through my bedclothes, he comes up empty-handed.

I have reason to worry. My notebooks are piling up. Ever since Nixon visited China, *Reference News* has been printing articles about American economic issues, and the members of the Construction Group have been taking turns stealing the newspaper from the cadres. Watergate, Carter's campaign speeches—finally a tiny window has opened on the American political and social system. A friend allows me to stash them, one at a time, in his workshop outside the gate. Thus I carry on my person only the notebook I am currently using. Mornings I take pains to check that my bunk contains nothing but mathematics and engineering. But any oversight, one stray page from my screenplay or from a political notebook, would be fatal.

I am relatively sure Director Zhou doesn't have any hard evidence, yet when I think of his grim, determined face, I panic. Old Liu's words come back to me: 'You must assume that everything you say will eventually be known, because they will use every means imaginable to encourage prisoners to divulge their secrets.'

It is distressing to think my conversations are being routinely communicated to the cadres. Any mention of politics by a political criminal is proof positive of 'political ambition'—latent 'political blight.' From the trouble that Director Song has given me, and from my experience in 'confessing and submitting to the law,' I have learned that the authorities do not care whether one's discussions are subversive in their intent or purely theoretical.

And yet, try as I might, I cannot keep my mouth shut. We politicals have a lot to talk over.

One month later my worst fears materialize. A particularly well-connected prisoner tells me that Director Zhou has begun to follow up on a recent KGB report that the Third Brigade houses a counterrevolutionary clique. The clique is said to link the dissident factions—the Democratic Party, the Labor, and Shengwulian. My head throbs, as if it is about to explode. For a moment, I cannot breathe. This investigation will lead them straight to me, for I am on equally friendly terms with members of the three major underground parties, with Rebels, and with Rightists. And at the core of Shengwulian.

During my ten-year imprisonment, virtually every one of my fellow inmates has been dubbed a 'cow-ghost, snake-spirit counterrevolutionary' at one time or another. Even common criminals such as Spartacus Li Gang were deemed to have committed 'political' errors. It is easy to imagine how much more serious a political sentence is doled out to inmates associated with unacceptable political ideas or organizations. Since Separate Handling, I have been housed almost exclusively with 'political' prisoners. Roughly one-third of the politicals in the Third Brigade belong to the category Master Wang calls 'true' counterrevolutionaries—men who have been sentenced for advocating underground political activities to launch another revolution and overthrow another regime.

I know inmates belonging to various spontaneously developed forms of the 'Labor Party,' the 'Democratic Party,' the 'Great Harmony Party,' and the 'Anti-Communist Salvation Army' of Taiwan, the latter encouraged by the Voice of Free China broadcasts from Taiwan. Little Ma, a former factory worker, insists that his Labor Party had absolutely nothing to do with Old Liu. In fact he is not acquainted with anyone at Reconstruction Farm who has been sent here on a Labor Party charge. But each of the Labor parties seems to have certain similarities—a Soviet style of socialism and a leadership consisting predominantly of Rightists, most of whom were killed early on.

I have just as many friends who belong to different branches of the 'Democratic' Party, also mutually unconnected. These people reject socialism, advocating instead a Western-style parliamentary system of democracy. One of these is Li Furen, a writer whose father was a Nationalist official who decided not to follow Chiang Kai-shek to Taiwan: 'Every dynasty needs businessmen; politicians won't ever bother businessmen.' But his father's judgment was off—his property was expropriated and he killed himself. It is clear that Li's own motivation for joining the party is strictly personal.

Unlike 'counterrevolutionary organizations,' 'counter-revolutionary cliques' are not organized underground parties, but 'salons,' groups of people who get together regularly. One Third Brigade 'counterrevolutionary clique' criminal is an elementary school teacher who had seen how, during the Great Leap, the Yueyang County Committee force the peasants to labor under cruel conditions during the construction of Green Mountain

Dam. This teacher had met frequently with his friends to see if anything could be done. During the Cultural Revolution he was sentenced to fifteen years for involvement in a counterrevolutionary clique.

Another case is a man named Zhou Yude who once worked in a mine on the outskirts of Yueyang. After the failure of the Great Leap Forward, he met monthly with his friends to discuss government policies. The group predicted the Communist dynasty would experience great political turmoil and viewed the Cultural Revolution as the fulfillment of their prediction. Though the majority of the 'clique' membership did not think that a power outside the Communist Party could overthrow it, they believed that secret plotters at the upper echelons of the Party could: 'People like Jiang Qing will rebel from within, just like Lin Biao rebelled from within the Party.'

But Jiang Qing never had a chance to establish her own power base. We heard from a free criminal in October 1976 how the Gang of Four had fallen. The 'counterrevolutionaries' of the Third Brigade were jubilant, thinking that perhaps the time was ripe for more moderate policies. The cadres also celebrated loudly with drums and gongs, but for different reasons: they saw the Gang of Four as symbols of the Rebels who challenged the authorities.

Most of the cases involving 'organizations' and 'cliques' trace back to the great famine of 1959. Like Bandit Xiang, my friend Zeng Aibin came from a village where many people starved during the Three Bitter Years. After witnessing the devastation of his family and neighbors, he became 'Commander' of one of the Anti-Communist Salvation corps in the early sixties and had taken advantage of the turmoil of the Cultural Revolution to conduct some sort of anti-government activities, the details of which he never shares. He and many other elderly prisoners from the countryside compared the chaos of the late sixties to the final days of the Qing Dynasty believing that the end of the Communist dynasty was near. Similar predictions were made by the adherents of the mystical group Doctrine of Coherence— peasants of various backgrounds who cited the 'Sesame Cake Song' and prophesied that millions of people would die after the Communists seized control, and who read fortunes to identify the emperor and prime minister of the next dynasty.

And so the days seem interminable. On edge, I cannot concentrate on my books. Nights I am awakened by the image of Old Liu bound in death shackles pounding on the door, or by the sober, silent face of Nine Dragons Zhang. I lie in my sweat-soaked clothes, reviewing case after case of prisoners who, having been accused during the Cultural Revolution of being involved in cliques, were ultimately executed. Though I try to calm myself with the thought I have never established any formal bonds, I know very well that all along I have been consciously reaching out to every conceivable type of prisoner, and especially to politicals, trying to understand them.

When I awake, I console myself with the fact that I have always embraced Confucius's strategy 'A man of virtue socializes, but does not form firm alliances,' cementing personal relationships across the political spectrum, leaving no traces of political linkage. The risks of such an approach were minimal with uneducated cadres such as Director Guan, Counselor He, and Brigade Leader Liu. But Old Liu had used the same strategy and ended up dead. If I run up against an adversary like the man who handled Old Liu's case during these last days of my term, a man, for example, like Director Zhou with his ideologically sensitive nose, I may never walk through the prison gate.

Day after day the senior cadres make life miserable for me, railing at the least little thing. One morning when I pause to check the plumb line against the wall, Brigade Leader Liu comes running over. 'Yang Xiguang!' he snarls. 'Stop loafing.'

Though I can't compete with Lu Guoan, I am one of the fastest masons in the Construction Group, and the counselor's remark makes me bristle. 'If you think I'm so slow, go out and grab somebody else to do the work. Snatching people and putting them to work is what you do best anyway!'

'You had better not let your head get swollen with counterrevolutionary notions, Yang Xiguang. If big-time counterrevolutionaries like Lin Biao and the Gang of Four aren't able to make it, how are *you* ever going to come out of this in one piece? Don't think for a moment we don't know about all your counterrevolutionary activities!'

I wonder what Director Zhou has been telling him. Every time something like this happens, I try meticulously to reconstruct just what I have said to whom, and who might be snitching. Days later, a friend warns me that the KGB might be Chen Sancai. It does seem that he is keeping his distance these days. And when we run into each other, instead of calling out 'Little Yang,' he ignores me altogether. I suddenly remember having seen him in Number Twenty-three at Zuojiatang. As a 1957 Rightist who had worked alongside Old Liu, even during the Cultural Revolution when they were fighting to rehabilitate themselves, he would be very clear about the nature of Liu's involvement in Shengwulian. If Chen is indeed the one who has been slipping notes to the cadres, I have to assume that they already know about this part of my past.

I spend another week in absolute terror. Then, inexplicably, things seem to quiet down. The other cadres seem to take little interest in Zhou's project. It may be that Director Zhou, as a newcomer, has not yet been able to secure the confidence and friendship of the farm cadres. Or perhaps, with the recent fall of the Gang of Four, moderation is indeed in vogue.

Whatever the reason, I privately rejoice. Had Director Zhou's investigation taken place in 1970, I could have been squashed effortlessly. Instead, on February 8, 1978, my tenth year of imprisonment, Brigade Leader Liu orders that I be transferred to the Exit Brigade, right on schedule.

But Director Zhou cannot resist a parting shot: 'Continue in this fashion, keep on refusing to be molded, and you'll never get rid of the counterrevolutionary cap on your head!'

◆

In the Exit Brigade, there are no walls, and we are close to Farm Headquarters. Suddenly we have freedom of movement; in fact inmates can now sneak home to Yueyang and Changsha, for even if they are caught, there will be no further sentence. Now, however, we find ourselves smack against another kind of wall. Residency status. Those who once lived in the city will soon have an opportunity to return there, while prisoners from the countryside must go back to their more humble origins. Because one may not choose—the 'household residency' system binds a person to live his entire life where he is born—and because the standard of living in rural areas is several times lower than in the urban, even lower than the labor camps, peasants will do anything they can to avoid a life sentence of living at home.

One of my new fellow inmates, a man named Yang Xiaowen, tells me that in his village a year's labor provides only the grain for his table. He never sees cash. If the family wants to buy salt or kerosene, he has to raise a few hens and sell eggs at the farmers' market. Regional Communist committees are also particularly zealous in their persecution of people with bad backgrounds. As a landlord, Yang Xiaowen's father had been targeted in every political campaign since 1949. Their home was ransacked, their livestock expropriated. Yang wants no more from life than to spend the rest of his days at Reconstruction

Farm. Here at least everyone labors together; no one will treat him as they did on the outside. And as a regularly employed worker, he can make about 20 yuan a month, more than he could make in a year in his village.

A large-headed cadre who we privately refer to as Fatty Zhou is responsible for making the post-prison assignments. Three days after my arrival, he convenes a meeting for newcomers. I am struck by his style, which is markedly different from that of other cadres. Never once does he lecture or scold, or bring up the matter of ideological reform. He is tough, but businesslike and to the point.

That night, as Fatty Zhou takes from his briefcase the stack of files which we know will decide our futures, the twelve of us hold our breaths. He calls out a name. A wiry old man stands up.

'Come up to the front!' Fatty Zhou smiles. 'How many people are in your family?'

'I don't have any family. Nope. No living relatives at all. Since I was sentenced in the Land Reform Movement, everybody's either died or moved away. It must be twenty years since I've heard from anyone.' This man, an historical counterrevolutionary incarcerated soon after the Communists assumed power, has probably spent half of his life in a prison cell.

Fatty Zhou stares at him for an instant, then says with considerable irritation, 'No family at all? How can that be? Now just because you haven't stayed in touch doesn't mean that there's nobody back there waiting. An old man like you, and you still want to hang around camp and let us support you? No, no; we're going to send a letter to your hometown, and persuade them to take you in. Don't be so set on staying.' He flicks his hand. 'Go back to your seat.'

The next to be called up is a youth from Changsha named Little Li. He is wearing a worker's uniform. Fatty Zhou looks at him intently. 'How many people are there in your family, son?'

Little Li tries to make his family's situation sound as good as possible. Both his parents work at a large state-run factory. His brothers have jobs. His little sister is a student. They write regularly every month. Fatty Zhou urges him to jot down his parents' exact address.

'Yang Xiguang!' I hear him call out at length. Director Zhou's pledge that I will continue to wear a counterrevolutionary cap even after my term is formally up, has made me realize just how important Fatty Zhou is to my fate.

He will read my files; he will write the memorandum to the Changsha Public Security Bureau. All decisions as to whether I will be able to return to Changsha, whether I will be permanently deprived of many rights, will be based on these documents.

'Are you the Yang Xiguang who wrote the reactionary essay?'

'Yes.'

Until now, Fatty Zhou has not asked about a prisoner's case all evening long, nor has he used judgmental language like 'reactionary.' What does he have in mind for me?

In a couple of hours, we are finished with the interviews. Based on appearances, Fatty Zhou is anxious to keep the strong and skilled workers at the farm, and send the less qualified people back home.

I have befriended a Changsha technician, a man by the name of Liu, who is finishing up a seven-year sentence for a critique he wrote of Mao Zedong. He tells me Fatty Zhou is a man of boundless greed, that he is hard on prisoners from the countryside, but for urban residents spares no pains to influence the local public security agencies. Every week Fatty Zhou travels about the province, making the necessary arrangements for prisoners to remain at the farm or return home. Fatty Zhou has been to Liu's home twice, and has let it be understood that a gesture of 40 yuan would be appreciated.

The paperwork which will enable Liu to settle permanently in Changsha is already in the works. If I give Fatty Zhou a suitable gift, Liu tells me, I will be guaranteed a return to my comfortable home in the provincial capital. The crucial first step is for the Changsha Public Security Bureau police substation where my father is registered to issue the 'certificate of acceptance' which will allow me to apply for residency. The second step is for Reconstruction Farm to issue a document agreeing to my return. Both documents must be processed by Fatty Zhou.

I remain skeptical. Will he openly ask for money? What exactly does one say in such cases? It is hard to imagine. To be prepared, I ask Liu to relate his experience to my father and Yang Hui as soon as he gets back to Changsha.

But in less than a week, I find myself sitting in Fatty Zhou's office. He wants my father's address. Could I possibly provide him with a few more details about his life? He nods vigorously as I relate to him how my father had been the head of the Agricultural Bureau of the provincial government before the Cultural Revolution and how, from 1968 to 1975, he was

confined in a May Seventh Cadres' School. Now he is back in
Changsha. Although his reputation is not what it used to be,
Father is currently Deputy Bureau Chief of the Provincial Bureau
of Light Industry. The title is more symbolic than substantive.
Perhaps Yang Hui can come to see me, suggests Fatty Zhou;
he would like to have a chance to chat with her.
She arrives about a week later, just before the Lunar New Year.
A recent college graduate, Yang Hui has been teaching at a
Changsha high school which is now closed for winter break.
During my imprisonment she has represented the family in
communicating with me, traveling up to the farm almost every
year. Fatty Zhou is extremely gracious and insists that she stay
at his home. The two of them talk for most of the afternoon.
The next day when I walk her to the bus station, she tells me
the situation. Fatty Zhou had gone out to reserve her return
ticket, carrying a large basket. After a while he returned with
the ticket, but without the basket. He had shaken his head and
said, 'Nowadays if you don't give a little something, you just
can't get anything done—can't even buy a bus ticket!'
Later that evening as Yang Hui sat with his family in front of
the fire, Fatty Zhou's wife remarked in passing that their oldest
son was about to be married and had almost everything he
needed. The only item that they were still missing was a
wedding quilt.
'That's it—that's what they want you to give them!' I
interrupt.
Yang Hui stares at me, unconvinced, until I remind her how
Fatty Zhou had solicited bribes from Liu and other prisoners.
Back in Changsha, Yang Hui goes out shopping and with my
father's money buys a traditional Hunanese red embroidered
quilt for 40 yuan—one month's salary for her. Then she mails
the large bundle to Fatty Zhou.
With some prisoners, there is just no oil to skim off the top.
I hear a story of one peasant who did not wish to return to the
countryside, but who was to be sent back nevertheless, the
village Party officials having expressed interest in watching over
this dangerous counterrevolutionary element and enemy of the
people. The peasant, knowing full well the treatment he could
expect at their hands, adamantly refused. Finally Fatty Zhou had
the hometown cadres send over a squadron of armed militia to
escort this labor reform 'released prisoner' home. The latter ran
away from his village as soon as he had a chance, returned to the
vicinity of Reconstruction Farm, and stole an untended water
buffalo at Junshan Farm, where he led the animal along the

highway, trying to sell it. He was soon arrested and packed back to camp.

It was only a matter of time before he came across Fatty Zhou. 'Now try sending me home!' he quipped, flashing a smile. Little Li's father arrives from Changsha, bringing with him two bottles of tigerbone wine, a costly product said to aid virility. That was what Zhou asked him for, Little Li tells me with a sigh. What Fatty Zhou does not know is that tigerbone wine *bottles* are all that he will be getting; having searched in vain all over Changsha, Li's father had to resort to buying ordinary herbal wine.

In time Fatty Zhou's venal behavior proves his undoing. Soon after I leave the camp, a number of prisoners about to return to Changsha go to the Provincial Public Security Department and bring charges against him. Even before the investigation at Reconstruction Farm is complete, Fatty Zhou is found near Farm Headquarters, hanging from a tree.

Technically my term has been up for a month, but there is still no news from Changsha. Like the other released prisoners who are 'regularly employed' at the camp, I now receive a monthly salary of 15 yuan. The salary scale for employees depends on whether the individual still wears a 'cap', which in turn depends on how obedient the prisoner was during his term. Counterrevolutionary or 'bad element' caps mean 10 to 15 percent less money. Members of the Exit Brigade do not know if they will be labeled until they actually leave. For the time being, our salaries are the same as the released prisoners who know they have caps.

It is not uncommon for prisoners whose terms are up to remain with the Exit Brigade for six months to a year before finally receiving clearance to go home. One of our fellow inmates named Little Yan just takes off for Changsha, where he greases the palms of local officials to speed things along. Then he returns to camp. That night in the barracks Little Yan gives us an update on what's new in Changsha. Young couples have started to hold hands in public, and girls are walking around in skirts— phenomena unheard of for over ten years. People are now sporting clothes made of a new luxury fabric called 'dacron.'

More sobering news is the report that Rebel leaders on the outside are once again being hunted down as the enemies of newly empowered cadres and thrown into jail. I think of the restorations of 1962 and 1972. Each had brought with it rationality and prosperity; but in each, the ascendant regime had lost no time in crushing its political adversaries. Why can't there be order and prosperity without persecution? In my years of labor reform, I have seen so many good people sacrificed. Never again can I naïvely embrace an order and a prosperity based on brutal oppression, an order which blots out its political enemies, making political upheaval inevitable. It is April again. My tenth April behind bars. The freshness of the spring air, the scents of rape blossoms and rice seedlings once again make my head spin. Throughout the country a period of enormous change is in the offing. My fate, like that of the nation, seems to be improving with each passing day of 1978. One morning I receive a letter from Little Liu, saying that my letter of acceptance will soon be issued. He has been to my home many times, the home of my dreams, the home that was also once the home of a wealthy Nationalist official. But there is no turning back. From now on I will identify with the Nationalists, with the underground parties, with the new wave of Rebel leaders who have just been imprisoned—with anyone who has ever been the victim of political persecution. The day that China's political situation finally stabilizes will be the same day that China's last group of persecuted individuals—her last group of Rebels—are set free. It troubles me that the Cultural Revolution has been rejected by the post-Mao government in its entirety; some revolutionary currents deserve to be remembered. I must believe the day will come when the Rebels' struggle against persecution will be vindicated.

◆

Yang Hui has come to take me home. Solemn and beautiful, she busies herself with my luggage, the shape of her face reminding me of our mother. Though we are close, my behavior in prison has not always been easy for her—when she learned that I had clashed with the cadres in 1972 after Director Song Shaowen informed on me, she wrote a letter begging me to give in. In my anguished response, I accused her of being 'half-livestock and half-devil, capitulating to a tyrannical government,' of 'acting peremptorily in the face of the innocent.' I, on the other hand, was 'half-beast and half-angel'; I swore that I would never heed her words and submit to those who would persecute me.

Now, as we sit side-by-side on the bus headed for Yueyang I can see she is ecstatic about my release. I fix my gaze on the moving fields outside the window, where the rice paddies are just turning green. In the distance I spot a bridge that I helped to build. Several men in blue uniforms are squatting on the bank. Though I ache to begin the life just ahead of me, a part of me lingers, clinging to this piece of earth and the prisoners here. The bus jostles on, passing the sluice. My heart is pounding. I think of the grassy stretch on the other side of the dike, and the anger, never very far below the surface, begins to build. Thunder Lei, Fu Zigeng, Huang Wenzhe—the aggrieved spirits of how many friends are still out there? I think of Liu Fengxiang and Zhang Jiulong—how good it would be if they were alive and I could talk with them. The day foreseen by Old Liu long ago, the day China would have its own Khrushchev, has finally arrived. The Mao era is being replaced by a new one.

Whatever the future holds for me, I vow not to let the events that have happened on this spot of earth slip into the darkness. My notebooks are already safely on the outside, thanks to the courage of friends. Let me write the unwritten history of the counterrevolutionary underworld I have witnessed, for my spirit will always be with the prisoners in the Third Brigades, in the Model Prisons, in the Number Nines.

◆

We have passed the cotton fields of the Tenth Brigade and crossed into Junshan Farm. On the horizon, the contours of Reconstruction Farm gradually flatten, receding farther and farther out of sight, until at length they are hidden completely by the tea trees atop Junshan Mountain.

Glossary

▼

Anti-Communist Salvation Army—A pro-Nationalist underground political party that was inspired by the Voice of Free China broadcast from Taiwan.

Anti-Rightist Campaign—Begun in June 1957, the campaign conducted by the Communist Party to repress the criticism generated in the Hundred Flowers Campaign.

August Storm—The movement in August 1967 characterized by battles between the Conservatives and the Rebels.

'Black' (as in 'black hand,' 'black categories', etc.)—The color black was used to describe anything related to undesirable backgrounds and was often used synonymously with 'counterrevolutionary.' See 'red.'

'Black categories'—Undesirable family-background identities including landlords, rich peasants, counterrevolutionaries, bad elements, rightists, and capitalists, used from the 1950s to the 1970s.

'Black hand'—A counterrevolutionary force acting behind the scenes to manipulate political events.

Cadres—A Chinese Communist Party official or other government official.

Central Cultural Revolution Group—An *ad hoc* group organized by Mao Zedong at the beginning of the Cultural Revolution (May 1966) in order to bypass the Central Committee. Key members were Kang Sheng, Jiang Qing, Yao Wenyuan, and Chen Boda.

Changsha Youth—A Rebel organization composed of former compulsory laborers and considered the desperadoes of the Rebel movement.

Conservatives, or 'Loyalists'—Supporters of the pre-Cultural

Revolution local Communist apparatus. They backed the local governments' suppression of the Rebels during the 'Cultural Revolution and took part in the discrimination against the 'black categories.'

Cultural Revolution Small Group—Another name for the 'Central Cultural Revolution Group.'

Democratic Alliance—A political group which was under control of the Communist Party and was regarded as a showpiece party.

Democratic Party—An underground, political party advocating Western-style, parliamentary democracy for China.

Eight-nineteen (8.19) Red Guards—A Rebel organization composed of Changsha high school students; the organization was named after the event occurring on August 19, 1966, in which a spontaneous student demonstration was labeled counterrevolutionary by the Communist forces.

February Countercurrent—A Conservative backlash against Rebel groups arising after a Central Working Conference in February 1967. This political shift, endorsed by Mao, targeted Rebel groups nationwide, especially those with military potential, and culminated in the 'Campaign to Suppress Counterrevolutionaries.' The movement essentially stemmed from a social conflict between 'Conservatives,' with interests vested in the establishment and the 'Rebels,' who wanted to change the power *status quo.*

Four Purifications Campaign of 1964—By 1961 the Communist apparatus had realized the seriousness of the flaws of the Great Leap policies leading to widespread famine. The Central Committee, headed by Liu Shaoqi, initiated the Anti-Five Winds Campaign directed against such practices as exaggerating one's performance, cheating, and exploiting the peasants. Embarrassed, Mao tried to regain control of the situation by taking over the leadership of the campaign and changing its name to the 'Four Purifications.' Whereas Liu had tried to keep his campaign within the scope of the 'Five Winds' and avoided communicating its activities outside the Party membership, Mao's campaign made a point of highlighting mistakes made earlier by Liu— for example, the fact that Liu had ignored the human rights of cadres when they were purged. As the first demonstration of a power struggle between Mao and Liu, the 1964 campaign was in some ways the first manifestation of the Cultural Revolution.

Golden Monkey Regiment—A Rebel organization composed of workers in small collective firms.

Great Harmony Party—An underground, political opposition group espousing the Confucian doctrine of 'great harmony.' Established by a bank clerk in 1960 in the aftermath of the great famine caused by Mao's Great Leap Forward, its members gathered regularly to discuss national politics. According to its leader, Yang Xuemeng (a cousin of the author), the group disbanded in the mid-1960s due to the economic recovery and the increasingly oppressive political atmosphere.

Historical Counterrevolutionaries—Political prisoners who were political enemies of the Communist Party before 1949.

January Storm, or January Revolution—The January 1967 event in which the Rebels were encouraged by Mao to overturn the local Communist apparatus.

'KGBs'—Prison jargon for a snitch or informant.

Labor Party—A pro-Soviet political party that criticized Mao's ultraleftist line in order to gain support from the people.

Mao Zedong Thought Red Guards—A Rebel organization composed of high school students, diametrically opposed to the Conservative Red Power Guardian Army.

March to Jinggangshan—Jinggangshan is the mountainous region where Mao built up a stronghold of Red Army troops during the Civil War period (1931–6). During the Cultural Revolution, more than one million Red Guards from every corner of China traveled on foot to Jinggangshan to demonstrate their adulation of Mao and to experience the same hardship that the Red Army had experienced.

May Sixteenth Elements (and 'Campaign to Single Out May Sixteenth Elements')—Lasting from 1971 to mid-1972, the May Sixteenth Campaign targeted against Rebel organizations signified Mao's shift of support from Rebels to Conservatives, allowing the Conservatives to exact revenge on the previously dominant Rebel forces.

Military Control Commission—Military authorities which took over administrative responsibilities from local governments when they became paralyzed in 1967–8.

October Party Central Work Meeting—A meeting called to plan Mao's strategy of taking advantage of the human rights problems. At this meeting, Mao called for the rehabilitation of those who had been labeled as counterrevolutionaries during the early stage of the Cultural Revolution and for more freedom of political association.

Paris Commune—A revolutionary republican commune set up in Paris in 1871 by workers and the lower-middle classes and ultimately ruthlessly suppressed. Socialists saw the effort as proof that only radical force could enable workers to overthrow the bourgeoisie.

People's Protection Group (PPG)—A secret police force organized during the Cultural Revolution by Kang Sheng in order to oppress political enemies.

Practicing Counterrevolutionaries—All dissidents, opposition elements, and prisoners of conscience who were labeled after 1949.

Provincial Revolutionary Committee Preparatory Goup—A provincial administrative body, comprising representatives of non-official rebel organizations and former government officials (deemed acceptable by Mao and Zhou Enlai) as well as military commanders.

Public Security Organs Headquarters (gongjianfa)—A conservative political organization consisting of staff from the public security organs, the procurators' organs and the judicial departments, persons, and agencies charged with the reform of criminals through labor during the period of 1967–8.

Purge of 1954—A political campaign designed to purge the political enemies of the Communist regime.

Purify the Class Ranks Campaign—A campaign beginning at the end of 1968 to purge dissidents, particularly Rebel forces.

Rebellion is Justified Army—A Rebel organization composed of high school students.

Rebels—As used by Mao in 1966, 'Rebels' were individuals who had been discriminated against by officials before the Cultural Revolution and who were critical of factions in power.

'Red'—A term used synonymously with 'revolutionary.'

Red Angry Fire—A Changsha terrorist organization composed of radical Conservatives.

Red Banner Army—A Rebel organization composed of disgruntled, demobilized veterans of the Civil and Korean Wars; the organization was highly proficient in military maneuvers.

'Red categories'—'Revolutionary' or 'pure-red' family backgrounds, including families of workers, poor and lower-middle peasants, soldiers, revolutionary cadres (individuals who participated in pre-Liberation activities), and revolutionary martyrs (individuals who died during the War of Liberation.)

Red Guards—A term often used generically to describe the first unofficial youth organizations formed during the Cultural Revolution; the first Red Guards were composed of the children of high-ranking cadres.

Red Guard Headquarters—An organization comprised of university students in Changsha which was the first of the Rebel organizations to clash with the local government in 1966. It later shifted its support to the Conservative Military Control authorities in the 1967 February Countercurrent.

Red Guard Pickets—A radical Conservative organization composed of Red Guards, most of whom were the children of high-ranking officials in Beijing.

Red Guardians—A Conservative organization composed of adult activists who were Communist Party members and worked in large state-owned factories.

Red High School Committee—A Rebel organization composed of high school students.

Red Power Guardian Army—A Conservative organization composed of the children of high-ranking cadres in power in August 1966, who advocated the 'blood line' and opposed the Rebel Mao Zedong Thought Red Guards.

Red Rebel Troupe—A Rebel organization composed of artists and writers who were persecuted by the old local Communist apparatus and by the Conservatives.

Red Rebels Association—A Rebel organization composed of high school students.

Restoration of 1972—After Lin Biao's death in 1971, Mao had to rely on Premier Zhou Enlai as his primary aid in purging Lin's followers. Zhou used this opportunity to criticize Lin's ultraleftist line, which both Lin and Mao had implemented during the Cultural Revolution. During this 'restoration,' Zhou rehabilitated many of the relatively conservative officials who had been purged during the Cultural Revolution, social order was restored, and many old social and cultural practices were revived. In this new climate, however, Rebels once again became a target of persecution.

Revisionists—Communists who opposed Mao's ultraleftist policies.

Revolutionary Committee Preparatory Group—A temporary, interim local institution existing from late 1967 and 1968, which acted as a *de facto* government when the local governments were paralyzed and the new authorities had yet to be established.

Right-wing Opportunists—Government officials who opposed Mao's Great Leap Forward policies in 1959 and who were subsequently purged by Mao.

Rightists—A label given to hundreds of thousands of individuals, especially intellectuals, in the Anti-Rightist Campaign of 1957.

Separate Handling—In 1972, the prison authorities revived the pre-Cultural Revolution regulation requiring political prisoners to be assigned only to brigades where there were no common prisoners. The purpose of this 'separate handling' was to prevent political prisoners from spreading their ideologies to the common prisoners and to keep prisoners from picking up habits from the common prisoners.

Shengwulian—'The Hunan Provincial Proletarian Revolutionary Alliance Committee,' Shengwulian was a Rebel umbrella group formed in October 1967. Consisting of more than twenty loosely affiliated organizations, each with its own grievance, it included Xiang River Storm, Teachers' Federation, Red Banner Army, and the Red High School Committee.

Sixteen Point Resolution—A directive issued by the Communist Party Central Committee in August 1966, initiating the 'Great Proletarian Cultural Revolution' and effectively legalizing the unofficial student organizations; the directive did not grant freedom of association for individuals other than students.

Socialist Education Campaign—The campaign from 1964 to 1966 in which work teams were sent from the cities into the countryside to reorganize the rural Communist apparatus.

Southern March—The final stage of the Civil War between the Nationalists and the Communists, in which the Communist Army conquered the entire nation, moving from the North to the South. It took place in 1949.

Strike One–Oppose Three Campaign—A campaign occurring in the spring of 1970 to strike down counterrevolutionaries and oppose common criminals, corruption, and waste. It signified the end of Mao's experimentation with the individuals' freedom of association during the Cultural Revolution.

Struggle session, or struggle meeting—A forum for denouncing counterrevolutionaries, first held during the Land Reform Movement of the 1950s and revived during the Cultural Revolution.

Teachers' Federation—A Rebel organization established in the Cultural
Revolution and composed of primary and secondary teachers who had
been persecuted for their bad-class backgrounds or for being Rightists
in the earliest stage of the Cultural Revolution.

Tertiary Education Storm—A Rebel organization composed of
university faculty and students who supported Xiang River Storm and
opposed the Red Guard Headquarters.

Three Bitter Years—1960–2; a period of famine, caused by the policies
of the Great Leap Forward.

Three-in-one-Combination—Revolutionary committees set up during
the Cultural Revolution, including representatives from rehabilitated
officials, from the military, and from Rebel groups.

Two-line Struggle—The power struggle between Mao's factions and that
of the high-ranking Communist officials who disapproved of Mao's
policies.

United Action—A Conservative organization composed of the children
of high-ranking Rebels.

Ultraleftists—Individuals who supported 'ultraleftist Marxist-Leninist
thought.' They were unhappy with the 'revolutionary committees,' and
sought to establish the people's commune and to overthrow the
bureaucratic bourgeoisie.

'Whither China?'—An essay written by Yang Xiguang in January 1968
in which he interpreted the events of the Cultural Revolution,
concluding that a bureaucratic 'class of red capitalists' had arisen that
needed to be forcibly overthrown in 'a new society of the Paris
Commune type.' The essay was declared reactionary and distributed
nationally by members of the Cultural Revolution Small Group as an
example of 'negative material to be criticized.'

Work groups or work teams and 'anti-work team activities'—In June of
1966, Mao expressed support for a poster displayed at Beijing University
which was critical of the leadership of Beijing University and the Beijing
Municipal Committee of the Communist Party. He called upon the
students to rebel against this 'black gang' and to challenge the heads of
the local Communist apparatus. Within days chaos developed
throughout the nation's high schools and universities.
    The Central Committee, along with the Communist Party, headed at
that time by Liu Shaoqi, ordered local Communist authorities to send
out 'work teams' to the campuses to regain control of these institutions.
Some students, a few of whom were aware that Mao might be
sympathetic to their cause, organized semi-underground organizations

to collect information about the work teams' activities and to hang defiant posters on the walls. Liu ordered the work teams to label all anti-work team organizations as counterrevolutionary. The students involved in anti-work team activities were then struggled against in early summer of 1966, when Mao purposely left Beijing to distance himself from all decision-making. He returned in August and convened a meeting of the Central Committee of the Communist Party, at which time he declared that persecuting students was the 'bourgeois reactionary line' and forced Liu to step down from his post as Vice President of the Central Committee.

Xiang River Storm—A Hunan Rebel organization composed of hundreds of thousands of people from various walks of life who were dissatisfied with the *status quo*, and who were oppressed by the military. The group included students, workers, and white-collar professionals from many counties advocating the rehabilitation of the persecuted.

Yijiawan—A village situated midway between Changsha and Xiangtan, where, in August 1967, Rebel forces defeated the Conservative forces largely due to the military strength of the Red Banner Army.

007 Affair—In late 1966, a young rebel in Changsha claimed to have found a slip of paper—later referred to as the '007 Document'—which constituted orders issued personally by Zhou Enlai that a Conservative coup be carried out against the leftist Central Cultural Revolution Group in early 1967. The slip of paper was given to 'Commander' Zhang Jiazheng of the Rebel organization Xiang River Storm, who responded by calling for all true Rebels to redouble their efforts against the 'counterrevolutionary evil plot of the bourgeoisie.'

In February 1967, a right-wing coup actually did break out under the support of Zhou and top military generals, causing many rebels to be labeled and imprisoned. In July 1967, after Mao rehabilitated and released the Rebels who had been labeled the previous February, 'Commander' Zhang attempted unsuccessfully to locate the 007 Document.

Chronology

▼

1948 Yang Xiguang is born in Dongfa, Jilin, on the eve of the Liaoxi-Shenyang Campaign (September 12–November 2, 1948). Yang's grandfather dies.

1949 Yang family moves to Changsha, Hunan. Mother becomes Vice Chair of the Hunan Provincial Federation of Trade Unions. Father becomes County Magistrate of Xiangtan County.

1949–50 Lives together with family of father's oldest sister in Zhuzhou.

1951 Enters Provincial Party Committee Nursery School for cadre children. The onset of a series of purges of 'all the fish who escaped the net': the 'Three Antis and Five Antis' campaigns.

1954 Father is appointed Secretary General of the Provincial Party Committee headquarters. The family moves to a suburb of Changsha.

1956 Hundred Flowers Campaign. Purge against counterrevolutionaries.

1957 Enters Guihuajing Elementary School. Father is demoted to Minister of the Hunan Provincial Department of Industry. Family moves into the Department complex in downtown Changsha. Anti-Rightist Campaign. Elder brother Yang Shuguang and uncle are labeled Rightists.

1958 The Great Leap Forward begins. Classes are canceled for two months. The backyard steel drive. Father is appointed Minister of the Provincial Party Committee's Department of the United Front. Family moves to father's Department compound. Yang Xiguang transfers to Datong Elementary School.

1959 Father is labeled a 'right-wing opportunist' and sent down to Junshan State Farm, where he becomes Deputy Farm Director. The rest of the family moves to his mother's unit, the Federation of Trade Unions.

1960 'Communization.' All youth are organized in 'Youth Houses.' The onset of famine and the 'Three Bitter Years.'

1962 Father is rehabilitated and returns to the Provincial Party Committee. Father and Xiguang move into the Provincial Party guesthouse along with families of other high-ranking cadres just rehabilitated. Xiguang passes the entrance exam for Changsha's key school, Changsha First Junior High.

1963 A series of political campaigns concurrent with the Socialist Education Campaign: 'Combat and prevent revisionism,' 'Raise successors to the revolution,' 'Politics takes command,' 'Learn from the People's Liberation Army,' and 'Revolutionization.'

1964 Xiguang is accepted into the Communist Youth League.

1965 Xiguang passes the entrance examination into Changsha First Senior High School.

1966
Anti-work group activities

May Afternoon classes are canceled and replaced with sessions to study the published documents on 'Studying the Cultural Revolution,' mostly clippings from newspapers.

June Classes are canceled altogether. Students put up posters criticizing teachers, Communist Party leaders, and work teams.

July Work team members label anti-work team students as counter-revolutionaries.

Students go to the countryside to assist in harvesting and planting.

Demonstrations against the Provincial Committee and the Municipal Committee

Aug. Rebel students distribute posters communicating the Party Central's 'Sixteen Point Resolution' which called for the disbanding of work groups. Mao Zedong supports the hitherto 'illegal' Red Guard organizations. Rebel workers and students demonstrate in the streets, protesting against the local Communist Party cadres in power, the Provincial Committee and the Municipal Committee.

Sept. Communist Party organizations initiate counterattacks against the Rebel students and workers. Some Rebel workers are labeled counterrevolutionaries.

Oct. Mao holds a Central Work Conference in support of the Rebels and orders their rehabilitation. The emergence of the first cross-sector, quasi-political parties.

Nov. Establishment of Shengwulian. Xiguang travels to Beijing again, this time to see Chairman Mao at Tiananmen Square.

Dec. Rebel attack on the Provincial Committee; incriminating 'black' files are seized. March to Jinggangshan.

1967

Jan. January Storm. Rebels unite to seize power from the Provincial Committee and barricade Communist newspaper presses. Xiguang first expresses support for Xiang River Storm.

Feb. February Countercurrent. Central Party pronounces the Red Banner Army to be a 'reactionary organization'. Members of the Rebel Xiang River Storm arrested en masse for belonging to a 'counterrevolutionary organization.' Xiguang is briefly imprisoned.

Mar. Xiguang is released from prison and joins the newly-formed Red Rebels Association. The Workers Union speak out against the military district officials and the provisional government's 'Red Union.'

Apr. Xiguang participates in anti-Zhou Enlai activities and helps barricade the provisional government newspapers.

May Xiguang travels to Beijing to understand the political situation and to gather materials about Zhou Enlai.

June Bloodshed. Rebels launch an onslaught against the headquarters of Conservatives' university-level organizations and Conservatives begin to fight back with weapons acquired through work-unit militias.

July The Rebel group Xiang River Storm is formally rehabilitated.

Aug. Xiguang attacks Zhou Enlai in big-character posters. Rebel forces seize weapons.

Sept. Large-scale military clashes between Conservatives and Rebels.

Oct. Establishment of the Revolutionary Committee Preparatory Group. Rebels split into two factions.

Dec. Xiguang goes to the countryside to investigate why educated youth are rebelling and writes 'Whither China?'

1968

Jan. Communist Party declares that Shengwulian is a counterrevolutionary organization. Xiguang flees to Hubei Province.

Imprisonment

Feb. Xiguang is captured and taken to Zuojiatang Detention Center.

1969

Oct. Xiguang is given a ten-year prison sentence.

Dec. Xiguang is sent to Reconstruction Farm labor reform camp.

1970

Apr. Xiguang returns to Changsha and is incarcerated in Model Prison. Strike One–Counter Three Campaign.

1971

Jan.   Xiguang is returned to Reconstruction Farm.

Sept.   Lin Biao Incident.

1972   Xiguang serves as a mason's apprentice in Construction Group.

1978   Yang is released and returned to Changsha.